Joshua Leavitt

EVANGELICAL ABOLITIONIST

Joshua Leavitt

EVANGELICAL ABOLITIONIST

Hugh Davis

LOUISIANA STATE UNIVERSITY PRESS
BATON ROUGE AND LONDON

99 98 97 96 95 94 93 92 91 90   5 4 3 2 1

Designer: Amanda McDonald Key
Typeface: Sabon
Typesetter: G & S Typesetters, Inc.
Printer and binder: Thomson-Shore, Inc.

Library of Congress Cataloging-in-Publication Data

Davis, Hugh, 1941–
    Joshua Leavitt, evangelical abolitionist / Hugh Davis.
        p.   cm.
    Includes bibliographical references.
    ISBN 0-8071-1521-5 (alk. paper)
    1. Leavitt, Joshua, 1794–1873.   2. Abolitionists—United States–
–Biography.   3. Slavery—United States—Anti-slavery movements.
4. Evangelicalism—United States—History—19th century.   5. United
States—History—1815–1861.   6. United States—Social conditions—To
1865.   I. Title.
E449.L46D38   1990
973.7'114'092—dc20   89-36161
[B]   CIP

The illustration of Joshua Leavitt, *ca.* 1860, on the title page is courtesy of
the First Congregational Church, Stratford, Connecticut.

For Jean, Andrew, Jenny, Mark, and Kate

CONTENTS

CONTENTS

PREFACE

Late in life, Joshua Leavitt sought to explain to his friend Salmon P. Chase why he felt compelled to speak out so forcefully on issues of the time. "When I *know* I am right," he stated, "I almost hear a voice saying Woe is me if I keep back the *truth*, which the nation and the world ought to know."[1] Throughout his reform career he acted on this conviction, seeking to root out practices he deemed contrary to God's will and injurious to Americans' well-being.

A native of New England who came from a Congregationalist, Federalist, and evangelical background, Leavitt typified the reformers who launched the great benevolent crusades of the early nineteenth century. He brought to his efforts a seriousness of purpose and sense of moral urgency that many of his contemporaries (and not a few twentieth-century scholars) considered self-righteous and narrowminded. His Manichean view of the world left little room for compromise and stimulated fears of conspiracy in him. To Leavitt and millions of other Americans—including large numbers who had been profoundly influenced by the evangelical revivals of the Second Great Awakening—dire forces produced by fundamental social and economic change seemed to threaten from all sides. With its emphasis on the dangers to the soul and society posed by a rising tide of immorality in the world, evangelicalism pointed toward a conservative social phi-

---

1. Joshua Leavitt to Salmon P. Chase, February 12, 1864, in Salmon P. Chase Papers, Library of Congress.

losophy. Yet the message of immediate repentance and human ability, as well as the moral duty to transform the world, which Leavitt and other evangelicals preached, also reflected the age's growing optimism that people could improve themselves and their society.

In the 1820s and 1830s Leavitt hoped that by uplifting sailors, prostitutes, workingmen, and the poor he and other benevolent activists could counteract the effects of rapid social and economic change and maintain an orderly, moral society. His tendency to emphasize the virtues of self-help, morality, hard work, and sobriety often seemed condescending to these groups—and, with blacks, could have definite racist connotations. Yet, unlike many evangelical reformers of his day, Leavitt came increasingly to adopt a humanitarian and democratic philosophy and to place more emphasis on freedom than on self-control as a prerequisite for moral progress, social harmony, and prosperity. More than most white Americans—more even than some abolitionists—he also transcended the prevailing racial prejudice. And, however inadequate his efforts may appear today, he was one of few middle-class Americans of the time who showed some concern for the plight of the urban working class.

Leavitt's powerful compulsion to do good and to serve as a Christian example goes far to explain his willingness to leave the prestigious professions of law and ministry and sacrifice life's comforts in order to embrace the calling of the reformer and, beginning in 1833, especially to devote his life to the highly unpopular cause of abolition. To Leavitt and other abolitionists, slavery was an unjust and oppressive system that presented Americans with a clear-cut moral choice. Although their moral outrage regarding slavery placed them within the emerging mainstream of opinion in the Western world, and their commitment to the republican ideals of freedom, human dignity, and even equality were abstractions most Americans endorsed (but did not act upon), the abolitionists were a despised minority in America.

Leavitt could be dogmatic, but this does not mean that he rejected new ideas. On the contrary, his ability to adapt to changing conditions and needs is striking. Less an original thinker than a synthesizer who developed and disseminated the ideas of others to a wider audience, he proved flexible and creative when espousing the new revival measures and a broad range of reform tactics. He made his most important and innovative contributions to the antislavery cause. During the 1830s and 1840s, he constantly searched for effective methods that would advance the cause of abolition.

Like many of his fellow abolitionists, Leavitt sought to reform rather than restructure American society. Even in seeking to destroy slavery, he did not reject American society as hopelessly corrupt. He repudiated the major political parties and bitterly criticized the churches because they refused to attack slavery. But, contrary to Stanley Elkins's thesis, he (and most other abolitionists) did not espouse an anti-institutional philosophy.[2] At a time when Americans were attempting to adapt to changing economic, social, and political realities, Leavitt was in fact an important architect of institutions that he hoped would serve as the foundation of the new order.

Unlike most prominent abolitionists, Leavitt has not previously received biographical treatment, in part because most of his correspondence with family members has been lost or destroyed and also because his career as an abolitionist spokesman effectively ended with the creation of the Free Soil party in 1848. Yet for twenty years he stood in the front ranks of the antebellum reformers, as a polished speaker, a prolific writer, a successful lobbyist, an influential Liberty party spokesman and tireless party organizer, a guiding force on the executive committees of numerous reform organizations, and perhaps above all, a respected and forceful editor of several religious and reform newspapers. Leavitt effectively espoused the causes he advocated, bringing to his efforts a wide-ranging knowledge, an enduring commitment to morality and justice, a facile pen, a dogged optimism, and enormous energy.

The dearth of personal letters has made it difficult to delve deep into Leavitt's private life. Moreover, though he wrote thousands of editorials, numerous published works, and many letters to friends and associates, he seldom revealed his deeper doubts and anxieties either in print or in private letters. Nevertheless, it is still possible to understand much about Leavitt the reform activist and the man. This biography examines Leavitt's life within its larger social context to explain why he became involved in numerous religious and social crusades, what his role was in these causes, and how he interacted with his fellow reformers. To understand Leavitt's life is to enrich our knowledge of the evangelical mentality as well as our understanding of the efforts of reform activists in Leavitt's generation to address the moral and social issues of their time.

2. Stanley M. Elkins, *Slavery: A Problem in American Institutional and Intellectual Life* (Chicago, 1959), esp. 140–206.

ACKNOWLEDGMENTS

During the years that I have worked on this book, I have accumulated many debts. The staffs of numerous institutions ably assisted my research: the American Antiquarian Society, the Boston Public Library, Columbia University, Cornell University, Essex Institute, Harvard University, the Historical Society of Pennsylvania, the Library of Congress, the Massachusetts Historical Society, the New Hampshire Historical Society, the New-York Historical Society, the New York Public Library, Oberlin College, the Ohio Historical Society, Syracuse University, the University of Michigan, the University of Rochester, and Yale University.

Several historians and friends, whose encouragement and criticism made this study better than it otherwise would have been, deserve special acknowledgment. John R. McKivigan read much of the manuscript and helped me avoid many errors of fact and interpretation. I owe my greatest debt of gratitude to Merton L. Dillon, who read the entire manuscript and offered eminently wise counsel and unflagging support from the book's inception. James Brewer Stewart read the early chapters and suggested a number of important interpretive and stylistic revisions. Richard Smith introduced me to the discipline of history as an undergraduate and has remained a source of inspiration. Finally, Robert Cole offered valuable advice on matters of style.

A sabbatical leave granted by Southern Connecticut State University facilitated my writing, and the university's Faculty Development Fund paid for the typing of the manuscript. I appreciate this generous institutional support. Rosemary Yanosik skillfully typed the final drafts. The editorial staff of Louisiana State University Press was most helpful and gracious throughout the process of revising and editing the manuscript.

This book could not have been written without the caring, understanding, and encouragement of my wife Jean and my children Andrew, Jenny, Mark, and Kate.

Joshua Leavitt

EVANGELICAL ABOLITIONIST

1

THE EARLY YEARS

Joshua Leavitt's social and economic background differed little from those of many others whose reform careers paralleled his. Born on September 8, 1794, he spent his childhood in Heath, Massachusetts, a village located in the northwestern part of the state. The immediate area had not been settled until the 1750s, but the availability of cheap land attracted many families to Heath between 1790 and 1810, pushing its population from 379 to 910 in these years. Despite this growth, Heath remained a provincial town throughout the nineteenth century, isolated from the major east–west transportation routes and the growing cosmopolitan urban centers of coastal New England. The professional middle class in the town was minuscule. A few residents raised sheep or prepared potash for sale in Boston, but most were small farmers who produced crops for local markets.[1]

With uneven terrain and unproductive soil, limited commercial activity, and small-scale manufacturing, Heath offered little opportunity for residents to accumulate wealth. Most farmers owned fewer than forty cleared acres, and their debts often exceeded the value of their land and livestock.[2] Yet discernible economic distinctions and well-

1. Edward Calver, *Heath, Massachusetts: A History and Guidebook* (Heath, 1979), 6–24, 56–57; Josiah Gilbert Holland, *History of Western Massachusetts* (Springfield, 1855), I, 388–411.

2. Joshua Leavitt, "God Helps Them That Help Themselves," *Christian Spectator*, I

defined social classes certainly existed. By any standard of measurement, Joshua's family stood very near the apex of Heath society.

Both of his grandfathers had been instrumental in founding Heath in 1785, when it broke away from the neighboring town of Charlemont, and were probably the most prominent men in the community during its early years. The Reverend Jonathan Leavitt, Joshua's paternal grandfather, was the great-grandson of John Leavitt, who had come to Dorchester, Massachusetts, from England in 1628. A Congregationalist minister, Jonathan was a strong-willed, authoritarian man with a penchant for shrewd investments in land as well as for controversy. He clashed with his parishioners in the 1770s over payment of his salary in depreciated currency and his lukewarm support for the American cause in the Revolution. The bitter salary dispute dragged on until late in the decade, when his congregation finally dismissed him. Then, after exhausting every available legal tactic, Jonathan actually forced his former parishioners to pay him his back salary.[3] Nevertheless, the old man exercised considerable influence in town affairs until his death in 1802. At the very least, for young Joshua his grandfather served as an object lesson in persistence and moving against the tide.

If Jonathan Leavitt was the most controversial figure in late-eighteenth-century Heath, Joshua's maternal grandfather, Colonel Hugh Maxwell, was the most respected resident. Born in Ireland in 1733 and brought to America while an infant, he served with distinction in the French and Indian War. He brought his family to Charlemont in 1773, and in 1775 he recruited a company of minutemen. Away from home for much of the next seven years fighting in numerous battles, he returned from the war a bona fide hero. He had difficulty providing for a large family by farming and surveying, but between 1795 and 1799 he served as the senior deacon of the Congregational church and held every major political office in Heath. Although Colonel Maxwell died when Joshua was a young boy, Joshua

---

(November, 1827), 584. For excellent treatment of the social and economic structures of somewhat comparable New England towns in this period, see Robert Doherty, *Society and Power: Five New England Towns, 1800–1860* (Amherst, 1977).

3. Emily Leavitt Noyes, *Leavitt: Descendants of John Leavitt, the Immigrant, Through his Son, Josiah, and Margaret Johnson* (Tilton, N.H., 1949), III, 20–22.

later spoke with admiration about his grandfather's courage and integrity.[4]

During the first sixteen years of Joshua's life, his father, Colonel Roger Leavitt, probably exerted the greatest influence on the young boy. The fifth of eleven sons of Jonathan and Sarah Leavitt, Roger married Chloe Maxwell, the youngest daughter of Hugh, in 1793 and proceeded to accumulate a sizable fortune for the period and the locality. By 1805 he paid the highest taxes in Heath. A large portion of his wealth came from his father's estate of hundreds of acres, which Roger inherited in 1802. But he was an intelligent businessman in his own right, becoming the most successful mortgage-holder and money-lender in the immediate area. From all accounts he was a man of integrity and grace, neither ostentatious in his life-style nor elitist in his bearing. Between 1800 and the 1830s he held nearly every important local office of public trust, including selectman, deacon of the church, representative to both houses of the Massachusetts legislature, and commander of a regiment of the state militia. If a rural aristocracy indeed existed in western Massachusetts, Joshua's father was a member in good standing.[5]

Some historians of the antebellum reform movements have maintained that the sons of men like Roger Leavitt joined these crusades because they could not otherwise achieve the social status that their fathers enjoyed. It is very doubtful whether this theory can legitimately be applied to Joshua—or to most other antebellum reformers, for that matter. In some respects Joshua did not preserve the social attainments of his father. He never approached Roger's level of wealth, and certainly inherited little of his business sagacity. With the possible exception of his tenure as a lawyer and then a minister in the 1820s, he was never part of any local power structure. Yet, had Joshua chosen to remain in a small town such as Heath, as his father had, and to remain

4. Howard Chandler Robbins (ed.), *1785–1935: Sesquicentennial Anniversary of the Town of Heath, Massachusetts, August 25–29, 1935* (Heath, 1935), 41–52. Several of Joshua's relatives on both sides of the family were prominent figures in Franklin County politics. See Francis M. Thompson, *History of Greenfield, Shire Town of Franklin County, Massachusetts, 1682–1900* (Greenfield, 1904), I, 289, 299, 308, 325, 600–602; II, 780, 783, 803–804.

5. Calver, *Heath*, 55–56; Leavitt Family Scrapbook, Heath Historical Society, Heath, Mass.

a lawyer or a minister, he might well have equaled or exceeded his father's social position. He never expressed a sense of social inadequacy or the feeling that he had failed to live up to his parents' expectations. In fact, he surpassed his father in the level of formal education and the degree of professional training he attained,[6] and his career as an editor and activist brought him far more national attention than his father ever received. Joshua's failure to achieve the social status that his father enjoyed was, in the final analysis, much more the result of than the reason for his decision to devote his life to advancing controversial causes.

The ideological context within which Joshua grew to maturity partly shaped his later decision to embark on a career of reform. Between 1790 and 1810, Heath remained an extremely homogeneous community, containing only one black, no Catholics, and a few immigrants from England. The great majority of the town's inhabitants belonged to the Congregational Church and the Federalist party.[7]

Joshua's parents were pious Christians who instilled in him and his four younger brothers and sisters a reverence for the Bible, a strong sense of obligation to practice their faith in daily life, and a belief that they should pay close attention to their own and their neighbors' spiritual state. At the age of thirteen Joshua became a member of the Congregational Church in the midst of a revival that swept through Heath and surrounding towns.[8] In later years he would be extremely critical of the churches for their complicity in the institution of slavery, but to the end of his life he remained a firm believer and a devoted Congregationalist.

In the early nineteenth century the Congregational Church often allied itself with the Federalist party in western Massachusetts. Massachusetts Federalists, like Roger Leavitt, who occupied high positions in the standing order were deeply committed to the ideals of unity, order, and stability and tended to see inroads by the Republican party

6. Edward P. Guild (ed.), *Centennial Anniversary of the Town of Heath, Massachusetts, 1785–1885* (Boston, 1885), 49–50, 106–108. For the most complete statement of the status revolution theory, see David Donald, "Toward a Reconsideration of the Abolitionists," in *Lincoln Reconsidered: Essays on the Civil War Era* (2nd ed.; New York, 1961), 19–36.

7. Calver, *Heath*, 178–79, 181.

8. Rev. Theophilus Packard, Jr., *A History of the Churches and Ministers and of the Franklin Association, in Franklin County, Mass.* (Boston, 1854), 226.

and the Baptists, Methodists, and other religious groups as part of a sustained threat to the underpinnings of a Christian republic. Their conservative preoccupation with social deference, tradition, and authority extended far beyond the upper ranks of society; less than a decade before Joshua's birth, Shays' Rebellion had attracted no discernible support in Heath, even though many farmers in the immediate area were saddled with heavy debts and taxes. At the turn of the century many people viewed this part of the state as the stronghold of political conservatism and religious orthodoxy.[9]

These Federalist concerns with social order helped to shape Leavitt's view of the world. His fear that the lower orders posed a threat to social stability explains in part his later efforts to combat immorality, intemperance, and a host of other vices. By the mid-1830s, however, he had come to reject much of the antidemocratic and elitist content of Federalist thought. But as James Banner has argued persuasively, neither Puritan theology nor Federalist thought was necessarily reactionary. Many of the New England clergy and those who headed the Federalist party had supported the Revolutionary cause and viewed themselves as virtuous, principled, and altruistic men committed to the republican ideology. An important part of Leavitt's motivation to reform derived from the Federalist—and certainly his parents'—emphasis on the virtues of disinterested efforts to relieve the plight of the unfortunate and to serve the general welfare. Roger Leavitt served as a powerful example for his children by participating in the incipient benevolent causes of the time, including temperance and education. Indeed, his decision in 1800 to limit significantly the amount of liquor he and his farm laborers consumed underscored for Joshua the importance of acting on one's convictions.[10]

In addition, the New England Federalists' criticism of the southern planter class (and, more obliquely, slavery) helped, as historians have noted, to shape the abolitionist beliefs of William Lloyd Garrison, Edmund Quincy, Arthur and Lewis Tappan, Elizur Wright, Wendell Phillips, Leavitt, and others who had Federalist antecedents. Many

9. Jacob C. Meyer, *Church and State in Massachusetts from 1740 to 1833: A Chapter in the History of the Development of Individual Freedom* (Cleveland, 1930), 137–46, 228–29.

10. James M. Banner, Jr., *To the Hartford Convention: The Federalists and the Origins of Party Politics in Massachusetts, 1789–1815* (New York, 1970), 72–73, 99–107; *Emancipator*, June 18, 1840.

Federalists directed their ire toward the three-fifths clause, which, they charged, permitted southern planters to control the national government. They often depicted themselves as a persecuted minority whose way of life (and that of Northerners generally) was threatened by the designs of southern slaveholders—a view of themselves which Joshua and his fellow immediatists held to when they undertook their great crusade in the early 1830s. Perhaps more important, many Federalists disliked slavery and—much as Joshua and other abolitionists would do—asserted that it degraded the South and its economy and rendered the planter class unfit for governing. Political considerations and fears of disorder prevented these Federalists from launching an antislavery crusade, but they instilled in their sons a sense that the national failure, for which the Virginia-dominated federal government was largely responsible, was essentially a moral one. Joshua and many others who later engaged in reform were conditioned by their fathers' belief that the fragile experiment in republican government could only be sustained by exertions of self-restraint and individual responsibility—which, they were convinced, the slaveholding classes lacked.[11] Thus, while abolitionists like Joshua transcended their fathers' gradualism, they did not so much rebel against that generation as they sought to act upon its stated ideals and thereby extend freedom to millions of Americans.

In all, Joshua's childhood was characterized by stability and security. His parents provided a warm and supportive home environment. As he noted to his brother Roger Hooker Leavitt in 1825, "I have never failed of receiving assistance, whenever I really needed it." Joshua enjoyed a warm and loving relationship with both his parents, and as an adult he came back to Heath to visit them whenever he could. He remembered his mother as a quiet, pious woman who devoted considerable attention to her children's spiritual state. He looked to his father for guidance and understanding, and respected his judg-

11. See, for example, David Hackett Fischer, *The Revolution of American Conservatism: The Federalist Party in the Era of Jeffersonian Democracy* (New York, 1965), 159–60, 166–67; Linda K. Kerber, *Federalists in Dissent: Imagery and Ideology in Jeffersonian America* (Ithaca, 1970), 24–29, 36–40, 59–66, 200–206; Bertram Wyatt-Brown, *Lewis Tappan and the Evangelical War Against Slavery* (Cleveland, 1969), 5–6, 20–21; James Brewer Stewart, "Heroes, Villains, Liberty, and License: The Abolitionist Vision of Wendell Phillips," in Lewis Perry and Michael Fellman (eds.), *Antislavery Reconsidered: New Perspectives on the Abolitionists* (Baton Rouge, 1979), 173–78.

ment and character. In the 1820s he advised his brother Roger Hooker to turn to their father for advice on a serious matter. "He has been young," Joshua counseled, "and has not forgotten the feelings, nor the ignorance and heedless acts of youth. . . . He is your father, and will see your best interest. He is a Christian, and will recommend to you to submit to the government of your country, for convenience sake. Though not a lawyer, he has the quick sense of right and wrong, and that accurate judgment of things. Such renders him a *safer* counsel than half the profession." [12]

Like many others whose parents emphasized benevolence toward others, moral uprightness, and concern for a proper balance between individuality and order, Joshua emerged from childhood with supreme confidence in his abilities and certain that he could help to ensure continued social progress and virtue in American society. This sense of being special also stemmed from the fact that he received the individual attention of his parents during the first seven years of his life (a sister born in 1797 died in infancy) and that his brothers were eleven and fourteen years younger than Joshua. [13] At no time in his life did he fundamentally depart from his parents' system of values. In later years, Roger and Chloe were extremely supportive of his career choices and were active in many of the same benevolent and social reform causes, including abolition.

Roger and Chloe Leavitt also assisted their son by providing a college education. For several years Joshua attended the common school in Heath. For some boys in Heath and surrounding towns, the installation of the Reverend Moses Miller as pastor of the local Congregational Church in 1804 provided a further educational opportunity. A graduate of Brown University (class of 1800), Miller remained a popular preacher in Heath until 1840, and became an important influence in Joshua's life. An innovative minister, Miller introduced religious

12. Joshua Leavitt to Roger Hooker Leavitt, January 5, 1825, and April 16, 1824, in Joshua Leavitt Papers, Library of Congress.

13. On the importance of child-rearing techniques and family environment for many who turned to religious benevolence and reform, see Bertram Wyatt-Brown, "Conscience and Career: Young Abolitionists and Missionaries," in Christine Bolt and Seymour Drescher (eds.), *Anti-slavery, Religion, and Reform: Essays in Memory of Roger Anstey* (Folkestone, England, 1980), 185–90; William G. McLoughlin, "Evangelical Childrearing in the Age of Jackson: Francis Wayland's Views on When and How to Subdue the Willfulness of Children," *Journal of Social History*, IX (Fall, 1975), 21–34.

education for children between church services and helped to prepare Joshua and other boys for college.[14]

In an era when fewer than 2 percent of young white males attended college, Joshua, the eldest son of a prosperous man who owned a large library, was an advantaged youth. Even when he began to prepare for entrance to college at the age of thirteen, there was little doubt that he would attend Yale College. In an earlier time, Harvard might have been seriously considered, but its divinity department had recently been "captured" by the Unitarians. On the other hand, many New Englanders considered Yale a bulwark of orthodoxy. Equally important, Joshua's paternal grandfather and two of his uncles were Yale graduates.[15]

The Leavitts selected the Reverend Joseph Lyman, the Congregational minister in Hatfield, Massachusetts, to assist the young Reverend Miller in preparing Joshua for college. A Yale graduate, a man of great influence in ecclesiastical circles in the state, a zealous Federalist, and later president of the American Board of Commissioners for Foreign Missions, Lyman lent considerable weight to the Leavitts' request that Yale admit their son. Under the careful guidance of his mentors, Joshua studied for the preliminary examination taken by all Yale applicants. A rigorous process that demanded at least as much perseverance as ability to analyze and comprehend, the examination required the incoming freshman to read and translate Greek and Latin and to prove his familiarity with "Vulgar Arithmetic." Yale, however, considered academic competence no more necessary for entrance than the need to present satisfactory evidence of a "blameless life and conversion."[16] A precocious youth of fifteen, Joshua was granted admittance and made the long trip to New Haven in the summer of 1810.

14. Spencer Miller, Jr., *Rev. Moses Miller of Heath, Mass., 1804–1840* (N.p., 1932), 3, 5.

15. Steven J. Novak, *The Rights of Youth: American Colleges and Student Revolt, 1798–1815* (Cambridge, Mass., 1977), 1; Franklin Bowditch Dexter, *Biographical Sketches of the Graduates of Yale College . . .* (New Haven, Conn., 1912), VI, 674; New York *Evangelist*, October 1, 1836.

16. See Z. E. Barstow's reminiscences in H. E. Parker, *A Discourse, preached in the First Congregational Church in Keene, N. H., Thursday, March 6, 1873, at the Funeral of the Rev. Zedakiah Smith Barstow, D. D., for fifty years pastor of the First Church in Keene* (Hanover, N.H., 1873), 21–23.

2

YALE COLLEGE AND
A LAW PRACTICE

Joshua's professors at Yale clarified and rein-
forced the basic beliefs to which he adhered when he arrived in New
Haven. There is little evidence that his mentors encouraged him either
to evaluate critically the world view of his parents or to challenge the
established order. At Yale, Joshua encountered ideas alien to his value
system, but this was primarily for the purpose of emphasizing the need
to repudiate them. Yet change as well as continuity marked his experience at Yale, where he received a thorough training. Timothy
Dwight, Yale's president, helped to shape the contours of Joshua's
evangelical beliefs and reform philosophy, while scholars such as
James Kingsley and Benjamin Silliman helped to awaken his intellectual curiosity. Although Joshua would always celebrate the virtues of
the small-town New England milieu from which he came, his years at
Yale broadened his horizons: New Haven was a much larger and more
complex community than Heath; more opportunity existed to debate
contemporary issues; and he came into contact with students from
other parts of the country.

Yale College occupied a secure and favored place within the New
Haven community and in Connecticut, counting among its alumni
most of the state's Congregational clergy, as well as its business and
political leaders. In the 1790s the college had experienced financial
problems and had come under attack from intellectuals who identified
with the philosophy of the French Revolution. But during Dwight's

tenure as president from 1795 to 1817, Yale's financial and academic position gradually improved.[1]

President Dwight was an excellent administrator who greatly expanded the size of the student body. Joshua's class of 1814, with eighty-two members, was the largest to attend Yale until 1826. By 1810, Yale's reputation was attracting students from throughout the nation. Dwight complained to Joshua and other seniors in 1814 that Yale still had to struggle for money for faculty salaries and scholarships, but during his presidency the physical plant and the curriculum expanded and the library holdings doubled. Moreover, while Dwight appears to have appointed faculty on the basis of character more than expertise, he was an astute judge of men. Joshua's professors were among the best minds of the time.[2]

Most undergraduates looked forward to the senior year with a mixture of eagerness and trepidation. At that time, they came under the personal guidance of Dwight, who instructed them in ethics, logic, rhetoric, and metaphysics, as well as presiding over their disputations on contemporary issues. Particularly in the disputations with the seniors—which most of them considered the capstone of their undergraduate careers—Dwight disseminated his views on issues he considered important. Here he was most effective as a teacher. Believing that Yale should, above all, create in the minds of students a proper regard for public and private morals, Dwight valued ideas primarily as ammunition against the forces of immorality and irreligion.[3] Silliman later claimed that Dwight wanted students to "differ with him and think for themselves." These disputations were indeed the freest period of discussion in Joshua's years at Yale, but even here Dwight chose the subjects that the students debated and concluded the debates with an elaborate "decision" on each issue. The lectures and discussions in Dwight's classes left a lasting impression on his students. They were awestruck by a man of Dwight's talents and reputation, who also had a commanding physical presence. Many years after graduating from

1. Charles R. Keller, *The Second Great Awakening in Connecticut* (New Haven, 1942), 17–25; Brooks Mather Kelley, *Yale: A History* (New York, 1974), 118.

2. Kelley, *Yale*, 128–30, 133–34, 137–40; Charles E. Cunningham, *Timothy Dwight, 1752–1817: A Biography* (New York, 1942), 181–90, 195–224.

3. *Theology, Explained and Defended, in a Series of Sermons, by Timothy Dwight, S.T.D., L.L.D., Late President of Yale College. With a Memoir of the Life of the Author* (2 vols.; Glasgow, 1821), I, 47.

Yale, Joshua fondly remembered "the attention and respect with which he [Dwight] impressed upwards of eighty giddy youths, by his admirable mode of giving instruction."[4]

While a student at Yale, Joshua followed a rigorous daily regimen, in which several prayer and worship services were interspersed with the academic schedule. Nearly forty pages of student rules regulated his conduct, along with the "parental system," wherein college officials frequently visited his room to admonish him. The officials expected him to "avoid profane language, gambling, and all indecent disorderly behavior and disrespectful conduct."[5]

Most college presidents of the time were preoccupied with order, for the period between 1798 and 1815 witnessed major student revolts and violent pranks on campuses. During Dwight's presidency, Yale experienced less disorder than under his predecessor or his successor, and fewer disciplinary problems arose than at Harvard or Princeton. Yale students did not rebel against Dwight's authority in part because they both feared and respected him and also because, as David Allmendinger has argued, Yale had "America's most pious student body."[6]

Yale did, however, experience unrest during Joshua's undergraduate days. The clash between students and "town boys"—particularly sailors—in 1812 was especially serious. Several hundred young men clashed with an assortment of weapons; many people were injured and dozens of students spent a short time in jail. Joshua went out of his way to assure his father that he had "hitherto been so fortunate as [to] keep out of all the difficulty and I hope I continue so." But he clearly sympathized with the jailed students, expressing the hope that the accuser, a deputy sheriff, would "come out at the little end of the horn with a broken head and empty pockets."[7]

In the end, Joshua's fear that actual involvement in the campus fracas would elicit the displeasure of his parents prevailed over both his

4. Quoted in Benjamin Silliman, *A Sketch of the Life and Character of President Dwight, Delivered as a Eulogium, in New Haven, February 12, 1817, Before the Academic Body of Yale College* . . . (New Haven, 1817), 23; Cunningham, *Timothy Dwight*, 246; New York *Evangelist*, December 28, 1833.

5. Cunningham, *Timothy Dwight*, 266–67.

6. Quoted in Kelley, *Yale*, 125; Novak, *The Rights of Youth*, 1, 24–25, 131–33.

7. Joshua Leavitt to Roger Leavitt, July 28, 1812, in Leavitt Papers. For an analysis of the Yale riots, see Kelley, *Yale*, 126–29.

incipient youthful defiance and what may well have been his desire for peer approval. Perhaps more important in explaining his failure to act on his sympathies was Dwight's powerful example, which led Joshua to direct his energies toward religious and benevolent activities. With the possible exception of his parents, Dwight had a greater impact on Joshua's beliefs than anyone else during the first thirty years of his life.

Dwight was in many respects a transitional figure in the evolution of Calvinist theology. The grandson of Calvinist philosopher Jonathan Edwards, he neither completely rejected Edwards's doctrines nor forcefully and systematically asserted freedom of the will. He believed in divine sovereignty, but rejected the harsher views of such disciples of Edwards as Samuel Hopkins and Nathaniel Emmons, who insisted that mankind lacked the moral ability to assist in achieving conversion and salvation. All obedience to God was voluntary, he repeatedly argued, and ministers must exhort sinners to use means of grace to achieve salvation.[8]

By inclination more an evangelist than an original thinker, Dwight preached a practical religion grounded in human reason and directed toward the defense of the evangelical revivals and the redemption of American society. At Yale his powerful preaching, weekly meetings for inquiry, and spiritual counseling of students helped to bring about several major revivals, including one during Joshua's junior year in 1812–1813.[9] He gave increasing prominence to the doctrine of works. As his emphasis moved from *being* good to *doing* good, his outlook became essentially moralistic and reformist. His was an active, vigorous Christianity. "Real religion," he stated, "is ever active; and always inclined to *do*, as well as to say." He frequently pointed out to Joshua and his classmates that they could glorify God by practicing self-denial and "by a regular extension of benevolence and beneficence to our fellow-man."[10]

8. Marie Caskey, *Chariot of Fire: Religion and the Beecher Family* (New Haven, 1978), 37–42.

9. Keller, *The Second Great Awakening in Connecticut*, 225–28. For Dwight's promotion of revivals at Yale, see James B. Reynolds, Samuel H. Fisher, and Henry B. Wright (eds.), *Two Centuries of Christian Activity at Yale* (New York, 1901), 66–67.

10. Quoted in *Theology, Explained and Defended*, II, 289; "Sermon XXVII. On the Love of Distinction. Preached to the Candidates for the Baccalaureate. In 1814," in *Sermons; by Timothy Dwight, D.D., L.L.D., Late President of Yale College* (2 vols.; New Haven, Conn., 1828), I, 507; also Kenneth Silverman, *Timothy Dwight* (New York, 1969), 112–13.

Dwight and other evangelicals were moved to attack intemperance, Sabbath breaking, and other vices by a mixture of fear and optimism: they were concerned to preserve order and morality in society, yet they also hoped to improve mankind and hasten the coming of the millennium. In 1812 Dwight joined other Connecticut church leaders to found the Connecticut Society for the Reformation of Morals and the Suppression of Vice, and he was a guiding force behind the creation of moral and benevolent societies on the Yale campus. Dwight's eloquent preaching and powerful example influenced Joshua to enter the world of organized benevolence while still a junior in college. In July 1813 he and several other students founded the Yale College Benevolent Society, which they hoped would assist "indigent young men of good talents and unblemished moral character in acquiring a liberal education." The society's success was assured, Joshua proudly informed his father, by the initial subscription of $1,000 among the students— one-half of this sum for immediate appropriation, and the remaining portion for establishing a permanent fund. Some money came from outside Yale, but Joshua and other students largely controlled the society's operations, with Dwight acting as the group's adviser.[11]

President Dwight influenced his students in still other ways. In his disputations with seniors he presented his views on many contemporary social and political issues, including slavery and the slave trade. At a time when antislavery sentiment was at a low ebb in New England, Dwight spoke out forcefully against slavery, as did a number of other Federalist leaders. Convinced that slavery constituted a barrier to mankind's movement toward a more perfect state and, more practically, that it enabled Virginia slaveholders to dominate the federal government, Dwight called for its end. The fact that many slaves had been converted to Christianity, he told Joshua and his classmates, was "of trifling importance" when compared to the need to end slavery. Society, he argued, must free the slaves and impart knowledge and "good habits" to them.[12] Most New Englanders in the early 1810s, including Dwight, did not seriously consider launching a concerted assault on slavery, and Joshua did not initially publish his own mis-

11. Cunningham, *Timothy Dwight*, 336; Joshua Leavitt to Roger Leavitt, July 20, 1813, in Leavitt Papers; "Constitution of the Benevolent Society of Yale College," Sterling Library, Yale University.

12. Timothy Dwight, Jr., *President Dwight's Decision of Questions Discussed by the Senior Class in Yale College, in 1813 and 1814* (New York, 1833), 160–61.

givings about the institution until the mid-1820s. But Dwight's direct attack on slavery, concomitant with his emphasis on the importance of ethical considerations in religion, would be a major factor in Joshua's eventual decision to devote his energies to abolition.

During the years from 1812 to 1814, the war with Britain, and not slavery, was the preeminent political issue in the United States. The British blockade brought the war to the doorstep of the college and dealt a severe blow to the economy of New Haven and much of the rest of New England. Both Joshua's father and Dwight sharply attacked the war. Their views on the conflict significantly influenced Joshua's perception of the events that occurred. In public meetings and from the pulpit, as well as in the disputations with the senior class, Dwight thundered against the Republican administration and the European powers—especially France. As the divisions and destruction wrought by the war became more serious, he increasingly saw the conflict as divine punishment for America's collective sins.[13]

Roger Leavitt shared many of Dwight's convictions regarding the war. When memorials presented by Massachusetts Federalists to Congress and the President had no effect on government policy, Roger and representatives from fifty-three towns met in Northampton, Massachusetts, in July 1812; they denounced the war as "neither just, necessary, nor expedient," condemned the Madison administration for disregarding the interests of New England, and demanded immediate peace with Great Britain. Roger was one of four men from Franklin County later selected to attend a state convention to discuss this issue.[14] His conviction that the federal government disregarded the interests of an aggrieved minority moved him to political insurgency; his protests and petitions served as a powerful example to Joshua, who in the late 1830s would repudiate the major parties in favor of third-party action (and would persuade his father to join the Liberty party) when he concluded that the major parties had completely ignored the wishes of abolitionists.

Joshua's sentiments regarding the war mirrored those of Dwight and his father in many ways. In light of their bitter opposition to the

13. Silverman, *Timothy Dwight*, 137–40.
14. *Proceedings of a Convention of Delegates from the Counties of Hampshire, Franklin, and Hampden, Holden at Northampton, the 14th and 15th of July, 1812* (Northampton, Mass., 1812), 3–12; also Banner, Jr., *To the Hartford Convention*, 306–10, 326–32, 343–44.

Madison administration's policies, it is not surprising that Joshua stood forth as a strong Federalist partisan. Convinced that he was on the side of right, he was quick to condemn the party's enemies. The salvation of the nation, he informed his father in 1813, required concerted Federalist opposition to that "fool and rascal" Madison and to a war that was "most unjust and foolish in its origin and disgraceful." He also questioned the motives of those who supported the war effort—as he was later inclined to do with critics of the new revival measures and various reform causes. When his roommate's father became "a highflying war-hawk," Joshua remarked facetiously to his father that "if he should be soon rewarded with a fat office the point would be more clear." This cynicism seems to have been in part the product of youthful disillusionment. While Joshua, like his father and Dwight, feared that the corruption and mistrust prevalent among the European nations, as well as the "selfish measures" of the American government, presented "almost insuperable obstacles to the accomplishment of the object," he was also an idealist who hoped that "it is true that the grand period has arrived when the nations of the earth shall war no more." [15]

In attacking the President and Congress, Joshua did not consciously intend to challenge constituted authority. The views expressed by most New England religious and political leaders reinforced his opposition to government policies, and he showed that he was prepared—as he would later be on the slavery issue—to condemn government policies he deemed illegal, unjust, or unwise. Nor was this an example of youthful rebellion against his parents' values, since he fully shared their view of the world. Indeed, Joshua, like his father, seemed politically alienated, yet also powerfully drawn to reforming politics, which they deemed rife with corruption and conspiracy. These convictions would later move both men to abolitionism and eventually the Liberty party.

As graduation drew near, Joshua came to consider various career options. He could choose from several occupations. In this era of rapid economic expansion some Yale graduates entered the business world,

15. Leavitt to Roger Leavitt, July 20, 1813, in Leavitt Papers. Writing to Charles Sumner in 1870, Leavitt recalled that he had supported the basic objectives of the Hartford Convention but denied that leaders at the meeting had demanded or desired secession. Joshua Leavitt to Charles Sumner, January 20, 1870, in Charles Sumner Papers, Houghton Library, Harvard University.

while a few others took up farming, as many of their fathers had. Joshua appears not to have given serious consideration to either of these options. Most Yale graduates chose the law, the ministry, and teaching; within a decade of his graduation, Joshua would enter each of these professions. The study of law attracted a large minority of Yale graduates, whereas, despite the periodic revivals of religion that occurred during Dwight's presidency, the percentage entering the ministry had been declining for many years.[16]

Joshua's mentors had prepared him well for Yale, and he devoted himself to his college studies. He was intellectually gifted. Equally important, his parents had emphasized dedication to one's tasks and the importance of intellectual pursuits as a means of acquiring knowledge and avoiding bad influences. Outside of his studies, Joshua seemed interested only in benevolent activities. Driven by a desire to excel and to gain recognition and respect from his peers and approval from his teachers and parents, he carved out a commendable academic record while at Yale. In his senior year he was a candidate for the Berkeley Scholarship, which provided its recipients with the opportunity to continue their studies at Yale. Established in 1733 by the philosopher George Berkeley, this prize was the oldest scholastic foundation at Yale and retained considerable prestige until well into the nineteenth century. The senior candidates for the scholarship underwent a rigorous series of written and oral exercises in Greek and Latin in the presence of the college president. Having successfully completed these examinations, Joshua was awarded a stipend that could be used for one, two, or three years of graduate studies, or simply accepted as an award. By the early nineteenth century, the revenues from Berkeley's lands provided insufficient funds to allow most recipients of the scholarship to remain at Yale. Although his parents certainly could have subsidized further study following graduation, Joshua followed the example of most recent recipients and left the college and New Haven in the summer of 1814.[17]

With no definite career plans and troubled by a persistent cough, Joshua returned home. He was seemingly the picture of health—tall and robust, even corpulent as he reached adulthood, with broad

16. Kelley, *Yale*, 123.
17. *Catalogus Collegii Yalensis* (Newport, R.I., 1835), 52; Ezekiel Porter Belden, *Sketches of Yale College* (New York, 1843), 85–87.

shoulders and piercing eyes. However, he had frequently been ill during his undergraduate years, and throughout his life often complained to family members and friends about his assorted ailments. Like many nineteenth-century Americans, he tended to focus in his correspondence more on *how* than *what* he was feeling. While in Heath, Joshua taught school for a few months. One of his students, a younger cousin, Jonathan Leavitt, later recalled that Joshua was a strict disciplinarian. Then in early 1815 Joshua accepted an offer to become preceptor of Wethersfield Academy, a private institution near Hartford that provided a basic education for young men. His one and a half years in Wethersfield seem to have been quite agreeable. His health recovered substantially, and he was committed to the task of educating youths. He informed his father in early 1816 that "the path of learning is a pleasant path." [18] Had it not been for another setback to his health, Joshua might well have continued teaching for several more years. As it was, he never again taught school after he returned to his parents' home in mid-1816 to recuperate. Nonetheless, he long remained interested in improving the quality of education provided by the common schools and in later years compiled several schoolbooks for children.

During this stay in Heath, Joshua must have frequently pondered his future. Twenty-two years old, once again living in his parents' home, unmarried, and yet to make a definite career decision, he still occupied a semidependent status. But as Joseph Kett has pointed out, this was not unusual for a young man of Joshua's age and experience; when he decided in late 1816 to begin the study of law, he was actually younger than many men at the time they made this choice. [19]

Joshua's decision was a logical one. Two of his uncles were prominent lawyers and judges in Greenfield, a nearby town on the Connecticut River, and Joshua certainly was aware of the respect accorded them in the community. Moreover, since he viewed himself as an altruistic and benevolent person, it is not surprising that he entered the

18. Jonathan Leavitt to Joshua Leavitt, January, 1815, February 21, 1816, in *Memoir of Jonathan Leavitt, A Member of the Junior Class in Yale College, Who Died at New Haven the 10th of May, 1821, Aged Eighteen Years and One Month* (New Haven, 1822), 27; Joshua Leavitt to Roger Leavitt, July 28, 1812, July 20, 1813, in Leavitt Papers.

19. For an excellent discussion of the mix of independence and dependence in the lives of young men in this era, see Joseph F. Kett, *Rites of Passage: Adolescence in America, 1790 to the Present* (New York, 1977), esp. 29–32.

teaching and legal professions, both of which had more to do with serving society than making money. Dwight also influenced his decision. Although Dwight acknowledged that some lawyers helped create disputes in order to profit from litigation, he often praised lawyers and attacked critics of the profession; he even argued before Joshua's class that "the lawyer stands between the oppressor and the oppressed." Prompted in part by Dwight's sentiments, nearly one-third of the Yale students during Joshua's undergraduate days became lawyers.[20]

Many young men in Massachusetts in 1817 could not seriously consider practicing law, for educational and financial requirements blocked their paths. Massachusetts had some of the nation's strictest requirements for admission to the bar, including a "good school education" and at least seven years devoted to "literary acquisitions." Before one could study law, it was necessary to undergo an examination on mathematics, ethics, logic, Latin, and other subjects before a committee of the bar. The Federalist leadership in the state viewed these requirements as a means of ensuring high standards of learning and pleading, as well as of preventing democratization of the profession's standards and procedures. Thanks to his Yale training, Joshua could easily meet these requirements. Moreover, a legal education was expensive. Only a young man of affluence or one who had patronage could afford the typical apprenticeship. Joshua probably had saved some money while teaching at Wethersfield, but his father almost certainly subsidized part of the cost of his legal studies.[21]

Joshua undoubtedly knew that he could count on such assistance. As he wrote to his brother Roger Hooker a few years later, "You know it was always our Father's wish to have his children cut for themselves, and though he tells a good deal about leaving them to shirk for themselves," he had always been there to help them. In Joshua's case, this financial support was substantial, for both a Yale education and a high-caliber legal apprenticeship were expensive. Joshua was indeed fortunate in comparison to his brothers Roger Hooker and Field. Shortly after Joshua completed his legal training, his father, at the age of fifty, experienced a second conversion in the revivals that swept the region.

20. Dwight, Jr. (ed.), *President Dwight's Decision*, 193, 198; Thompson, *History of Greenfield*, I, 473, II, 783, 803; Kelley, *Yale*, 123.
21. Anton-Hermann Chroust, *The Rise of the Legal Profession in America, Vol. II: The Revolution and the Post-Revolutionary Era* (Norman, Okla., 1965), 131–32; Banner, Jr., *To the Hartford Convention*, 186–87.

He informed Joshua that he would make no more money but rather would devote the rest of his life to advancing the welfare of mankind. As for his younger children, Roger now insisted that if they desired more, they would have to obtain it by industry and economy, as he had done. While the meager family correspondence gives little indication of sibling resentment toward Joshua, it is clear that he felt some sense of guilt regarding the largesse his parents had bestowed upon him. He expressed to his brother Roger Hooker the wish that their father had not "exhausted his means upon one" but acknowledged that "if he has I am sorry."[22]

In the early nineteenth century most young men who wished to study law continued the long-standing practice of serving an apprenticeship in the office of a lawyer or a judge. Joshua was again fortunate to have Eli P. Ashmun of Northampton as his mentor. Although an intelligent and diligent young man with an excellent academic record, he was not averse to trading on his family's reputation and contacts within the ranks of the Massachusetts elite. The facts that his father and his uncle Jonathan were members of the political and social elite in western Massachusetts and had been colleagues of Ashmun in the Massachusetts legislature certainly eased the way for him to study with a man of Ashmun's stature. A self-made man whose parents had been able to provide him with only a minimal formal education, Ashmun had risen rapidly in the legal profession and in Massachusetts politics. As one of three lawyers in Hampshire County, he served from 1806 until his death in the capacity of official examiner for the state bar, as a member of both houses of the state legislature for several terms, and as a member of the Governor's Council. In 1816, the year before Joshua came to Northampton to study law with him, the legislature selected Ashmun to fill the vacancy in the U.S. Senate that had been created by the resignation of Christopher Gore.[23]

The legal education one received by close association with, and observation of, a practicing lawyer or judge varied greatly in quality. In lesser law offices much of the process was mechanical, and the student determined how much he read and learned. Leavitt received perhaps the best training available in the nation at the time. It was neither

22. Joshua Leavitt to Roger Hooker Leavitt, January 5, 1825, in Leavitt Papers; *Emancipator*, June 18, 1840.

23. *Biographical Directory of the American Congress, 1774–1949* (Washington, D.C., 1950), 794; *Hampshire* (Mass.) *Gazette and Public Advertiser*, July 6, 1819.

sporadic nor perfunctory, despite the facts that Ashmun frequently stayed in Washington in 1817 and 1818 and—following his resignation from the Senate in 1818 because of family considerations, financial problems, and poor health—was at times incapacitated during the last year of his life.[24]

Joshua later recalled Ashmun as an experienced practitioner and able teacher, as well as "a man of the strictest and most elevated moral principles I ever knew." During the required three years of study, Joshua and the other two legal trainees under Ashmun's tutelage—one of them Lewis Strong, the son of Caleb Strong, many times Massachusetts governor and U.S. senator—received both a practical and theoretical training in the law and the basic procedures and responsibilities of a legal practice. He read the great historical and legal commentaries of Hume, Vattel, Blackstone, Gibbons, and Coke, discussed legal principles and theory with Ashmun and the other students, and copied legal documents by hand.[25]

During his legal apprenticeship, Joshua became involved in the community life of Northampton. Located along the Connecticut River, Northampton in the late 1810s was still a close-knit and homogeneous town whose 3,000 residents generally engaged in farming or home manufacturing and owed their allegiance to the Federalist party and the Congregational Church. Soon after he arrived in Northampton, he joined the First Congregational Church, whose minister of forty years, the Reverend Solomon Williams, was a powerful voice of orthodoxy in the struggle against the Unitarians and a committed Federalist. (Fifteen years earlier he had bitterly attacked the Jeffersonian Republicans from the pulpit as "damned rascals.") In 1817 Joshua met Williams's daughter Sarah, a pious young lady of nineteen who had become a member of the church in 1816.[26] Their courtship continued through his years in Northampton.

24. Chroust, *The Rise of the Legal Profession in America*, II, esp. Chap. 4, "Training for the Practice of Law," 173–223; *Hampshire* (Mass.) *Gazette and Public Advertiser*, July 6, 1819.

25. New York *Evangelist*, September 14, 1833; Chroust, *The Rise of the Legal Profession in America*, II, 174–75; Joshua Leavitt to Charles Sumner, January 20, 1870, in Sumner Papers.

26. The Tercentenary History Committee (comp. and ed.), *The Northampton Book: Chapters from 300 Years in the Life of a New England Town, 1654–1954* (Northampton, Mass., 1954), 66, 77, 386–87; William S. Leavitt, *First Parish, Northampton. Historical Sketch, 1653–1878* (Northampton, Mass., 1878), 18–20.

At the peak of the local revival of religious enthusiasm in 1819, the church gained more new members than ever before in any one year. The revival had a profound effect on Joshua. He paid close attention to the developments in the community and to his own and others' spiritual state. It was, he wrote his brother Roger Hooker, "a wonderful season" that raised his hopes that the revival would spread to Heath and other towns in the region. He was particularly concerned that his brother, who was then thirteen—an age when many young people had a religious experience—should immediately examine his soul. In counseling his brother, Joshua showed himself to be not only a deeply pious young man but also one inclined to deal with his younger siblings in a rather paternalistic manner—a relationship that, in the case of his brother Roger Hooker, carried through much of their lives. Joshua cautioned him that, while the pursuit of education was extremely important, "the learning of the Bible, a knowledge of the Character of God, as a Wise and Just and Holy Being, and of your obligations to Him, as your Creator and Continual Preserver, of your own character as a sinner exposed to the eternal and insufferable vengeance of God, and of the way," was a "higher kind of learning." This must not be delayed, he warned ominously, for "wealth, learning, honor, and esteem must all be left behind, none of them can save or even comfort you in the hour of death." [27]

In the midst of the revival, Joshua received the required character reference, completed three years of study, and was duly admitted to the bar. Far from being a rebel or part of an unpopular minority in Massachusetts society, he was now associated with talented and well-connected men of power and prestige and was about to enter the inner circle of the state's professional and social elite. He probably could have practiced law anywhere in the Northeast, yet he chose to return to Heath to establish a practice. Although Heath was removed from centers of power, Joshua's decision to move there had a compelling logic behind it. From a professional standpoint, the prospect of success appeared favorable. Heath's population stood at 1,100 in 1819— nearly double that of two decades earlier—and it had never been served by a resident lawyer. Also, he knew most of the town's residents

27. *The Church Book of the First Church of Christ in Northampton, 1860* (Northampton, Mass., 1860), 44; Joshua Leavitt to Roger Hooker Leavitt, February 28, 1819, in Leavitt Papers.

and wished to pursue his courtship with Sarah Williams, who lived less than fifty miles away.[28]

Equally important, settling in Heath permitted frequent contact with his parents, as well as his brothers and sisters, to whom Joshua felt very close. Although in his mid-twenties, and seemingly confident of his abilities, at this time in his life his emotional dependence on his parents and his attachment to the familiar surroundings of Heath remained quite strong. A few years later he urged his brother Roger Hooker to accept a teaching position in the West, noting philosophically that "as to leaving home, it is a trial, but in the course of nature home will change if we try to stay there. We cannot make it perpetual. Perhaps it will be best for us to scatter a little."[29] But in 1819 Joshua seemed reluctant to move far from his family and his community of origin.

During his two years as a lawyer in Heath, Joshua experienced considerable satisfaction and a sense of stability in his personal life, and immense frustration and a feeling of uncertainty in his professional career. As a lawyer just beginning his practice, he needed to attract clients, especially since, as a bachelor of twenty-five, he should also marry and begin a family. Sarah Williams, as a member of a solid Federalist family and the daughter of a prominent Congregational minister whom Roger Leavitt had known for several years, was certainly acceptable to Joshua's family. Sarah and Joshua were married in Northampton on November 1, 1820.[30]

Joshua's marriage to Sarah added stability to his life and completed his passage from youth to manhood. Now settled in a career and responsible for a family, his deep roots in the community were further strengthened; townspeople now expected him to play an active public role. As pious Christians committed to advancing the evangelical revivals and hastening the coming of the millennium, Joshua and Sarah naturally involved themselves in the church. While a young legal trainee in Northampton, with no roots in the community, Joshua had done little more than observe the religious revivals then sweeping the region. In Heath, where he was a respected and well-known member of the community and enjoyed a close relationship with the Reverend

28. Noyes, *Leavitt*, III, 39.

29. Joshua Leavitt to Roger Hooker Leavitt, January 5, 1825, in Leavitt Papers.

30. *Ibid.*; *Vital Records of Heath, Massachusetts, to the Year 1850* (Boston, 1915), 96.

Miller, the Congregational minister, he immersed himself in the affairs of the community. Above all, he set out to combat religious indifference in the church and the community. Following a revival between 1816 and 1818, there had ensued, as Miller later recalled, a period of "unprecedented coldness and stupidity in the church as a body, and much thoughtlessness and vanity prevailed in the community." According to Miller, Joshua and a few other church members sought to rectify this situation with a "universal spirit of prayer."[31] Convinced that the spiritual welfare of the congregation was at stake, Joshua thus determined—as he so often would during his reform career—to move against the tide and lend his considerable energies to the task of converting the unbelieving majority to the path of righteousness.

Encouraged by Miller and influenced by Dwight's beliefs that children instinctively revered religion and that religious education played a significant role in preparing the way for regeneration and salvation, Joshua established the first Sabbath school in the area in 1819 and served as its superintendent and Bible class teacher. By the mid-1820s, Joshua had fully incorporated into his evangelical theology Dwight's emphasis on the education of the child as an important means of grace; throughout his life he remained an ardent supporter of the Sunday school movement.[32]

In 1822, the year after Joshua and Sarah left Heath, a major revival of religion occurred in the community—an event that the Reverend Miller credited to the efforts of Joshua Leavitt and others. Joshua must have derived some satisfaction from these developments, but the same could not be said of his professional life. Contrary to his expectations when he returned to Heath in 1819, his law practice provided only limited financial rewards and produced considerable frustration. Few residents of the town felt the need for legal advice, and many of those who did were delinquent in paying his fees.[33]

With a dearth of clients and with a wife to support, Joshua decided in 1821 to move to Putney, Vermont. As in his earlier decision to es-

31. *A Historical Discourse Delivered by Rev. Moses Miller, October 13, 1852* (Shelburne Falls, Mass., 1853), 27.

32. *Independent*, January 23, 1873.

33. Guild (ed.), *Centennial Anniversary of the Town of Heath*, 44–49. For a discussion of the responsibilities of a small-town lawyer in the early nineteenth century, see Catherine Fennelly, *Life in an Old New England Country Village* (New York, 1969), 76–82.

tablish a practice in Heath, he seems to have been attracted to Putney by the presence of one of his father's brothers, David, who owned a general store in the town. Joshua did not view his professional troubles in Heath as a sign of personal failure. Never one who could easily concede defeat or question his own abilities, he dealt with whatever disappointment he felt by plunging into his work and building a respectable practice. Fortunately, Putney was a prosperous Connecticut River community that held out greater promise of a successful law practice than had Heath. Joshua's practice provided an adequate income for him and Sarah and their infant son William, the first of six sons, who was born in 1822.[34]

As one of two lawyers in town, with impeccable credentials, two years of experience in his profession, and a growing family, Joshua was immediately accepted into the community and became one of its bright young lights. The town meeting appointed him to a committee charged with discussing the needs of Putney. Moreover, the Congregational church selected him to serve on a committee that resolved disputes among its members and elected him a deacon in 1823—a signal honor and a clear indication that, though only twenty-eight years old, Joshua was respected in both the church and the community.[35]

Joshua also joined the Putney Musical Society, an evangelical organization founded in 1817 by persons who believed in "the importance of sacred music in the worship of God." As a member of the society, in which he served as secretary in 1822 and 1823, he pledged to listen to only "real and substantial music," such as that by Handel, Arnold, and Giardini, as opposed to many of the secular pieces of the time, which, in the members' opinion, were "calculated rather to excite levity than the spirit of true devotion."[36]

In 1823 Joshua signaled his commitment to religion in a dramatic way by deciding to return to Yale as a student in its first theological

34. William Leavitt, *A Sketch of the Life and Character of Rev. Jonathan Leavitt: The First Minister of Charlemont, Mass.* (n.p., 1903), 7; Leavitt Family Scrapbook.

35. Meeting of September 2, 1822, in "Town Meeting Records, Vol. II (1796–1833)," Putney Historical Society, Putney, Vermont; Meetings of March 8, 1822, February 17, March 20, 1823, in "Records of the Church of Christ in Putney, Beginning June 25th, 1807," Putney Historical Society, Putney, Vermont.

36. "Records of the Putney Musical Society, 1820–1840," Putney Historical Society, Putney, Vermont.

class. Many other men of his age and circumstances would have chosen to remain where they were, earning a comfortable living as a small-town lawyer and serving as a pillar of the community. Intelligent, ambitious, and with family and Yale connections throughout the region, Joshua's horizons could have extended far beyond Putney. Yet he chose to uproot himself and his family in order to prepare for a new career—a decision that would dramatically alter the course of his life.

3

THEOLOGICAL STUDIES AND
THE STRATFORD YEARS

When Joshua Leavitt enrolled in Yale Theological Seminary, he joined a growing number of young men in their late twenties and early thirties who had chosen the ministry as a career. Some of these men had been forced to postpone a college education until they had earned sufficient money; others, like Leavitt, were part of the increasingly common phenomenon of "track switching," which moved in several directions but especially toward the ministry in this time of rising religious enthusiasm.[1]

For Leavitt, the grandson and son-in-law of ministers, the decision to enter the ministry was not unexpected. More important, his father's recent religious experience and new baptism served as a powerful stimulus for this pious young man, who was already deeply involved in the life of the church. His decision to undertake theological studies must have greatly pleased his father and mother. His choice of Yale also was not surprising, though other options were certainly available to him. Some Congregational ministerial candidates still received their training from well-known ministers, who provided a solid grounding in the day-to-day functions of a minister. By the early nineteenth century, however, many church leaders had concluded that this system could not meet the growing demand for ministers and that many training ministers were too busy to attend to the needs of their students and did not possess adequate libraries.[2]

1. Kett, *Rites of Passage*, 32–33.
2. William Warren Sweet, "The Rise of Theological Schools in America," *Church History*, VI (1937), 260–73.

Leavitt probably gave serious consideration only to Andover and other theological seminaries, which since 1800 had trained most ministerial students. Many Yale graduates had attended Andover since its founding in 1808 as the union seminary for Congregationalists, but a growing number of church leaders, including Dwight and Lyman Beecher, had concluded that Andover's graduates lacked sufficient revival enthusiasm and were too conservative, or Hopkinsian. These concerns helped to steer Leavitt toward the newly created Yale Theological Seminary. Yale was a logical choice: he felt a deep sense of loyalty toward the college; he knew most of the professors, themselves ardent supporters of the evangelical revivals; and a small class encouraged close contact with instructors.[3]

A theological school of sorts had been conducted for many years in conjunction with Yale, with President Dwight and, in later years, Professors Eleazar T. Fitch, James Kingsley, and Chauncey A. Goodrich instructing a number of ministerial candidates. When students petitioned in 1822 to be organized into a theological class, the Yale faculty and corporation founded the seminary.[4]

Yale Theological Seminary was established in an era of growing professionalization of studies in law, medicine, and the ministry. Many people came to view a seminary education as essential for entrance into the professional religious community. Within the seminary the introduction of a formal curriculum, divided into a series of subjects taught by professors who specialized in certain areas of expertise, altered traditional methods of instruction.[5]

The seminary at Yale was assured an auspicious beginning with the appointment of Nathaniel William Taylor—a former student of Dwight and for ten years a successful revival preacher at Center Church in New Haven—as Professor of Didactic Theology. During Leavitt's years as a student, the faculty also included Fitch, Professor of Homiletics; Goodrich, who offered a course in the Pastoral Charge; and Kingsley, who taught Hebrew until Josiah Willard Gibbs was hired in 1824 as Professor of Sacred Literature and Biblical Teaching.

3. John Terrill Wayland, "The Theological Department in Yale College, 1822–1858" (Ph.D. dissertation, Yale University, 1933), 66; Joshua Leavitt to Roger Hooker Leavitt, March 16, 1824, in Leavitt Papers.

4. Wayland, "The Theological Department in Yale College," 52–62, 67.

5. On the professionalization of the ministry and the standardization of ministerial training, see Donald M. Scott, *From Office to Profession: The New England Ministry, 1750–1850* (Philadelphia, 1978), 63–64.

These men instructed only a handful of students in the early 1820s—
two in the first year, four more in 1823, when Leavitt entered, and
thirteen in 1824. The seven men who graduated with Leavitt in 1825
had much in common: Most were natives of Connecticut who had
graduated from Yale several years before they decided to study for the
ministry.[6]

The seminary's curriculum differed little from that of other seminaries of the time; courses were offered in the classical languages and
philosophy, the composition and delivery of sermons, the duties of the
pastoral office, and especially exegetical, systematic, and applied theology. The training Leavitt received was far superior to that offered by
individual ministers, despite deficiencies in the areas of both curriculum and instruction.[7]

The heart and soul of the theological faculty was Taylor, a highly
original and creative thinker. With advice and support from his colleagues and from Lyman Beecher—a powerful preacher, polemicist,
revivalist, and Taylor's close friend—Taylor developed in the late
1810s and 1820s a system of theology that was variously termed
"evangelical Christianity," "Taylorism," and the "New Haven theology." These doctrines, which the faculty passed on to Leavitt in the
classroom, the chapel, and private conversations, represented both a
significant shift in emphasis within the framework of New England
Puritanism and a clarification and extension of Dwight's views.

To preserve a common front among the evangelical forces, the New
Haven theologians consciously eschewed strict adherence to minutely
defined doctrines. The fundamental problem they debated was how to
reconcile the tenets of Calvinism with successful efforts to win souls
to God. If salvation was entirely the work of the Holy Spirit and
people were totally depraved, they asked, how could the evangelist
exhort his audience to accept the offer of the Gospel? As practical men
seeking to advance the revivals, they did not concern themselves as
much with building a coherent scheme of theological thought as with
winning converts. Imbued with a revival spirit, they desired a theology
that would render Calvinism more acceptable to their society and

6. See Roland H. Bainton, *Yale and the Ministry: A History of Education for the
Christian Ministry at Yale from the Founding in 1701* (New York, 1957), 84–88; Wayland, "The Theological Department in Yale College," 120.

7. Wayland, "The Theological Department in Yale College," 178, 188–219.

would thus stem the inroads of the Methodists, the Episcopalians, and especially the Unitarians.[8]

In the process of answering the Unitarian charges that Calvinism denied human free will and made God the author of sin, the Yale theologians sought to improve and clarify certain doctrines developed by Edwards and his successors. Taylor drew back from the uncompromising logic of the consistent Calvinists; even more than Dwight, he based his theology on the conclusions of common sense and reason. He and Dwight (and for that matter William Ellery Channing, the leading Unitarian spokesman) shared the conviction that, for a generation raised on Enlightenment rationalism, the Bible must be tested by the rules of internal consistency and conformity to experience. By the 1820s, the Scottish Common Sense philosophy—developed by Thomas Reid, Dugald Stewart, and others during the eighteenth-century Enlightenment in Scotland—had become dominant at evangelical colleges such as Yale. For Taylor, Beecher, and other evangelicals, the Scottish philosophy, by affirming the human ability to perceive God's natural order and moral law, provided a convincing rationale for evangelical rationalism and moralism and, at the same time, a clear refutation of skepticism. It represented, above all, a persuasive intellectual defense of their belief that God was a benevolent despot and humans free moral agents.[9]

Common sense and reason, the New Haven theologians argued, showed that people sin and are punished for sins they freely choose to commit. Strict Calvinists contended that sinners could repent if they would but always followed their inclination, of which God is the ultimate cause—an argument that Taylor as well as the Unitarians believed rendered God the author of sin and people responsible for what they could not help. Instead, these men insisted that human consciousness of freedom is not a mere illusion. "Moral agents," stated Taylor, "are the proximate efficient causes of their own acts."[10]

Taylor was drawn powerfully to discussion, reasoning, and argumentation on doctrinal points, but he was preeminently a dogmatist.

8. Sidney Mead, *Nathaniel William Taylor, 1786–1858: A Connecticut Liberal* (Chicago, 1942), 97–100.

9. Sydney E. Ahlstrom, "The Scottish Philosophy and American Theology," *Church History*, XXIV (1955), 263–64.

10. Quoted in Mead, *Nathaniel William Taylor*, 125–26.

29

The idea of an "eternal" truth, to which he sought to make his doctrines conform, lay at the core of his system of theology. He believed that if he presented doctrines clearly and rationally, and if others engaged in unlimited investigation of his views, only perversity or mental deficiency could account for anyone's rejection of them. Consequently, Taylor could not appreciate Josiah Gibbs's attempt to occupy a balanced position between different interpretations of a subject. Dwight's grandson and namesake recalled Taylor saying that "I would rather have ten settled opinions, and nine of them wrong, than to be like my brother Gibbs with none of them settled." [11]

Since Taylor believed that investigation would bring anyone to accept his views, he magnanimously insisted that his students "be thorough and independent thinkers—to call no man master, and to go for the truth themselves." Yet, convinced that his theology was the "truth," he became impatient with students who doubted the validity of his opinions and often brushed aside their objections in a somewhat cavalier fashion. He was persuasive. Not only did his students admire his superior intellect and commanding personality, but also, as one of his students noted, "Who could stand out against logic and tears?" [12]

Taylor exerted a real and lasting influence on his students. They admired his courage and independence and exulted with him in his theological victories. His enthusiasm and sincere interest underscored for them the importance of their calling as ministers. During the 1830s, Leavitt gained notoriety as an outspoken defender of the New Haven theology against attacks from its conservative critics. In urging him to "follow the truth if it carries you over Niagara," Taylor helped to shape Leavitt's reform philosophy and his conviction that a person must pursue the path of righteousness even if most others do not. Yet Taylor's insistence on self-reliance and independent thought also at times led Leavitt to arrive at a "truth" rather different from his mentor's. This was most evident in the slavery issue, on which Leavitt became a pioneer abolitionist while Taylor remained a colonizationist until his death in 1858. [13]

11. Wayland, "The Theological Department in Yale College," 89–93, 97, 102, 108–12; Timothy Dwight, Jr., *Memories of Yale Life and Men, 1845–1899* (New York, 1903), 260, 262, 265–66.

12. S. W. S. Dutton, *A Sermon Preached in the North Church, March 14, 1858, the First Sabbath after the Death of Rev. Nathaniel W. Taylor, D. D.* (New Haven, Conn., 1858), 17; Mead, *Nathaniel William Taylor,* 162

13. See Mead, *Nathaniel William Taylor,* 161, 236.

Hard work and a flexible curriculum enabled Leavitt to complete the program in one and a half years. In August 1824 he was licensed to preach. This was a commendable record, especially in view of the fact that in early 1824 he had been so ill with what appeared to be consumption that he contemplated giving up his studies. He and Sarah and their son, William, moved a few miles from New Haven; the daily walks to the seminary appear to have helped him regain his health.[14]

In November 1824, at the very time that Leavitt completed his theological training, Sarah gave birth to their second son, John Hooker, named for two of Joshua's uncles. Leavitt, an excited and proud father, expressed to his younger brother Roger Hooker the fond hope that his newborn son would "grow up a good boy, and be a greater and better man than any that have gone before him."[15] At the age of thirty, with a wife and two children to support and at the end of yet another stint of professional training, he awaited a satisfactory call to a pastorate.

He planned to become a minister but did not know when a call to a pastorate would be made. Remaining in New Haven through the fall of 1824, he earned some money by traveling periodically to his parents' home and preaching in Heath and surrounding towns—"much to the satisfaction of his hearers," according to his mother. Finally, in November 1824 the First Congregational Church in Stratford, Connecticut, asked him to preach for several weeks, with the understanding that if he satisfied them he would receive a formal call. His performance duly impressed the congregation. Yet, while awaiting a call to the Stratford church, Leavitt had second thoughts. As a student of the highly respected Taylor and with an outstanding academic record, he may well have expected a more prestigious church. Yet he masked whatever disappointment he felt by expressing indifference about the post, noting regretfully that Stratford had declined "in wealth and habitation til the world is going to N[ew] York" and that religion was "at rather a low ebb here, and improvement in anything is extremely difficult." Three and a half years later Leavitt himself would join the migration to New York. But, despite his misgivings, when the Stratford church voted unanimously in January 1825 to call him to settle

14. *A General Catalogue of the Theological Department in Yale College* (New Haven, Conn., n.d.), 4; Joshua Leavitt to Roger Hooker Leavitt, March 16, November 1, 1824, in Leavitt Papers.
15. Joshua Leavitt to Roger Hooker Leavitt, November 1, 1824, in Leavitt Papers.

as its pastor, he quickly accepted the offer; in February, Professor Taylor presided at his ordination ceremony.[16]

The profession that Leavitt now entered had been undergoing change for many decades. In the eighteenth century the ministry had been an occupation as well as a form of public office; the clergy had viewed themselves as part of a broader officialdom. With the disestablishment of the Congregational Church and the growth of religious pluralism, the ministry in New England ceased to be a public office. Instead, by the 1820s it had largely become a profession that offered a specialized service to a self-selected clientele. Congregations now expected ministers to lead exceptionally blameless lives and to maintain the growth of the church, or face dismissal.[17]

During his years in Stratford, Leavitt performed all the time-honored tasks of a settled minister, including visiting members of his congregation in their homes, meeting with deacons and other lay leaders, exchanging pulpits with ministers in nearby towns, and attending church meetings held throughout New England. He was especially interested in providing religious education for youths in his church. In early 1825 he became a manager of the Connecticut Sunday School Union and the next year established a Sunday school in his church. He served as superintendent of the school and sometimes taught classes in which students memorized passages from the Bible and various hymns.[18]

Leavitt's primary responsibilities as a minister were preaching the Word to his congregation and bringing new members into the fold. As a student of Dwight and Taylor, he naturally tended to display more enthusiasm for gaining converts than for maintaining doctrinal purity. He argued forcefully that a "real" revival was eminently desirable. As he saw it, the critics of revivals unfortunately focused only on the

16. Chloe Leavitt to Roger Hooker Leavitt, October 30, 1824, Leavitt to Roger Hooker Leavitt, November 1, 1824, January 5, 1825, in Leavitt Papers; "Ordinations and Installations," *Christian Spectator*, VIII (March, 1825), 167.

17. See Scott, *From Office to Profession*, xi-xii.

18. Entries for January 4, 21, 1828, in "Church Record Book, 1813–1833," First Congregational Church, Stratford, Connecticut; *Proceedings of the General Association of Connecticut, 1825–1828*, (1825), 5; (1827), 3; (1828), 4–7; F. Stanley Sellick, *The First Congregational Church of Stratford, Connecticut, 1639–1939* (Stratford, 1955), 21, 59; *The Annual Report of the Connecticut Sunday School Union, Presented at the Second Annual Meeting of the Society* (New Haven, 1825), 5–6, 9, 23; (1826), 6, 20; (1828), 69.

blemishes, while ignoring or minimizing the enormous benefits that flowed from successful revival efforts—"the salvation of a vast number of precious souls."[19]

In this era congregations came to expect their ministers to organize revivals and maintain a high level of religious excitement. Leavitt wished to satisfy these expectations. Although he viewed revivals as divine events that could not be provoked at will, he and many of his fellow ministers tended to approach revivals as projects for preachers and churches to undertake rather than as gifts bestowed upon the congregation by the Holy Spirit. In this endeavor numerous techniques and institutions could be used to encourage church members to recognize the need to repent and seek salvation; these included home visits, ministerial associations, Friday and Monday services, and study and inquiry societies.[20]

Attendance at public worship in Leavitt's church increased, and in 1828 he noted that a church committee had "found general harmony and good feelings and piety more than was anticipated." Yet there is no evidence that a revival occurred in his church. His predecessor, the Reverend Matthew R. Dutton, had been a vigorous pastor from 1814 to 1821, adding 153 members to the church.[21] It is entirely possible that Leavitt's ministry came during a lull following intense revival activity—a not altogether uncommon occurrence. Try as he might to work the congregation into a state of readiness, the major revival he desired seems not to have materialized.

Leavitt was rather defensive about his failure to provoke a sustained revival within his church. He declared to his congregation in 1828 that "as regards my discharge of ministerial duty among you, I suppose that in preaching, lecturing, teaching the young, visiting, etc. I have labored more than my predecessors, and perhaps as much as most ministers in this vicinity."[22] One might conclude on the basis of this statement that he felt insecure about his ability to fulfill the expectations of his parishioners and his fellow ministers. Yet in fact Leavitt

19. Scott, *From Office to Profession*, 36–37; Joshua Leavitt, "Thoughts on the Revival under Whitefield," *Christian Spectator*, n.s., II (April, 1828), 175, 177–78.
20. Daniel H. Calhoun, *Professional Lives in America: Structure and Aspiration, 1750–1850* (Cambridge, Mass., 1965), 108.
21. Quoted in entry for January 4, 1828, in Stratford Church Record Book; Sellick, *The First Congregational Church of Stratford*, 59.
22. Entry for February 27, 1828, in Stratford Church Record Book.

had enormous confidence in his abilities. Well-born and well-educated, intelligent, and articulate, he was an important voice in the community and was respected by his congregation. He certainly did not feel threatened by the lay leaders in his own church. Far too many ministers, he stated in an 1827 article, were "so afraid of encroachments upon their office, that they wish to make a very wide separation between themselves and all the other servants of their master." He proposed, instead, that ministers abandon the notion that deacons should only assist at the communion table. Their duties, he argued, should include managing the finances of the church, watching over members and disciplining wayward souls, helping to restore backsliders, and conducting religious conferences and prayer meetings. In his own church he welcomed a sharing of such responsibilities as a means of lessening the burden he experienced as a recently settled minister.[23]

During his years in Stratford, Leavitt was a conscientious and hardworking minister. He necessarily directed most of his time and energy toward his manifold duties as pastor. Yet, during these years, the range of his activities and interests gradually expanded to include a number of secular and religious causes that had emerged in the 1820s. His involvement in these causes took the form of delivering public lectures, serving as a traveling agent, and writing for religious journals. Foremost among these journals was the *Christian Spectator*, an evangelical magazine founded in New Haven in 1819. Closely associated with the Yale community, this magazine became the organ of the New Haven theologians in their battles with the Unitarians and the strict Calvinists. Though initially addressed to the "better part" of the community, the *Christian Spectator* primarily sought to bring its readers into the evangelical camp and to enlist them in the cause of religious benevolence.

In contributing numerous pieces to the *Christian Spectator*, Leavitt joined other young men then entering the ministry, who felt at ease in looking beyond the local parish to a larger, anonymous evangelical audience in a regional or national setting. In doing so, he sought to achieve personal and clerical recognition.[24] He was an ambitious

23. Joshua Leavitt, "On the Office and Duty of Deacons," *Christian Spectator*, n.s., I (June, 1827), 287–88.

24. Scott, *From Office to Profession*, 66–67, 72. At the same time, because Leavitt, like many ministers, was sensitive to the prevailing sentiments of his parish, his pieces on controversial as well as mundane matters appeared anonymously under such pseu-

man. The accumulation of wealth never interested him greatly, though on occasion he entered into ventures that promised—but uniformly failed—to provide a healthy return on his investment. But he did have a considerable ego, viewing himself as a well-bred, well-educated, and well-informed man whose views on contemporary issues were worthy of public consideration. Further, both his parents and Timothy Dwight served as powerful examples of the need for an active Christianity, and growing numbers of laymen were expecting him to provide leadership in efforts to improve the morals and manners of the community and the nation.

During his Stratford years, Leavitt spoke out forcefully in favor of the causes of temperance, Sunday schools, and educational reform and called for an end to lotteries and slavery. He viewed these efforts as crucial to the attainment of a well-ordered, moral society peopled by sober and industrious men and women. If we are to understand why Leavitt and other evangelicals feared that immorality and depravity threatened to overwhelm American society, it is necessary to look beyond the evangelicals' tendency to see the secular world as inherently corrupt. What perhaps proved most disturbing to them were the effects of fundamental social and economic changes then occurring in towns like Stratford, Connecticut, Concord, Massachusetts, Rochester, New York, and many other communities in the North.

In Stratford and similar towns, increasing numbers of farmers were being pulled inexorably into the competitive market economy. In accommodating the demands of the marketplace, they planted new crops and altered their traditional ways. In the process they abandoned habits and practices they now considered wasteful and inefficient and relied on hired hands rather than on family labor. By the 1820s, Stratford contained tinware factories, tanneries, textile shops, mills, mercantile houses, and other business establishments. Stratford manufacturers, master craftsmen, and merchants established close business ties with the commercial farmers in the surrounding countryside. Some Stratford residents were, as Leavitt had lamented in 1825, moving to New York City, but the community was in fact feeling the stirrings of modernization.[25]

---

donyms as "S.F.D." and "J.L." His authorship is indicated in copies of the *Christian Spectator* located in Sterling Library at Yale University.

25. See Robert A. Gross, "Culture and Cultivation: Agriculture and Society in Tho-

In many such communities these groups adapted to an expanding market economy by imposing rigid controls on their workers in the name of productivity and profit. Yet, as Paul Johnson notes, in reorganizing work these entrepreneurs encouraged their workers to move into their own neighborhoods, where they were free of traditional controls on their social behavior. The owners' desire for profit and domestic privacy had a number of important consequences. One was a mounting anxiety regarding their workers' drinking, gambling, and infrequent attendance at church; another was their wives' assumption of a new moral authority and consequent efforts to draw all family members into the church.[26]

The commercial farmers, manufacturers, master craftsmen, and others enmeshed in commercial and industrial capitalism, as well as some of the workers, filled the pews in Leavitt's and other churches and enlisted in the benevolent causes to which he lent his active support in the mid- and late 1820s. These men, joined by large numbers of women, sanctioned an acquisitive economic order and viewed temperance and other causes as necessary for permanent moral and material progress. Though Leavitt had no direct stake in these entrepreneurs' profits or in American economic growth, he strongly identified with their emphasis on self-discipline as promoting individual and national progress and morality.

During Leavitt's years in Stratford, many of the fears of these businessmen and the clergy focused on the problem of drinking. The efforts of some eighteenth-century Americans to educate the public to the harmful effects of distilled spirits had had little impact on drinking patterns. In fact, between 1790 and the 1830s, grain surpluses, improvements in the distillation process, and lower transportation costs combined to make available large quantities of distilled spirits at low prices and to move per capita consumption to the highest levels in the nation's history. Yet an organized crusade against the use of ardent spirits did not begin in earnest until 1826, when the American Society

---

reau's Concord," *Journal of American History*, LXIX (June, 1982), 42–61; Paul E. Johnson, *A Shopkeeper's Millennium: Society and Revivals in Rochester, New York, 1815–1837* (New York, 1978), 6, 16–31; William H. Wilcoxson, *History of Stratford, Connecticut, 1639–1939* (Stratford, 1939), 613–14.

26. Johnson, *A Shopkeeper's Millennium*, 38–52, 55, 108; see also Mary P. Ryan, *Cradle of the Middle Class: The Family in Oneida County, New York, 1790–1865* (Cambridge, England, 1981), 12, 60, 83–104.

for the Promotion of Temperance (often called the American Temperance Society) was established. Clergymen played an important role in the early years of the movement, as did farmers and entrepreneurs who were concerned about their workers' drinking habits—much as Roger Leavitt had been a quarter of a century earlier—while at the same time they themselves were discouraged by their pious wives from drinking.[27]

Leavitt probably drank in moderation until the 1820s, and even acknowledged that he and many other Americans had become rather indifferent to the mounting evidence of alcohol's destructive effects. Yet, in the same year that the American Temperance Society was founded, he addressed a broad appeal to Christians to stem the tide of intemperance, warning that it was *"the source of the greatest and most numerous class of evils with which mankind were ever visited."* He and most other temperance reformers believed that intemperance was linked directly to crime, poverty, insanity, and a host of other social problems and was especially prevalent among workers and the poor. They sought not only to reestablish traditional social controls that had been weakened as a result of the widening gulf between employers and workers but also to preach the gospel of self-control and salvation.[28]

For these temperance activists, the control of desire was the key to moral action. Temperance would strengthen the values of self-mastery, industry, and moral consistency by providing new means of controlling and rationalizing emotions. As Leavitt charged, those who drank liquor committed a great sin by failing to regulate their behavior. Both the emerging agricultural and industrial capitalism and the evangelical revivals of the time were grounded in the belief that one could achieve self-improvement only by avoiding indulgence and idleness. Leavitt insisted that intemperance violated God's laws; if left unchecked, it would destroy millions of souls and create further social disorder. Alcohol was the devil's agent, which cut off drinkers from eternal salva-

27. See W. J. Rorabaugh, *The Alcoholic Republic: An American Tradition* (New York, 1979), esp. 11–21, 25–38, 95–122, 149–83; Johnson, *A Shopkeeper's Millennium*, 55–60.

28. Joshua Leavitt, "The Use and Abuse of Ardent Spirits," *Christian Spectator*, VIII (June, 1826), 303. The most extensive application of the status revolution theory to the early temperance activists is Joseph Gusfield, *Symbolic Crusade: Status Politics and the American Temperance Movement* (Urbana, Ill., 1963), esp. 3–5, 38–44. For persuasive criticism of Gusfield's principal arguments on this point, see Robert L. Hampel, *Temperance and Prohibition in Massachusetts, 1813–1852* (Ann Arbor, 1982), 2–4, 27–31; Rorabaugh, *The Alcoholic Republic*, 188, *passim*.

tion by hardening their hearts. The pledge to abstain from the use of ardent spirits thus became a symbol of conversion and the decision to change one's habits and lead a new life.[29]

In his 1826 article on the temperance question Leavitt told his readers that the triumph of the cause depended on its supporters doing more than writing essays and preaching the Word from the pulpit. Less than two years later, he heeded his own advice by agreeing to serve on a part-time basis as one of the first traveling agents for the American Temperance Society. He clearly wished to get out among the people beyond his parish in order to enlist others in the cause. His selection by the society attests its confidence in his speaking and organizational talents and his ability to work with both clergy and lay leaders. The decision to ask him to serve was probably based on his 1825 *Christian Spectator* article and his strong support in the General Association for a resolution recommending the formation of temperance organizations in all Connecticut towns.[30]

Appointed in May 1828, Leavitt spoke in support of the cause in thirteen towns in Connecticut and eight in Massachusetts and collected several hundred dollars for the national society during a period of two months. Typically, he wrote ahead to ministers in a town to seek support for the cause. Upon his arrival he presented a public address in one of the churches, urged clergymen and prominent citizens to form a temperance society, and provided a model constitution for such an organization.[31]

During his years in Stratford, Leavitt also devoted attention to other causes that, like temperance, were linked to the maintenance of an orderly, moral, and productive society. One of these was the education of youth, which he considered important not only because it helped to develop mental discipline but also because it served as a vital force in the struggle against immorality and irreligion. His *Easy Lessons in Reading*, first published in 1823 and issued in a second edition in 1825, represents his most direct and lasting contribution to the cause of secular education in the 1820s. Many readers—the most common schoolbooks in this era—consisted of little more than a series of

29. Leavitt, "The Use and Abuse of Ardent Spirits," 301, 303, 304. The links between abstinence and the evangelical revivals are discussed in Rorabaugh, *The Alcoholic Republic*, 208–14; Hampel, *Temperance and Prohibition in Massachusetts*, 29–31.

30. John Allen Krout, *The Origins of Prohibition* (New York, 1925), 111–12.

31. *Proceedings of the General Association of Connecticut*, (1828), 9; Rorabaugh, *The Alcoholic Republic*, 193, 210.

lengthy selections culled from plays and essays and bore little relationship to the pupil's grade in school. Leavitt sought to remedy these
deficiencies by compiling a reader suitable for use before pupils were
ready for an English or American reader. "A habit of easy, animated,
and forcible reading," he argued, could be formed by reading materials that focused on real life. Yet as a pious evangelical he viewed moral
development as ultimately more important than the development of
the mind in the educational process. His reader would be a success, he
stated in the preface to the second edition, if it encouraged students to
lead "a life of piety and morality."[32]

In the 1820s Samuel J. May, a Unitarian minister in Brooklyn, Connecticut, and a few other reformers established the Friends of Education, a group that sought to arouse public concern about the quality
of education in the state's schools. Leavitt did not join this group, but
he expressed some of the same concerns stated by May and his colleagues—especially that the schools could not be improved unless the
public was willing to insist upon better training and salaries for teachers. He had little confidence, however, that this would soon happen.
As he complained to his brother in 1824, "Our old towns are like the
old people; the most of them had rather have things go on in the old
way, even if they are fully convinced that a new one is better."[33]

Although Leavitt played only a minor role in the debate on education reform that emerged in the late 1820s, his arguments helped to
stimulate that debate. For example, he urged that a classifying system,
in which students moved through several stages and took annual examinations, should replace the so-called Lancastrian system, which
saved money by having older students teach younger children. He also
insisted that excitement, more than money or talent, would ultimately
improve the system. Such reforms, he argued, would enable students
to function more effectively in an increasingly complex society. Yet,
notwithstanding his prediction that the benefits of reform would more
than offset the unsettling effects of new ideas and policies, Leavitt was

32. Joshua Leavitt, *Easy Lessons in Reading: For the Use of the Younger Classes in
Common Schools* (2nd ed.; Keene, N.H., 1825), 5–6; Ruth Miller Elson, *Guardians of
Tradition: American Schoolbooks of the Nineteenth Century* (Lincoln, Neb., 1964),
3–5. His reader was still selling at a brisk pace in the early 1830s. New York *Evangelist*,
September 14, 1833.

33. Paul H. Mattingly, *The Classless Profession: American Schoolmen in the Nineteenth Century* (New York, 1975), 2–3; Joshua Leavitt to Roger Hooker Leavitt, November 1, 1824, in Leavitt Papers.

in fact a social conservative who feared that the rapid social and economic changes occurring in many communities had produced a dangerous decline in moral standards. He and other evangelicals felt
strongly that the church must instill in children the values necessary
for the preservation of a society guided by Christian precepts. Since
disestablishment had largely ruled out religious education in the
schools, it seemed imperative to the clergy and leading laymen in Connecticut that the Sunday school assume that crucial responsibility.[34]
These activists preached the message of moral uplift, self-control, and
social control. As the American Sunday School Union stated in 1828,
it wished "to lay in the children's minds the foundation of obedience
to their governors in church and state, to make them contented with
the station which providence has appointed to them in the world, to
teach them the subjugation of their passions, and the avoiding of the
company of dissolute and profligate and vicious characters."[35]

By disseminating such values as morality, respectability, productivity, punctuality, usefulness, and upright manners, Leavitt and other
Sunday school proponents sought to create an effective counterforce
to "idleness or vicious pursuits" and, in a larger sense, to "insure the
existence of our civil institutions." These evangelicals believed that
virtue and order were products of choices made by morally responsible
individuals. Thus, children, workers, and others were free moral
agents who were accountable for their actions; it was the duty of parents and employers, not to discipline these groups in traditional ways,
but to educate them and change their hearts. Those who had turned
to Christ must, in Leavitt's opinion, unite for moral action to counteract the dreadful effects of immorality and social fragmentation. "The
enemy of souls," he warned in an 1825 article, "is at this moment
making a desperate effort to poison the minds of the *young*, by circulating the sneers of infidelity and universalism, in the form of cheap
books, newspapers, etc." He feared that unless the Sunday and Bible
schools acted immediately, "we shall in a few years find, with surprise,
that iniquity has come in like a flood."[36]

34. Joshua Leavitt, "Common Schools," *Christian Spectator*, VII (November, 1825),
582–83; Ann M. Boylan, "Sunday Schools and Changing Evangelical Views of Children in the 1820's," *Church History*, XLVIII (September, 1979), 320–33.

35. Quoted in Paul Boyer, *Urban Masses and Moral Order in America, 1820–1920*
(Cambridge, Mass., 1978), 42.

36. *Third Annual Report of Connecticut Sunday School Union*, 12; *Second Annual*

Leavitt's deep-seated fear that immorality and depravity would overwhelm American society also prompted him to condemn the lottery, an institution long established in most states as a means of raising money to build bridges, public buildings, and factories and to support education. In the mid-1820s the clergy began to object to the lottery, and in 1828 Leavitt added his voice to the ranks of its opponents. Speaking as a supporter of all institutions "calculated to promote religion, improve the morals, warm the patriotism, relieve the distress or advance the happiness of his fellowmen,"[37] he launched a sweeping assault on the lottery, condemning it as a threat to the nation's morality and happiness.

Certainly the most controversial subject that Leavitt addressed during his years as a settled minister was American slavery. In his articles on "People of Colour," which appeared anonymously in the *Christian Spectator* soon after he arrived in Stratford, he charged that "the natural effects of slavery on the morals, industry, population, strength, and elevation of character are so destructive" on both masters and slaves.[38] At this time, he did not condemn slaveholding as a sinful act or call for its immediate end; rather, he focused largely on the dangers that slavery posed to the nation and the need for Americans to discuss the issue and develop some plan of action.

Slavery had existed in America for nearly two hundred years, but not until the late eighteenth century did the Revolutionary ideals of liberty and human dignity lead some Southerners to free their slaves. In the North, Revolutionary sentiment, the doctrines of the Enlightenment, and the expansion of the middle class moved all of the northern states to undertake gradual emancipation by 1804.[39]

From the 1790s on, antislavery sentiment continued to grow in both the North and South. Several state legislatures passed antislav-

---

Report of Connecticut Sunday School Union, 8; Joshua Leavitt, "Sunday School Magazine," *Christian Spectator*, VII (November, 1825), 583–84.

37. Joshua Leavitt, "To the Trustees and Directors of those Institutions which hold grants or charters for Lotteries," *Christian Spectator*, n.s., II (August, 1828), 402–403; Keller, *The Second Great Awakening in Connecticut*, 161–63.

38. Joshua Leavitt, "People of Colour," *Christian Spectator*, VII (March, 1825), 134–35. For proof that Leavitt wrote these articles, see Leonard Bacon, *Slavery Discussed in Occasional Essays, From 1833 to 1846* (New York, 1846), iv n.

39. Donald L. Robinson, *Slavery in the Structure of American Politics, 1765–1820* (New York, 1971), 24–38.

ery resolutions, numerous antislavery societies were formed, and the Methodists and Presbyterians publicly attacked slavery as inconsistent with the laws of God. Yet during the half-century following the Revolution, apathy and indifference on the slavery question prevailed in the free states, and southern antislavery agitation—always severely hampered by white racial fears—tended to be conservative and defensive. Even Benjamin Lundy and other early-nineteenth-century abolitionists, who condemned slavery as contrary to natural law and destructive of republican values, generally subscribed to a gradualist philosophy and the colonization principle.[40]

The American Colonization Society appealed to many who were troubled by slavery and wished to end it, yet who also wished to remove from America a people they considered alien and inferior. It promised to hasten America's millennium by solving the slavery and race problems at home while expanding missionary and civilizing work in Africa. Most of its southern supporters, however, viewed colonization as a means of ridding the region not of slaves but of free blacks, whom they believed to be a potentially dangerous element.[41]

The colonization scheme had its doubters and detractors. Free blacks feared that colonizationists would soon resort to forced expatriation and seriously questioned whether the program offered their people any real benefits. Slaveholders generally feared its adverse effects on slavery, while many northern colonizationists suspected that slaveholders supported removal of free blacks in order to strengthen the slave system. Moreover, from its inception the society experienced serious financial, constitutional, and logistical problems that severely limited the number of blacks sent as colonists in any year.[42]

In spite of the paradoxes inherent in the colonization movement, the American Colonization Society represented for many Americans a conscientious alternative to acquiescing in the existence of slavery and

40. See Gordon E. Finnie, "The Antislavery Movement in the Upper South Before 1840," *Journal of Southern History*, XXXV (August, 1969), 319–42; John W. Christie and Dwight Dumond, *George Bourne and the Book and Slavery Irreconcilable* (Wilmington, 1969), 26–27, 35–58, 63–64; Merton L. Dillon, *Benjamin Lundy and the Struggle for Negro Freedom* (Urbana, Ill., 1966), 81–82.

41. For an excellent analysis of the paradoxes inherent in the colonization scheme, see P. J. Staudenraus, *The African Colonization Movement, 1816–1865* (New York, 1961), vii-viii, 22, 28–29.

42. Donald G. Mathews, *Slavery and Methodism: A Chapter in American Morality, 1790–1845* (Princeton, N.J., 1965), 88–90.

a relatively painless way of dealing with a complex moral and social problem. As the only organization in the 1820s capable of effecting a union of conservative antislavery elements and evangelical activists, it attracted the support of nearly all the major religious denominations, including the Congregationalists. In 1825 Leavitt and his colleagues in the General Association of Connecticut pledged to contribute to the colonization cause in the hope that it would "ultimately do much for the illumination and salvation of benighted Africa, as well as the improvement of the temporal and spiritual interests of the people of color in the United States."[43]

By the mid-1820s, it was becoming increasingly difficult for opponents of slavery to believe that any gradualist scheme, let alone colonization, would bring slavery to an end. Slavery had not been kept out of Missouri in 1820 and, despite the letter and spirit of the Northwest Ordinance, had nearly been legalized in Illinois in 1824. At a time when Britain abolished the slave trade and began a decade-long debate on general emancipation, and when the new Central and South American republics abolished slavery, the institution in the United States steadily expanded and gained strength. These developments served to escalate the rhetoric of those who publicly condemned slavery.[44]

Leavitt was familiar with these recent developments as well as the history of slavery in the Americas. In his *Christian Spectator* articles he exhibited little of the militancy and sense of moral outrage that would later characterize his views on slavery. Convinced that slavery was wrong, yet aware of the enormous difficulties involved in ridding the nation of the institution, he assumed a cautious and at times confused stance on the slavery question. He did not consider personal liberty an absolute right and even went so far as to argue that because slaves were in a degraded state, "incapable either of appreciating or enjoying liberty," at present no choice existed for the master but to keep his slaves in bondage. Despite the apologetic tenor of these statements, however, Leavitt was desperately searching for some means of effecting emancipation. His hopes that slavery would die a natural death had been dashed by the virtual political moratorium on the slavery debate following the Missouri controversy and by the contin-

43. *Proceedings of the General Association of Connecticut*, (1825), 7.
44. See Betty Fladeland, *Men and Brothers: Anglo-American Antislavery Cooperation* (Urbana, Ill., 1972), 144–45, 160–61, 177–83; Dillon, *Benjamin Lundy*, 104–108.

ued spread of slavery into the deep South. He had lost patience with those who did little more than wring their hands. "Philanthropy," he warned, "has been put off for many years with fair speeches and pathetic lamentations over the evils of slavery, and the difficulty of applying a remedy. It is time to do something; neither can the urgency of the case be satisfied with half-way measures. We may as well look the subject fairly in the face, and make up our minds that the point to be aimed at is the entire and speedy abolition of slavery."[45]

He also expressed contempt for the "extraordinary" argument that discussion of slavery presented a greater danger than slavery itself. The welfare of the slave—held in a system that was "an evil, a great abomination," Leavitt argued—required prompt action. Beyond this, he feared that internal pressures mounted by an oppressed people, as well as the external models of abolition movements in other parts of the Western world, posed the imminent danger of a war of extermination in the South.[46]

On a general level Leavitt knew what must be done. Because slavery was "our guilt, our full, dark, unmitigated guilt," Northerners must join Southerners in going "to the seat of the disease." "It must be a national business," he maintained. "The whole nation shares in the disgrace of slavery, in the guilt of introducing and perpetuating it, and in the danger which threatens our free institutions, our national union, and our friendly intercourse with other nations."[47]

When it came to devising a specific means for ridding the nation of slavery, Leavitt seemed as perplexed by the magnitude and complexity of the task as did most other thoughtful Americans who wrestled with the problem. In lawyer-like fashion he contended that the slave should receive equal protection under the law during an apprenticeship preceding emancipation, but he never explained how the concept of equal protection could apply to people still in slavery. He called for speedy abolition and argued that the slaves' degradation resulted from slavery, not a biological inferiority; he also insisted that slaves would remain unsuited for freedom until they had acquired sufficient industry and morality. Further, while praising slaveholders for their love of liberty, he concluded that because they would always resist emancipation, abolition probably would have to be carried out by the nonslave-

45. Leavitt, "People of Colour," 133, 239.
46. *Ibid.*, 130–31, 135–36.
47. *Ibid.*, 134, 240.

holding population over the protests of the slaveholders. Leavitt's uncertainty also extended to the relationship between the U.S. Constitution and slavery; in the end, confronted with the imposing presence of the concept of states' rights, he suggested the possibility of amending the Constitution. Finally, he was ambivalent regarding the ability or the desire of the American Colonization Society to deal with the problem of slavery. While willing to see blacks sent out as colonists, he suspected Southerners' motives in supporting the plan and viewed the colonization approach as far too slow and ineffectual.[48]

In the final analysis, Leavitt as much as acknowledged that he knew of no practical solution to the slavery question. "If God is just," he concluded wistfully, "something will be done." Yet he did not intend his articles to be so much a detailed prescription for ending slavery as an attempt to underscore the manifold dangers inherent in the present situation and the need to act. Few Americans, however, heeded his call for a rational and thorough discussion of this explosive issue. Especially in the South, his articles came under fire not only because many considered it improper for such pieces to be included in a religious periodical but, more importantly, because they believed his arguments to be inflammatory. Leonard Bacon, pastor of the Center Church in New Haven, recalled two decades later that Leavitt's pieces produced a "violent sensation" in Charleston, South Carolina, where the *Christian Spectator* "was immediately put upon the *Index librorum prohibitorum* of his holiness Judge Lynch."[49]

Three months after his second article appeared, the American Colonization Society reacted defensively to criticism leveled by Leavitt and other Northerners, reminding them that American slavery was two hundred years old and a legally recognized institution. If the editors of the *African Repository and Colonial Journal* believed that Leavitt had repudiated the colonization movement, they were mistaken. For not until 1833 did he thoroughly and irrevocably abandon hope that the American Colonization Society would uplift blacks here and in Africa and, ultimately, destroy slavery.[50]

In the early fall of 1828 Leavitt's tenure as pastor of the Congregational Church in Stratford came to an end when he accepted an offer from the American Seamen's Friend Society, one of the recently estab-

48. *Ibid.*, 132–35, 240–46.
49. *Ibid.*, 230; Bacon, *Slavery Discussed in Occasional Essays*, iv n.
50. *African Repository and Colonial Journal*, I (August, 1825), 161.

lished benevolent organizations headquartered in New York City, to serve as its secretary and general agent and editor of its magazine. This was a difficult decision to make. He and Sarah had overcome their negative feelings about the community of Stratford soon after their arrival. His manifold responsibilities had at times been burdensome, and he and Sarah had been dealt a severe blow in the summer of 1828 when their second son, John Hooker, died at the age of three. Yet in all they had, as he noted at the time they left for New York, enjoyed a "pleasant situation" with "so many comforts and such kind friends" during their years in Stratford.[51]

In his letter requesting that the church members dissolve the pastoral relationship, Leavitt sought to reassure them that the American Seamen's Friend Society's offer was "very far from anything I should have sought or chosen for myself, and I have made all the reasonable objections I could against leaving my present settlement." It would have been indiscreet and perhaps damaging for him to have appeared eager to break the bonds with his congregation. Yet, he hesitated only briefly before accepting the offer. He recognized the personal and professional opportunities that this new position afforded him. And, notwithstanding his ritual confession that he feared the new responsibilities would be "too vast for my humble abilities,"[52] he was a self-assured, ambitious young man ready to move beyond the somewhat circumscribed world of Stratford, Connecticut.

There were compelling reasons for accepting the offer. The Stratford church was not one of the choice plums of Connecticut Congregationalism. Leavitt and a growing number of young, energetic Congregational ministers found no ladder to climb within the denomination beyond that of pastor. Above all, he left Stratford in order to become an integral part of the expanding benevolent empire. His movement from a settled pastorate to the arena of organized benevolence was part of a larger and rapidly changing relationship that developed in the 1820s between the new benevolent organizations

51. *Second Annual Report of the American Society for the Promotion of Temperance*, (1829), 8; Joshua Leavitt to Roger Hooker Leavitt, July 14, 1828, in Leavitt Papers; letter to congregation, October 13, 1828, in Stratford Church Record Book.

52. *Sailor's Magazine and Naval Journal*, I (November, 1828), 89 (hereinafter cited as *Sailor's Magazine*); letter to congregation, October 13, 1828, in Stratford Church Record Book.

and the major Protestant denominations. These societies increasingly called upon local churches to devote Sunday services to preaching about, and raising funds for, causes such as missionary work and tracts. Leavitt himself had sought to mobilize Christian America in behalf of systematic benevolence. Convinced that the churches had failed to lead the way in establishing a program of systematic contributions to benevolent organizations, he urged them to launch an aggressive grass-roots campaign designed to advance the cause of religious benevolence: "The age calls for action and the interest of Christ's kingdom requires, not only that the large concerns of empires and provinces should be attended to, but that Christian benevolence should extend its operations to every town and hamlet. Attention to minute details is as necessary to success, as boldness of plan, and perseverance in execution."[53]

The national benevolent societies that emerged during the late 1810s and 1820s created a growing number and variety of non-pastoral posts—editorships, secretaryships, and agencies—which, as Leavitt fully realized, were highly valued for their service to the evangelical cause. A prestige ladder in the ministry came into being, which subtly undercut the sanctity of the ordination bonds and eroded the tradition of pastoral permanence. Young men like Leavitt who entered the ministry in the 1820s began to envision a career as a process composed of a number of positions of ever-greater prestige and influence; they now looked beyond the community and parish for personal and professional recognition and achievement. Clerical leaders themselves often encouraged this willingness to break ordination bonds by recruiting the most dedicated and talented ministers for posts that both parties now considered more important to the larger cause than a pastorate. Leavitt acknowledged as much in his letter requesting that his pastoral obligations be dissolved, stating that his position with the American Seamen's Friend Society "opens to me a vast field of labor."[54]

53. Scott, *From Office to Profession*, 66; Leavitt, "Sunday School Magazine," 583; also, Joshua Leavitt, "Systematic Charity," *Christian Spectator*, VII (November, 1825), 645.

54. Scott, *From Office to Profession*, 71–72; letter to congregation, October 13, 1828, in Stratford Church Record Book.

In leaving the security of a pastorate and uprooting his family for a position with a new and struggling organization, Leavitt took a decided risk. But, as would happen so often during the next twenty years, his belief that he had embarked on the path of righteousness and that he could help to advance an important cause more than offset whatever anxiety or regret he may have felt. With the church's concurrence, his career as a settled minister ended.

4

ORGANIZED BENEVOLENCE AND THE AMERICAN SEAMEN'S FRIEND SOCIETY

When Leavitt arrived in New York City in October 1828, he entered a social and economic milieu that differed radically from Heath, New Haven, or Stratford. By the late 1820s, New York's population had reached nearly 200,000, with ever-growing numbers of people streaming in from the farms and villages of upstate New York and New England, as well as from England, Ireland, and the German states. While still largely confined to the lower reaches of Manhattan, the city had inexorably expanded northward; six-story buildings now lined the city streets, and real estate values spiraled as the demand for land intensified.[1]

New York City's location, size, wealth, and commercial importance made it a major world port. By the 1820s, it enjoyed a three-to-one edge in combined imports and exports over its closest American rivals, Boston and Philadelphia. The city led the way in a period of enormous growth in American deep sea commerce; registered tonnage rose from 600,000 in 1820 to 757,000 in 1828, and the whaling fleet from 203 vessels in 1829 to 393 in 1833. The number of American seamen engaged in the foreign and coastal trade and whaling likewise increased, approaching a peak of nearly 100,000 nationwide in the 1830s, 30,000 of whom entered the port of New York each year.[2]

1. See Raymond Mohl, *Poverty in New York, 1783–1825* (New York, 1971), 4–6; Carroll Smith-Rosenberg, *Religion and the Rise of the American City: The New York City Missionary Movement, 1812–1870* (Ithaca, N.Y., 1971), 30–34.

2. Winthrop L. Marvin, *The American Merchant Marine: Its History and Romance from 1620 to 1902* (New York, 1910), 180–83, 219–20; Elmo P. Hohman, *The*

When he moved to New York to minister to the physical and spiritual needs of this important occupational group, Leavitt entered fully into the world of organized benevolence. Largely a product of the evangelical revivals that had steadily gained momentum through the early nineteenth century, by the mid-1820s the benevolent empire consisted of numerous voluntary societies that were seeking to remake America into a moral Christian republic and to usher in the millennium. Like their counterparts in England, they drew much of their support from the evangelical wings of the Protestant denominations, though they had no formal connection with the churches. Many of the societies' leaders were Presbyterians or Congregationalists, but Episcopalians, Dutch Reformed, Baptists, and Methodists also occupied important leadership positions.[3]

The American Seamen's Friend Society represented the culmination of benevolent endeavors in behalf of sailors. Several societies founded in the late eighteenth and early nineteenth centuries had assisted widows and orphans of sailors, distributed tracts, and preached to sailors. But, like their counterparts in Britain, these organizations received little public support. By 1825, the movement's prospects had improved, and dozens of Marine Bible societies, Bethel unions, seamen's churches, and floating chapels were scattered along the Atlantic coast. The American Seamen's Friend Society was established in January 1826, but severe financial problems soon forced it to cease operations. Not until mid-1828 did it slowly begin to revive[4]—a process accelerated by the founding of the *Sailor's Magazine* and the hiring of Leavitt.

As editor, general agent, and corresponding secretary of the society, Leavitt became part of an organizational structure similar to that of most benevolent societies of the day. Many of its officers and leading

---

American Whaleman: A Study of Life and Labor in the Whaling Industry (New York, 1928), 41; Sailor's Magazine, IV (June, 1832), 300.

3. See, for example, Clifford S. Griffin, *Their Brothers' Keepers: Moral Stewardship in the United States, 1800–1865* (New Brunswick, N.J., 1960), 23–36; Charles I. Foster, *An Errand of Mercy: The Evangelical United Front, 1790–1837* (Chapel Hill, 1960), 115–16, 138–45.

4. Israel P. Warren, *The Seamen's Cause; Embracing the History, Results, and Present Condition of the Efforts for the Moral Improvement of Seamen* (New York, 1858), 3–15; *Report of the Society for Promoting the Gospel Among Seamen in the Port of New-York* (New York, 1821), 4–7, 11–12; *The Acts of the Apostles of the Sea: An Eighty Years' Record of the Work of the American Seamen's Friend Society* (New York, 1909), 6–7, 9–10.

benefactors were prominent politicians, philanthropists, shipowners, and merchants from New York City and other eastern ports. Smith Thompson, an associate justice of the United States Supreme Court and former secretary of the navy, served as president of the society until 1831. Both he and his successor, Adrian VanSinderen, a New York merchant, helped to shape its policies. The society's numerous vice presidents and directors did little more than attend annual meetings and lend their names and prestige to the organization. Most of the small contributors did not even attend the annual meetings, held in the city in May in concert with other benevolent associations.[5]

Real authority resided in the society's executive committee. Composed principally of New York City clergymen, merchants, and shipowners, it called meetings, allocated funds, assigned personnel, and lent assistance to the several dozen local seamen's organizations and women's auxiliaries throughout the eastern United States. Leavitt and his colleagues sought constantly to maintain a balance between central direction and local initiative and control. Their frequent disclaimers of any desire to dictate to the auxiliary societies indicate the sensitivity of many local leaders on this issue. Nevertheless, the executive committee believed strongly that only a vigorous national organization could provide the desired coordination and cohesion within the movement. As Leavitt stated emphatically in 1832, "The seamen's cause is one."[6]

Leavitt was by far the most important member of the executive committee. His responsibilities included corresponding with leaders of local seamen's organizations; editing the society's monthly magazine; traveling around the city and throughout the Northeast to address clerical conventions, prospective contributors and missionaries, and meetings of other benevolent groups; and lobbying in Albany and Washington. Although he traveled extensively, most days found him at the society's offices on Nassau Street (and later Fulton Street) in the heart of the city's commercial and financial district, near City Hall and the Customs House and, perhaps most important, within blocks of the headquarters of the national Bible and tract societies. Thus, each day

---

5. *Sailor's Magazine*, I (September, 1828), 2, III (June, 1831), 332. For a study of the society during the first decade of its existence, see Hugh Davis, "The American Seamen's Friend Society and the American Sailor, 1828–1838," *American Neptune*, XXXIX (January, 1979), 45–57.

6. *Sailor's Magazine*, III (June, 1831), 310, IV (June, 1832), 294.

Leavitt was within easy reach of many of the leading patrons of the cause as well as the sailors and ship captains who congregated at the city's wharves. Crowded into the society's small offices during Leavitt's tenure as agent and editor were a reading room and library with "appropriate" materials and a Register Office listing acceptable boarding-houses as well as ships that neither left port on the Sabbath nor carried liquor aboard.[7]

Of all his responsibilities perhaps the most important, and certainly the most time-consuming, was editing the *Sailor's Magazine*. The magazine served a number of practical purposes, especially that of raising funds for the society's operations. Leavitt had to devote an inordinate amount of his time and energy to fund raising, for when he came to the society it had little money and the *Sailor's Magazine* had virtually no subscribers. The organization grew steadily in size and strength, and by the end of Leavitt's tenure its annual receipts totaled more than $5,000. Many of the society's largest contributors were merchants in New York and other Atlantic ports, but it depended most heavily on small contributors who bought life memberships in the society for their ministers and on Sunday school students who contributed pennies to uplift and save the sailor. Yet its constant appeals for funds elicited limited financial support—especially from the clergy, whom Leavitt expected to be committed to all good benevolent causes. As he declared angrily in 1831, the clergy wanted benevolent societies to collect as much money as possible, "but they do not lift a finger to aid nor assume a particle of responsibility on the subject."[8]

The *Sailor's Magazine* itself was a constant financial drain on the society. The number of subscribers rose steadily, in spite of the society's dilemma of not being able to hire agents to obtain subscribers because few would work on a percentage basis so long as the magazine had few subscribers. Following unsuccessful efforts to sell copies to sailors on the docks of New York and other ports, Leavitt and his colleagues generally gave away a majority of the magazines printed.[9] Yet the failure of the *Sailor's Magazine* to turn a profit did not particularly concern the society's officers, for they viewed it as the principal means of

7. *Ibid.*, III (November, 1830), 94.

8. *First Annual Report of the American Seamen's Friend Society* (ASFS) (New York, 1829), 24–25; *Sailor's Magazine*, II (June, 1830), 313, IV (June, 1832), 299, 307, III (December, 1830), 125, (July, 1831), 343–45.

9. *Sailor's Magazine*, I (June, 1829), 314, III (June, 1831), 322.

keeping interested persons abreast of the society's operations and sustaining and, it was hoped, increasing public interest in the cause.

Although Leavitt proved himself a hard-working editor, the *Sailor's Magazine* was a rather pedestrian publication, consisting largely of items reprinted from other journals and rather insipid stories and poems intended to inspire and uplift its readers. Leavitt and the magazine had their share of critics. One of the most vociferous of these was Nathaniel Ames, a veteran of both the U.S. Navy and the merchant service, who branded the magazine "an exceedingly silly periodical" written "in a style too puerile, too silly, for children of five years old." He implored Leavitt and others in the sailor's cause to "address seamen as though they were speaking to people who have wit enough to go below when it rains." [10]

Many sailors shared Ames's sentiments and refused to patronize the society's institutions, in part because they resented its condescending references to their character and life-style. Leavitt and his fellow reformers indeed tended to stereotype sailors with such sweeping descriptive terms as "wicked," "profane," "rough," "generous," and "feeling" and to assume that sailors could not take care of themselves. As the society stated in its first annual report, sailors "of course are little fitted to look out for their own interests, when thrown upon their own resources." [11] Thus, the language of the *Sailor's Magazine* was at times puerile because the society's leaders tended to view sailors as dependent children who needed guidance and protection, and because the magazine was mainly read by men and women who held to the same views.

Some historians have argued that Leavitt and other benevolent activists viewed themselves as trustees of the Lord who were therefore obligated to bring others to conform to God's—and their own—ways. In the name of benevolence, they contend, these men and women condemned as immoral every practice in which they did not indulge and, particularly with groups such as journeymen, sailors, and prostitutes, tended to attribute their poverty and misery to a weakness of character and a lack of religious conviction. [12]

10. Nathaniel Ames, *Nautical Reminiscences* (Providence, R.I., 1832), 47–48.

11. *Sailor's Magazine*, I (December, 1828), 122, II (January, 1830), 144; *First Annual Report of the ASFS*, 3–4.

12. See, for example, Griffin, *Their Brothers' Keepers*; John R. Bodo, *The Protestant Clergy and Public Issues, 1812–1848* (Princeton, N.J., 1954).

In some respects Leavitt fits quite comfortably into this mold. An intense moralism, which distinguished clearly between proper and improper behavior and emphasized the necessity of striving constantly for moral improvement, underlay his commitment to sailor's reform, temperance, and other benevolent causes. Although he may have judged himself harshly as a sinner before God, he believed that his values and modes of behavior were exemplary and should be inculcated in those groups in society that had not yet sufficiently adopted them. If this were accomplished, he assumed, these people—and, ultimately, American society—would benefit. In the pages of the *Sailor's Magazine* and in numerous speeches and pamphlets, Leavitt constantly urged sailors to turn away from drinking, gambling, tobacco, Sunday sailings from port, theater-going, brothels, profanity, and many other "vicious habits" so that they might improve their socioeconomic conditions and open the way for the Holy Spirit. At times he seemed to emphasize moralism at the expense of benevolence. For instance, in an address he prepared for the New-York City Temperance Society, which he helped to establish in 1829 and periodically served as general agent between 1829 and 1831, Leavitt argued not for the reformation of those already addicted to alcohol but for the proposition that "the method of *prevention* being all that *can* be done, is all that we propose to do." Thus, he tended to appeal to people like himself who already abstained from the use of alcohol. Moreover, on occasion he implied that if sailors would only conduct themselves in an exemplary manner, they could resist those who sought to exploit them.[13]

The fact that Leavitt and other benevolent partisans sought to uplift and improve sailors and other workingmen certainly raises the possibility that they hoped to control potentially unruly groups and thus maintain order in American society. In truth, they were aware of, and deeply concerned about, the consequences of the startling changes then occurring in New York and many other towns and cities.

A growing number of poor immigrants, as well as young men and women from the small towns and rural areas of the Northeast, were flooding into New York. At the same time, as Sean Wilentz has shown, merchant capitalists, petty proprietors, and other employers in the ex-

13. *An Address to Physicians, by the Executive Committee of the Board of Managers of the New-York City Temperance Society* (New York, 1829), 4; *Sailor's Magazine*, II (January, 1830), 144.

panding manufacturing sectors (and to a lesser degree in commerce) functioned in an increasingly competitive market economy that placed a premium on efficient labor. With the disappearance of household manufacturing and other traditional methods, many workers came to live in their own autonomous neighborhoods in the city. Thus, employers might control their workers' behavior on the job, but in the working-class wards and districts they frequently observed disorderly, intemperate behavior and feared that the situation would only worsen unless their workers adopted the values and habits of the virtuous classes.[14]

To Leavitt and other evangelicals in the city, the situation appeared extremely threatening. Not only did many workers drink, attend circuses and theaters, gamble, play cards, and frequent houses of prostitution, but government and the churches, which had long served as instruments of social control, seemed increasingly unable effectively to preserve established social practices and forms. Based on his reading of the few available city records and his observations at Five Points, the wharves, and other areas of the city where sailors and workers lived, Leavitt warned the public in a New-York City Temperance Society pamphlet: "Intemperance is filling our Alms-houses with paupers, our Hospitals with patients, our Asylums with madmen, our Penitentiaries with criminals, and our streets with vagrants."[15]

Here, as in his earlier benevolent activities, Leavitt had no direct financial stake in the drive by master craftsmen, manufacturers, shipowners, ship captains, and other employers for an orderly, sober, and industrious work force. But he also had no complaint against the profit motive. More important, Leavitt shared the employers' vision of an orderly, moral society. He and most of the entrepreneurs who enlisted in various benevolent causes did not, as some historians have claimed, seek to impose on workingmen and the poor a harsh moralism, bereft of compassion, for the sake of maintaining the social status quo. However, by bringing the message of discipline, responsibility, and self-improvement to others, they hoped to impose order on a society that seemed increasingly beyond their control.[16]

14. See Sean Wilentz, *Chants Democratic: New York City and the Rise of the American Working Class, 1788–1850* (New York, 1984), 10–11, 146, 281–82.

15. *An Address to the Inhabitants of the City of New-York, by the Board of Managers of the New-York City Temperance Society* (New York, 1829), 5.

16. Among the major statements of the social control theory are Mohl, *Poverty in New York*; Bodo, *The Protestant Clergy and Public Issues*; Griffin, *Their Brothers'*

Yet we must not ignore the fact that Leavitt and many of the businessmen who supported the sailor's reform, temperance, moral reform, and other causes were dedicated evangelicals who carried into their endeavors a profound sense of moral purpose and of their obligation to save their own and others' souls. While one need not accept at face value Leavitt's emphasis on the doctrine of disinterested benevolence as the primary factor responsible for his involvement in these movements, that doctrine profoundly influenced him. Promulgated by Samuel Hopkins, and later subscribed to by both Dwight and Taylor, the doctrine proclaimed that all virtue or holiness was an outgrowth of a disinterested affection that glorified God by seeking the highest degree of good for all beings. This generated a powerful impulse to evangelical moral reform.[17]

The "only right course," in Leavitt's opinion, "was the benevolent object of pleasing God"; virtue was synonymous with choosing the happiness of others. The act of relieving the oppressed would also bring immense pleasure to the benevolent Christian—"a heavenly pleasure, unknown but to those that are beneficent and liberal." Timothy Dwight's belief that preaching and meditative piety were not sufficient to carry the gospel successfully into the world always informed his philosophy of benevolence. All Christians, Leavitt argued in the *National Preacher*, must practice an active faith by serving as "a living epistle every day of their lives" and by being pious in the sense of "going about doing good."[18]

Sailors, mechanics, the unemployed, and other elements of the lower ranks in the city were important objects of Leavitt's benevolent endeavors. Not content with composing editorials in the American Seamen's Friend Society's office, he spent many hours each week during these years with Lewis Tappan, a pious merchant active in numerous benevolent causes, distributing tracts and Bibles among workers and others along the wharves of the East River and in the stores and taverns of Five Points and the countinghouses of State and Wall streets.

Keepers; Charles C. Cole, Jr., *The Social Ideas of Northern Evangelists, 1826–1860* (New York, 1954).

17. Oliver Wendell Elsbree, "Samuel Hopkins and His Doctrine of Benevolence," *New England Quarterly*, VIII (December, 1935), 534–50.

18. New York *Evangelist*, August 18, 1832; *Sailor's Magazine*, II (November, 1829), 91, V (October, 1832), 48; see also Joshua Leavitt, "The Living Epistle," *National Preacher*, V (December, 1830), 106–12.

Working under the auspices of the New York City Tract Society, which had been formed in 1827 by a number of prominent philanthropists to disseminate the truth of revealed religion to the unchurched and deprived of the city, Leavitt served on one of the committees created in each of the city's wards to distribute tracts. He had the responsibility of contacting approximately sixty families each month and urging them to discuss their religious life, join a church, and enroll their children in a Sunday school. He and Tappan gave a tract to each person they met; after each foray, these two earnest moralists would, as Tappan noted, talk at length "about exerting ourselves systematically for the good of the poor and ignorant of the city."[19]

The well-known evangelical preacher Charles Finney made his initial visit to the city in 1829, and from this time Leavitt also helped to establish free churches in the city as a means of bringing the working classes back to the Reformed Dutch and Presbyterian churches. In 1830 Leavitt, Arthur and Lewis Tappan, and other zealous evangelicals founded the First Free Presbyterian Church, with the Reverend Joel Parker, Finney's friend from Rochester, as pastor. In this and other free churches membership was open to all, and pews were not sold. Here, Leavitt, master craftsmen, wealthy philanthropists, and others sat with the few pious workers and their families who attended. Through these contacts they hoped to recruit additional workers and thereby advance the evangelical revivals.[20]

While serving as general agent for the New-York City Temperance Society, Leavitt also made overtures to workingmen in their meeting halls. Brushing aside the concerns of "some influential citizens" who believed that such contacts were a waste of time because workers were entirely hostile to the temperance and other benevolent causes, he addressed the Typographic Union and other labor organizations. "I hope an impression was made in favor of our general object," he informed the Temperance Society's officers. "The question is one of considerable importance whether it is expedient to push our object before these various societies. I do not doubt that great good would result if we could have access to all these meetings in such a way as not to produce

19. Entry for October 18, 1829, Lewis Tappan Journal, Lewis Tappan Papers, Library of Congress; Smith-Rosenberg, *Religion and the Rise of the American City*, 4, 70–71.

20. Charles C. Cole, Jr., "The Free Church Movement in New York City," *New York History*, XXXIV (July, 1953), 284, 288–89, 293–94.

an unpleasant impression at the outset."[21] In the name of social order, moral uplift, and spiritual salvation, he thus sought to bridge the chasm between the "respectable" classes and the working classes that had widened so dramatically through the early nineteenth century.

Yet Leavitt by no means brought this message solely to the workers. He frequently called upon all groups—including wealthy bankers and merchants, ship captains, naval officers, shopkeepers, ministers and their congregations, and physicians and lawyers—to avoid the manifold vices that constantly tempted them and to engage in a systematic program of moral improvement. In some ways Leavitt and other early urban missionaries, working through organizations such as the New-York City Temperance Society, seemed most intent on reaching and converting "respectable" citizens like themselves. They did so largely because they assumed, quite correctly, that these people were the guardians of morality and order in the city and that they would respond most favorably to the message. Unlike workers in Rochester, Utica, and many other communities in the North, however, few workers in New York City were converted in the evangelical revivals or joined the temperance and other benevolent organizations, in part because the city's ethnic and religious diversity was so great, its working classes (especially the sailors) so mobile, and its distractions so numerous; in addition, the city's economy was based more on commerce than on manufacturing.[22]

Leavitt certainly wished to make workers sober, pious, and well-behaved, and he clearly did not believe in the idea of social equality. Yet he was far more interested in making everyone equally good and pious by persuading them to practice self-control than he was in protecting the rule of the elite. For example, he repeatedly urged all New Yorkers to adopt total abstinence. The moderate drinker must be won to the cause, he warned, because moderate consumption of alcohol represented the failure to control one's appetite; this, in turn, led inevitably to excessive consumption. "All this talk about moderate use, temperate use, innocent use," he intoned, "must be abandoned; and the only kind of use we allow ourselves, must be *no use at all.*"[23]

21. Entry for April 4, April 11, 1829, in "Minutes of Proceedings of the Executive Committee, of the New-York City Temperance Society, 1829–1842," New York Public Library.

22. Smith-Rosenberg, *Religion and the Rise of the American City*, 70–71; Wilentz, *Chants Democratic*, 10, 156, 279–80.

23. *Sailor's Magazine*, II (September, 1829), 24.

In declaring that sailors could not take care of themselves, Leavitt and his colleagues in the sailor's movement essentially argued that sailors could not control their appetite for the vices that tempted them. Their declaration also represented an admission that while on shore between voyages, sailors' lives were generally not subject to control or regulation by either their employers or the benevolent activists. Though both paternalistic and patronizing, this view of sailors was in some measure an accurate assessment of the realities that confronted most of them. In fact, as Elmo Hohman has pointed out, in this era sailors experienced worsening conditions, which they found increasingly difficult to control. With ever larger numbers of sailors being young, inexperienced, foreign-born, or from the lower classes, working and living conditions on board many vessels deteriorated. Many sailors experienced strict and often harsh discipline with virtually no redress of grievances available, cramped quarters, abuse, hardship, and much lower wages than those earned even by unskilled workers on shore.[24]

It is not surprising, therefore, that many sailors viewed life ashore as freedom from discipline and a respite from hardship. While in port they also had insistent needs—whether shelter, clothing, entertainment, or sex—which they sought to satisfy during the brief periods between voyages. In all, these factors made possible the systematic exploitation of sailors by shipping agents, outfitters, boardinghouse and grogshop owners, and prostitutes. To make matters worse, as a rootless and diverse group, sailors faced an unsympathetic public that considered them moral pariahs.[25]

In response to the plight of the sailor, the American Seamen's Friend Society emphasized the need for voluntary self-restraint (though it did not object to shipowners and captains banning liquor on board their ships). Although Leavitt himself generally refrained from the standard middle-class practice of blaming the victim, he at times lapsed into this posture. In all, he and other urban benevolent activists went far beyond most of the "respectable" classes, who tended to limit themselves to contributing small sums of money and avoided any contact with sailors and other urban working-class groups. However dogmatic, pa-

24. Elmo P. Hohman, *History of American Merchant Seamen* (Hamden, Conn., 1956), 7, 21–22; *The American Whaleman*, 48–58.

25. Elmo P. Hohman, *Seamen Ashore: A Study of the United Seamen's Service and of Merchant Seamen in Port* (New Haven, Conn., 1952), 202–206.

ternalistic, and narrow-minded these religious humanitarians were at times, and however much they emphasized the virtues of an orderly and moral society, the fact remains that they stood nearly alone in showing concern for the physical and spiritual welfare of these groups.[26]

To some degree these benevolent activists recognized and sought to rectify the serious social and economic problems that plagued sailors. In his editorials Leavitt often argued that many of the sailors' problems stemmed from the fact that they were paid in the form of advances and allotments. Quickly learning that it could do no more than request that shipowners abandon this practice, beginning in 1829 the society founded a number of savings banks for seamen. Guided by the assumption that economic virtues such as thrift and prudence were also moral virtues, this undertaking proved a practical venture that brought real benefits to a growing number of sailors.[27]

Efforts by the American Seamen's Friend Society and its auxiliaries to maintain, or to encourage others to establish, "reformed" boardinghouses were less successful. In an attempt to drive existing boardinghouses out of business, the society sought to provide accommodations at a fair price and to safeguard sailors' personal belongings. Commendable as this may have been, its rigid policies banning liquor, obscene language, gaming, dancing, carousing, and all other forms of behavior that Leavitt and others considered immoral made it difficult for these boardinghouses to compete with others that permitted— indeed, often encouraged—such behavior. Most sailors viewed these policies as intrusive and repressive and refused to frequent these establishments. The same held true on board most ships, where the society's efforts to distribute moral and religious literature had little effect on the lives of seamen. Even William McNally, a former sailor and a friend of the cause, stated that he "never knew any real benefit derived" from tracts written specifically for sailors, observing that they were "not used in any way except as an ornament on top of the mess can, or the mess chest."[28]

26. For an important challenge to the social control theory, see Lois Banner, "Religious Benevolence as Social Control: A Critique of an Interpretation," *Journal of American History*, LX (June, 1973), 23–41.

27. *Sailor's Magazine*, II (December, 1829), 111–12, III (September, 1830), 12; *The Seamen's Bank for Savings in the City of New York: One Hundred Fifteen Years of Service, 1829–1944* (New York, 1944), 8–10, 14.

28. *Sailor's Magazine*, II (June, 1830), 314, VI (May, 1834), 288; William McNally,

On occasion, the executive committee acted to protect sailors' legal and financial interests in their dealings with both private parties and state and federal officials. It had little success in protecting the wages of sailors whose vessels were sold or who fell ill or were discharged while on a voyage. Thanks in part to Leavitt's lobbying efforts in Albany, however, the society persuaded the New York legislature to place at the disposal of sick and disabled sailors revenue from the quarantine tax imposed upon entering New York harbor. Most sailors supported this measure because it seemed to be free of moral judgments.[29]

The society, which had important contacts in Washington, also dealt with federal officials on a broad range of issues that affected enlisted men in the U.S. Navy. The reformers' highest priority was repeal of the grog ration for navy personnel, which appears to have had more support among the society's members and politicians than among sailors. This practice, the society maintained, destroyed sailors' morals and led to widespread flogging. Following the introduction of a resolution in the House of Representatives in 1829, which requested a report on the effects of the grog ration on sailors and the navy, Leavitt urged that each sailor who did not draw the ration be paid for the cost of the liquor. The House, as well as John Branch, secretary of the navy, supported the resolution. Buoyed by this success, Leavitt traveled to Washington in February 1830 to present a memorial requesting that Branch make the grog ration voluntary. Following meetings with Branch, Senator Robert Hayne of South Carolina, chairman of the Senate Naval Committee, and other congressmen, Leavitt spoke at length with President Andrew Jackson on a broad range of issues. The president, Leavitt reported, "seemed much interested, approved such objects, spoke freely of the importance of morality among seamen." A few months later the new secretary of the navy, Levi Woodbury, implemented the society's original suggestion by decreeing that all sailors who voluntarily relinquished the grog ration would receive six cents per ration.[30] In his lobbying efforts in Albany and Washing-

Evils and Abuses in the Naval and Merchant Service Exposed; With Proposals for their Remedy and Redress (Boston, 1839), 154.

29. *Sailor's Magazine*, I (April, 1829), 246–47, III (February, 1831), 182–83, VII (September, 1834), 12–13.

30. *Ibid.*, I (April, 1829), 143–45, II (March, 1830), 223–24, III (January, 1831), 149; Harold D. Langley, *Social Reform in the United States Navy, 1798–1862* (Urbana, Ill., 1967), 127–28, 210–14, 217–29.

ton, Leavitt gained experience that proved valuable a decade later when he established his antislavery agency in the nation's capital.

The society considered these efforts to improve conditions confronting sailors in port and on board ship extremely important. But its principal objectives were the sailors' conversion and the spread of Christianity throughout the world in preparation for the coming of the millennium. As Leavitt stated in 1832, "All reformation is skin-deep, and will not last, unless the heart is changed by religion." To awaken sailors to their sinful ways and bring them to repent and accept God into their hearts, the society sought to create an institutional structure that would facilitate the task of bringing the gospel message to seamen. Toward this end, Leavitt oversaw the formation of Bethel Floating Committees and Bethel Unions, which held public worship and monthly prayer concerts and distributed religious and moral literature on ships anchored in harbor.[31]

In addition, the society founded several mariner's churches in various Atlantic ports. Two principles that Leavitt and other evangelical activists held dear guided the operation of these churches: No fees were charged for pews, and services were conducted on a nonsectarian basis. Here, as with other institutions the society established, the objective was to bring sailors into contact with the evangelical groups and their message. Ministers who labored for the society at home and abroad belonged to several Protestant denominations; all were instructed to avoid the "niceties of theological disquisition" and to concentrate solely upon "the most important and obvious truths" in their dealings with sailors. The society emphasized moral action and spiritual awakening, rather than adherence to denominational creeds. This evangelical, interdenominational theme characterized the *Seamen's Devotional Assistant, and Mariner's Hymns*, which Leavitt compiled in 1830 for use in the mariner's churches and aboard vessels. Urged by several seamen's preachers to compile a hymnbook that sailors would find relevant and useful, he hoped that it would serve to further the evangelical revivals.[32]

Throughout these years, Leavitt and other national officers consid-

31. *Sailor's Magazine*, IV (January, 1832), 133, II (January, 1830), 135, III (February, 1831), 194, (July, 1831), 359.

32. *Second Annual Report of the American Seamen's Friend Society* (New York, 1830), 5–6; Joshua Leavitt, "Seamen's Friend Society," *Quarterly Christian Spectator*, III (June, 1831), 253–67.

ered the maintenance of seamen's chaplains in foreign ports at least as important as the society's varied domestic activities. Practical considerations helped to shape the activists' interest in this field of operations. As Leavitt noted in 1829, the fact that seamen were absent from American ports approximately 80 percent of the time, combined with "their unrestrained exposure to temptation, while in our ports, forbid the hope of a very general reformation among them by means of domestic operations alone." Thus, the society would follow sailors around the world in order to ensure that they held to the same standards of conduct as its officers.[33]

The great surge of enthusiasm for foreign missions in the 1820s and 1830s also deeply influenced these evangelicals. Christianity had always been a proselytizing religion, seeking to convert others to the true faith. Throughout this era, foreign missions inspired the activities of reform organizations such as Bible, tract, education, Sunday school, and sailor's organizations. The enthusiasm for foreign missions emerged from, and served as an outlet for, the energies unleashed by the evangelical revivals of the Second Great Awakening. These revivals created an aggressive, activist mentality within the evangelical ranks. It was necessary, evangelicals believed, to bring Protestantism and American civilization—a religion and a culture that were assumed to be superior—to people throughout the world. With the deepening of the chiliastic strain in evangelical Protestant thought, an increasing sense of urgency developed among those who sought to convert the world to Christianity.[34]

Leavitt and his colleagues viewed the American Seamen's Friend Society as an integral part of the worldwide missionary movement and sailors as an important vehicle for the movement's advancement. The presence of seamen's chaplains in foreign ports would, they hoped, hasten the conversion of sailors, whom the society feared "would otherwise have been exposed to all the pollution of heathenism with-

33. *Sailor's Magazine*, I (March, 1829), 217.
34. For treatments of the foreign missionary movement in the early nineteenth century, see Clifton Jackson Phillips, *Protestant America and the Pagan World: The First Half Century of the American Board of Commissioners for Foreign Missions, 1810–1860* (Cambridge, Mass., 1969); John A. Andrew, *Rebuilding the Christian Commonwealth: New England Congregationalism and Foreign Missions, 1800–1830* (Lexington, Ky., 1976); J. Orin Oliphant, "The American Missionary Spirit, 1828–1835," *Church History*, VII (1938), 125–37.

out an interposing barrier." Yet, in some respects they viewed American seamen less as an end in themselves in either a secular or spiritual sense than as a means for converting the world to Christianity. Sailors must be converted, Leavitt editorialized in 1831, because "there is no class of persons whose 'living epistle' bears so extensive a testimony concerning the Christian religion." In this crusade to conquer the world for Christianity, the seamen's chaplains were to be the field officers, the sailors the front-line troops, and the society and other benevolent organizations the general staff plotting strategy and deploying men and supplies. The society hoped that the chaplains, with the assistance, or at least the positive example, of thousands of converted seamen, would gain access to and proselytize the vast multitudes in other parts of the world. Leavitt, like many evangelicals, felt contempt for the religion and morals of the non-Christian—and for that matter, non-Protestant—peoples of the world, frequently labeling them depraved, ignorant, and profligate. For all his education and training, in many ways he remained something of a parochial bigot throughout his life. Despite his contact with at least a small number of sailors (usually pious ones amenable to the society's overtures), he was unable to transcend a rather stereotypical view of them. And he made no apparent effort to understand groups whose cultures differed dramatically from his. As he stated to a group of seminary students in 1829, one of the greatest rewards of serving as a missionary for the society was "to remove by example, some of the darkness and ignorance that now hangs over many popish, mohammedan, and pagan countries." [35]

The idea of sending seamen's chaplains abroad did not begin to take shape until 1829, when David W. C. Olyphant, a prominent New York merchant engaged in the China trade, offered free passage and a year's lodging in Canton for a missionary. Following extended consultations between Leavitt and officials of the American Board of Commissioners for Foreign Missions, the two organizations agreed that the Reverend David Abeel would occupy the Canton mission. The Chinese government restricted Abeel's field of service to Canton and Whampoa, where most foreign ships were anchored. During the early 1830s Leavitt constantly urged the society to expand the scope of its opera-

35. *Sailor's Magazine*, VI (May, 1834), 282–83, III (March, 1831), 208, I (May, 1829), 282; see also Joshua Leavitt, "Review on Missions to China," *Quarterly Christian Spectator*, II (June, 1830), 299–321.

64

tions abroad. Yet, despite his grandiose plans for founding missions throughout the world, the society created only a few during his tenure as general agent—one in Honolulu, the principal port for whaling ships in the Pacific; others, in conjunction with resident missionaries employed by other organizations, in Cronstadt and Le Havre.[36]

Here, as with so many other projects that Leavitt helped to initiate before his departure from the society in September 1832, the achievements seldom matched his expectations. On occasion, he expressed disappointment about the society's limited success. "It is somewhat discouraging to our natural feelings," he admitted in 1830, "to establish regular boarding-houses, register offices, savings banks, and the like, and have the body of sailors treat them with neglect."[37] However, he generally remained optimistic, believing that sailors could be persuaded to lead moral and productive lives and that the evangelical revivals would continue to bring growing numbers of converts into the Christian fold. These converts would then fill the ranks and the coffers of the benevolent organizations at home and the missionary movement abroad. As an evangelical committed to the advancement of the revivals then sweeping the nation, Leavitt never really doubted that all sinners would eventually be swept up in the revivalist tide and American society would be renewed and purified.

36. *Sailor's Magazine*, I (January, 1829), 143, (April, 1829), 234–38, II (October, 1829), 38–40, (April, 1830), 258, IV (March, 1832), 228; Phillips, *Protestant America and the Pagan World*, 173–74.
37. *Sailor's Magazine*, IV (January, 1830), 143.

5

THE NEW YORK
EVANGELIST AND THE
NEW MEASURES REVIVALS

The evangelical revivals that Leavitt sought to
extend to the far corners of the world had grown in intensity and scope
since the 1790s and reached their zenith in the 1820s and 1830s.
Spreading from the western frontier to the maturing regions of central
and western New York and Pennsylvania, they eventually took root in
the burgeoning cities of the East. A number of evangelists led successful revivals and enjoyed a measure of notoriety; a few played significant roles in shaping the evangelical theology of the time and advancing the revivals. Foremost among these men was Charles Grandison
Finney, who developed his evangelical theology between 1826 and
1835 in the course of conducting mass revivals in upstate New York
and then in Boston, Philadelphia, and New York City. Increasingly,
Finney came to repudiate the main tenets of Calvinism. He was a complex man—an optimist who believed in progress, the benevolence of
God, and the dignity of the individual, but who was also deeply pessimistic, especially in his belief that sinners were unwilling, not unable,
to do all that God required.[1] Like Taylor, who by 1831 had come to

1. James E. Johnson, "Charles G. Finney and a Theology of Revivalism," *Church
History*, XXXVIII (September, 1969), 338–58; William G. McLoughlin in Charles
Grandison Finney, *Lectures on Revivals of Religion*, ed. William G. McLoughlin
(Cambridge, Mass., 1960), viii-ix; Leonard I. Sweet, "The View of Man Inherent in
New Measures Revivalism," *Church History*, XLV (June, 1976), 206–208. Johnson
and McLoughlin tend to see Finney as an optimist who was a child of his age, whereas
Sweet emphasizes the conservative and pessimistic features of Finney's thought. For the

applaud Finney's work, Finney sought to harmonize human responsibility with the doctrine of absolute sovereignty. While Finney believed that the Holy Spirit energized people's minds, he emphasized human ability even more than did the New Haven theologians. Because free moral agency was the key to the human condition, the preacher must employ measures designed to bring sinners under a degree of excitement, wherein they could either reject the truth presented or repent and submit to God.[2]

Tired of small-town life, and convinced that the urban populace needed to be saved, Finney in 1828 brought his revival from upstate New York to Philadelphia, the bastion of Old School Presbyterianism. During Finney's stay in Philadelphia, Arthur and Lewis Tappan, Anson G. Phelps, David Low Dodge, and other transplanted New England Calvinists sought to bring him to New York City. These successful merchants and bankers, who belonged to a group called the Association of Gentlemen, subscribed to Taylor's theological views and desired a greater lay voice in church matters than was possible in the structured hierarchy of the Presbyterian Church. Part of a resurgent evangelical Protestantism, they viewed Finney as a vital force in preparing the nation for the coming of the millennium and advancing the religious benevolence in which they were deeply involved. After many pleas from members of the association, Finney came to New York in 1829; buoyed by enthusiastic crowds at his revivals, he stayed in the city well into 1830.[3]

The Tappans and their associates believed that if Finney was to succeed in converting the city to God, an independent weekly paper, "on the side of revivals and deeply experimental and practical," must be established. This idea had been advanced in 1827 by Dodge, who with other pious New Yorkers was disturbed by the unwillingness of

---

best recent analyses of the revivals of the Second Great Awakening, see William G. McLoughlin, *Modern Revivalism: Charles Grandison Finney to Billy Graham* (New York, 1959); and William G. McLoughlin, *Revivals, Awakenings, and Reform: An Essay on Religion and Social Change in America, 1607–1977* (Chicago, 1978).

2. Johnson, "Charles G. Finney and a Theology of Revivalism," 338–58; Charles G. Finney, *Memoirs* (New York, 1876), 12, 42–51, 57, 154–57.

3. Marion L. Bell, *Crusade in the City: Revivalism in Nineteenth-Century Philadelphia* (Lewisburg, Pa., 1977), 49–77; Zephaniah Platt to Charles G. Finney, August 6, 1828, David Low Dodge to Charles G. Finney, September 19, 1828, in Charles Grandison Finney Papers, Oberlin College.

the New York *Observer* and other orthodox religious newspapers to print the arguments of those who supported the "new measures" revivals. Finney's arrival in 1829 sparked interest in the project, and in March 1830 the Association of Gentlemen launched the New York *Evangelist*.[4]

Leavitt participated in all of the discussions that led to the founding of the paper. He did not belong to the Association of Gentlemen and was not one of the city's *nouveaux riches*, and he ultimately proved far less cautious and conservative on important social issues than were many association members. Nonetheless, Leavitt was a logical choice as editor of the New York *Evangelist*. He shared with these wealthy philanthropists a belief that the preservation of an orderly, moral society and the coming of the millennium required the promotion of revivals and an aggressive advocacy of benevolent causes, such as the Bible, tract, missionary, and temperance movements. Since his arrival in New York City in 1828, he had gained the attention and respect of the Tappans and other association members through his tireless and dedicated efforts to minister to the spiritual needs and morals of the poor, sailors, and other groups. He had also developed a reputation as an able and intelligent editor who did not mince words with the opponents of religious benevolence and a modified Calvinism.

Not long after the paper was founded, the association offered Leavitt the editorship. Because of his busy schedule as editor and general agent for the American Seamen's Friend Society he declined, though he ultimately edited approximately half of the paper's issues during 1830 and 1831. Even when he accepted a second offer and assumed the task of editing the New York *Evangelist* on a full-time basis in December 1831, he continued to devote a portion of his time to his duties at the society's office until August 1832, when a replacement finally arrived.[5]

Leavitt made his most significant contribution to the evangelical revivals as editor of the New York *Evangelist*. He stood forth as an ardent defender of the new measures revivals in the face of increasingly severe criticism from the Hopkinsian Congregationalists and Old School Presbyterians. Under his guidance the paper offered to thou-

4. David Low Dodge to Charles G. Finney, December 18, 1827, in Finney Papers; New York *Evangelist*, April 17, 1830.
5. New York *Evangelist*, October 22, December 10, 1831.

sands of readers a thorough—though frequently one-sided—discussion of all aspects of the evangelical crusade. Well-grounded in biblical scholarship and familiar with the complex theological currents of the day, he nevertheless cared more about advancing a practical, activist Christianity than about speculating on or analyzing esoteric theological doctrines. A persuasive and cogent writer, Leavitt was more a popularizer than an original thinker. He proved especially adept at distilling others' theological views and summarizing information concerning the state of religion and the progress achieved by the evangelical forces. The stream of editorials he wrote in defense of the revivals helped to marshal widespread support for Finney and other evangelists, as well as a host of benevolent enterprises. Leavitt made the New York *Evangelist* one of the most influential organs of the evangelical Calvinist camp in the 1830s. When his tenure as editor of the paper ended in 1837, his friend Theodore Weld calculated that Leavitt had had "more actual influence over the giving, doing, daring, praying, and accomplishing part of the Church than any other man."[6]

At the same time, Leavitt's combative nature, which periodically surfaced in his editorial battles with the anti-evangelical forces as well as with those whom he considered lukewarm supporters of the new measures, alienated some of his readers. He often seemed convinced that his critics were wrong or, even worse, guided by sinister motives. He was not alone among the evangelical reformers in exhibiting a Manichaean view of the world. This tended to breed a certain dogmatism, for if one was wrong, the consequences for one's soul, and indeed for the cause of religion, could be catastrophic. Not all of Leavitt's fellow evangelicals were as reluctant as he was to brook dissent or challenge. He had great confidence in his abilities and the soundness of his opinions. Years later Lewis Tappan, who worked closely with Leavitt during the 1830s and who himself was at times censorious and dogmatic, referred to Leavitt's "natural obstinacy, pugnacity, etc." As he noted to Gamaliel Bailey in 1843, "Brother Leavitt's *manner* is sometimes arrogant, and his temper hasty. If you reply with spirit he will defend himself, but a 'soft answer' will steer away his wrong feelings. He is a sound minded man, with a very good opinion of himself, and does not like to be put in the wrong." Even Weld, a close friend

6. Theodore Weld to James Birney, June 26, 1837, in Dwight L. Dumond (ed.), *Letters of James Gillespie Birney, 1831–1857* (2 vols.; New York, 1938), I, 390.

who believed Leavitt to be one of the wisest and most able men in the nation, noted in the mid-1830s that he had "now and then criticized his spirit."[7]

Leavitt did not consider himself intellectually superior to those with whom he differed. Rather, he believed so deeply in the causes he supported that he at times felt compelled to personalize the battles. He placed his name on the masthead of the *Evangelist*, scorning those "who hide themselves from public indignation by cowardly concealment of their names." This practice, of course, tended to encourage the paper's critics to attack him personally, and he responded in kind. Only occasionally could he acknowledge that in the heat of battle he failed to abide by the Christian rule of charity.[8] His total dedication to the causes he embraced proved a source of strength in the face of adversity, yet his sharp tongue and acerbic pen at times antagonized even some of his closest associates.

Leavitt's certainty that his views were correct explains in part the stubborn independence that he exhibited throughout his journalistic career. He consistently refused to bend to pressure from either benefactors or associates to follow a particular editorial line. Upon assuming the editorship of the New York *Evangelist*, he pledged to maintain the founders' views on Christian doctrine and practice. But he pointedly declared his right to dissent from views with which he disagreed and to determine what should be inserted in the paper. It would be his paper, and he alone would be responsible for its contents. He was extremely protective of his journalistic integrity and proud of his professional ability, even to the point of placing other editors' ringing endorsements of the paper in the columns of the *Evangelist*.[9]

Over the years Leavitt experienced many difficulties and frustrations in his job. One of the problems was avoiding financial ruin. Never a shrewd businessman, he struggled for nearly six years to earn a living from the paper, which he and the religious publisher Seth Benedict owned from 1833 on. Also, like many other editors, he constantly had to contend with subscribers delinquent in their payments.

7. Lewis Tappan to Joshua Leavitt, January 8, 1848, Lewis Tappan to Gamaliel Bailey, March 20, 1843, Lewis Tappan Papers; Theodore Weld to James Birney, October 10, 1836, in Gilbert H. Barnes and Dwight L. Dumond (eds.), *Letters of Theodore Dwight Weld and Angelina Grimké Weld and Sarah Grimké, 1822–1844* (2 vols.; New York, 1934), I, 342–43.

8. New York *Evangelist*, November 3, 1832.

9. *Ibid.*, December 31, 1831.

When he resigned as editor in 1837, he was on the verge of bankruptcy. In addition, while he realized that he could never please all of his readers, at times he complained that if he took a forthright stand on an issue it inevitably elicited criticism from some quarters. He felt a bond of sympathy with all other religious editors. "The multitudes of subscribers," he noted to Amos A. Phelps, a Congregational minister and reformer, "have no sort of sympathy with an editor—especially one who goes ahead—and for the least mistake or difference of opinion they just kick him or turn him adrift." Yet, he also confided to Finney that some readers' convictions were so weak they would accept virtually any doctrine "if only seasoned with a little pious talk." [10]

These pressures prompted Leavitt at one point to call his editorship an "unwelcome and thankless job." [11] Nevertheless, he fully recognized the power of the press to mold public sentiment and viewed his paper as an important instrument for moving mankind toward the millennium. That prospect, as well as praise from associates and readers, went far to satisfy his considerable ego. Whenever the opportunity arose to edit a paper, Leavitt seldom hesitated to step into the breach.

Especially in the early 1830s Leavitt included in the columns of his paper detailed reports of the progress of the revivals and discussion of various doctrines. He also informed his readers—many of whom, like him, were New Englanders who had moved to New York City and central and western New York—of his own religious beliefs. His stand on both doctrines and measures was similar to that of Taylor, as well as Finney, whom he had come to know well during Finney's stay in New York in 1829 and 1830. Leavitt's attempt to translate and clarify Taylor's modifications of orthodox Calvinism for a lay audience only partially attuned to the intricacies of the New Haven theology, and to defend Finney's measures without further alienating the conservatives, required considerable skill. Like Taylor, Leavitt carried this off with some success, but not without executing a number of semantic somersaults. For instance, he hedged on the doctrine of divine imputation, stating that Adam's fall caused all people to sin, yet also insisting that people's depravity was moral, not physical, in nature. Moreover, he declared his belief in the doctrine of election and the importance of

10. *Ibid.*, November 3, 1832; Joshua Leavitt to Amos A. Phelps, November 8, 1833, in Amos A. Phelps Papers, Boston Public Library; Joshua Leavitt to Charles G. Finney, February 26, 1832, in Finney Papers.

11. New York *Evangelist*, November 3, 1832.

divine agency, yet at the same time clearly opened the way for human agency when he stated "that no created power or influence can add to this number, except by the *free choice* of the non-elect; and they *will* not. I believe, that God has fore-ordained whatsoever comes to pass, but yet in such a sense as does not militate against human agency. So that men, considered as free agents, have the power to do differently, and this to frustrate the decrees of God—only they will *not*." [12]

Leavitt believed that because people were, as Taylor and Finney contended, moral agents, they were thus culpable for sin and must be held strictly accountable. His belief in human ability underlay his uncompromising support for Finney's new measures revivalism. Leavitt insisted that the corruption that permeated the secular world could not effectively be counteracted and the world prepared for the coming of the millennium without revivals. "Revivals of religion," he declared, "are necessary to the accomplishment of God's purposes. Great means will be necessary to bring their great purposes to pass. But great things never will be done, without great revivals of religion. All the orthodoxy in the world will not do it. . . . Theoretical systems will do nothing, unless warmed by revivals." [13]

In issue after issue of his paper Leavitt berated the opponents of revivals. But he saved his sharpest barbs for the "devoted and efficient" friends of revivals who gave their support with the condition that revivals be restrained and decorous, with no new measures being employed. He denounced these "lukewarm" supporters as misguided hypocrites whose constant carping encouraged the decided enemies of revivals to intensify their attacks on "energetic" Christians. With these people—as with moderate drinkers and others whom he viewed as false allies—Leavitt resorted to the tactic of calling their motives into question, charging that they applauded revivals only "when they come in such a way as to build up their own congregation, or party, or to give a seeming sanction to their mode of preaching, or their theological views." [14] Such charges infuriated those whose sincerity he questioned, but this seldom bothered him. He simply could not understand why such people did not commit themselves unreservedly to a cause or an idea that he believed was correct and potentially beneficial to

12. *Ibid.*, May 22 (my italics), August 21, 1830, August 23, 1836; also September 15, 1832, December 7, 1833.

13. *Ibid.*, May 22, 1830, January 1, 1831; also April 23, 1831, September 15, 1832, September 21, 1833.

14. *Ibid.*, January 21, September 15, 1832.

mankind. Indeed, in some ways he seemed more tolerant of the true believers who disagreed vehemently with him, for at least they believed deeply in something.

Leavitt also devoted considerable space in his paper to defending and explaining the new measures in the face of attacks by conservative Calvinists. He conceded that some itinerant evangelists aroused more excitement than piety in revivals, but he believed that, whatever the dangers of excess, excitement was a necessary instrument for moving sinners toward God. Using a sailing metaphor, he maintained that "if we know our own minds, we would greatly prefer a dash through the billows towards the wished for port, before a strong wind—even if a sail should now and then be torn, a plank sprung, or a spar lost; rather than remain with flapping canvas, in the safe indolence of a calm." Leavitt therefore stood forth as an uncompromising supporter of such measures as the protracted meeting, the anxious seat, the use of itinerant evangelists in support of settled pastors, calling out for a sinner to repent immediately, and frequent visitations in the home. He, like Finney, was a dedicated pragmatist on this issue. Results were what counted, and excitement helped to produce the desired results. The conservatives, he argued, deserved to be condemned primarily because, content simply to avoid doing any harm, they failed to advance the cause of religion one iota. It was, he editorialized, a "palpable and soul destroying error" for a minister, church members, and impenitent sinners to "go to sleep together, waiting for a 'direct operation' upon their souls." While the influence of the Holy Spirit made regeneration possible, without measures there could be no revival. "The salvation of men," he stated in a wide-ranging statement of faith in 1830, "is effected by God's people using means, adapted to the end, and so well adapted that they would accomplish it alone, if the wickedness of men were not so very great as to resist all means. And where the proper measures are used, with a proper sense and honor to God's sovereignty, he will not fail to add his blessing." Leavitt and Finney fully agreed that whatever measures proved successful—"subject only to the limitations of charity, decency, and order"—should be employed with vigor; those that failed should be discarded. As Finney so often stated, success in saving souls showed that divine truth was preached, for God sanctified success.[15]

15. *Ibid.*, October 20, 1831, September 15, 1832, May 22, 1830, July 30, 1836; also January 21, April 7, 1832, November 30, 1833, October 22, December 17, 1836.

Leavitt did not devise or employ the new measures as a minister or a lecturer. Instead, he lent his considerable energies and prolific pen to the cause primarily as a propagandist. He devoted much of his time to editing the New York *Evangelist*, a task that kept him at the office from dawn until nearly dusk six days a week.[16] Yet he also found time to labor on other fronts in behalf of the evangelical crusade. The *Christian Lyre*, a book of hymns for use in revivals, which he compiled in 1830 and 1831, stands as one of his most direct and lasting contributions to the new measures revivalism.

The Congregational and Presbyterian churches only slowly abandoned the hymns of Isaac Watts and Timothy Dwight. Asahel Nettleton's *Village Hymns for Social Worship*, which went through several editions in the 1820s, displayed an exuberance that previous hymnals had lacked. But to avoid the vulgarizing influence of the folk hymns used in the Methodist camp meetings in the West, Nettleton carefully separated the hymns deemed appropriate to "social worship" from the popular hymns that were part of the intense conversion experience of the revival.[17]

The Finney revivals, in which the view of conversion as a private experience gave way to a "social religion" that included shared religious experiences, such as the protracted meeting and discussion of theology and morals, made this distinction between public and private religious exercises increasingly difficult to maintain. Leavitt believed that Nettleton had supplied "in a good degree" the needs of churches. But prayer meetings, devotional groups, and similar social gatherings were necessary instruments for advancing the revivals, and they required somewhat lighter and more songlike hymns. Leavitt's interest in religious music dated back at least as far as his membership in the Putney Music Society in the early 1820s. At the time Finney conducted his 1829 revival in New York City, they frequently discussed the need for new and different hymns for use in revivals. Convinced that no one else would undertake such a project, in late 1830 Leavitt began to collect and print in the New York *Evangelist* the favorite tunes and hymns of various Protestant denominations, which were published in 1831 as two volumes of the *Christian Lyre* and a supplement.[18]

The *Christian Lyre*'s hymns placed less emphasis on a hierarchical

16. *Ibid.*, May 19, 1832.
17. Sandra S. Sizer, *Gospel Hymns and Social Religion: The Rhetoric of Nineteenth-Century Revivalism* (Philadelphia, 1978), 26, 64, 66–67.
18. Louis F. Benson, *The English Hymn: Its Development and Use in Worship* (New

universe and a mysterious God than had Watts's or Nettleton's. Much like the late-nineteenth-century hymns of Dwight Moody and Ira Sankey, those Leavitt selected for his hymnal focused on the themes of guilt, pardon, redemption, and salvation. Many nineteenth-century hymnals depicted the individual as a passive victim, helpless in the face of hostile forces; metaphors of refuge and hiding abounded. A number of the *Christian Lyre*'s hymns contained images of storms, shipwrecks, wandering, and a safe harbor. But this emphasis can be attributed more to the fact that Leavitt still served as general agent for the American Seamen's Friend Society than to his view of the individual. The individual in his hymnal was consciously evil, having the ability but not the will to repent and obey God's will. His hymns almost invariably expressed an aggressive activism; the mission of the church was ideological conquest—to spread the gospel to the farthest reaches of the globe.[19]

The *Christian Lyre* stands as one of the most important Protestant hymnals published in America during the nineteenth century. Used extensively in protracted meetings and missionary and temperance gatherings, it went through nine editions in the first six months and seventeen more by 1842. Not everyone welcomed the *Christian Lyre*, however. The Finney revivals and those led by Lyman Beecher and Taylor in the late 1820s had generated widespread debate on the influence of folk hymns in revivals. Leavitt's hymnbook added fuel to the fire. By including popular songs in a collection designed for social worship and by consciously seeking to engender excitement through singing, Leavitt broke through the boundaries that Nettleton (and Leavitt himself as a member of the Putney Musical Society in the early 1820s) had sought to maintain. Leavitt believed that bold and assertive rhythms and lyrics served a useful purpose. "If the hymns in general are almost exclusively of a doubting, depending, timid, unresolved cast," he asserted in the preface to the *Christian Lyre*, "they will tend very powerfully to keep Christians in such a state. The use of sacred songs of a more energetic and stirring character is believed to be one of the means by which the church is to be strengthened for millennial achievements."[20]

York, 1915), 37; New York *Evangelist*, December 25, 1830, July 23, 1831; Joshua Leavitt to Charles G. Finney, November 15, 1830, in Finney Papers.

19. Sizer, *Gospel Hymns and Social Religion*, 28, 30–31, 35–37, 42–46.

20. McLoughlin, *Modern Revivalism*, 99n; Benson, *The English Hymn*, 377; Joshua

This sentiment shocked many conservatives who were already deeply disturbed by the new measures revivalism, which transformed conversion from a private to a public and intensely social event by bringing sinners into public contact with praying Christians—often wives and other family members. Foremost among Leavitt's critics were Thomas Hastings and Lowell Mason, well-known lecturers and writers, who published *Spiritual Songs for Social Worship* in 1832 in an attempt to counteract the baneful influence of the *Christian Lyre*. Having striven for several years to improve musical standards in public worship, they believed that Leavitt had degraded hymnody by borrowing tunes from "the current love songs, the vulgar melodies of the street, of the midnight reveler, of the circus and ballroom." As conservative Calvinists they also vigorously rejected the expression of emotions in hymn singing, even "in the mildest of strains." They argued that, instead, the hymnal should "cultivate the finer emotions and edify the Christian." Leavitt reacted defensively to these assaults. As so often happened when challenged, he quickly went on the attack, accusing Hastings of imitating his placement of hymns and music side by side. In the final analysis, however, the hymnal's success counted most to him; he regarded its widespread use in revivals throughout the North as the best evidence of its worth.[21]

As these revivals achieved a high level of intensity and popularity in the small towns and rural areas of New York and New England, Leavitt, the Tappans, and a few other supporters of the new measures renewed their efforts to bring Finney to New York City on a long-term basis. As early as the summer of 1830, Arthur Tappan offered to contribute to a new church for Finney, and the Synod granted permission to Leavitt and other evangelicals to establish the Third Presbytery in the city, which they rapidly made into a "revival presbytery."[22]

In 1831 Leavitt proved as persistent as any in urging Finney to come to the city. He conceded that few of the city's ministers supported such a move, but argued that lay support for Finney would

Leavitt, *Companion to the Christian Lyre* (New York, 1833), iii-iv; Leavitt to Finney, November 15, 1830, in Finney Papers.

21. Thomas Hastings and Lowell Mason, *Spiritual Songs for Social Worship* (Utica, 1832), 4–6; *Sailor's Magazine*, III (November, 1830), 95; New York *Evangelist*, September 10, October 15, 1831.

22. A. Brown to Charles G. Finney, September 30, 1830, in Finney Papers; McLoughlin, *Modern Revivalism*, 58–59.

prevent ministerial opposition from coalescing. Always optimistic that Finney's triumphs in upstate New York and Philadelphia eventually would lead the city's clergy to welcome him, and determined to persevere in the face of all opposition, Leavitt went so far as to predict that a reconciliation could be achieved between Nettleton and Finney and that Finney's presence would convert at least 20,000 sinners in the city.[23]

Unfortunately, frustrated by Finney's reluctance to come to New York, Leavitt ended up hurting Finney's feelings by tactlessly advising him to "look a little minutely at your inside, and see what it is, precisely, that makes you want *all* the ministers in the city to take off their hats to you. . . . I can tell you I have sometimes found there was a *specie* of pride, where I thought I was only standing up for my character and means of usefulness." Leavitt soon apologized for the slight, but at the same time offered the rather lame explanation that his remark had been intended as "a little pleasantry to turn off your mind from the apprehension that it was necessary for you to wait until all the ministers are ready for you to come." More important, he sought to brush off the incident and put it behind them, saying, "But I suppose you have forgiven and forgotten it. So now let it pass." Thus, whatever apology Leavitt was able to muster was a qualified one, which he simply assumed Finney would accept. Finney, a strong-willed man in his own right, did forgive, if not forget, the slight, and he and Leavitt worked closely together in the Lord's vineyard for several years to come. In 1831, however, Finney agreed with those in the city who feared that his presence would produce further discord, for he accepted Lyman Beecher's invitation to bring his revival to Boston, where he made many converts yet also deepened the gulf between supporters and opponents of the new measures.[24]

Leavitt and a handful of friends in the city ultimately prevailed. These men, like Theodore Weld, had common roots in rural and small-town America and agreed that the city was corrupt and materialistic. But, whereas Weld concluded that the West must therefore be

23. See Hammond Norton to Charles G. Finney, February 21, 1831, Joel Parker to Charles G. Finney, February 21, April 4, 1831, Lewis Tappan to Charles G. Finney, February 21, March 17, March 18, 1831, Joshua Leavitt to Charles G. Finney, February 24, 28, April 7, 1831, in Finney Papers.

24. Leavitt to Finney, February 28, April 7, 1831, in Finney Papers; McLoughlin, *Modern Revivalism*, 78.

converted before the great cities, they concurred with Lewis Tappan's assertion that "the city must be converted or the nation is lost. Do what may be done elsewhere, and leave this city, the headquarters of Satan, and the nation is not saved." [25]

Convinced that New York was ripe for the revival message, Finney left Boston in April 1832. When he arrived in New York, Leavitt, Tappan, Joel Parker, and a few other friends, whom Tappan characterized as "the *avant garde* revival nucleus," met him at the dock. Rejoicing that Finney had finally returned after an absence of two years, they quickly organized the Second Free Presbyterian Church and moved it to the Chatham Street Chapel, with Finney as its pastor. [26]

Leavitt watched with great anticipation as the tide of religious fervor rose ever higher. A crucial moment in history seemed at hand. With the evangelical elements within the Protestant denominations acting in concert, it would be only a matter of time before all were swept up in the great revivals and the world converted to Christ. He indeed hoped that "the millennium had actually dawned." Throughout the early and mid-1830s Leavitt stood forth as one of the most outspoken advocates of interdenominational cooperation. "There never was a time," he exulted in 1832, "when the evangelical portions of the various sects were so near to each other, or so disposed to help and encourage each other in their respective plans for promoting the salvation of sinners." No good reason existed, he argued, for revivals to be carried on exclusively by a particular sect. As late as 1835 he still hoped that the Protestant groups would soon become "so united in spirit, in love, in aiming at the salvation of sinners, as to make the points on which they differ appear as unessential as they really are." [27]

Leavitt's spirited call for Christian unity clearly excluded Catholics. Many Protestants exhibited a blatant anti-Catholic bias. In the 1820s and 1830s, rising levels of German and Irish Catholic immigration, the spread of the evangelical revivals, and the proliferation of the benevolent societies combined to increase significantly the intensity and

25. Theodore Weld to Charles G. Finney, February 26, 1832, Lewis Tappan to Charles G. Finney, March 16, 1832, in Finney Papers.

26. Susan Hayes Ward, *The History of the Broadway Tabernacle Church: From Its Organization in 1840 to the Close of 1900, Including Factors Influencing Its Formation* (New York, 1901), 23–24.

27. New York *Evangelist*, December 27, 1834, January 7, 1832, October 17, 1835; also November 2, 1833, March 26, May 27, 1836.

scope of anti-Catholicism. It is not surprising that Leavitt lent his voice to the growing assault on the Catholic Church. As an enthusiastic promoter of the evangelical revivals, he viewed Protestantism as a positive force to be advanced in order to create a Christian republic and to convert the world in preparation for the millennium. In addition, his Congregationalist predilections ran counter to the rigid hierarchical structure of the Catholic Church. Leavitt's wholehearted endorsement of the conspiracy theory promulgated by the more rabid anti-Catholics, however, indicates that on this issue his zeal for evangelical Protestantism warped his powers of reason. Catholic immigrants, he warned in 1833 in terms that became the stock in trade of the nativist movement, owed absolute allegiance to the Pope and planned "to subvert the fair fabric of American liberty and religion, by overrunning our land with Popish emigrants, and filling it with Popish churches, convents, and schools." [28]

The fact that many Protestant Americans agreed with this statement does not make Leavitt's paranoid ramblings any less bigoted. His assaults were never as vitriolic as those of seasoned Catholic baiters such as George Bourne, and he never condoned violence against Catholics. But the inclusion of such sensational charges in his paper—not much different from those that the anti-abolitionists would hurl at Leavitt and other opponents of slavery—helped to create an atmosphere of fear and distrust in which anti-Catholic mob action would occur. [29]

The union of these evangelical Protestant activists, in part in response to the perceived Catholic threat, as well as Finney's arrival in New York in 1832, provided a powerful impetus to the evangelical cause in the city. During the next two years, with revival enthusiasm at a peak of intensity, Finney and other preachers converted large numbers of New Yorkers. Several historians have maintained that these revivals represented an antidote for the confusion and anxiety experienced by rootless individuals in a society undergoing rapid social and economic change. Thus, revivals were a means of restoring order and a sense of purpose among people suffering from a sense of

28. Ray Allen Billington, *The Protestant Crusade, 1800–1860: A Study of the Origins of American Nativism* (Chicago, 1964), 41–108; New York *Evangelist*, August 3, 1834, July 27, 1833.

29. See New York *Evangelist*, November 29, 1834.

cultural disorientation.[30] Yet studies of recruits to Finney's revivals in Philadelphia, Rochester, New York City, and Utica indicate that these converts did not come primarily from groups experiencing instability and dislocation in their lives but rather from the most stable elements in the community—the artisans (who were themselves often masters), the manufacturers, and, to a lesser extent, the merchants. These groups tended to be located in high prestige occupations, were church members or husbands of women active in the church, and were wealthier than those who shunned the revivals. They viewed the evangelical doctrines as a religious solution, not so much for the social upheaval in their own lives as for the disorder and immorality they observed among the increasingly autonomous working classes in their communities.[31] Leavitt fully expected that these men and women would unite to form a Christian army to destroy sin and usher in the millennium.

30. See McLoughlin, *Revivals, Awakenings, and Reform*, 12 ff.; Scott, *From Office to Profession*, 38–41; Donald G. Mathews, "The Second Great Awakening as an Organizing Process, 1780–1830: An Hypothesis," *American Quarterly*, XXI (Spring, 1969), 23–43; T. Scott Miyakawa, *Protestants and Pioneers: Individualism and Conformity on the American Frontier* (Chicago, 1964).

31. See Robert W. Doherty, "Social Bases for the Presbyterian Schism of 1837–1838: The Philadelphia Case," *Journal of Social History*, II (Fall, 1968), 69–79; Johnson, *A Shopkeeper's Millennium*; Wilentz, *Chants Democratic*, 277–83; Ryan, *Cradle of the Middle Class*, 12, 60–62. Bell (*Crusade in the City*, 76–77) contends that Finney appealed largely to the less educated lower classes in Philadelphia but provides little supporting evidence for this claim.

6

EVANGELICALISM AND THE
EXPANDING WORLD OF REFORM

From its inception the New York *Evangelist* had been "Devoted to Revivals, Doctrinal Discussion, and Religious Intelligence." But Leavitt gave increasing attention to a number of benevolent enterprises. He and many other New Yorkers responded to the mounting religious enthusiasm by demanding the immediate end to all compromise with sin. To fail to direct one's efforts toward the eradication of sinful habits and practices, they believed, would not only impede the progress of Christianity but also make one an accomplice to the evil that existed in the world. Souls were lost and sin continued to hold sway because men chose to sin. This thinking underlay Leavitt's advocacy of the manual labor, temperance, antiprostitution, and antislavery causes.

Leavitt and other evangelicals who founded the manual labor movement in the early 1830s were inspired by the work of Philip Emanuel von Fellenberg, an eighteenth-century Swiss educator who established a regimen of manual labor in academies for the purpose of teaching students the value of correct conduct. Oneida Institute of Science and Industry in Whitesborough, New York, and Andover Theological Seminary in Massachusetts instituted this system in the 1820s as a means of preserving students' health and helping them to pay for instruction and living expenses.[1]

1. Charles Alpheus Bennett, *History of Manual and Industrial Education Up to 1870* (Peoria, Ill., 1926), 182–88.

Leavitt, the Tappans, and other benevolent activists established the Society for the Promotion of Manual Labor in Literary Institutions in 1831, in the hope that manual labor education would help to swell the ranks of missionaries and that colleges and other educational institutions would adopt the manual labor system. A mixture of vigorous physical labor and education, they believed, would instill in young men the values of productivity, usefulness, moral deportment, and above all self-control, thus helping them to resist the constant temptation to indulge in immoral practices. Like temperance and other reforms that Leavitt advocated, manual labor was intended to instill discipline and a willingness to forego gratification in those who engaged in it. As Theodore Weld, who served as the society's general agent in 1831–1832, stated in the report he submitted when he resigned his post: "Sufficient exercise would be a preventive of moral evils *by supplying that demand for vivid sensation so characteristic of youth*, whose clamors for indulgence drive multitudes to licentious indulgence, or to ardent spirits, tobacco, and other unnatural stimulants. It would preserve the equilibrium of the system, moderate the inordinate demands of immoral excitability, and quell the insurrection of appetite."[2]

The manual labor movement never gained widespread support, partly because the continuous labor kept students from their studies. In addition, the vigorous discipline and Puritan asceticism that Leavitt and his colleagues sought to inculcate in the students did not appeal to many, and the movement never directed its energies toward young workingmen.[3] But for Leavitt, manual labor education represented only one of many means that God-fearing Americans must utilize to combat the corrupting influences of the world and to prepare the way for the ultimate triumph of the gospel. Another means was a succession of moral reform societies designed to root out immorality and licentiousness wherever they existed. In the early and mid-1830s he served the moral reform cause as editor, general agent, and executive committee officer.

In the course of distributing tracts, visiting the waterfront, and carrying out his other benevolent responsibilities, Leavitt observed the

2. New York *Evangelist*, June 18, 1831; *First Annual Report of the Society for Promoting Manual Labor in Literary Institutions* (New York, 1833), viii, 3.
3. See *First Annual Report of the Manual Labor Society*, 93–97.

poverty and crime that increasingly characterized the urban scene. In the Five Points area, located only a few blocks from his office, as well as in other sections of the city, Irish and black laborers and other New Yorkers lived in squalor and poverty in decaying buildings. Numerous prostitutes—including growing numbers of recent arrivals from small towns and rural areas—openly solicited clients, and men from all social classes frequented the brothels. These conditions were abhorrent to Leavitt and other moralists, who believed that prostitution, adultery, and lewd thoughts and language violated the Seventh Commandment. As in their sailor's reform and temperance activities, they hoped to reestablish the social controls that had existed in the preurban social order and to persuade those who violated the Seventh Commandment to exercise self-control in their lives. They were disturbed by the horror stories that circulated widely concerning young women and men from pious families who were either lured into prostitution or tempted to visit the brothels, but they were also worried by the fact that in this urban setting the cloak of anonymity permitted residents to commit a host of moral transgressions. Equally troubling to these moralists, many prostitutes and their clients were poor and working-class New Yorkers whose values and life-styles differed significantly from theirs and whose lives seemed largely beyond their influence. To many of the transplanted rural and small-town Americans who joined this moral crusade, the city—particularly areas such as Five Points, which most respectable New Yorkers avoided entirely—seemed alien and threatening. As the *Journal of Public Morals*, the organ of the American Moral Reform Society that Leavitt helped to edit in the mid-1830s, stated: "The sin of Sodom is steadily increasing with the increasing population, and if nothing is done to prevent this, our cities must soon become as corrupt as those of Europe."[4]

Leavitt and other evangelical Protestants sought to awaken Christian America to the pervasiveness of sexual sin and the need to oppose it and to reform the city's prostitutes. John R. McDowall, a dedicated, idealistic Princeton divinity student who came to the city in 1830 to do volunteer work in the Five Points slums, launched the moral reform movement. He and several women converted in the Finney revivals

4. Carroll Smith-Rosenberg, "Protestants and Five Pointers: The Five Points House of Industry," *New-York Historical Society Quarterly*, XLVIII (October, 1964), 327; *Journal of Public Morals*, I (May, 1836).

hoped to "reform depraved and abandoned females, and the profligacy in the vicinity of noted places of vice," and thus remove a major obstacle to municipal regeneration. In 1831 McDowall and his supporters, including Arthur Tappan, established the New-York City Magdalen Society and opened a "House of Refuge." The society received little public notice until McDowall claimed in the first annual report in 1832 that 10,000 prostitutes worked in the city and that men from the city's most respected families regularly patronized the brothels. Even in the millennial America of the 1830s, many people regarded prostitution as a taboo subject; it is no wonder that the Magdalen Society's clinically detailed exposé of the effects of prostitution shocked and angered many New Yorkers. Even Lewis Tappan, a member of the society, later admitted that McDowall's "zeal and courage were greater than his judgment."[5]

If Leavitt had any reservations about McDowall or the report, he did not express them. He was convinced by his work with the Seamen's Friend Society that prostitution was an integral part of the system that exploited and degraded sailors and that it—like intemperance, gambling, and other vices—represented the failure to control one's appetite. Thus, he praised the Magdalen Society's officers for having the courage and honesty to investigate the evils of prostitution. Unable to comprehend how anyone could refuse to support efforts to preserve the moral order and to combat such an egregious sin unless guided by ulterior motives, he accused the moralists' critics of either profiting from prostitution or despising the society's leaders for their "well known liberality, in patronizing benevolent objects, and their zeal for religion and temperance." He thus satisfied himself, as he did in similar circumstances with other causes he supported, that the unregenerate and timid were responsible for the outpouring of scorn and abuse. His success in locating villains, however, provided little comfort for the cause, for public opinion—including not only Tammany Hall and groups associated with it but also many religious leaders and members of the city's elite—was so negative, and the society's success so negligible, that the Magdalen Society was dissolved in 1831.[6]

5. Smith-Rosenberg, *Religion and the Rise of the American City*, 99; see also *First Annual Report of the New-York City Magdalen Society* (New York, 1831), 3–4, 6–7; O. Brown to Charles G. Finney, January 6, 1831, in Finney Papers; Lewis Tappan, *The Life of Arthur Tappan* (New York, 1870), 114

6. New York *Evangelist*, August 6, 1831; *Sailor's Magazine*, III (July, 1831), 359;

Even McDowall, who with a simple country view of city vice came to exhibit a fascination with prostitution and licentiousness, conceded that "the Society rose in confusion, was sustained in discord, and perished in anarchy." In the dark days of 1832 McDowall, who at Leavitt's urging had begun to serve as a correspondent for the New York *Evangelist*, came to Leavitt's home to discuss his plans for the future. Buoyed by Leavitt's promise to assist him in every way he could, McDowall established *McDowall's Journal* in early 1833. Soon thereafter, Leavitt and other die-hard moralists formed a number of moral reform organizations; their efforts culminated in the creation of the American Society for Promoting the Observance of the Seventh Commandment, in which Leavitt served as chairman of the executive committee.[7]

In 1832 Sarah Leavitt, Finney's wife, and other evangelical women in the city, motivated by a desire to reform prostitutes and to warn God-fearing Christians of the pervasiveness of sexual sin and the need to combat it, founded the Female Benevolent Society of the City of New York. Sarah served as a manager of this organization and of the New York Female Moral Reform Society, which she helped to establish in 1834. Both organizations sought to promote chastity and good morals and insisted that prostitutes were victims of lascivious and predatory males who endangered the nation's spiritual life. Perhaps the most controversial of their activities were their visits—in the company of Joshua and other male moralists—to the brothels, where they prayed with and exhorted the prostitutes and their patrons. Their tactic of reading Bible passages, singing hymns, and observing and noting the identity of customers—some of them prominent figures in the city or their sons—had a deterring effect in the more expensive brothels, but in the poorer areas it often generated curses and angry threats.[8]

With several young sons at home, including William, who was approaching his teenage years in the early 1830s, Sarah was bound to be sensitive to the temptations that confronted young men in the urban

---

Memoir and Select Remains of the Late Rev. John R. McDowall (New York, 1838), 184–85.

7. New York *Evangelist*, January 19, 1833, January 2, 1837.

8. *First Annual Report of the Female Benevolent Society of the City of New York* (New York, 1834), 2–8, 21–22; Carroll Smith-Rosenberg, "Beauty, the Beast and the Militant Woman: A Case Study in Sex Roles and Social Stress in Jacksonian America," *American Quarterly*, XXIII (October, 1971), 562–63, 565–84.

setting. Yet her activism and her willingness to endure hostility and ridicule stemmed from more than her concern for her sons' moral welfare or her husband's devotion to the cause of moral reform, or, indeed, than the evangelical conviction that God commanded her work. In the Leavitts' and other evangelical households the mother had increasingly come to be viewed as the moral governor responsible for the improvement of all family members. Joshua obviously exerted moral influence as well, but in exercising new forms of moral authority and becoming active in temperance, moral reform, and other causes Sarah moved away from the traditional subordinate feminine roles. Her authority was, if anything, augmented by the fact that Joshua was often absent from home at least fourteen hours a day, six days a week, editing his newspaper, attending meetings, and addressing groups in the city and throughout the Northeast. This left Sarah in charge of much of the child rearing.

Neither Joshua nor Sarah was prepared to reject the prevailing view that men should establish policy for the religious and benevolent organizations and that women should occupy subordinate positions in these causes. In 1834, while noting that women could play important roles in advancing religion by assisting in the church, dispensing charity, distributing tracts and Bibles, and forming female auxiliaries, Joshua argued that they should not engage in "*authoritative* acts, which are inconsistent with their relation to the other sex." It is therefore not surprising that Sarah devoted much of her energy outside the home to serving on the executive committee of the female auxiliary of the Seventh Commandment Society and other benevolent associations. Yet Joshua and Sarah seem to have had a companionate marriage, with each being supportive of the other's roles and responsibilities. Indeed, in encouraging Sarah's active participation in the temperance, moral reform, and other causes—especially in visiting brothels—Joshua gave his approval to actions that many Americans still considered improper for women.[9]

In the mid-1830s the men's and women's moral reform organiza-

9. New York *Evangelist*, August 30, 1834; *McDowall's Journal*, II (June, 1834), 42, 44. On women's changing place within the evangelical home and the central place of women in religious life, see Ryan, *Cradle of the Middle Class*, 105, 116–23; Johnson, *A Shopkeeper's Millennium*, 107–108; Ann Douglas Wood, *The Feminization of American Culture* (New York, 1976); Smith-Rosenberg, *Religion and the Rise of the American City*, 97–124.

tions increasingly went their separate ways, addressing different constituencies and following different paths toward the goal of eradicating licentiousness and prostitution. The women focused on establishing asylums for prostitutes, while the men emphasized the need to protect virtuous males from contamination by the manifold evils that surrounded them. Much as they labored in the temperance movement to convince moderate drinkers to abstain, rather than seeking to regenerate alcoholics, Leavitt and his associates called upon ministers, teachers, parents, and editors to "promote purity of thought, language, and life" so as to protect the nation's youth from "adultery, fornication, and kindred crimes." As McDowall stated in his paper, which served as the semiofficial organ of the Seventh Commandment Society, "*To stay the influx of new victims should be our chief aim.*"[10] Thus, they essentially acknowledged that they could not influence the lives of many of those who were already engaging in sexual vice.

The Seventh Commandment Society made little progress and endured constant public ridicule during its first year. The religious community provided negligible support and, with the exception of Leavitt's New York *Evangelist* and a few other religious newspapers, the press condemned the crusade. Leavitt's refusal to retreat an inch in the face of this hostility is indicative of a new form of militance on his part. Notwithstanding his criticism of slavery in 1825, he had continued to support the colonization effort. That cause and the temperance and sailor's reform crusades drew much of their support from evangelical activists. In the late 1820s he had also supported the Sabbatarian movement, which had sought to ban Sunday mail delivery. The public ridicule directed toward that effort, and its consequent failure, as Bertram Wyatt-Brown has noted, led Leavitt, the Tappans, and other evangelicals increasingly to see themselves as an unpopular minority who could not trust expedient politicians to labor for civic virtue and morality. Yet Leavitt had not been nearly as directly and deeply involved in the Sabbatarian movement as he was in the moral reform cause. Not only did public condemnation now rain down upon him and his family, but much of that denunciation came from the very people he counted on to support the cause—the clergy, the religious editors, and the benevolent activists. His sense of social isolation and his willingness to endure scorn and contempt in order to advance

10. *McDowall's Journal*, II (January, 1834), 1, 7.

a highly unpopular cause certainly influenced his thinking in the summer of 1833 when he made the difficult decision to embrace abolitionism.[11]

Predictably, Leavitt blamed the timid and the self-serving for generating much of the criticism of the Seventh Commandment Society. However, the critics' motives were more complex than that. Moved by wounded city pride, a Victorian delicacy, and a dislike for the moralists' proclivity for graphic details and harsh accusations, a grand jury investigated charges that McDowall's paper "inflames the passions of the young," and the Third Presbytery arraigned McDowall on charges of financial mismanagement, unministerial conduct, misrepresentation, and slander. Leavitt fought vigorously in defense of his friend, lashing out at the presbytery for having censured "a great reformer" who had engaged in "self-sacrificing labors" for the cause it had ordained him to serve. At McDowall's funeral after his untimely death in December 1836 he praised him for the "boldness of his course, and the disclosures he made" and expressed deep regret that during the last years of his life his friend had suffered "a series of vexations and oppressions."[12] Leavitt could be extremely generous and caring toward friends, perhaps especially those, such as McDowall (and Charles Torrey a decade later), whom he considered victims of injustice and abandoned even by many of their friends.

Only with the founding of the American Moral Reform Society in 1836 did the cause experience a rebirth. Leavitt remained in the forefront of the movement, serving on the society's executive committee and as one of several editors of its official organ, the *Journal of Public Morals*. This organization, like its predecessors, argued that if the rising tide of licentiousness were not reversed, the evangelical cause could not triumph. Yet both subtle and obvious differences existed between this society and earlier organizations. First, it was more self-consciously a male-oriented society. Second, Leavitt and his colleagues

11. Bertram Wyatt-Brown, "Prelude to Abolitionism: Sabbatarian Politics and the Rise of the Second Party System," *Journal of American History*, LVIII (September, 1971), 316–41; Merton L. Dillon, *The Abolitionists: The Growth of a Dissenting Minority* (DeKalb, Ill., 1974), 24–30.

12. William Brown and D. Fanshaw to Theodore Weld, March 17, 1834, in Barnes and Dumond (eds.), *Weld-Grimké Letters*, I, 130–31; *McDowall's Journal*, II (April, 1834), 31, (December, 1834), 92–95; New York *Evangelist*, April 30, December 17, 1836.

came to accept the female moralists' argument that low wages were responsible in part for forcing women to turn to prostitution. Thus, they proclaimed the movement for higher pay "a righteous cause." Finally, these would-be censors now devoted attention to the harmful influence of the theater and "immoral" books. Seeking to determine the limits of respectability in literature and entertainment, they insisted that theaters be closed and books of "immoral tendency" be suppressed.[13]

Leavitt and his fellow moralists met with some success during the society's fourteen-month existence. They managed to persuade 10,000 men to pledge "to discountenance licentiousness," and by 1837 the *Journal of Public Morals* had 8,300 subscribers. Yet the society, like its predecessors, did not engender much enthusiasm among the urban population, whose moral standards it sought to elevate. The poor and the working classes stood largely beyond the reach of the evangelical moralists, separated from them by the barriers of class and religion. In the moral reform cause, as in the temperance and sailor's reform movements, Leavitt and his colleagues remained outsiders in many neighborhoods in the city, missionary visitors whose encounters with the objects of their benevolence were often fleeting and impersonal. Much of what little financial support the society received came from evangelical groups in the towns and villages of the "Burned-over District" of upstate New York, as well as in towns in New England such as Heath, where Joshua's younger brother Roger Hooker served as president of the Young Men's Moral Reform Society. With the onset of the 1837 depression, the society disbanded.[14]

From the establishment of the organized movement, Leavitt and his associates had managed to alienate most New Yorkers by their self-righteous denunciations and graphic exposés. Although well-meaning and sincere, these rural and small-town churchmen only partially understood that poverty and social dislocation underlay many of the problems they sought to eradicate. Moreover, the city's populace was simply too diverse to permit the imposition of effective social controls. In their defense, however, it must be remembered that most Americans were not prepared to discuss the subject of prostitution at all. These reformers stood practically alone among the respectable classes in the

---

13. *Journal of Public Morals*, I (November, 1836), (February, 1837).
14. *Ibid.*, II (June, 1837); Ryan, *Cradle of the Middle Class*, 116–23.

city in attempting to do anything about eradicating this complex phenomenon. Mathew Carey and a few other social commentators of the time pointed to low wages for women as a factor underlying the spread of prostitution but, much like the evangelical activists, they looked to a moral awakening among the respectable groups as a solution to urban misery. And the call for cheap land and education and bank reform made by such secular reformers as Fanny Wright, Robert Dale Owen, and George Evans scarcely represented a realistic solution to the pressing needs of the urban poor.[15] Leavitt and other evangelicals of his generation failed in their effort, but so too has each succeeding generation.

Leavitt's conviction that prostitution and licentiousness could be removed from society was grounded in his perception of his own experience: self-control and Christian virtue had allowed him, as they would others, to resist temptation. He applied this same reasoning to abstinence from alcoholic beverages. Both the temperance and moral reform causes would, he insisted, enable people to achieve control over their animalistic instincts. Alcoholics and those who indulged in sexual license were prisoners of their baser appetites. Thus, freedom had to be redefined. To be truly free, Leavitt reasoned, one must control these impulses by developing moral values and by sacrificing personal interest to the general good.[16]

In the early and mid-1830s Leavitt enunciated this theme as a leading spokesman for the radical wing of the temperance cause. The temperance movement underwent dramatic changes in these years. At a convention in 1833, which Leavitt attended as a reporter, delegates formed the American Temperance Union. Here, heated debate arose on two issues. One concerned the liquor traffic. Some delegates wished to condemn the traffic as morally wrong, while others feared that this would undermine efforts to persuade liquor dealers to abandon the traffic. In the end, the convention condemned the liquor traffic, which Leavitt denounced as "inhuman and infamous, a species of piracy upon the rights and happiness of society." Debate on the second issue, the abstinence pledge, proved more divisive. Many moderates called for total abstinence from the use of ardent spirits, whereas a radical

---

15. See Smith-Rosenberg, *Religion and the Rise of the American City*, 40–42.
16. See Rorabaugh, *The Alcoholic Republic*, 200–201.

minority sought to include beer, wine, and cider in the pledge. After much controversy, the moderates prevailed.[17]

In numerous editorials in the New York *Evangelist* and in debates in state and local temperance conventions, Leavitt vigorously called for abstinence from all intoxicating drink. Before the early 1830s, he had not insisted that beer, cider, and wine be included in temperance pledges because he believed that, used in moderation, these substances did not intoxicate. He now concluded that if alcohol was a sinful compound, a slight quantity could not change its fundamental nature. Moderate use would only encourage progressively wider deviation into error. In defense of his stance on the issue, he declared in 1835: "All that those who are agitating the question desire to know, is *truth* and duty. When they gain this, they will adopt such a course as they shall be satisfied is according to the will of God. There is no other 'ultraism,' nor 'radicalism,' nor 'over-wise-ness,' nor 'intemperance' but a desire to go to all lengths with the laws of God, to effect a radical extermination of all sin, to understand exactly 'the mind of the Spirit,' to be 'always zealously affected in a good thing.'"[18]

The fact that Leavitt only recently had come to judge the moderate consumption of beer, cider, and wine as wrong did not concern him greatly, for he believed that God's plan unveiled itself to believers. He now grasped an absolute moral truth; neither public censure nor schism within the temperance ranks would move him from that position. For Leavitt and others whose evangelical mentality inclined them to locate moral absolutes, there was no room for moderation. The world was neatly divided between the kingdom of God and that of Satan. Immorality, evil, and sin must be rooted out wherever they existed. Leavitt held to this view of the world throughout his life.

This absolutist reasoning led Leavitt inexorably to conclude that because the use of tobacco represented the triumph of one's lower desires over conscience and will it, too, was wrong. For the same reason, he initiated and strongly supported the campaign to replace wine with grape juice in the communion service. Declaring that God had "never cautioned his children against going too fast and too far in abandoning that which is wrong and pursuing that which is right," he stated

17. New York *Evangelist*, November 30, 1833; Krout, *The Origins of Prohibition*, 132–33.
18. New York *Evangelist*, August 22, 1835.

to his readers that "the use of fermented wine, at the communion table, is a powerful barrier to the progress of the temperance cause, and a stumbling block to the impenitent." This campaign eventually gained some support among temperance advocates, but it also produced a bitter and divisive dispute within the movement and in the churches. Believing purity of doctrine to be of the utmost importance, Leavitt exhibited little concern about the possibility that such a novel stand might seriously divide the movement. Yet many Christians could not accept his interpretation of the Scriptures. Indeed, some temperance activists warned him and other radicals that even their demands for abstinence from *all* intoxicating drink would ultimately destroy the very cause they espoused. These fears were nearly realized at the American Temperance Union's convention in 1836, where a majority of delegates, now in the radical camp, pushed through a pledge binding temperance advocates to "totally abstain from all that can intoxicate." The convention placated the moderates by calling for voluntary acceptance of the pledge, but even this compromise alienated many temperance advocates.[19]

Despite these growing divisions, the temperance movement steadily gained strength during the 1830s. The number of temperance societies in the United States more than tripled during the first half of the decade; by the mid-1830s, more than one million people belonged to temperance organizations. During these years Leavitt was active in the effort, headed by Gerrit Smith and Arthur Tappan, to establish hotels owned and operated by temperance men that refused to serve alcoholic beverages as well as refusing to accept people who traveled on the Sabbath. Despite stiff opposition and financial problems, they succeeded in establishing temperance hotels in several cities in the 1830s.[20] A veritable flood of pamphlets and books fed this upsurge in temperance enthusiasm. The distillers of liquor, who for decades had been an honored group in society, bore the brunt of these attacks. In 1835 George B. Cheever, a young Salem, Massachusetts, minister, published *Inquire at Amos Giles' Distillery*, which led to a libel trial that became the *cause célèbre* of the temperance movement in the 1830s. Before the trial, Leavitt collected money for Cheever's defense

19. *Ibid.*, September 21, 1833, January 11, 1834, August 22, 1835, April 26, 1834, August 20, 1836.
20. *Ibid.*, March 30, 1833, March 28, 1835; Ralph Volney Harlow, *Gerrit Smith: Philanthropist and Reformer* (New York, 1939), 69–71.

and frequently corresponded with him. He reacted angrily to the guilty verdict of the Massachusetts Court of Common Pleas, charging that "some decided drinkers on the jury refused to find him innocent." But he believed the verdict to be essentially irrelevant, in that the moral question transcended the legal issue, or even the legal vindication of Cheever; the case would serve as a valuable means of mobilizing public support for the cause.[21]

Toward this end, Leavitt, Lewis Tappan, and Edward Delevan, a leading New York temperance advocate, overruled those who advised settlement outside of court and rejected Daniel Webster as Cheever's lawyer on the grounds that Webster, a drinker of some reputation, would hardly be an appropriate person to defend a temperance man. Leavitt recommended that Rufus Choate manage the legal process and that Cheever defend himself by presenting a temperance sermon "to the conscience of the multitude, such as they have never heard before." "Show your flag too as a firm believer in an eternal hell," he counseled Cheever, "and turn the court room into an anxious meeting. . . . Make a Christian business of it, and then if you fail, you will have a hold on the hearts and prayers of Christians."[22]

Cheever agreed with Leavitt's plan of attack. When he appeared before the Massachusetts Supreme Court, he read his defense—an hour-long, carefully prepared assault on drunkenness and its evils. Although the court upheld the ruling of the lower court, sentencing Cheever to three days in jail and a fine of $1,000, Cheever's diatribe against intemperance became an effective tool in the hand of temperance agitators. Leavitt applauded Cheever's speech, believing that "it has shown the vindictiveness of transgressors and called attention to the truth."[23] He had calculated correctly. As a seasoned propagandist for a number of movements, he clearly understood the importance of publicity and of gaining public sympathy for those persecuted for espousing a cause.

Leavitt believed that Cheever's triumph—and that of the larger tem-

21. Robert M. York, *George B. Cheever, Religious and Social Reformer, 1807–1890* (Orono, Me., 1955), 72–75; New York *Evangelist*, July 4, 1835.

22. Joshua Leavitt to George B. Cheever, November 12, 1835, in Cheever Family Papers, American Antiquarian Society.

23. York, *George B. Cheever*, 77–78; George B. Cheever to Charlotte Cheever, December 4, 1835, Joshua Leavitt to George B. Cheever, January 14, 1836, in Cheever Papers.

perance movement, as well as sailor's reform, moral reform, and other benevolent causes—would help to cleanse the nation of evil and prepare the world for the millennium. His conviction that Christian duty obliged him to combat sin wherever it existed in the world also led him in these years to demand the immediate abolition of slavery, a system that by 1833 he had come to view as the greatest evil afflicting American society.

Leavitt followed a long and tortuous path from the colonization principle to immediatism. He gave little attention to the subject of slavery in the late 1820s; when he did, he invariably viewed the colonization scheme favorably. He believed that the moral standards of blacks could be improved. As general agent for the New-York City Temperance Society, for example, he urged blacks to adopt the temperance pledge. Yet he, like many other benevolent activists who supported the colonization cause, was alarmed by the underclass of free black paupers and criminals he observed during his forays into the waterfront and Five Points areas. These blacks, as well as poor whites, seemed an alien and threatening element in the city; at this time he was unable to see a connection between their condition and the systematic discrimination they encountered. In all, he was largely insensitive to the feelings of blacks. In 1829, for example, he expressed concern that intemperate and immoral black servants might exert a deleterious effect on children placed in their care. Black servants, he warned in the *Evangelist*, "have, to a great extent, the power to make early and deep impressions upon the white young generation. They are in our houses, and have freer access to our children than we do ourselves." [24]

Such considerations prompted him and Sarah to contemplate sending to Liberia a young, unmarried black woman who had been a servant in their home for two years. Writing as a "friend of Colonization" in 1829, he conveyed to Ralph R. Gurley, secretary of the American Colonization Society, his fear that the servant, who he believed was pregnant for a second time, would endanger the morals of his young

24. See Leavitt, "Systematic Charity," 645; Minutes for April 4, 1829, New-York City Temperance Society (New York Public Library), 11–12; New York *Evangelist*, June 19, 1830. For a study of the colonization movement that emphasizes the importance of racist attitudes and republican values, see David M. Streifford, "The American Colonization Society: An Application of Republican Ideology to Early Antebellum Reform," *Journal of Southern History*, XLV (May, 1979), 201–20.

sons. Confessing some ignorance of conditions that would confront her in Liberia, he asked Gurley whether it would be wise to send her there.[25]

Leavitt's pointed inquiry regarding conditions in Liberia may also have been provoked by disquieting rumors that the Colonization Society allowed rum to be sold to the Liberian people. This news shook his confidence in the organization. "On this point," he warned, "may be suspended perhaps the question, whether the colony is to flourish or decline; whether it is to prove a blessing or a curse to Africa." Yet soon thereafter, assured by the society that it was doing everything it could to rectify the situation, he appeared to conclude that it deserved the support of benevolent people; in late 1831 he praised naval officers for lending assistance to the settlement in Liberia.[26]

Others were not so charitable toward the colonization movement. By 1830, a handful of men and women—including William Lloyd Garrison, an intense, pious activist who had been arrested and imprisoned for accusing a shipmaster of piracy for transporting slaves to the South—had come to condemn slavery as a great national and personal sin that must be immediately and unconditionally eradicated. Garrison feared that unless slavery was soon ended, a bloody race war would engulf America—a fear that seemed to be confirmed only a few months after Garrison's founding of the *Liberator* newspaper, when Nat Turner and a few supporters cut a bloody swath through the Virginia countryside, spreading panic throughout the South. In addition, his denunciation of the colonization scheme in his *Thoughts on African Colonization* converted Elizur Wright, Beriah Green, and Charles Storrs—all professors at Western Reserve College in Ohio—to immediatism. Following discussions with Wright and others, Theodore Weld, a brilliant, sensitive young man who had been converted in the Finney revivals and was deeply committed to the temperance and manual labor movements, also began to move toward immediatism.[27]

For reasons that are not altogether clear, Leavitt remained apart

25. Joshua Leavitt to Ralph R. Gurley, October 20, 1829, in American Colonization Society Papers, Library of Congress.

26. *Sailor's Magazine,* II (September, 1829), 33, IV (September, 1831), 8; *Fourteenth Annual Report of the American Society for Colonizing the Free People of Colour of the United States* (Washington, D.C., 1831), 11–12.

27. See John L. Thomas, *The Liberator, William Lloyd Garrison: A Biography* (Boston, 1963), 106–13; Henry Wilson, *History of the Rise and Fall of the Slave Power in*

from this incipient movement. He had frequent contact with Weld and Arthur Tappan, a silk importer and benevolent activist who was also gravitating toward the abolitionist orbit. Moreover, he certainly knew of Garrison's activities in Boston. In an 1831 editorial in the New York *Evangelist*, Leavitt indeed sounded much like Garrison when, following Nat Turner's revolt, he condemned slavery as a "national SIN, as well as evil." At this time, he sought to make his point "kindly, and without occasioning offence or gulf," and did not wish to insist on exactly how slavery should be abolished. But he was certain that "until this is effected, the dangers, and alarms, and evils, attendant on slavery, will continue to multiply." Nevertheless, he did not repudiate colonization. This may be explained in part by the fact that the Seamen's Friend Society had many southern supporters. He argued in 1829 that sailors needed benevolent assistance more than did slaves because slaves were cared for when infirm or aged.[28]

The Seamen's Friend Society's supporters, of course, expected such special pleading. But, in fact, Leavitt did not regard abolition as an objective of the highest priority to which Christians must lend their energies. Rather, he believed that in this time of widespread religious enthusiasm the gospel must be brought to slaves and free blacks alike in order to advance the evangelical revivals. In May 1833 he expressed sentiments with which many evangelical Protestants agreed: "I confess that much as I love freedom and detest slavery, when I hear of the triumph of the gospel among the slaves, I cannot help thinking how small a thing is the emancipation of the body, compared with the salvation of the soul. Let the religion of the gospel reign in both masters and servants, and slavery would cease of itself." [29]

The violent reaction to the efforts of Arthur Tappan and Simeon Jocelyn to establish a black college in New Haven in 1831 probably further convinced Leavitt that the time was not propitious for joining the infant movement. He did not hesitate to lend support to the highly unpopular Magdalen Society. But he had not yet come to view slavery (as he did licentiousness and prostitution) as a heinous example of the

---

America (Boston, 1872), I, 223–28; Theodore Weld to James Birney, September 27, 1832, in Dumond (ed.), *Birney Letters*, I, 27.

28. New York *Evangelist*, October 1, 1831; *Sailor's Magazine*, I (February, 1829), 185.

29. New York *Evangelist*, May 25, 1833; also December 24, 1831, April 27, 1833.

sin of self-gratification, which impeded salvation and the coming of the millennium. In the final analysis, his belief that the evangelical revivals must succeed in order for American society to be redeemed, as well as his conviction that the Colonization Society was "the only means of raising blacks to their proper rank in the scale of humanity and the only flexible plan for Christianizing and civilizing the vast continent of Africa," largely explain his reluctance to disavow colonization.[30]

The first hint of movement toward repudiating colonization came in a June 1833 editorial in the New York *Evangelist*, in which Leavitt advised "intelligent Christians" to contribute to benevolent organizations other than the Colonization Society, arguing that this "would do more for the benefit of the colored race, more to promote true liberty, more to bless Africa, more to free our country from its greatest danger, more to strengthen the bonds of our union, more to promote the glory of God and the salvation of men."[31]

This statement represents a significant shift in Leavitt's thinking, for he now dissociated the evangelical and benevolent impulses from the colonization cause. He was not yet prepared to commit himself fully and openly to the doctrine of immediatism. Even his warning in August 1833 that "something must be done about slavery" differed little from what he had said eight years earlier. Unlike the situation in 1825, however, there now existed a fledgling antislavery society and a newspaper in Boston, as well as a tentative organizational effort in New York City. With Arthur Tappan as the chief benefactor and driving force, New York City was fast becoming a center of antislavery activity.[32]

Finally, following months of intensive soul-searching, Leavitt announced his conversion to the doctrine of immediatism in the summer of 1833. A combination of experiences and personal traits led to his

30. Robert Austin Warner, *New Haven Negroes: A Social History* (New Haven, Conn., 1940), 53–59; New York *Evangelist*, December 24, 1831.

31. New York *Evangelist*, June 29, 1833. Gilbert Hobbes Barnes, *The Antislavery Impulse, 1830–1844* (New York, 1933), 33–36, states that in mid-1831 Leavitt, Lewis Tappan, Weld, and a few other men met in New York City to plan the establishment of a national antislavery organization but that the New Haven mob action against Arthur Tappan forced them to abandon the idea. This assertion, however, is not documented, and this author has found no evidence to support it.

32. New York *Evangelist*, August 24, 1833; Wyatt-Brown, *Lewis Tappan*, 102–103.

conversion. The impulse toward immediatism varied from individual to individual. While those who embraced the abolitionist cause had much in common, no "abolitionist personality" existed; they were a diverse group in terms of their psychological makeup as well as their views on many issues.[33]

Neither a fertile imagination nor a personality disorder moved Leavitt to condemn slavery. Prominent Americans of the Revolutionary generation, as well as growing numbers of people in Europe and the Western hemisphere, had come to denounce the institution.[34] In 1825 he had warned that slavery had become ever more tightly woven into the fabric of American society and that nothing was being done to reverse this trend. By 1833 the situation had, if anything, worsened. The South seemed more determined than ever to resist any form of emancipation. Only recently, South Carolina had threatened to nullify federal law, largely to protect slavery from outside interference, and then had gained tariff concessions from the Democratic party. The cotton culture had spread inexorably into the Lower South and the Southwest, in the process funneling hundreds of thousands of slaves onto these new lands. Moreover, the always weak southern antislavery movement had virtually disappeared by 1830. Slavery, therefore, stood in a much stronger position in 1833 than it had in 1825. Moderate ideas and programs had proved hopelessly inadequate; it was time for bold action and insistent demands.

The fact that only a handful of Americans had come to espouse immediate emancipation by the summer of 1833 did not dissuade

33. For treatments of the broad range of experiences and attitudes among abolitionists, see Martin B. Duberman, "The Abolitionists and Psychology," *Journal of Negro History*, XLVII (July, 1962), 183–91; Betty Fladeland, "Who Were the Abolitionists?" *Journal of Negro History*, XLIX (April, 1964), 99–115. Ronald G. Walters, *The Antislavery Appeal: American Abolitionists After 1830* (Baltimore, 1976), emphasizes characteristics that abolitionists had in common but does not lump them together indiscriminately.

34. See Duberman, "Abolitionists and Psychology." Nor does Leavitt appear to have been moved to embrace abolition because of status anxiety. For penetrating critiques of the status revolution theory as it has been applied to abolitionists, see Robert W. Doherty, "Status Anxiety and American Reform: Some Alternatives," *American Quarterly*, XIX (Summer, 1967), 329–37; Robert Allen Skotheim, "A Note on Historical Method: David Donald's 'Toward a Reconsideration of Abolitionists,'" *Journal of Southern History*, XXV (August, 1959), 356–65; Gerald Sorin, *The New York Abolitionists: A Case Study of Political Radicalism* (Westport, Conn., 1971), 101–15.

Leavitt from publicly endorsing the cause, for he had already encountered widespread hostility and scorn from opponents of the moral reform cause. His sense of Christian obligation helped him to overcome whatever trepidation he may have felt about joining the small cadre of immediatists. As he recalled in 1837, "We profess that we entered on the work of emancipation as a religious duty." The relationship between his evangelical beliefs and his conversion to abolitionism, however, was complex. After all, his tendency to view reform as an adjunct of the Great Revival had been instrumental in delaying his conversion. Also, other evils had seemed more threatening to the soul than did slavery. For instance, he and other temperance activists had argued that drunkennesss was more sinful than slavery because, while slaves lost control of their bodies, drunks lost control of their souls.[35]

Yet, at the same time, the evangelical image of intemperance (and licentiousness, prostitution, gambling, and other vices) as self-gratification and the inability to control one's basic instincts helped to condition Leavitt to view slavery in a similar light. As Ronald Walters has shown, for many abolitionists slavery easily became the analogue for disorder and debauchery. With unchecked authority resting in the hands of masters, charged the abolitionists, the system permitted them to fall prey to lascivious instincts and to become the slaves of passion, thus corrupting both themselves and their slaves and spreading depravity throughout the South. Only the end of slavery, they insisted, would bring civilization and self-control to the South.[36]

Leavitt, Weld, the Tappans, and other converts to abolitionism shared with many Americans of their time the belief that licentiousness represented an enormous threat to a moral, orderly society. All of the causes in which Leavitt had been involved during the late 1820s and early 1830s emphasized this theme. To him, the failure to control the "animal nature," which invariably led to human depravity, was evident throughout American society. He now believed, however, that slavery was the clearest example of the prevalence of sexual immorality.[37]

Leavitt had now concluded that all of these practices—prostitution, licentiousness, gambling, drinking, and slaveholding—were sinful. It

35. *Emancipator*, August 17, 1837; see, for example, Rorabaugh, *The Alcoholic Republic*, 214.
36. Walters, *Antislavery Appeal*, 70–78.
37. *Ibid.*, 80–85.

made no difference if one seldom frequented a brothel or entertained lewd thoughts, or was a moderate drinker, an occasional gambler, or a kind slaveholder. Moreover, to condemn these practices—by signing an abstinence pledge for the temperance or moral reform causes or by declaring for immediate emancipation—constituted, in his opinion, "a moral act, a triumph of conscience over the lower desires"—that is, an act of self-liberation. Such an act, he declared, would generate additional revival activity. "We may reasonably expect," he stated, "to see revivals follow in the train of *every* great struggle, by which conscience gains a triumph over passion, and truth becomes ascendent in the public sentiment." Further, his evangelical belief in the human ability to repent and in the concept of immediate conversion pointed naturally toward the conclusion that anyone who did not denounce slavery and demand immediate emancipation was guilty of the sin of slavery.[38]

Leavitt never regretted his decision to endorse immediatism, even though, as he acknowledged a few years later, "we clearly saw that abolition of slavery was one of the most difficult and laborious undertakings."[39] He had wrestled with this issue since at least 1825, but now he suddenly broke with most of the benevolent activists with whom he had worked closely for several years in the colonization, temperance, sailor's reform, moral reform, and other causes. He would soon come into bitter conflict with these former friends and associates. Thus, he did not merely endorse a highly unpopular cause; in doing so, he separated himself from the inner circle of benevolent activists that had been such an important part of his life.

The immediate factor underlying his momentous decision was the impending abolition of slavery in the British West Indies. In August 1833 Arthur Tappan initiated a series of conferences with Leavitt, Elizur Wright, William Goodell, editor of the *Genius of Temperance*, and a few other men to discuss the feasibility of establishing an antislavery society following action by the British Parliament. British emancipation stirred the imagination and raised the hopes of these men. Now that the leading power in the world was finally ending a system that had endured for centuries, success seemed possible in the United States

38. New York *Evangelist*, January 11, August 23, 1834; see also Donald M. Scott, "Abolition as a Sacred Vocation," in Perry and Fellman (eds.), *Antislavery Reconsidered*, 72–73.

39. *Emancipator*, August 17, 1837.

as well, after so many years of frustration and discouragement. As Leavitt noted to his *Evangelist* readers with great expectation: "No man or body of men, or class of men, or human safeguards, or bulwarks, can keep from our shores the moral influence, the speaking voice of the act of abolition."[40]

Their attempts to emulate the English action, however, generated deep fears and hostility in both the North and South. New York was the leading American port for cotton exports, and numerous merchants and others in the city relied on that trade for their livelihoods. Moreover, white workers feared competition from blacks for jobs. Soon after a committee headed by Leavitt issued a call for a meeting on October 2, 1833, for the purpose of organizing an antislavery society, these groups—as well as colonizationists and others who disliked Leavitt and his friends for their benevolent meddling—threatened violence. Encouraged by vitriolic attacks by the press and politicians, an angry mob assembled outside Chatham Street Chapel as fifty abolitionists met hurriedly and established the New York City Anti-Slavery Society, adopted a constitution, and chose Leavitt, Lewis Tappan, William Goodell, and a few others to serve on its executive committee. Leavitt and his friends were forced to disperse, with some of them being rescued by a policeman.[41]

Leavitt was shocked and outraged by the incident. Neither the burning of his *Christian Spectator* article in the streets of Charleston and other southern cities eight years earlier nor the intense hostility directed toward him and other moral reform activists had prepared him for the fury of the mob. "Who could have thought," he declared, "that the disgraceful scenes of Columbia, S.C. would so soon be attempted in New York? In New York, where not a slave is to be found, and where, if a man brings his slave, he becomes instantly free! SPIRIT OF SLAVERY!"[42]

Some of the city's papers expressed mild regret at the disturbance, but other journalists, especially James Watson Webb, the truculent editor of the New York *Courier and Enquirer*, urged New Yorkers to

40. *National Anti-Slavery Standard*, October 24, 1844; New York *Evangelist*, September 12, 1833.

41. Joseph G. Rayback, "The American Workingman and the Antislavery Crusade," *Journal of Economic History*, III (November, 1943), 152–63; *Liberator*, October 12, 19, 1833.

42. New York *Evangelist*, October 5, 1833.

crush "this many headed Hydra in the bud, expose the weakness as well as the folly, madness, and mischief of these bold and dangerous men." The mob action intensified Leavitt's determination to continue on the path he had so recently chosen, regardless of the personal consequences. Not long before, his hatred of slavery had been tempered to some degree by the realization that sincere people who wished to resolve the slavery question faced a difficult task. Now, he edged closer to the uncompromising position that all who refused to attack slavery were insensitive to their moral obligation. Yet he also sought to attract support and forestall further attempts to suppress the fledgling movement by signing the new organization's address to the public, which disclaimed any intention of arousing slaves to rebellion or employing political pressure against slavery.[43]

While these abolitionists hoped to convince Americans that the concept of immediatism did not necessarily mean that emancipation would occur immediately, they condemned gradualism as morally bankrupt and a failure and insisted that all Americans begin immediately to demand the end of slavery. Whatever would follow emancipation must be left to those whose consciences moral agitators had touched. As Leavitt stated categorically, "whatever provisions of legislation, education, guardianship, etc. either prudence or humanity may decide to be necessary for such a multitude thus delivered from slavery, should all take effect subsequent to emancipation; for they are all necessarily inconsistent with even the temporary existence of slavery."[44]

43. Quoted in *Liberator*, October 13, 1833. For interesting speculation regarding the impact of violence on the abolitionists' commitment to the cause, see Silvan S. Tomkins, "The Psychology of Commitment: The Constructive Role of Violence and Suffering for the Individual and for His Society," in Martin B. Duberman (ed.), *The Antislavery Vanguard: New Essays on the Abolitionists* (Princeton, N.J., 1965), 270–98.

44. *Address of the New-York City Anti-Slavery Society, to the People of the City of New-York* (New York, 1833), 4–5, 11; New York *Evangelist*, July 26, 1834. For analyses of the concept of immediatism, see David B. Davis, "The Emergence of Immediatism in British and American Antislavery Thought," *Mississippi Valley Historical Review*, XLIX (September, 1962), 209–30; Anne C. Loveland, "Evangelicalism and 'Immediate Emancipation' in American Antislavery Thought," *Journal of Southern History*, XXXII (May, 1966), 172–88; Donald G. Mathews, "The Abolitionists on Slavery: The Critique Behind the Social Movement," *Journal of Southern History*, XXXIII (May, 1967), 172–75.

Chastened by the October riot, Leavitt and his New York colleagues now urged caution in launching a national antislavery organization. But as the result of pressure from Garrison and Evan Lewis, the Quaker editor of *The Friend* in Philadelphia, a convention held in that city (which Leavitt did not attend) founded the American Anti-Slavery Society. In its Declaration of Sentiments Garrison branded slavery a national crime and a personal sin and declared that congressional authority extended to the interstate slave trade and slavery in the territories and the District of Columbia.[45] With the launching of the national antislavery society, Leavitt threw himself fully into the cause as a strategist and propagandist. During the next few years, the movement would attract many new supporters, but for both Leavitt and the cause these would also be years of crisis and challenge.

45. *Liberator*, May 23, 1831, December 14, 21, 1833; Samuel J. May, *Some Recollections of our Antislavery Conflict* (Boston, 1869), 79–80; Declaration of Sentiments and Constitution of the American Anti-Slavery Society, in Anti-Slavery Papers, Library of Congress.

7

ABOLITIONISM AND
EVANGELICALISM
UNDER SIEGE

Several formidable tasks confronted Leavitt, the Tappans, and others appointed to the American Anti-Slavery Society's executive committee in December 1833. They immediately began to form auxiliary groups throughout the North; disseminate newspapers, tracts, and books; raise funds; and mobilize support among the churches and benevolent societies. Leavitt also served on the committee on agencies, which, in Elizur Wright's opinion, "must put on the muscle and transfuse the warm blood and breathe into it [the movement] the breath of life." The society needed effective agents in order to gain converts and bring needed revenue into the coffers. During the first year, the committee experienced little success in recruiting agents, but in the mid-1830s Theodore Weld and numerous other abolitionists preached the gospel of antislavery in hundreds of northern towns and villages and brought thousands of converts into the movement.[1]

The abolitionists launched their crusade with ebullient spirits and an unbounded faith that God would not allow their cause to fail. Despite the fact that hundreds of millions of dollars' worth of chattels and two centuries of deeply ingrained racist habits were at stake, Leavitt and his colleagues fully expected that slavery would soon

1. Elizur Wright to Amos A. Phelps, December 31, 1833, in Phelps Papers; entries for December 13, 16, 1833, August 5, 1834, in "Minutes of the Committee on Agencies of the American Anti-Slavery Society, 1833–1840," Boston Public Library; John L. Myers, "The Beginning of Anti-Slavery Agencies in New York State, 1833–1836," *New York History*, XLIII (April, 1962), 149–81.

crumble and a new and glorious era of justice and freedom be ushered in. In January 1834 Leavitt declared that British emancipation had doomed American slavery "to a speedy termination." Many others shared his optimism. Theodore Weld, for example, predicted that "within *twenty years* Slavery in these United States will be at an end."[2]

Both Leavitt and Weld were part of what Lawrence Friedman has termed the "Tappan Clique" of moral stewards, which also included William Jay, son of John Jay and a Westchester County, New York, landowner of aristocratic bearing; Arthur and Lewis Tappan; and a handful of other evangelical abolitionists. It was a disparate group. For example, Weld's hair was long and unkempt and his clothes ill-fitting, while Lewis Tappan presented an impeccable appearance. Weld held organizational activity in contempt, whereas Leavitt and Tappan had developed a high level of bureaucratic skills and thrived on organizing and mobilizing others. At the same time, Leavitt tended to be more charismatic and capable of relating to others at a deeper emotional level than did Tappan. But despite their differences, during the 1830s the group's members developed respect and affection for one another. In the case of Leavitt, Weld, and Tappan, their close friendship emerged from working together in numerous benevolent enterprises dating back to the late 1820s. They also shared an attachment to the revival theology of Charles Grandison Finney, which viewed humans as moral agents capable of seeking salvation and obligated to perform good works—and God as ultimately righting all wrongs in the world. Their confidence in God's beneficent design, as well as their bond of friendship, gave these men a sense of purpose and a resilience that sustained them through trying times and, in the case of Leavitt and Tappan, permitted them to transcend their differences over antislavery politics at the end of the decade.[3]

Some cause for optimism indeed existed. In the months following the formation of the national organization, an average of two new antislavery societies were founded each week. Moreover, at Lane Seminary in Cincinnati the students, led by Weld, came to support abolition and declared the American Colonization Society unworthy

2. New York *Evangelist*, January 4, 1834; Theodore Weld to James Birney, June 19, 1834, in Dumond (ed.), *Birney Letters*, I, 119.

3. See Lawrence J. Friedman, *Gregarious Saints: Self and Community in American Abolitionism, 1830–1870* (Cambridge, England, 1982), esp. 70–77.

of Christian patronage. Leavitt added his voice to the mounting assault on colonization, declaring it morally and financially bankrupt. Hoping to witness the death knell of the colonization movement, he traveled to Washington in early 1834 to report on the society's annual meeting. What he observed convinced him, predictably, that the movement would soon die a natural death. On the basis of Leavitt's "spirited and accurate reporting," Elizur Wright concluded that "*The victory is ours.*" Both Leavitt and Wright were certainly premature in their predictions of the imminent demise of colonization, but even the society's director, Ralph R. Gurley, feared that if the South did not soon give some indication of being willing to abolish slavery, the colonization cause could not survive.[4]

Yet, the abolitionists' optimism could not hide the fact that the cause confronted a number of problems. Despite generous contributions by Arthur Tappan and other wealthy merchants, the fledgling organization soon found itself strapped for funds and forced temporarily to suspend publication of both the *Emancipator* and the *Anti-Slavery Reporter.* The executive committee sought to break the dependence on Arthur Tappan and his associates, but this required time and organization, and Tappan's cautious ways tended to inhibit experimentation and growth. The society also failed to draw the Bible Society and other benevolent organizations into the antislavery orbit.[5]

The abolitionists also exaggerated Southerners' willingness to hear their message and underestimated the depth of northern racial prejudice. The physical threat posed by people both virulently racist and antiabolitionist became clear within months of the founding of the American Anti-Slavery Society. The publicity given the founding of the national society and the intensifying agitation of the slavery question in subsequent months produced mounting tension in New York City. The abolitionists' attacks on the colonizationists released a torrent of invectives from the local press. The widespread belief that emancipa-

---

4. New York *Evangelist,* March 22, 1834; Joshua Leavitt to Gerrit Smith, March 31, 1834, in Gerrit Smith Miller Collection, Syracuse University; Elizur Wright to William Lloyd Garrison, January 30, 1834, in Elizur Wright Papers, Library of Congress; Ralph R. Gurley to James Birney, December 17, 1833, in American Colonization Society Papers.

5. Wyatt-Brown, *Lewis Tappan,* 111–12; Clifford S. Griffin, "The Abolitionists and the Benevolent Societies, 1831–1861," *Journal of Negro History,* XLIV (July, 1959), 196–97.

tion threatened property rights and, ultimately, the Union itself also fueled the fires that would soon erupt in mob violence. Rapid social and economic change—characterized by startling urban growth, the rise of mass politics, and mounting immigration rates—created amorphous, though real, fears for the future. With rising unemployment rates, many white workers feared that emancipation would cause a flood of blacks into the cities.[6] But more than anything else, a violent antipathy toward blacks, which existed at all levels of society, precipitated the rioting that occurred.[7] It was no accident that in the course of the July 1834 riots in New York City, the mob directed far more of its fury at the black sections than at those inhabited by white abolitionists.

Even many abolitionists who sympathized with the plight of blacks were, as scholars have reminded us, ambivalent on the race issue. From the beginning of the cause, its leaders consciously sought to link the need to improve the conditions of free blacks with that of emancipation. The American Anti-Slavery Society hoped "to elevate the character and conditions of the people of color, by encouraging their intellectual, moral, and religious improvement, and by removing public prejudice, that by this they may according to their intellectual and moral worth, share an equality with whites, of civil and religious privileges."[8]

For Leavitt and many other white abolitionists, increasing contact with blacks had made them more sensitive to blacks' feelings. In the late 1820s he had supported colonization and had been concerned far less about the physical and emotional impact of white racism on black

6. *First Annual Report of the American Anti-Slavery Society* (New York, 1834), 15, 34. For analyses of the fears generated by the prospect of emancipation, see Lorman Ratner, *Powder Keg: Northern Opposition to the Antislavery Movement, 1831–1840* (New York, 1968), 131–41; Michael Feldberg, *The Turbulent Era: Riot and Disorder in Jacksonian America* (New York, 1980), 44–45, *passim*; Linda K. Kerber, "Abolitionists and Amalgamators: The New York City Race Riots of 1834," *New York History*, XLVIII (January, 1967), 28–39.

7. This point is argued persuasively by Ratner, *Powder Keg*, 18–23; Merton L. Dillon, "The Abolitionists as a Dissenting Minority," in Alfred Young (ed.), *Dissent: Explorations in the History of American Radicalism* (De Kalb, Ill., 1968), 93–94; Leonard L. Richards, *"Gentlemen of Property and Standing": Anti-Abolition Mobs in Jacksonian America* (New York, 1970), 35–37, 114–15.

8. Declaration of Sentiments and Constitution of the American Anti-Slavery Society, in Anti-Slavery Papers, Library of Congress; see also Friedman, *Gregarious Saints*,

Americans than about the deleterious effect that blacks might have on the morals of whites. By 1834, he could plead with whites, on the basis of "common humanity and the first principle of Christian piety," to do everything they could to gain the confidence of blacks. Whether or not whites saw fit to assist blacks, he argued, nothing could prevent their elevation in America.[9]

Some abolitionists seemed content to denounce the South without making a serious effort to improve conditions for blacks at home in the North. This was not entirely true of Leavitt. In 1834 he, Lewis Tappan, and a few other white abolitionists joined Samuel Cornish, Peter Williams, and other black clergymen in the Phoenix Society, an organization founded and operated by blacks that sponsored adult schools, operated libraries and reading rooms, and encouraged vocational training and moral uplift for blacks in the city. Through this organization and their contacts within the American Anti-Slavery Society, Leavitt and his white friends gained some degree of familiarity with the problems and aspirations of northern blacks. Nevertheless, they were not free of racial prejudice. A genuine concern for the welfare of blacks led them to assert that blacks could gain the respect of whites only by educating themselves, working hard, and leading blameless lives—a message they had also preached for years to the white lower classes. But in viewing themselves as exemplars of morality whose middle-class evangelical values and standards should be inculcated in blacks, they exuded the patronizing air of a superior class, implied that black self-help and advancement were intended more for the benefit of the antislavery cause than for the sake of free blacks themselves, and came close to saying that blacks' involvement in immoral activities produced white racism. Notwithstanding the fact that black leaders such as Cornish agreed that blacks could advance only by adopting the ways of the white middle class, many blacks resented the white abolitionists' tendency to stereotype them as childlike, irresponsible, and impulsive. Clearly, as Friedman argues, this "chord of prejudice" helped maintain the emotional distance between the races. Leavitt, for example, never really became close to Theodore Wright, a New York City clergyman, Cornish, and other black co-

---

160–80; Jane H. Pease and William H. Pease, *They Who Would Be Free: Blacks' Search for Freedom, 1830–1861* (New York, 1974), 79–80.

9. New York *Evangelist*, May 24, 1834; see also Friedman, *Gregarious Saints*, 14.

workers in the cause. Equally troublesome, many white abolitionists never devoted much energy to combatting segregation and discrimination in the North. During the 1840s, Leavitt, a cofounder of the antislavery Liberty party, and other party leaders increasingly subordinated the race issue to other concerns.[10]

Leavitt's record on the matter of race, however, was better than that of some of his associates, whose blatant prejudice deeply disturbed him. Following Charles G. Finney's veto of Lewis Tappan's effort to end segregation in the Chatham Street Chapel in 1836—on the grounds that the amalgamation issue would severely damage the abolition movement—Leavitt clearly had Finney in mind when he bitterly attacked the churches for exhibiting a "*spirit of caste*, and not the *spirit of Christ*" toward blacks. But overt racism also existed within the abolitionist ranks. Few blacks attained positions of influence in the cause. William Jay, John Rankin, and William Green, who were all members of the national society's executive committee, especially objected to having blacks participate in leadership positions. Leavitt could not understand how one could be an abolitionist and still be so insensitive to the feelings of blacks. "The moment any one admits the elementary idea of abolitionism, that colored people ought to be regarded and treated simply as persons," he asserted in the New York *Evangelist*, "he immediately realizes that they have feelings, and that their feelings are as much a part of their happiness or misery, and are entitled to as respectful consideration by their friends, as those of any other persons." Thus, he went far beyond most Americans in attempting to relate to blacks as equals. Yet, in the final analysis, he and most other white abolitionists only partially succeeded in transcending the pervasive racial prejudice of their time.[11]

Abolitionists repeatedly denied charges that they were amalgamationists, but to no avail. Rumors that they engaged in, or expressed support for, race mixing stirred the wrath of northern whites. In New

10. *Address to the People of Color, in the City of New York, by Members of the Executive Committee of the American Anti-Slavery Society* (New York, 1834), 3–8; Friedman, *Gregarious Saints*, 166–67, 169–78; William H. Pease and Jane H. Pease, "Antislavery Ambivalence: Immediatism, Expediency, Race," *American Quarterly*, XVII (Winter, 1965), 689–92, 695.

11. New York *Evangelist*, March 18, 1837, July 19, 1836; Charles G. Finney to Arthur Tappan, April 30, 1836, in Finney Papers; Wyatt-Brown, *Lewis Tappan*, 177; Dillon, "The Abolitionists as a Dissenting Minority," in Young, *Dissent*, 96–98.

York City this anger exploded into a full-fledged riot in July 1834, during which a frenzied mob brought the city to the brink of anarchy. The rioting began in earnest on July 9 and lasted for nearly a week. The rioters—including skilled workers who generally lived in close proximity to blacks, as well as middle-class professionals and businessmen who feared that the abolitionists threatened their moral leadership, values, and traditions—were constantly encouraged by James Watson Webb of the New York *Courier and Enquirer* and other editors.[12]

The mob seriously damaged several churches as well as the homes of Lewis Tappan, Samuel H. Cox, and other white friends of Leavitt. The black community suffered far worse destruction. Leavitt, with good reason, was extremely apprehensive. He was an imposing figure, tall and powerfully built, but was obviously no match for the bands of marauders that roamed the streets nearly at will, at times wreaking havoc in a random manner, especially in the black sections, and at other times methodically attacking selected targets. There was no way to know where the mob would strike next. Leavitt feared that it would destroy the *Evangelist* office and his house and harm his family. "On Tuesday evening," he wrote his parents three days after the rioting began, "the word came that they were destroying Dr. Cox's house, and were coming to Mr. [Henry] Ludlow's next, and would probably take mine. I thought it fundamental to leave the house with my family; about 10 o'clock we were safely housed at another place. Yesterday, the spirit of the mob seemed to be rising instead of declining, and we left the house in the afternoon. . . . Our office is threatened, McDowall's office and house, etc." Leavitt's house and office were spared, and Sarah managed to remain "very calm," but he informed his parents that "the fatigue and watching have made her tired." The tension became so great for him and Sarah that he seriously considered taking the family out of the city, as had a few other abolitionists. But the situation was so confusing and frightening that he did not know what to do. "Whether I shall leave town today," he wrote his parents, "I know not. . . . Where it will end we know not, but we all have faith in God."[13]

What made the situation even more frightening was that the few

12. Richards, "*Gentlemen of Property and Standing*," 150–55; Kerber, "Abolitionists and Amalgamators," 28–39.

13. Joshua Leavitt to parents, July 12, 1834, in Leavitt Papers; Richards, "*Gentlemen of Property and Standing*," 113–22.

night watchmen on duty were thoroughly outnumbered and intimidated, so they disappeared until after the riots had subsided. To make matters worse, during much of the rioting—in which at least sixty homes and six churches were destroyed, many more seriously damaged, and several blacks killed—the city's political leaders seemed utterly indifferent to the fate of either the black population or the white abolitionists. This indifference led the rioters to grow increasingly intrepid. Finally, Cornelius Lawrence, the Democratic mayor, placed the city under martial law and called up elements of the city militia. The militia, however, proved largely ineffectual, in part because the rioters knew that it was under orders not to fire on them. This policy, patently favoring the mob, infuriated Leavitt, but his rage partly stemmed from a feeling of impotence. He knew that any resistance to the mob would be foolhardy, and he cautioned blacks that even the threat of violence on their part would "only increase the ferocity of their enemies, and may lead to disastrous consequences." But he was also furious that the rioters had "ill treated a good many colored people in the streets." He directed much of his anger and contempt toward Mayor Lawrence and the militia. "Our police and military," he sneered, "have no decision. Two regiments were out last night, and the damage was done under their nose." In fact, Mayor Lawrence finally took action only when rumors surfaced that the mob might begin systematically to loot homes and stores belonging to middle-class and wealthy New Yorkers. With the press and city officials suddenly committed to law and order, the rioting tapered off gradually.[14]

Even before the chaos and tumult had completely subsided, both the abolitionists and their critics set forth post-mortems of the riots; each group interpreted the impact and fixed the blame according to its own perspective and needs. Most New Yorkers probably agreed with Philip Hone, a patrician businessman, who attributed the riots to the actions of "a set of fanatics who are determined to emancipate all the slaves by a *coup de main*." But Leavitt, with considerable justice, denounced the police and politicians for doing nothing to control the mob and charged the press with encouraging the rioters—an assessment with which even the procolonization New York *Observer* and New York *Evening Post* partly concurred.[15]

14. Leavitt to parents, July 12, 1834, in Leavitt Papers; Kerber, "Abolitionists and Amalgamators," 28–39; *Emancipator*, July 15, 22, 1834.

15. Allan Nevins (ed.), *The Diary of Philip Hone, 1828–1851* (New York, 1927),

In the aftermath of the riots a few newspapers accurately predicted that the antiabolition riots might increase the fervor and numbers of abolitionists. Most abolitionists indeed responded to the July riots by rededicating themselves to the task at hand. But, despite the abolitionists' defiant optimism and their critics' continuing accusations, the riots had a chastening effect on both groups. In the short term, Leavitt and his fellow reformers sought to prevent a recurrence of violence by assuring Mayor Lawrence that they had addressed no appeals to slaves, had broken no laws, did not wish for Congress to violate the Constitution, and had no desire to promote racial "mongrelization." Likewise, when a recurrence of mob violence seemed possible three months later during a visit to the city by George Thompson, a fiery British abolitionist, Leavitt and a majority of the American Anti-Slavery Society's executive committee urged him to leave the city. The wisdom of such caution in these volatile times soon became apparent when abolitionists were mobbed in Boston and several other New England communities. The July riots also made a deep impression on "gentlemen of property and standing" in New York City. When an equally dangerous situation developed there a year later, the business and political leaders quickly moved to limit its scope.[16] Such restraint, however, was exceptional among the opponents of abolition. During the 1830s, antiabolitionist and antiblack riots represented the commonest form of collective violence in the United States.

This was an extremely trying period in Leavitt's life. At the same time that angry mobs threatened his family, home, and office, he confronted a crisis that nearly ruined the New York *Evangelist* and forced him to consider leaving New York City. His paper had ridden the rising tide of religious fervor in the years following Finney's return to New York in 1832, its circulation increasing from 3,000 subscribers in early 1831 to 6,000 by the end of 1833. But Leavitt's conversion to

---

I, 314; Leavitt to parents, July 12, 1834, in Leavitt Papers; New York *Observer*, July 19, 1834; New York *Evening Post*, July 8, 12, 1834.

16. See New York *Evening Post*, July 8, 1834; Ratner, *Powder Keg*, 83–84; enclosed in Lewis Tappan to Ralph R. Gurley, July 18, 1834, in American Colonization Society Papers; Lewis Tappan to Theodore Weld, September 29, 1834, in Slavery Manuscripts, Box II, New-York Historical Society; New York *Evangelist*, September 27, 1834; Wyatt-Brown, *Lewis Tappan*, 121. On Thompson's American tour, see C. Rice Duncan, "The Anti-Slavery Mission of George Thompson to the United States, 1834–1835," *Journal of American Studies*, II (April, 1968), 13–31.

the cause of immediate emancipation had disastrous consequences for the paper. As he hammered away at the theme of the sin of slavery and the duty of Christians to repudiate it, the rumbling of discontent among his readers increased noticeably. On the eve of embarking on a cruise to the Mediterranean in early 1834 to recover from the effects of cholera, Finney admonished him "to be careful not to go too fast in the discussion of the antislavery question, lest he destroy the paper." Leavitt would not listen. As he stated obstinately to his readers, "If it were not for the cost of an unguilty conscience and a displeased Heavenly Father we have every other inducement to retrace our steps."[17]

In his enthusiasm for the cause Leavitt clearly had moved far ahead of what many of his readers deemed acceptable. His zealous advocacy of abolition may well have been morally correct, but it was bad business policy. During the first six months of 1834, he lost nearly one-third of his 6,000 subscribers. Most of the subscribers were Northerners. While many of them eventually joined the antislavery movement, others disliked Leavitt's incessant attacks on slavery and cancelled their subscriptions. Within a few months, virtually all of his southern subscribers had cancelled: some because, as one irate reader said, the paper's course was "injudicious, and full of danger to the southern slave-holder"; others, no doubt, because they were afraid to pick up the paper at their post office.[18]

Leavitt's expectation that his evangelical readers would recognize their Christian duty and flock to the antislavery ranks did not prepare him for this turn of events. By the summer of 1834, he became so depressed that he considered resigning his editorship and, as he informed his mother, "finding a retreat in your 'east room' down the hall." "I felt," he added a few months later, "as if there was a storm coming, and I did not know what to do. Nothing afforded me encouragement, nothing excited me to action."[19] For a man who normally exuded self-confidence, this was an extraordinary confession (though one he probably would not have made publicly). It certainly indicates that he could confide his deepest anxieties to his parents and that their home remained a refuge from the storms that buffeted him. It is not surprising that he was filled with self-doubt and a sense of foreboding,

17. Joshua Leavitt to Amos A. Phelps, November 8, 1833, in Phelps Papers; Finney, *Memoirs*, 328–29; New York *Evangelist*, January 18, 1834.

18. New York *Evangelist*, January 18, June 21, 1834.

19. Joshua Leavitt to Chloe Leavitt, January 17, 1835, in Leavitt Papers.

for the *Evangelist* provided much of the income needed to support Sarah and their four sons. Moreover, this crisis came in the wake of the riots, an event that steeled his determination to forge ahead but also provided frightening evidence of the extent and degree of northern hostility toward blacks and the abolition cause.

With the advantage of hindsight, Leavitt viewed his concern as having been "as foolish as it was groundless."[20] It was almost as if he was embarrassed by his earlier confessions of impotence in the face of adversity, even though he probably had confided only in his parents and Sarah. But in July 1834 the problem seemed very real indeed.

The situation was in fact so critical that on the day Finney returned to New York, Leavitt rushed to the pier to greet him. Years later, Finney claimed that Leavitt admitted he had not heeded Finney's warning and that the paper could not survive more than a few months at the current rate of cancellations. Finney's recollection of the conversation undoubtedly was self-serving; after all, he was never as committed to abolitionism as was Leavitt. But the loss of sixty subscribers a day clearly alarmed Leavitt. He proposed that Finney resolve the crisis by writing several articles on revivals for the New York *Evangelist*. After briefly considering this idea, Finney decided to deliver a series of Friday night lectures on revivals before his congregation at Chatham Street Chapel. Leavitt had no knowledge of shorthand, but his keen memory and his experience in reporting on the proceedings of dozens of religious and benevolent meetings over the years enabled him to capture the essence of Finney's lectures. At each of the twenty-two lectures delivered between December 1834 and April 1835, Leavitt sat in the front row of the church and wrote down words in abbreviated form; the following morning he rewrote the lecture from his notes and sent it to the printer.[21]

Finney's lectures had the desired effect. One month after the lectures began, Leavitt informed his mother that they were "exciting a good deal of interest" and that "the clouds began to break away." Subscriptions increased at the rate of 200 a day. He now decided to ride out the storm. In all, he added nearly 5,000 new subscribers—many of them converts to abolitionism—in 1835. Finney's lectures

20. *Ibid.*
21. Finney, *Memoirs*, 329–30; Charles G. Finney to wife, November 24, 1834, in Finney Papers. Finney's lectures appeared in the New York *Evangelist*, December 13, 1834, to May 2, 1835.

had saved the day, but Leavitt, who continued to condemn slavery in almost every issue during the months that he printed Finney's lectures, deserves much of the credit for making the paper a major force for abolition among the northern evangelical groups.[22]

Leavitt's version of Finney's lectures, published in November 1835 under the title *Lectures on Revivals of Religion*, sold 12,000 copies as quickly as they could be printed and earned substantial royalties for both Leavitt and Finney—each of whom received 20 percent of the book's receipts. Beyond this, as one of Finney's most important statements on doctrines and measures, the lectures informed and inspired countless thousands of middle-class evangelicals through the nineteenth century.[23]

The warm reception accorded the lectures by the evangelical community delighted Leavitt, but as an abolitionist he found little in the lectures that was heartening. In none of the lectures did Finney denounce slavery, and in one he charged that the denunciatory spirit of the abolitionists was unchristian and served to weaken the revivals. Finney participated in a number of reform movements and called for the end of slavery. But he believed that spiritual salvation must take precedence over abolition, for a better world could not be made until God changed the human heart. Moreover, he regarded slavery's sinful nature as one of God's gradual revelations of moral truth. He clearly stated his sense of priorities when he told Theodore Weld that if abolition "can be made an appendage of a general revival of religion all is well." [24]

Finney's refusal to come out boldly in favor of abolition deeply offended some abolitionists. Lewis Tappan accused him of being a coward, and Elizur Wright said as much, noting sarcastically that Finney's credo was "You must not lift a hammer or sound a note lest the noise should disturb the meditations of anxious sinners." Leavitt, who had helped to move Finney toward abolitionism, did not so quickly con-

22. Joshua Leavitt to Chloe Leavitt, January 17, February 7, 1835, in Leavitt Papers; New York *Evangelist*, January 2, 1836.

23. Finney, *Memoirs*, 330; Agreement, dated March 1, 1835, in Finney Papers; Finney, *Lectures on Revivals of Religion*, viii.

24. McLoughlin, *Modern Revivalism*, 107, 109–10; Charles G. Finney to Theodore Weld, July 21, 1836, in Barnes and Dumond (eds.), *Weld-Grimké Letters*, I, 319. For an excellent analysis of Finney's ambiguous stance on reforms such as abolition, see James H. Moorhead, "Social Reform and the Divided Conscience of Antebellum Protestantism," *Church History*, XLVIII (December, 1979), 416–30.

demn him. After all, they had served together for several years in what Finney would later term a "very intimate and permanent friendship," seeking to reap souls in the Lord's vineyard. Beyond this, Leavitt owed Finney a debt of gratitude for saving his paper and agreed with Weld that Finney was a courageous man who sincerely desired an end to slavery.[25]

Leavitt never criticized Finney directly for his priorities, probably because he realized that to do so would only strengthen the hand of opponents of the new measures and abolition. Indeed, between 1835 and 1837 they continued to struggle side by side against the Old School Presbyterians and for the cause of Congregational denominationalism. Nevertheless, Leavitt believed that Finney had misconceived his Christian duty. He could not countenance Finney's insistence that the antislavery cause would eventually destroy the evangelical revivals. For him, the relationship between evangelical Christianity and reform was complex and symbiotic: both were dynamic forces that gave meaning and substance to the vision of a moral republic. Contrary to Finney's stance, Leavitt considered the cause of immediate emancipation, like the temperance crusade, a great moral and religious struggle that would stimulate revival activity.[26]

Leavitt had managed to weather his personal and professional crises in the mid-1830s. At the same time, however, the antislavery cause came to an important crossroads in its history. As William Lloyd Garrison and other abolitionists escalated their attacks on those who refused to condemn slavery, it was probably only a matter of time until an organization such as the American Union for the Relief and Improvement of the Colored Race emerged. Founded in 1835 by Lyman Beecher and other benevolent activists who believed that the abolitionists' accusatory spirit alienated many Americans from the cause, the union sought to employ moderate means to overcome sectional mistrust and racial prejudice and to unite abolitionists and colonizationists in a common cause. But, unable to generate much excitement or support, the union soon sank into oblivion.[27]

25. Theodore Weld to Lewis Tappan, November 17, 1835, in Barnes and Dumond (eds.), *Weld-Grimké Letters*, I, 242–43; Elizur Wright to Beriah Green, March 7, 1835, in Wright Papers; *Independent*, February 6, 1873.

26. New York *Evangelist*, January 11, 1834.

27. Wyatt-Brown, *Lewis Tappan*, 134–38, 140–42; Thomas, *The Liberator*, 224–27.

Leavitt and most other members of the American Anti-Slavery Society's executive committee realized that the cause needed a more vigorous campaign to bring the message to millions of Americans. This, rather than a more restrained rhetoric, would generate enthusiasm and advance the cause. Sustained by their faith in the efficacy of moral suasion, they sent dozens of agents into the field, established and maintained several newspapers, and flooded the nation with a vast array of literature. Yet the violent southern reaction to their propaganda ended, for all practical purposes, any reasonable hope that the South could be won over to the cause and forced Leavitt and his colleagues to concentrate on mobilizing northern public opinion.[28]

The postal campaign also evoked a negative response in the North. The press subjected abolitionists to a constant stream of invective, and mob action became increasingly common in 1835. For example, Weld and other antislavery agents experienced the public's wrath in numerous towns and hamlets in New York state and the West; and in October, on the same day that a mob led Garrison through the streets of Boston with a noose around his neck, residents of Utica, New York, harrassed Leavitt and other abolitionists.[29]

Leavitt and Elizur Wright had devoted several weeks to planning the Utica convention, which was scheduled to establish the state antislavery society. News that 700 abolitionists planned to converge on the town led the local press, both Whig and Democratic, to urge that the convention be "put down." More ominously, one month before the convention an Oneida County grand jury had declared that abolitionists were guilty of sedition and their publications should be destroyed. In this tense atmosphere the call for the convention went out. Under intense pressure, the Utica Common Council rescinded its permit allowing the abolitionists to use the town's courtroom; organizers then switched the convention to a local Presbyterian Church.[30]

When the delegates assembled on October 21, Leavitt joined his

28. See Myers, "The Beginning of Anti-slavery Agencies in New York State," 167, 170–71; Bertram Wyatt-Brown, "The Abolitionists' Postal Campaign of 1835," *Journal of Negro History*, L (October, 1965), 227–29; Clement Eaton, "Censorship of the Southern Mails," *American Historical Review*, XLVIII (January, 1943), 266–80.

29. Wyatt-Brown, *Lewis Tappan*, 151–53; Richards, "*Gentlemen of Property and Standing*," 41–42, 50–52, 64, 93–100.

30. Elizur Wright to Amos A. Phelps, September 4, 16, 1835, in Wright Papers; Richards, "*Gentlemen of Property and Standing*," 86.

father and his brother Hart. Abolitionism had become a family affair for the Leavitts. Although there is no evidence regarding the sentiments of Joshua's sisters Clarissa and Chloe on the issue, they were probably sympathetic to the cause. His parents and brothers had been active for a few years in the temperance and moral reform movements, and during a visit to Roger and Chloe's home following the 1834 riots, Joshua had had a long talk with his father about the overriding importance of abolitionism and had converted him and his mother. Through the 1830s they remained active in the cause, Roger serving as an officer of the local antislavery society and Chloe collecting signatures on petitions calling for abolition in the District of Columbia. In his abolition and other reform endeavors, Leavitt never doubted that his family was entirely supportive and proud of his efforts.[31]

Immediately after the convention had begun its deliberations, a large, well-organized mob gathered, composed primarily of middle-class professionals, merchants, bankers, politicians, and clerks who feared that the abolitionists would undermine traditional patterns of power, influence, and deference—perhaps especially by welcoming both men and women from all social classes into their ranks. The mob attacked the delegates, destroyed antislavery documents and hymnals, and shouted down the meeting. Because the abolitionists did not resist, violence was minimized. Nevertheless, the residents forced the meeting to disband and retreat to Gerrit Smith's estate in nearby Peterboro, where the delegates succeeded in founding the New York State Anti-Slavery Society.[32]

Some abolitionists viewed mobs as a stimulus to the cause. But with the Utica and New York City riots still fresh in his mind, Leavitt was not so certain. "Our views of the influence of sin do not lead that way," he editorialized. "Our hope and our confident expectation was, that we should meet in peace. We believed that, by the blessing of God, the truth can abolish slavery, better and sooner without mobs than with them, if our opponents would cease stirring up violence."[33]

The attempts to stifle the voices and pens of the abolitionists ulti-

31. *First Annual Report of the New York State Anti-Slavery Society, Held at Peterboro, October 22, 1835* (Utica, 1835), 13, 15, 45; *Emancipator*, June 18, 1840; F. Packard to Caroline Weston, September 23, 1836, in Chapman Family Papers, Boston Public Library.

32. Richards, "*Gentlemen of Property and Standing*," 89–92, 134–35.

33. New York *Evangelist*, November 7, 1835.

mately extended to the highest circles of government. Several northern governors requested that abolitionists end their campaign voluntarily, and President Jackson and Postmaster-General Amos Kendall urged the passage of laws prohibiting the dissemination of incendiary literature. Although Congress did not accept President Jackson's proposal, the administration proceeded simply to permit the southern states to censor the mails.[34]

Yet the abolitionists' postal campaign was not a failure. Their sustained propaganda barrage made it increasingly difficult for Northerners to ignore the slavery question. The striking contrast between the antiabolitionists' threats, violence, and violations of fundamental rights, on the one hand, and, on the other, the abolitionists' nonviolent tactics and their warning that their opponents' actions jeopardized the civil liberties of all Americans evoked sympathy for the cause (though not necessarily for slaves or free blacks) among growing numbers of Northerners.[35]

Leavitt fully realized that the struggle also had to be made on other fronts if the cause was to prevail. Convinced that the success of the new measures revivals and that of abolitionism were intertwined, he insisted that the churches be converted to both evangelicalism and the antislavery cause. The rapid growth of the antislavery societies' membership rolls in the mid-1830s heartened Leavitt. But at the same time, his hopes that both the new measures and the antislavery cause would prevail within the religious community were disappointed. To some degree each cause eroded the other's strength: the antislavery movement drained some of the vital energies from the revivals, and a growing number of evangelicals, inspired by Finney, focused their attention on a more purely pietistic religiosity.[36]

Leavitt was deeply disturbed by the declining intensity and scope of the revivals, calling the situation "a mournful picture" in late 1834. Following several years of sustained revival activity, it was perhaps inevitable that the high level of enthusiasm would diminish, but he

34. Eaton, "Censorship of the Southern Mails," 266–80.

35. Protest of the American Anti-Slavery Society to President Jackson, in *A Collection of Valuable Documents* (Boston, 1836), 42–45; Russell B. Nye, *Fettered Freedom: Civil Liberties and the Slavery Controversy, 1830–1860* (East Lansing, Mich., 1949), 32–54.

36. Moorhead, "Social Reform and the Divided Conscience of Antebellum Protestantism," 416–30.

chose to attribute this decline to "party politics" within and among the Protestant denominations.[37] Sectarian and intradenominational squabbling indeed intensified during the 1830s, at the expense of the revivals and the sense of Christian unity that for years had bound many Protestant activists together. By 1837 the Presbyterian Church, which he had hoped would be a major force propelling the revivals and the antislavery cause, had been captured by conservative Calvinists hostile to both movements.

The Plan of Union, an ecclesiastical agreement reached between the Presbyterians and the Congregationalists in 1801, formed a central pillar of the Christian unity that had made significant advances during the early nineteenth century. Designed to limit conflict between these denominations and to facilitate missionary works in New York state and the Northwest, the accord made eminent sense, for they shared a common Puritan heritage and allegiance to the Westminster Confession, and their ministers had long moved between pulpits of the denominations. The Congregationalists especially wished to cooperate with the Presbyterians because they believed the Presbyterian ecclesiastical organization could be more effective in the religiously pluralistic environment of the West.[38]

Both churches enjoined missionaries to promote a spirit of accommodation and established a basic formula for determining the structure of individual churches and the location of ecclesiastical jurisdiction. The founding of what many termed "Presbygational" churches— essentially Congregational churches that retained their name and church government while functioning under the jurisdiction of presbyteries—advanced the spirit of the Plan of Union after 1808. Yet, due to their church's less aggressive denominational spirit, most Congregationalists who moved into upstate New York and New York City between 1800 and 1830 came under the jurisdiction of the Presbyterian Church.[39]

When Leavitt moved to New York in 1828, he joined Dr. Gardiner Spring's Brick Presbyterian Church in Manhattan. Given Spring's

37. New York *Evangelist*, October 27, 1834, December 17, 1834.
38. See Robert Hastings, "The Plan of Union in New York," *Church History*, V (March, 1936), 32–33.
39. Gaius Glenn Atkins and Frederick L. Fagley, *History of American Congregationalism* (Boston, 1942), 136–38, 142–57; Samuel D. Alexander, *The Presbytery of New York, 1738–1888* (New York, 1888), 101–23.

avowed orthodoxy and his attacks on the theology and methods of Finney and Taylor, Leavitt's choice of this church is rather puzzling. The most plausible reasons for his decision are that Spring was a prominent minister, a Yale graduate, and an active participant in benevolent enterprises. Leavitt's decision not to join a Congregational church upon his arrival in the city is easier to understand. Spring's recent veto of Lewis Tappan's proposal to create a chain of Congregational churches in the city and the marginal position that the few Congregational churches occupied in the city's religious community certainly influenced any thoughts Leavitt may have had of advancing the cause of Congregationalism in New York.[40] Moreover, many transplanted New Englanders with whom he would labor in the benevolent empire belonged to the Presbyterian Church.

Yet even in the early 1830s mounting conflict between the evangelical and conservative wings of the Presbyterian Church had begun to narrow Leavitt's vision of Christian unity in America. The Old School Presbyterians—many of whom were Scotch-Irish from Pennsylvania and the Upper South—viewed the Plan of Union as a mixed blessing: The influx of Congregationalists into the Presbyterian ranks had helped to swell church membership, but it also had the effect of extending the New England Theology into New York and the West. Ever vigilant for any deviation from the letter of the Westminster Confession, conservative Presbyterians increasingly attacked what they considered doctrinal error—in the American Board of Commissioners for Foreign Missions, the American Home Missionary Society, and other voluntary associations that performed missionary functions within the church; in the new measures revivals, tinged with Taylorism and Beecherism, and, ultimately, Finneyism; and in the Presbygational churches, many with ministers trained at Andover and later at Yale and Williams.[41]

In the face of this Old School criticism, Leavitt moved toward an advocacy of Congregational denominationalism. An unabashed admirer of the Congregational polity, he claimed in an 1831 article

40. H. Shelton Smith, *Changing Conceptions of Original Sin: A Study in American Theology Since 1750* (New York, 1955), 134–35; Jonathan Greenleaf, *A History of All Denominations in the City of New York, From the First Settlement to the Year 1846* (New York, 1846), 352–57; Wyatt-Brown, *Lewis Tappan*, 62.

41. Sydney E. Ahlstrom, *A Religious History of the American People* (New Haven, Conn., 1972), 462–65.

(which Leonard Bacon, one of the church's leading theologians in the nineteenth century, praised as the "first intelligent and consistent lessons concerning the ecclesiastical polity of New England") that the Congregational system had "been the means under God, of nearly all the civil and religious liberty in the world." Though disturbed by the fact that most New England Congregationalists who moved west of the Hudson River came under the jurisdiction of the Presbyterian hierarchy, at this time his call for Congregationalists to rally to the defense of the church was primarily a response to what he perceived as unjust and unwarranted assaults on Congregationalists by their Presbyterian brethren. In 1831 he went so far as to question the worth of the Plan of Union. "The compromise," he stated, "has never produced peace; for the time has never been, when New England doctrines and New England men were not subjected to obloquy and jealousy among rigid Presbyterians. It has done nothing towards the purity of the church, either from false doctrine or corrupt practices." But this did not mean that Leavitt questioned the value of Christian union. Indeed, he believed that Congregational principles would serve as the foundation of any such union. "And if the time shall ever come, when all Christians and all churches, shall unite with perfect catholicism in promoting the kingdom of Christ," he stated, "they will of necessity unite on pure congregational ground; i.e., the equality of churches, and the right of self-government."[42]

The evangelical revivals created the New School group within the Presbyterian Church. The New School had much in common with the evangelical Congregationalists, emphasizing moral reform, revivalism, evangelical piety, and interdenominational cooperation. Moved by an intensely evangelical spirit, they viewed the benevolent societies as effective means of converting the West and the nation.[43] The basic tenets of the New School program were dear to Leavitt's heart, and he aligned himself closely with them as the struggle between the New and Old School factions escalated through the 1830s. With the exception of 1831, he attended every meeting of the Presbyterian General Assem-

42. *Independent*, January 30, 1873; "Review of Hawes' Tribute to the Memory of the Pilgrims," *Quarterly Christian Spectator*, III (September, 1831), 338, 365–75, 377, 391–92, 380.

43. See George M. Marsden, *The Evangelical Mind and the New School Presbyterian Experience: A Case Study of Thought and Theology in Nineteenth-Century America* (New Haven, Conn., 1970).

bly between 1830 and 1837, supplying extensive editorial correspondence and commentary for the columns of the New York *Evangelist*. One of the first editors of a religious newspaper to report on the proceedings of a denominational meeting, he threw himself wholeheartedly into the conflict as an outspoken critic of the Old School faction.

Leavitt exulted in every triumph achieved by the New School forces. When they easily defeated Old School attempts to censure "doctrinal errors" in 1832, he rejoiced in the assembly's success in "subduing the brow-beating spirit" that had sought to "prostrate the church to the purposes of bigotry." Returning for the 1833 session, he expressed satisfaction that "the triumph of peace, and of a catholic spirit" permitted him to remain in the Presbyterian Church, where he felt he belonged in the name of Christian unity.[44]

The Philadelphia faction, however, shattered the peaceful interlude in 1834. In its "Act and Testimony," the ultraconservatives threw down the gauntlet to both the New School and the Congregationalists by rejecting the legitimacy of any presbytery or synod formed on principles that smacked of Congregationalism. This proposal elicited sharp criticism not only from Leavitt and other evangelicals but also from the moderate Princeton faction of the Old School, which adhered to traditonal doctrines and church polity and severely condemned the New Haven "errors" for subverting the foundations of the church's creed. But they did not wish to see the church divided by the actions of either the New School or the ultraconservatives. Alienated by the demands of the Philadelphia group, the Princeton faction had often voted with the New School on crucial issues.[45]

Not surprisingly, the "Act and Testimony" gained little support within the church. Yet Leavitt and other evangelicals had little cause for elation. By 1835, the Old School faction, determined to force all within the church to adhere to its standards, used its majority position to strengthen the denominational machinery as a means of enforcing doctrinal conformity and uniform church polity and to minimize cooperation with the Congregationalists and the Evangelical United Front.[46]

44. New York *Evangelist*, June 2, 1832, June 29, 1833.
45. "The Present Prospects of the Presbyterian Church," *Biblical Repertory and Theological Review*, VII (January, 1835), 56–72; Marsden, *The Evangelical Mind and the New School Presbyterian Experience*, 57–58.
46. *Minutes of the General Assembly of the Presbyterian Church in the United States*

Leavitt tended to see the enemies of evangelical Christianity all about him, but his growing conviction that many Old School Presbyterians intended to drive from the church all those who deviated from their narrow sectarian ways was essentially correct. In the face of their onslaughts he seemed uncertain in which direction to move. At times he reiterated his commitment to the ideal of Christian unity. "We believe," he stated in the summer of 1835, "that the Presbyterian and Congregational churches in the United States are, and of right ought to be, one united body of Christians." Yet, as the conflict intensified and the conservative forces became bolder in their denunciations, Leavitt's vision of Christian unity narrowed considerably. The conservatives' actions so angered him that in 1835 he urged the "sectarian disorganizers" in the Philadelphia party, for the sake of peace within the church, to leave its ranks and carry on their destructive action elsewhere.[47] Thus, in a very real sense he had come to be no more wedded to the idea of a unified church than were his enemies.

Leavitt did not yet wish to lead an exodus from the Presbyterian Church, for he still felt a strong bond with the New School faction. He was prepared, he wrote in 1835, to make "any sacrifice but those of conscience and Christian liberty to perpetuate the Union." But, given the fact that he valued these principles above all others, this pledge was very conditional. In fact, he warned that unless the General Assembly granted representation to the Presbygational churches, abolished the sectarian boards, and condemned slavery, he and many other members would leave the Presbyterian Church.[48]

Leavitt sincerely believed that once the sin of slavery was exposed, all Christians would demand its immediate end. But his hopes in this direction were soon dashed. It became abundantly clear that the vast majority of Christians had chosen one of three courses of action: to remain silent on the slavery question; to repudiate the antislavery cause and attack its leaders; or to defend slavery. Frustrated by the church's refusal to recognize its sacred trust, Leavitt concluded that only harsh criticism would bring Christians to the path of duty. He

---

of America; With an Appendix, A.D. 1835 (Philadelphia, 1835), 27–30; Rev. E. H. Gillette, History of the Presbyterian Church in the United States of America (Philadelphia, 1864), II, 446–51.

47. New York Evangelist, August 8, 1835, March 12, 1836.

48. Ibid., August 8, 1835, March 12, 1836.

seemed to realize, if only vaguely, that this might further alienate many from the cause. But, he reasoned in 1835, it was worth the risk: "The church, as all must see, is the grand shield of slavery, because the church is the main regulator of public morals on all subjects. So long as the church sanctions and sustains it, slavery is impregnable against all moral influences. Whenever the church shall wash her hand of the stain the downfall of slavery is nigh at hand."[49]

Leavitt, the Tappans, and Weld, among others, believed that they could convert the Presbyterian Church to immediatism through a campaign of education and pressure. After all, such prominent New Schoolers as Albert Barnes and N. S. S. Beman were avowed abolitionists, and thousands of New Schoolers subscribed to the New York *Evangelist*. But the task of lobbying the General Assembly, which Weld undertook in 1835, proved a formidable one. Since its condemnation of slavery in 1818, the Presbyterian Church had routinely welcomed slaveholders to its communion and strongly endorsed the colonization movement. Thanks to Weld's effective lobbying efforts at the 1835 annual meeting, however, delegates presented to the General Assembly several resolutions condemning slavery. Hoping to avoid open conflict, a large majority of delegates voted to submit the matter to a committee, with instructions to report back to the next General Assembly.[50]

Leavitt was absolutely determined to push the slavery issue to its conclusion, even if it meant that Southerners would leave the Church. "Yet our southern brethren," he declared, "may be assured that nothing on earth can prevent our laboring as we can to deliver them from sin and their colored brethren from oppression. If they remain with us, or withdraw from us, we shall continue to think that slavery is a sin." But many Presbyterians, and especially an influential minority of New School delegates led by Lyman Beecher, feared that the issue would thoroughly divide the church. Beecher's forces prevailed at the 1836 General Assembly. The committee's recommendation that the subject be indefinitely postponed passed by a vote of 154–87, with

49. *Ibid.*, November 21, 1835; also June 14, 1834, January 2, November 12, 1836. For an excellent treatment of the abolitionists' assault on the churches for refusing to repudiate slavery, see John McKivigan, *The War Against Proslavery Religion: Abolitionism and the Northern Churches, 1830–1865* (Ithaca, N.Y., 1984).

50. C. Bruce Staiger, "Abolitionism and the Presbyterian Schism of 1837–1838," *Mississippi Valley Historical Review*, XXXVI (December, 1949), 396–97.

abolitionists and southern representatives voting against it for very different reasons: the former because they wanted the assembly to condemn slavery; the latter because they feared that any future compromise might lead to slaveholders being excluded from the church. The fact that one day after this vote the New School majority annulled most of the Old School actions of the previous year indicates how divided the New School was on the slavery issue. Leavitt welcomed these New School advances, but the assembly's refusal to condemn slavery tempered his enthusiasm. Rejoicing that "so little evil was done," he expressed disappointment that "so little good was done—so very little that will contribute to the *advancement* of religion."[51]

In light of these reverses, many Old Schoolers had to decide whether to secede or to attempt to throw out the New School. Even some interested observers had concluded that a division was both inevitable and desirable. Nathaniel Taylor, for example, urged the Presbyterians to "divide not on the ground of heresy, and with mutual hate and denunciation, but divide for peace's sake." Taylor's entreaty fell on deaf ears. At the 1837 General Assembly the Old School, hoping to eliminate Congregational influence within the church and to arrest the "widespread and ever restless spirit of radicalism," which it believed had "driven to extreme fanaticism the great cause of revivals of religion, of temperance, and of the rights of man," prohibited the American Home Missionary Society and the American Education Society from operating in any Presbyterian churches and abrogated retroactively the Plan of Union of 1801—thereby eliminating from the church one Ohio and three New York synods with more than 60,000 members. The stunned and confused New School forces that remained in the General Assembly soon withdrew and joined their excluded brethren.[52]

Leavitt's response to this dramatic development was mixed. He was angered by what he considered an "unconstitutional and unlawful"

51. New York *Evangelist*, March 19, 1836, June 11, 18, 1836; Ratner, *Powder Keg*, 90–95; *Minutes of the General Assembly of the Presbyterian Church*, 247–50, 271–73, 286–87.

52. Nathaniel Taylor to Lyman Beecher, March 3, 1837, in Charles Beecher (ed.), *Autobiography, Correspondence, etc. of Lyman Beecher* (New York, 1864), II, 48; *Minutes of the General Assembly of the Presbyterian Church*, 507; also 419–22, 440–46, 504–505; *Presbyterian Reunion: A Memorial Volume. 1837–1871* (New York, 1870), 51–53.

act, but even more than that he felt a deep sadness and sense of fore-boding about the prospect of achieving the millennium and maintain-ing the union of American states. He wrote:

> It is a sad spectacle! One of the largest, and most enlightened Christian denominations in our land, and that bid fair to do most of the salvation of the world, perpetrated, by its highest representative body, a public breach of faith scarcely paralleled in the annals of national profligacy. The Pres-byterian Church dismembered, and virtually dissolved. . . . It is a solemn spectacle. . . . The cords of religious confidence and affection between the churches of the north and south have begun to break, severed by the hands of the slaveholder. The brilliant anticipations with which we have so long fed our dreams, are covered with a cloud.[53]

At the same time, Leavitt expressed the hope that evangelical Pres-byterians and Congregationalists would continue their joint venture. Yet this desire to perpetuate the evangelical union was tempered by the fact that even before the schism he and others with strong Congrega-tionalist predilections had begun to move inexorably toward a self-conscious denominationalism. Indeed, he seized upon the schism to urge the excised synods to abandon Presbyterianism and become thor-oughly Congregationalist in their church government and fellowship. He believed that the Old School's expulsion of the Presbygationalists from the Presbyterian Church would permit them to see the "true vir-tues of Congregationalism." The men who created the Plan of Union had been "actuated by the best intentions," he explained to these Pres-bygationalists, "but they never *could* have done as they did, had they been intelligently and conscientiously grounded in the Congregational principles of John Cotton and Thomas Hooker."[54]

This denominationalist movement had begun in earnest in 1836, when Leavitt, the Tappan brothers, Joseph Thompson, David Hale, and other proponents of the new measures and the Congregational system of church polity founded the Broadway Tabernacle. They in-stalled Finney, who had long been disenchanted with the Presbyterian hierarchy and doctrines and had become a Congregationalist in the mid-1830s, as pastor. The Tabernacle covenant, Leavitt stated in his charge to the people at Finney's ordination, defined the congregation as a complete church and subject to no authority but God's. In the

53. New York *Evangelist*, June 10, 1837.
54. *Ibid.*, June 10, 17, 1837.

months before and after the Presbyterian schism, they held several meetings to plan the organization of Congregational churches in New York and New Jersey. While they made overtures to the New School Presbyterians on the basis of their shared belief in revivals and benevolent action, their denominational consciousness had developed to the point that any formal union would have had to take place on their terms.[55]

The Presbyterian Church thus lay in ruins, largely the victim of the Old School's unwillingness to tolerate diversity and innovation within its ranks, but also of a gradual waning of an interdenominational spirit among evangelicals such as Leavitt. In the end, neither the Old School nor Leavitt and other Congregationalist enthusiasts found sufficient reason to attempt to keep the church whole.

As an astute, though scarcely objective, observer of the conflict and an active participant in it, Leavitt recognized (as have a number of scholars who have studied the schism) that numerous issues— including church polity, the new measures, church control of missionary and educational organizations, and slavery—had moved the church toward division.[56] But because he had come to view nearly every public issue as somehow related to the slavery question, he naturally concluded that "slavery has turned the scale in the Presbyterian conflict." He conveniently cast the antislavery forces in the role of in-

55. New York *Evangelist*, April 16, 1836, January 28, 1837; Samuel C. Pearson, "From Church to Denomination: American Congregationalism in the Nineteenth Century," *Church History*, XXXVIII (March, 1969), 45–77; Rev. James H. Hotchkin, *A History of the Purchase and Settlement of Western New York, and of the Rise, Progress, and Present State of the Presbyterian Church in That Section* (New York, 1848), 246–48.

56. For assessments of the causes of the Presbyterian schism, see Marsden, *The Evangelical Mind and the New School Presbyterian Experience*, esp. 60–101; Irving Stoddard Kull, "Presbyterian Attitudes Toward Slavery," *Church History*, VII (1938), 106–108, 111; Elwyn A. Smith, "The Role of the South in the Presbyterian Schism of 1837–38," *Church History*, XXIX (1960), 45, 60; Timothy Smith, *Revivalism and Social Reform in Mid-Nineteenth-Century America* (New York, 1957), 26–27; Earl R. MacCormac, "Missions and the Presbyterian Schism of 1837," *Church History*, XXXII (March, 1963), 32–45; Earl A. Pope, "New England Calvinism and the Disruption of the Presbyterian Church" (Ph.D. dissertation, Brown University, 1962), 367–69, 411; Robert Hastings Nichols, *Presbyterianism in New York State*, ed. James Hastings Nichols (Philadelphia, 1963), 129–33; Staiger, "Abolitionism and the Presbyterian Schism," 413–14.

nocent victims, insisting self-righteously that "slaveholders struck the blow, Abolition men had nothing to do in the case."[57]

Leavitt's post-mortem was both self-serving and incorrect. Many Old Schoolers indeed wished to end all debate on the slavery question by throwing the New School out of the church. But Leavitt and other abolitionists were equally unwilling to compromise on the matter. Also, it is difficult to determine whether southern Presbyterians' fears of abolitionism attracted them to the Old School forces more than did their doctrinal concerns. The Old School often emphasized the connection between the New School theology and abolitionism, and solid southern support for the Old School position at the 1837 General Assembly provided the conservatives with a comfortable margin of victory. But in the end, the schism probably would have occurred even without the existence of the slavery issue.[58]

The schism of 1837 was, as Leavitt believed, an ominous event. In truth, the Presbyterian Church had divided only in part along sectional lines. The Old School retained a large southern contingent until the Civil War, and even the New School forces managed to hold on to their small southern wing until 1857 by refusing to discipline slaveholders within their ranks. But the fact remains that the slavery question had helped to push the antagonists over the brink. The internal bonds of an important national institution were severed, thereby weakening those that bound the Union together. Less than a decade later, the slavery issue would be even more instrumental in dividing the Baptist and Methodist churches along sectional lines, and the Whig party would begin to break apart under the strain of the slavery question. Leavitt did not radically overstate the case when he warned in 1837 that "the fabric of American Union has begun to crumble."[59]

The schism also had disturbing implications for Leavitt's editorship of the New York *Evangelist*. It soon became apparent that many of the New Schoolers who subscribed to his paper wished to remain in the Presbyterian Church and mobilize their forces in preparation for the next General Assembly. Theodore Weld reported "a simulta-

57. New York *Evangelist*, June 10, 1837.
58. Othniel A. Pendleton, Jr., "Slavery and the Evangelical Churches," *Journal of the Presbyterian Historical Society*, XXV (September, 1947), 157–58; Marsden, *The Evangelical Mind and the New School Presbyterian Experience*, 96–101.
59. New York *Evangelist*, June 10, 1837.

neous cry to *arms* and the din of marshaling is everywhere." These developments deeply concerned Leavitt, who assumed correctly that the New School leadership would seek to establish a paper in the city to lead the struggle against the Old School, thereby cutting sharply into his subscription lists. For their part, the New Schoolers confronted something of a dilemma: On the one hand, according to Weld, they preferred Leavitt "to anybody else" and realized that they could not compete successfully with the *Evangelist's* great influence in the religious community; on the other hand, they realized that Leavitt cared far more about espousing Congregationalism and abolitionism than about leading the New School back into the Presbyterian Church. Thus, they moved to buy the paper and hire a new editor.[60]

Under most circumstances Leavitt would not have considered relinquishing the editorship or selling the paper. He had enjoyed the past six years as editor and hoped to continue in this capacity for many more years. When he did sell the paper, he confessed to his father that he experienced "some pain in retiring from the editorial chair." Indeed, at first he resisted the New School's overtures, but financial distress eventually forced him to reconsider. Though he had more than 10,000 subscribers by late 1836, he was also plagued by delinquent subscribers. This problem had forced Leavitt and his partner Seth Benedict to borrow $2,000 to continue printing the paper. A far greater financial burden was acquired when, during the halcyon days of financial speculation in 1837, he and Benedict borrowed thousands of dollars at high interest rates for the purpose of constructing an office building near Fulton Street. Leavitt was probably sincere when he protested to Gerrit Smith that he was "not greatly addicted to the love of money," but on this occasion he risked what little money he had in the hope of profiting from an investment. Even when this investment had begun to go sour, he wrote his father that "the question whether it makes us rich or poor will depend chiefly *on the times*." Unfortunately, the times were not propitious for such a venture; in May, when the financial crisis came, he and Benedict were among thousands of investors and businessmen caught in it.[61]

60. Theodore Weld to James Birney, June 26, 1837, in Dumond (ed.), *Birney Letters*, I, 389; Joshua Leavitt to Roger Leavitt, July 25, 1837, in Leavitt Papers.

61. Joshua Leavitt to Amos A. Phelps, December 26, 1836, in Phelps Papers; Leavitt to Roger Leavitt, July 25, 1837, Joshua Leavitt to Roger Hooker Leavitt, January 3, 1837, in Leavitt Papers.

His editorship jeopardized, his role as provider seriously threatened, and his future clouded, Leavitt at the age of forty-two experienced what we would term a mid-life crisis. Particularly depressing was the financial disaster that threatened him with bankruptcy and debts he feared he could never honor. He confessed to Smith that he was concerned the situation would "not only swallow up the little earnings of the past, but I fear entail a load of embarrassment, debt and dishonor upon the future." Equally disturbing was the prospect of not being able to provide for Sarah and the boys. This had often troubled him during the past several years, and now it seemed a reality. This point was brought home forcefully when he had to inform Jeremiah Day, president of Yale, that he must withdraw his eldest son William from the freshman class for lack of funds. For a proud man who valued education, who had sent his eldest son to his beloved alma mater, and whose father had provided a college education for him, this must have been a humiliating experience. These financial problems deeply distressed him. As he acknowledged to Smith, "pecuniary care and embarrassment always paralyzes my mental powers, and unfits me for what I [ought] to do to serve my generation."[62]

The fact that Leavitt was forced to sell the *Evangelist* added to his mental anguish. He had devoted enormous energy to the task of editing the paper and had derived a great deal of satisfaction from his labors. Equally important, the sale left his future very much in doubt. There were rumors that he would be named editor of the *Emancipator*, the organ of the American Anti-Slavery Society, but he was uncertain whether he wanted this, or whether he would be appointed. Weld in fact reported that Leavitt "has about made up his mind to leave the city and go to preaching." Leavitt confided to his father that he would accept "any lawful calling, only with a preference for one in which I may still aid, in some way, the abolition cause." But for the moment he felt he must stay in the city in order to earn money to send Sarah and the boys to Heath: "If I find employment I shall be able to lay in winter stores. If not, I do not see but I must come back to the old hive."[63] To make matters worse, recent events had called into question

62. Joshua Leavitt to Jeremiah Day, May 17, 1837, in Jeremiah Day Papers, Beinecke Library, Yale University; Joshua Leavitt to Gerrit Smith, August 23, 1837, in Smith Miller Collection.

63. Theodore Weld to James Birney, June 26, 1837, in Dumond (ed.), *Birney Letters*, I, 389; Joshua Leavitt to Roger Leavitt, July 25, 1847, in Leavitt Papers. Leavitt later

his expectation that the churches would be in the vanguard of the assault on slavery. In the Presbyterian Church the antiabolitionist Old School had prevailed, and abolitionist sentiment had made only limited headway among the New Schoolers. Moreover, by 1837 the movement's rate of growth had begun to slow down.

Some relief came with the sale of the *Evangelist* for $18,000, which left Leavitt and Benedict with the printing machines and $20,000 due from subscribers and agents. Yet he still faced a very difficult situation, and friends such as the Tappans, who normally could have assisted him, had financial problems of their own. Thus, he was forced to appeal to the wealthy Gerrit Smith—whom he respected but who was not a close friend—for a loan of $2,000. He was desperate, confessing to Smith that if he did not lend him the money, "I have no earthly friend to whom we can apply." He pleaded with Smith not to "voluntarily turn the old Hack Horse of Reform adrift unpitied"—certainly a humbling experience for a fiercely independent man. In the end, Smith loaned him $1,000.[64]

There was still the possibility of editing the *Emancipator*. The paper had a checkered history. None of its editors had proved themselves capable of generating much enthusiasm. The executive committee had made it a weekly paper in early 1836, but the new editor, Amos Phelps, though a good writer, was, in Elizur Wright's estimation, "not passionate, moving, electrifying." In early 1837 the committee reorganized the American Anti-Slavery Society's national headquarters by bringing Weld, John Greenleaf Whittier, and Henry B. Stanton to New York to assist the hard-working Wright, its secretary. "Weld, Whittier, Stanton, Wright," exclaimed Wright, "what a pestilent, dangerous clump of fanatics all in our little room plotting freedom for the slaves."[65]

Leavitt did not know whether he wished to join these men at antislavery headquarters. He told his close friend Weld that he was "a good deal worn down from editing" and needed a change of occupa-

---

said that he had been asked several times since 1833 to edit the *Emancipator* but was "too well satisfied" with his situation at the *Evangelist* to leave. *Emancipator*, December 7, 1843.

64. Joshua Leavitt to Gerrit Smith, August 23, 1837, in Smith Miller Collection.

65. Elizur Wright to Theodore Weld, March 24, 1836, in Barnes and Dumond (eds.), *Weld-Grimké Letters*, I, 279; Elizur Wright to parents, July 20, 1837, in Wright Papers.

tion, including the possibility of returning to the ministry.[66] It is difficult to imagine that, having been a prominent participant in numerous
reform causes for several years, he would have been content to return
to the relative obscurity of a church pastorate. The prospect of losing
his services to the antislavery cause disturbed some of Leavitt's friends.
Weld, in particular, proceeded to lobby vigorously for Leavitt's appointment as editor of the *Emancipator*. Having worked closely with
Leavitt in several causes over the years, he admired Leavitt and felt
uniquely qualified to comment on his attributes. He believed, as he
informed Lewis Tappan in 1836, that Leavitt was not only an extremely wise man whose knowledge of the slavery question and "clear,
calm philosophic candid and solemn manner" were impressive, but
also a hard worker who accomplished "an immense amount for the
cause in a multitude of ways which most other men would never
dream of." If Leavitt were to edit the *Emancipator*, Weld wrote Birney,
"its subscription list would double if not triple very rapidly on account
of the *personal* hold which he had upon a multitude of persons." Finally, he warned that "if Leavitt should leave the city one half of the
actual bona fide energy, practical wisdom and prompt execution of
the Executive Committee is either utterly taken away or thrown *hors
de combat*. And the remaining half would move on with feeble and
divided counsels." Weld's opinion carried significant weight. In August
the American Anti-Slavery Society offered Leavitt the post of editor, at
a salary of $1,500 a year, which he considered quite adequate.[67] Not-
withstanding the rigors of the past few years, he promptly accepted
the offer. With this new position he came to direct his energies almost
entirely to the antislavery cause and the controversies that were beginning to surface within its ranks.

66. Quoted in Theodore Weld to James Birney, July 10, 1837, in Dumond (ed.),
Birney Letters, I, 394–95; Joshua Leavitt to Roger Leavitt, July 25, 1837, in Leavitt
Papers.
67. Theodore Weld to Lewis Tappan, October 10, 1836, in Barnes and Dumond
(eds.), *Weld-Grimké Letters*, I, 342–43; Weld to Birney, June 26, 1837, in Dumond
(ed.), *Birney Letters*, I, 390; *Emancipator*, December 7, 1843.

8

SCHISMS IN THE
ANTISLAVERY MOVEMENT

When he became editor of the *Emancipator* in August 1837, Leavitt entered a new phase in his reform career. During the next ten years, he continued to support the evangelical revivals and a number of benevolent causes, but the demands of the job and his belief in the overriding importance of the antislavery crusade led him to subordinate other endeavors to his abolition work.

Leavitt commuted daily from Bloomfield, New Jersey, a small town near Newark where he and Sarah had moved in 1835 to provide a healthier environment for their five sons, the last of whom was born in that year. He spent much of his workday at the antislavery headquarters, where he shared a small office with James Birney, one of the secretaries of the American Anti-Slavery Society; John Greenleaf Whittier, who headed the petitions campaign; Theodore Weld, who had come to New York to study the slavery question; and Henry B. Stanton, who supervised fund raising. Each day they sat at their desks, mapping out the details and planning the strategy they hoped would ultimately achieve the destruction of slavery.[1]

They were a rather disparate group. Elizur Wright, whose calculating mind and organizational skills served him well as one of the secretaries of the national society and would later be applied successfully in helping to develop the life insurance industry, tended to be direct,

1. Theodore Weld to Lewis Tappan, April 5, 1836, in Barnes and Dumond (eds.), *Weld-Grimké Letters*, I, 286; Elizur Wright to parents, July 20, 1837, in Wright Papers.

impatient, and caustic in dealing with others. Even Leavitt, who could be brusque and tactless at times, seemed steady and reserved by comparison. Wright himself admitted that under Leavitt's guidance the *Emancipator* would be "*calmer* and more convicting than I could make it, and that is what we want." Birney, a soft-spoken, genteel former slaveholder, and Whittier, a moody, introspective Quaker poet, were gentler souls who stood in contrast to Leavitt and Wright, as well as to Stanton, who was young, energetic, and ambitious. Given these personality differences and competitive instincts, it is not surprising that the men occasionally made unflattering remarks about each other. Wright, for example, confided to Beriah Green that Leavitt had "*buttressed*, not *sharpened*" the *Emancipator*, while Stanton noted that Whittier "has no power of originating, is rather poetical in his temper i.e. *unstable*, subject to low spirits, hypo, etc.—is a Quaker from head to foot, is rather careless in his business habits." For his part, Weld pointedly referred to Wright's "asperity and undignified snappishness" and Stanton's "air of 'recklessness' and 'harem-Scarem.'"[2] Yet in the final analysis the group managed to work together in harmony.

Leavitt continued to serve on several subcommittees and as the recording secretary of the American Anti-Slavery Society, which entailed keeping minutes of annual and executive committee meetings, but his principal task was editing the *Emancipator*. Unlike the *Evangelist*, which he and Benedict had owned after 1833, the *Emancipator* was the official organ published by the executive committee and in theory reflected the views of the organization's officers. However, Leavitt enjoyed considerable editorial autonomy. Fiercely independent, opinionated, and sensitive to perceived restraints, he insisted on conducting the paper according to his own "best judgment," feeling that "no man could do justice to himself or to the cause, without a certain degree of personal freedom and discretion." An experienced and polished editor who possessed a wide-ranging knowledge of the slavery issue, he breathed new life into the paper and made it, in Lewis Tappan's estimation, the best antislavery paper in the United States.[3]

2. Elizur Wright to Beriah Green, August 14, 1837, in Wright Papers; Theodore Weld to James Birney, May 23, 1837, Henry B. Stanton to James Birney, August 7, 1837, in Dumond (ed.), *Birney Letters*, I, 382, 405–406; Bennet Whitman, *Whittier: Bard of Freedom* (Chapel Hill, 1941), 113–14.

3. *Emancipator*, January 11, 1838; Lewis Tappan to Gamaliel Bailey, October 24, 1839, in Tappan Papers.

In 1837 abolitionists could point to definite signs of progress in their crusade against slavery. Thousands of Americans had flocked to the cause, and the number of antislavery societies had risen steadily. In his maiden editorial Leavitt hailed the "momentous achievements" of the past four years: "Not a reverse has occurred of sufficient importance to stop our program. Not a single important measure has failed. Not a step of any moment has been retraced. Not a shot has recoiled. Not a sentiment has reacted."[4] Leavitt's ebullient spirit, however, led him to exaggerate the extent of progress achieved by the movement. Major obstacles stood in the path of abolition. Perhaps more than ever before, the South was determined to resist any agitation of the slavery question, and most Northerners—including political, business, and church leaders—remained implacably opposed to the abolitionists' goals of immediate emancipation and racial equality. Their bitter opposition to the cause deeply disappointed and angered Leavitt, William Lloyd Garrison, and other abolitionists.

Garrison, strong-willed, impatient, and contentious, had long chafed at the cautious and conservative ways of Arthur Tappan and other businessmen among the New York abolitionists. Before 1837 little overt antagonism existed between Garrison and the American Anti-Slavery Society's executive committee, but this changed as Garrison's thinking underwent a significant transformation. He had become increasingly disillusioned with politics and the churches as the major parties and religious groups refused to condemn slavery. A meeting in 1837 with John Humphrey Noyes, who argued that Christians must purge themselves of sin and reject all human authority, helped to clarify and strengthen Garrison's propensity for moving reform in a more ultraist direction. In the columns of the *Liberator* he began to assert that because all civil government was grounded in violence or the threat of force, one must withdraw from an impure society. Combining pacifist and millennialist ideas, Garrison came to condemn all institutions and practices that he deemed coercive and, therefore, obstacles to the quest for absolute purity. In particular, he began to attack the New England churches and the ministry as an embodiment of human authority.[5]

4. *Emancipator*, August 17, 1837.
5. See Thomas, *The Liberator*, 218, 221, 223–34, 239–40; Lewis Perry, *Radical Abolitionism: Anarchy and the Government of God in Antislavery Thought* (Ithaca, N.Y., 1973), 58–59, 64–70.

The response from the clergy was not long in coming, most importantly in the form of the Appeal of Clerical Abolitionists on Anti-Slavery Measures. Garrison responded to these attacks by questioning the clergy's claims of authority and religious supremacy and by turning to the national society's executive committee for support. He received, instead, an uneasy silence, which both concerned and outraged him. "It behooves them to remember that 'silence gives consent,'" he informed George Benson, "and if they refuse to answer the appeal, the enemy will construe their silence into a virtual approval of it." In truth, some members of the committee wished to maintain a strict neutrality, while others hoped to isolate Garrison within the movement in order to free it from his intemperate remarks and his heresies.[6]

A mutual suspicion between the Garrison and New York cliques had existed beneath the movement's surface for some time; a more overt hostility now developed. For his part, Leavitt generally refrained from openly attacking Garrison for a year following the Clerical Controversy. As editor of the national society's official organ, he thought it advisable to remain neutral. During the last half of 1837, he therefore did little more than request that both parties "cease to expend their ammunition upon one another, and see which can do the most for the poor slave."[7]

Fundamental philosophical differences between the two men go far to explain Leavitt's refusal to rush to Garrison's defense. Although identified in the public mind as a radical because he challenged the almost universal racist assumptions of white Americans and called for the destruction of an institution deeply rooted in the nation's fiber, Leavitt was in fact more a reformer than a radical. He did not seek to create a brave new world based on untested models, but rather to improve the existing society through ameliorative reforms. He objected not to American society's stated ideals, but rather to its failure to live up to the standards implied in its assumptions. Indeed, he believed American society to be essentially sound. The only major insti-

6. William Lloyd Garrison to George Benson, August 26, 1837, in Wendell Phillips Garrison and Francis Jackson Garrison, *William Lloyd Garrison, 1805–1879: The Story of His Life Told by His Children* (New York, 1885), II, 159; Elizur Wright to Amos A. Phelps, October 20, 1837, in Phelps Papers; James Birney to Lewis Tappan, September 14, 1837, in Tappan Papers; Henry B. Stanton to James Birney, September 1, 1837, in Dumond (ed.), *Birney Letters*, I, 420–23.

7. *Emancipator*, November 9, 1837.

tution that he sought not to change and reform but to destroy was slavery. Once slavery disappeared, he believed, the social order would be rejuvenated and the Union preserved and strengthened. As he editorialized in 1837, "We only come right up to the mark of truth and righteousness, and there is no *ultraism* in that and moreover, we are laboring on the truest principles of conservatism, to save both the church and the nation, from impending destruction, by endeavoring to persuade both to put away their sins."[8]

Leavitt's emphasis on conservative principles was in part a rhetorical ploy designed to reassure Americans that abolitionists were not wild-eyed fanatics. But he was not a radical of the "come outer" mold. Stanley Elkins's contention that abolitionists were so anti-institutional and individualistic that they isolated themselves from the centers of power, thus preventing any practical or peaceable reform, scarcely applies to Leavitt, or for that matter most other abolitionists.[9] Leavitt bitterly criticized the churches and the major parties for their silence on the slavery question and left the Presbyterian Church in part, and the existing parties wholly, for this reason. He did not, however, repudiate institutions or institutional means *per se*, but rather those he considered corrupted by their connections with slavery. In fact, he valued institutions, helping to create or sustain the Liberty party, benevolent organizations, and the Congregational Church as means of organizing and ordering society in an era of rapid change and, above all, as weapons to be employed against slavery.

Leavitt harshly criticized not only those institutions he believed helped to sustain slavery but also "Northern Capitalists" for the "bitterness and persecution" they directed toward the abolitionists and for their unholy alliance with slaveholders. "Every merchant or manufacturer," he editorialized in 1837, "therefore, who has southern debts to collect, becomes more anxious than ever, to keep all quiet, and prevent any agitation, that will hazard the stability of commercial arrange-

8. *Ibid.*, September 14, 1837.
9. Elkins, *Slavery*, esp. 140–205. For excellent critiques of Elkins's thesis as it applies to the abolitionists, see Aileen S. Kraditor, *Means and Ends in American Abolitionism: Garrison and His Critics on Strategy and Tactics, 1834–1850* (New York, 1969), 16–22; Walters, *Antislavery Appeal*, 6–9; James Brewer Stewart, "Politics and Beliefs in Abolitionism: Stanley Elkins' Concept of Antiinstitutionalism and Recent Interpretations of American Antislavery," *South Atlantic Quarterly*, LXXV (Winter, 1976), 74–97.

ments, *until the debts are collected.*" These selfish business interests deserved, in his opinion, nothing but contempt from "the middling class of society"—i.e., those who had launched the antislavery movement and "who live by their own earnings, and think their own thoughts, who daily offer up a prayer, and who deem the privilege of working with *their own* hands, and eating *their own* bread, and choosing their own rulers, and doing good unto all men as they have opportunity, as infinitely surpassing in value the pride of wealth, or the advancement of the manufacturing and banking interests, or any other exclusive aggrandizement."[10]

Although Leavitt considered the greed and materialism he observed in northern life to be antithetical to Christian brotherhood, his criticism of the entrepreneurial classes did not represent a repudiation of the emerging economic order. His complaint was not that these businessmen made money but that they placed their profits above their moral obligation to condemn slavery. As Bertram Wyatt-Brown has argued, most abolitionists thought more in terms of "the respectability"—self-supporting, civic-minded, and God-fearing men and women—than of the middle class in economic terms and identified more with these bourgeois elements, with whom they shared a similar socioeconomic background, education, manners, evangelical beliefs, and aspirations, than they did with the workingmen.[11]

Leavitt certainly fits into this mold. He increasingly came to espouse democratic principles, and he had suffered a disastrous financial setback following the Panic of 1837. In addition, his attachment to the principle of Christian brotherhood prevented him from being a blind supporter of the capitalist status quo or espousing a philosophy based on pure self-interest. But this does not mean that he was anticapitalist or antibusiness. His evangelical beliefs, which tended to associate both salvation and success with the values of sobriety, hard work, and self-control, were quite compatible with the idea of economic competition. Indeed, he, like many other abolitionists, accepted social inequality as a natural reflection of individual differences in ambition and talent.[12]

Leavitt firmly believed in the American Dream, insisting that the

10. *Emancipator*, September 7, 1837, October 10, 1839.
11. Bertram Wyatt-Brown, "Proslavery and Antislavery Intellectuals: Class Concepts and Polemical Struggle," in Perry and Fellman (eds.), *Antislavery Reconsidered*, 311–19; see also Walters, *Antislavery Appeal*, 112–18.
12. *Emancipator*, December 31, 1840.

opportunity for upward mobility existed even for industrial workers and that northern wage laborers were far better off than were southern slaves. In branding as "utterly false and pernicious" Orestes Brownson's contention that "true social democracy" did not exist in America, Leavitt stated, on the basis of his limited observation of manufacturing towns in the Northeast: "The truth is, that the *great body* of the young men of New England, and a large portion of the young women, work for wages in the beginning of life, and by the surplus of their wages, acquire the means of becoming either employers or operatives in their own shops or on their own farms. To assume the existence of a distinction between employers and paid workmen, as a permanent state, is either to dream or to deceive." Because employers took risks and contributed special skills, he added, they had a larger claim to profits than did their workers. He drew back from criticizing the workers, in part because he realized that artisans constituted an important element of the antislavery constituency in New York City in the 1830s, in some instances providing more support than did the benevolent activists. The distinction he drew between the entrepreneurial class and those who worked with their hands represented at least a partial acknowledgment of that support. Yet Leavitt and most other abolitionists held to a highly individualistic conception of slavery and freedom; saw the end of slavery, not higher wages, as a prerequisite for the elevation of free labor; and emphasized that factory owners were proslavery, not that they exploited their workers. As a result, they could neither understand nor cooperate with the labor reformers of the time.[13]

Garrison, much like Leavitt, did not question the legitimacy of the capitalist system or the emerging industrial order, nor did he call for civil disobedience to government. Further, he repudiated the clergy's

13. *Ibid.*; also October 10, 1839. For treatments of the abolitionists' attitudes toward the northern working class, see Eric Foner, "Abolitionism and the Labor Movement in Antebellum America," in Bolt and Drescher (eds.), *Antislavery, Religion, and Reform*, 254–66; Walters, *Antislavery Appeal*, 117–19; Bernard Mandel, *Labor: Free and Slave; Workingmen and the Anti-Slavery Movement in the United States* (New York, 1955), 81–92; Jonathan A. Glickstein, "'Poverty is not Slavery': American Abolitionists and the Competitive Labor Market," in Perry and Fellman (eds.), *Antislavery Reconsidered*, 200–204, 213–17; Williston H. Lofton, "Abolition and Labor," *Journal of Negro History*, XXXIII (October, 1949), 249–83. On the changing composition of the antislavery constituency in the city, see John B. Jentz, "The Antislavery Constituency in Jacksonian New York City," *Civil War History*, XXVII (June, 1981), 101–22.

claim of authority, not the Christian religion itself. But while Garrison did not thoroughly repudiate all institutions, he was genuinely a radical in that he believed American society to be immoral, with slavery being only the worst of its numerous sins. His perfectionist ideas drove him to seek a radical transformation of the society's institutional structure and ideology. Thus, the social order he envisioned differed greatly from the one Leavitt desired.[14]

These philosophical differences inevitably shaped Leavitt's view of Garrison and his role in the movement. In addition, from a practical standpoint he feared that Garrison's harsh attacks on the clergy might well preclude any opportunity to convert Christian America to the cause. His growing conviction that Garrison wished to create a multiple reform admixture of abolitionism, nonresistance, and women's rights, thereby distracting attention from the cause and alienating potential converts, added to his concern.[15]

The American Anti-Slavery Society's executive committee looked to Leavitt as one who could have a calming influence on the warring factions. Given his tendency to be blunt, opinionated, and at times tactless, one might question the committee's faith in him as a conciliator. Yet he could also be charming, persuasive, and reasonable. Perhaps more important, he was respected by all parties in the emerging conflict. "The induction of bro. Leavitt into the editorial chair of the Emancipator," Stanton noted in 1837, "will exert a calming influence. He has the confidence of all, and especially of the disaffected party [the New England clerical abolitionists]." Yet, within two months of his ascension to the editorial chair, Leavitt's studied silence had deeply disturbed Garrison. "The Emancipator alone is dumb," Garrison thundered. "What does it mean?"[16] It meant that Leavitt was becoming progressively disenchanted with Garrison's ways.

The controversy surrounding the Lovejoy incident in late 1837 served further to drive a wedge between them. An Alton, Illinois, mob had killed Elijah Lovejoy, a passionate young abolitionist editor, but only after Lovejoy and his supporters shot a member of the mob in the process of defending Lovejoy's press. The national executive committee moved immediately to exploit the shock of this event, and during

14. See Thomas, *The Liberator*, 233–35.

15. See, for example, *Emancipator*, November 9, 1837.

16. Henry B. Stanton to James Birney, September 1, 1837, in Dumond (ed.), *Birney Letters*, I, 423; *Liberator*, October 6, 1837.

the following weeks the abolitionist press expressed outrage at the brutal killing. Yet abolitionists did not all approve Lovejoy's use of violence to defend his newspaper. The great majority—including many affiliated with the American Peace Society, which under the leadership of William Ladd during the 1830s had moved slowly toward a renunciation of all wars, both offensive and defensive—were ambivalent concerning the affair, praising Lovejoy as a martyr while condemning his use of force even in self-defense and for the sake of slaves. Leavitt, Wright, Wendell Phillips, and other abolitionists, convinced that Lovejoy was a martyr to the cause of liberty, could not accept this assessment. Never a pacifist, Leavitt generally approved of the American Peace Society's principles but refused to condemn self-defense. Following Lovejoy's death, he rushed to his defense, insisting that Lovejoy had committed "justifiable homicide" while acting "under the deepest conviction of duty." [17]

Leavitt breathed a sigh of relief when the executive committee did not officially disclaim Lovejoy's actions. To have done so, he warned, would have meant that abolitionists "could never again ask the civil authority to interfere for their protection" and that the law would be reduced to "a mere nullity of *good advice*, or soft entreaty." Garrison and other advocates of nonresistance, however, had other ideas. At the 1838 annual meeting of the American Anti-Slavery Society, they presented a resolution urging abolitionists to "continue patient under the manifold provocations, forgiving their enemies, not relying upon physical strength for their defense against the violence of others." The delegates overwhelmingly defeated this resolution, but the issue was far from dead.[18]

It appeared to Leavitt that Garrison and his associates wished to link nonresistance to the antislavery movement, thus making it a condition for membership in the national society. The founding of the New England Non-Resistance Society in late 1838 by Garrison and approximately fifty others, who proceeded to denounce all wars and disavow all human government, heightened his suspicion. He now openly attacked Garrison, accusing him of giving "credit and currency to the Non-Resistance Society by identifying its projectors with those

17. Merton L. Dillon, *Elijah P. Lovejoy: Abolitionist Editor* (Urbana, Ill., 1961), 159–79; Carleton Mabee, *Black Freedom: The Nonviolent Abolitionists from 1830 Through the Civil War* (New York, 1970), 42–48; *Emancipator*, November 23, 1837.
    18. *Emancipator*, January 4, May 10, 1838; also April 11, 1839.

of the Anti-Slavery Society." In truth, Garrison did not wish to transform the antislavery societies into nonresistance or universal reform organizations. But Leavitt's concern that Garrison's advocacy of nonresistance at antislavery conventions and in the columns of the *Liberator* (even if placed on the last page of the paper) might confuse the public about the connection between the two causes seems well founded. Indeed, Garrison was not certain where he stood on this matter. He stated to George Benson in 1837: "I feel somewhat at a loss to know what to do—whether to go into all the principles of holy reform, and make the abolition cause subordinate, or whether still to persevere in the *one* beaten track as hitherto." [19]

Relations between Garrison and the New York committee continued to deteriorate in 1838 as he became more convinced that they wished to force him from the movement. The leaders of several state antislavery societies agreed with Garrison and his Massachusetts supporters that the state organizations should have more autonomy, particularly in the area of fund raising. Caught in a financial squeeze between the national society and local organizations during the worsening economic depression, the delegates to the 1839 annual meeting resolved that henceforth the state societies would pledge a stipulated sum to the parent society. [20]

This financial arrangement, which forced the national officers to depend on the state societies for their operating funds, experienced difficulties from its inception, especially between the national committee and the Massachusetts society. The antagonism engendered by the Clerical Controversy and subsequent disputes culminated in early 1839 in the founding of the Massachusetts Abolition Society by Amos Phelps, Orange Scott, and others closely allied with the New York leaders. Garrison's intransigence and self-righteousness had helped to precipitate the schism. But Leavitt and others on the New York committee were also culpable in this deteriorating situation, through their silence in the midst of the Clerical Controversy and their rather autocratic methods of dealing with the financial issue. In particular, their

---

19. Merle E. Curti, "Non-Resistance in New England," *New England Quarterly,* II (January, 1929), 43–46; *Emancipator,* October 18, 1838; Garrison to Benson, August 26, 1837, in Garrison and Garrison, *William Lloyd Garrison,* II, 160.

20. William Burleigh to Henry B. Stanton, March 24, 1838, in Weston Family Papers, Boston Public Library; *Fifth Annual Report of the American Anti-Slavery Society* (New York, 1838), 12.

declaration that they would send agents back into the states to collect $10,000 for the national society deeply disturbed many Garrisonians and other abolitionists.[21]

However much Leavitt may have wished to remain apart from the fray, by early 1839 his close ties with the leaders of the Massachusetts Abolition Society and his hard line on the financial issue not surprisingly had led many Garrisonians to view him as one of the enemy. Yet neither the Garrisonians nor the non-Garrisonians was a monolithic group. On one of the most emotional issues that divided abolitionists during these turbulent years—the role of women in the antislavery movement—Leavitt, Weld, Gerrit Smith, and others stood much closer to many of the Garrisonians than they did to more socially conservative abolitionists such as Lewis Tappan, Birney, and Phelps. A few women had attended the founding convention of the American Anti-Slavery Society, but few delegates challenged the gender division of the benevolent societies: men directing the operations and women joining separate and subordinate auxiliaries that held sewing bees and bazaars. Sarah and Angelina Grimké (and the Garrisonians generally) neither denied the existence of a "woman's sphere" nor sought to reorganize the division of labor within the home. In demanding that women have access to a broader public sphere, however, they used prevailing ideas concerning women's traits to justify an expansion of their social roles.[22]

Many men within the movement were not prepared for the Grimké sisters or their message. At the same time, a substantial majority of female abolitionists, including Sarah Leavitt, seemingly felt comfortable in separate female auxiliaries. These women, like most others in America, were content to let men speak for them in public and make the basic decisions, though their involvement in the antislavery and

21. Thomas, *The Liberator*, 264–71; entries for May 10, June 21, 1838, January 3, May 2, 11, 1839, in "Minutes of the Executive Committee of the American Anti-Slavery Society, 1837–1841," Boston Public Library; Henry B. Stanton to Elizur Wright, February 11, 1839, in Wright Papers; *Emancipator*, March 14, 1839; *Sixth Annual Report of the American Anti-Slavery Society* (New York, 1839), 42.

22. For treatments of the abolitionists and the early women's rights movement, see Blanche Glassman Hersh, "'Am I Not a Woman and a Sister?' Abolitionist Beginnings of Nineteenth-Century Feminism," in Perry and Fellman (eds.), *Antislavery Reconsidered*, 254, 257–62; Ellen DuBois, "Women's Rights and Abolition: The Nature of the Connection," *ibid.*, 240–42, 244–46; Friedman, *Gregarious Saints*, 130–31, 140, 144, 153.

other causes certainly allowed them to transcend traditional roles for women. The emerging Garrisonian stance on the issue inevitably antagonized many abolitionists. The issue came to a head at the 1839 annual meeting of the American Anti-Slavery Society. In response to a resolution stating that only "men, duly constituted, shall constitute the roll," Leavitt joined a majority of the delegates—including Weld, Wright, and Smith—in passing a resolution declaring that the names of "all persons, male and female," be placed on the roster.[23]

Lewis Tappan and Birney were furious, warning in a sharply worded protest that the principles upon which the majority based its actions posed a threat to the social order and to unity within the movement. Leavitt resented the tone of the protest and even considered writing a rejoinder, but ultimately chose not to do so. In his maiden editorial in the *Emancipator*, he had supported the right of the Grimké sisters to speak before audiences of men and women. Convinced that some of the abolitionists' shrill warnings about the consequences of women participating in the cause were absurd, he resorted to sarcasm to make his point: "Horrible! What are we coming to? Why, the efforts of the last thirty years to educate and elevate the sex has actually infatuated some of the dear creatures to make them think that women have souls, and intellects, and the capacity of forming opinions, even on such intricate subjects as the right or wrong of slavery." Notwithstanding his belief that women should be permitted a decision-making role in the movement, he never endorsed the full equality of the sexes. He consistently subordinated the issue to abolitionism and warned that it should not be allowed to create a serious rift in the movement. Thus, he reassured the protesters that the 1839 convention's acceptance of the resolution "cannot be justly regarded as committing the Society for or against any party on the question of Women's Rights." His fear that the abolitionists' constant bickering would permanently cripple the cause led him, despite his friendship with a number of Garrison's enemies in Massachusetts who had created the Massachusetts Abolition Society, to vote with James Gibbons, the only Garrisonian on the national executive committee, as a minority of two opposing its recognition of the Massachusetts society as an auxiliary of the national organization on the grounds that such action was "unusual."[24]

23. Blanche Glassman Hersh, *The Slavery of Sex: Feminist-Abolitionists in America* (Urbana, Ill., 1978), 10–35; Thomas, *The Liberator*, 272–73.

24. *Emancipator*, August 17, 1837; Joshua Leavitt to Gerrit Smith, May 15, 1839,

Thus, even as late as mid-1839 Leavitt sought to act as a peace-maker between the warring factions. Yet, ironically, his vocal advocacy of political action helped to push the strife-torn cause closer to open rupture at this time. In debating this issue, his relationship with Garrison, which had so far been characterized by a certain distance yet never by overt hostility, was strained to the breaking point.

From the movement's inception, abolitionists had viewed political action, in the form of voting for sympathetic politicians and petitioning Congress and state legislatures, as a valuable weapon in the war against slavery. As Birney stated in 1835, "With the political action of political men, and holy action of religious men, there is, here, no inconsistency that is irreconcilable." Important developments within and outside the movement, however, soon caused abolitionists to disagree not only on the propriety and feasibility of specific forms of political action but even on the morality of political action in any form. As early as 1836, the congressional gag laws had led most abolitionists to abandon the petitions campaign in favor of questioning candidates about their views on slavery. Borrowing from the British system of interrogation, they sought to hold the balance of power through concerted action, without being corrupted by party politics.[25]

By 1838, however, Leavitt and other advocates of interrogation encountered growing challenges. A few abolitionists, most notably Alvan Stewart, believed the South's evident refusal to brook any criticism of slavery necessitated a radically new conception of abolitionist means. A witty and charming though volatile New York lawyer who served as president of the New York State Anti-Slavery Society, Stewart developed the most startling constitutional theory presented by abolitionists in the 1830s. Convinced that voluntary emancipation was inconceivable, at the 1838 annual meeting of the national society he attempted to amend the society's constitution by striking from it the clause that acknowledged the right of each state to exclusive control over slavery within its boundaries. He based his proposal on the

---

in Smith Miller Collection; entry for June 6, 1839, in Tappan Diary, Library of Congress; Henry B. Stanton to James Birney, June 13, 1839, in Dumond (ed.), *Birney Letters*, I, 490.

25. James Birney to Lewis Tappan, February 3, 1835, in Dumond (ed.), *Birney Letters*, I, 177; *Emancipator*, May 3, 1836, October 19, 1837.

grounds that slavery violated the due process clause of the Fifth Amendment of the U.S. Constitution.[26]

Leavitt, Birney, William Jay, and Wendell Phillips—all of whom had legal training—strongly criticized Stewart's theory as unhistorical and unrealistic. Stewart's constitutional arguments, Leavitt informed Jay, were "dangerous and seductive sophistry" based upon a fundamental misreading of the U.S. Constitution. The resolution failed to receive the needed two-thirds vote to amend the society's constitution. However, the fact that a "solemn pledge" not to interfere with slavery in the states had nearly been rescinded, thereby threatening to undermine public confidence in the cause, disturbed Leavitt and others. They also feared that Stewart desired the creation of an abolition party—a move that Leavitt warned would be "suicidal." "Abolitionists will not become a political party," he declared. "They will identify themselves with no party. . . . Their object is not office, honor, emolument, or aggrandizement, for themselves, their relations, party, state or section." As these abolitionists saw it, a new party responsive to the abolitionists' entreaties would endeavor to capture control of Congress. The South could conveniently be ignored, for a congressional majority could be recruited from the North; if successful, this party would then proceed to declare slavery unconstitutional throughout the United States. However implausible this scenario may appear, Stewart and a few other abolitionists were indeed toying with the idea of a third party, and disillusionment with existing abolitionist tactics was spreading through the ranks.[27]

At the same time, Garrison and other advocates of the nonresistance philosophy repudiated the act of voting (though not petitioning or questioning) as coercive and sinful. Although Garrison carefully emphasized that all those whose conscience permitted them to vote should do so, many abolitionists chose not to believe his protestations. Those who emphasized the need for unity at the polls and rejected Garrison's nonresistance philosophy responded by setting forth a suc-

26. Luther R. Marsh, "Sketch of Alvan Stewart," in Alvan Stewart Papers, New York State Historical Society.

27. Joshua Leavitt to William Jay, May 15, 1838, in John Jay Collection, Baker Library, Columbia University; *Emancipator*, May 17, 31, June 7, 1838; *Friend of Man*, March 22, May 23, 1838; *Letter of Gerrit Smith to Hon. Henry Clay* (New York, 1839), 25–26; *Pennsylvania Freeman*, April 26, 1838.

cession of ever stronger declarations on the duty to vote. Leavitt's reference to voting as "a sacred trust" was quite mild in comparison to others' statements that, by implication, questioned the nonvoting abolitionists' commitment to abolition. For example, William Goodell, editor of the *Friend of Man*, the organ of the New York State Anti-Slavery Society, remarked in 1838: "To talk of being an *abolitionist*, and not in favor of *political action* against slavery, is a contradiction in terms."[28]

In the midst of this rising tide of controversy, Leavitt stood opposed to both Stewart's tentative moves toward third-party action and Garrison's repudiation of voting. By the spring of 1839, he had fully entered the fray against Garrison, repeatedly denouncing nonresistance and even printing Birney's strongly worded "Letter on the Political Obligations of Abolitionists" in the *Emancipator* without editorial comment.[29] This infuriated Garrison, who blasted the *Emancipator* for its "prostitution to party purposes." He was even more caustic in private, commenting to Samuel May that Leavitt's remarks "show a disturbed state of mind." Leavitt did not reply in kind at this time, but he was sufficiently exasperated by Garrison's carping at political action to imply in an editorial that if the Garrisonians did not appreciate the way the society conducted its business, they could leave.[30]

Leavitt had moved far from his original conviction that the moral weight of the churches, led by a clergy committed to cleansing America's collective and individual sins, would destroy slavery. For a man who had served as a settled minister and religious editor and whose closest friends were devoted to church-based antislavery action, the decision to adopt political action as the principal abolitionist tactic was a difficult one. By at least 1837, however, he had become bitter and disillusioned about the churches' record on slavery. As he charged angrily, "Time was, when these ministers and churches were the very foremost in measures for the general reformation of mankind. . . . But

28. *Fifth Annual Report of the Massachusetts Anti-Slavery Society* (Boston, 1837), xxxviii; Massachusetts Anti-Slavery Society, *An Address to the Abolitionists of Massachusetts on the Subject of Political Action* (Boston, 1838), 13–16; *Friend of Man*, October 24, 1838; see also Richard H. Sewell, *Ballots for Freedom: Antislavery Politics in the United States, 1837–1860* (New York, 1976), 29–33, 37–40.

29. *Emancipator*, May 16, 1839.

30. *Liberator*, July 26, 1839; William Lloyd Garrison to Samuel May, June 22, 1839, in Garrison Papers, Boston Public Library; *Emancipator*, April 18, 1839.

when the cry of the suffering slave came up . . . we find these brethren, as a body, not only standing aloof, but employing their whole influence, almost, as a body, to smother the cry, and cast obstacles in the way of every effective measure of relief." He stated a year later that "the war-ecclesiastical is intended to be a war of extermination."[31]

The combined effort by the conservative and evangelical clergy to crush the abolitionist movement did not, however, lead Leavitt to repudiate religion, as it did some abolitionists. He remained a devoted evangelical Congregationalist, active in the affairs of the church. Yet by the late 1830s his sense of priorities, as he informed Myron Holley, a New York abolitionist, was then moving rapidly toward third-party action: "We want to set forth the issue and evil of slavery, its character as a political apostasy, its arrogance, usurpation, continued encroachment, danger, etc. Also the duty of American citizens to meet it in the very citadel of power, vis., in politics. I am convinced its peculiar power is here, rather than in the church, i.e. it is resistless in the church because it is resistless in the State. We are eminently a political people."[32]

Yet Leavitt's vocal support for political action and his condemnation of nonresistance represented only a temporary substitute for a coherent political strategy. By late 1838, the questioning method had proved unsatisfactory as a means of forcing the major parties to endorse abolition. In isolated instances, especially in New England, abolitionists held the balance of power and helped elect candidates sympathetic to the cause. More frequently, however, candidates either refused to reply to the abolitionists' entreaties or answered them evasively.[33]

By the late 1830s, the second party system, which had begun to emerge with the creation of the Democratic party a decade earlier, had reached maturity. In many of the states, especially in the North, sharp competition developed between organized, coherent political parties. Campaigns were characterized by appeals to the common man, mass meetings, and enormous enthusiasm on the part of the electorate and

31. *Emancipator*, November 2, 1837, December 6, 1838.
32. Joshua Leavitt to Myron Holley, July 12, 1839, in Miscellaneous Manuscripts, New-York Historical Society.
33. See *Emancipator*, October 25, November 1, 8, 1838; Gerrit Smith to William Jay, October 9, 1838, in Luther Bradish Papers, New-York Historical Society.

produced high levels of voter participation. Particularly among the Democrats, but increasingly among those who came to identify with the recently established Whig party, strong partisan loyalties took root. While personalities counted for much in the parties' appeals to their constituents, the parties differed in their views on the relationship between government, society, and the individual as well as on specific issues. But most Democrats and Whigs agreed, in the name of party unity and sectional harmony, that the slavery question must be kept out of the national political debate.[34]

It became increasingly apparent to some abolitionists that these political realities meant that the questioning method would frequently be undermined. In addition, as long as relatively few people cared intensely about abolition, the parties did not need to take the abolitionists seriously. These developments discouraged a growing number of abolitionists, perhaps no one more than Gerrit Smith, who proposed the creation of new antislavery societies that would require their members to pledge to vote only for abolitionists. But Leavitt and many other political abolitionists questioned the value of pledges. By this time, they believed that a convention should be called to discuss "the duties of abolitionists in the present state of the cause." The 1839 annual meeting of the American Anti-Slavery Society provided for such a national meeting, to be held in Albany from July 31 to August 2.[35]

Leavitt played a major role in organizing the Albany Convention and wrote much of its Address, which stated that slavery "must be driven out and destroyed by the only force which can reach the citadel—THE BALLOT BOX." But following three days of intense debate, a restatement of Birney's resolution calling voting a duty was tabled in the face of considerable opposition. Many delegates were not prepared

34. For analyses of the political culture and the second party system, see William E. Gienapp, "'Politics Seems to Enter into Everything': Political Culture in the North, 1840–1860," in Stephen E. Maizlish and John J. Kushma (eds.), *Essays on American Antebellum Politics, 1840–1860* (College Station, Tex., 1982), 15–57; Ronald P. Formisano, *The Transformation of Political Culture: Massachusetts Parties, 1790's-1840's* (New York, 1983), 245–62, 268–79, 300–316; Daniel Walker Howe, *The Political Culture of the American Whigs* (Chicago, 1979); Edward Pessen, *Jacksonian America: Society, Personality, and Politics* (Homewood, 1978), 197–260; Michael F. Holt, *The Political Crisis of the 1850's* (New York, 1978), 33–38.

35. Gerrit Smith to Amos A. Phelps, December 28, 1838, in Phelps Papers; *Liberator*, December 1, 1838; *Emancipator*, May 16, 1839.

to make independent nominations. Some feared that such a resolution would preclude supporting John Quincy Adams and others with anti-slavery predilections who did not favor immediatism, while others opposed nominations under any circumstances. A third group, which included Leavitt, considered such a course of action "unadvised and premature." Thus, in the end, the convention left nominations to the discretion of abolitionists in local areas.[36]

Stewart sharply attacked the convention's tepid declaration on political action, calling Leavitt's and others' hope that the major parties somehow could be forced to repudiate slavery "an infinite absurdity." Yet Leavitt's position was based more on expediency than on principle. Many arguments had been voiced against third-party action. Most abolitionists—Garrisonians and non-Garrisonians alike—feared that the scramble for office and power would destroy the moral foundations of the cause and that an antislavery party would be an ineffective minority with no chance to influence the policies of the major parties.[37]

Leavitt had stated these arguments for months in the *Emancipator*. In the fall of 1839, however, he moved steadily away from "an ill-fitting neutrality" and toward open support for independent nominations. Following a "long and earnest mental struggle against the proposition for having anti-slavery nominations," he endorsed the idea in several editorials in October. He credited a series of treatises in the Rochester *Freeman*, edited by Myron Holley, a recent convert to abolitionism, with dispelling many of his objections. Leavitt now declared that because the major parties were antiabolitionist, abolitionists were effectively disfranchised. Moral suasion directed toward the South, agitation within the churches, and the interrogation of candidates had all failed. Thus, the only feasible option that remained was to nominate and elect candidates who would be true to their avowed principles and would eventually hold the balance of power in national politics. He realized that many abolitionists distrusted partisan politics, but he pointed to the successful experience of the temperance

36. Joshua Leavitt and Henry B. Stanton to George Bancroft, June 20, 1839, in George Bancroft Papers, Massachusetts Historical Society; *Emancipator*, August 8, 15, 1839.

37. Alvan Stewart to Edwin W. Clarke, September 14, 1839, in Slavery Manuscripts, Box II; see also Alvan Stewart to Samuel Webb, August 5, 1839, in Stewart Papers; Sewell, *Ballots for Freedom*, 53–54.

activists who had turned to politics. Above all, he believed that abolitionists were morally superior to the average politician. It was inconceivable to him that an antislavery party (if and when established)
would attract to its ranks the more conventional type of politician who
might emphasize votes over principles.[38]

Within little more than a year, Leavitt had come full circle on the
question of independent nominations. He now joined a small group
of activists in the vanguard of political abolitionism. In November,
Holley and Stewart persuaded a Warsaw, New York, convention to
nominate Birney for president and Francis J. LeMoyne of Pennsylvania
for vice president. Even though Leavitt, Elizur Wright, Stewart, and
others applauded the nominations, the nominees declined on the
grounds that the Warsaw vote was premature.[39]

Convinced that he had embarked on the correct course, Leavitt was
prepared to argue the case for independent nominations no matter
what others thought. It was only a matter of time before he clashed
with Lewis Tappan and other stewards who believed that the movement must continue to rely on the tried and true methods of interrogation, petitioning, and evangelical church-centered abolitionism. For
several years Leavitt had worked closely with these men. Now, without consulting with them, he became the first member of the national
executive committee to endorse third-party action; worse still, he
trumpeted his views in the official organ of the American Anti-Slavery
Society. The committee, which found his weekly editorials on the
subject totally unacceptable, reacted angrily and unanimously. They
sought first to silence him and, when that failed, to dissociate the committee from his position. Tappan, convinced that his friend had lost
sight of "first principles," was especially shocked by Leavitt's apostasy.
As he warned in a letter, which Leavitt printed in the *Emancipator*,
the creation of a third party would destroy the movement both by
causing abolitionists to lose their sense of moral purpose and their
claim to be the conscience of society and by corrupting it for political
ends. Because Leavitt had chosen to advance his ideas in the columns

38. *Emancipator*, October 10, 17, 1839. For an analysis of the relationship between
revivalism and political abolitionism, see John L. Hammond, *The Politics of Benevolence: Revival Religion and American Voting Behavior* (Norwood, N.J., 1979),
68–105.

39. *Friend of Man*, November 13, 20, 1839; Elizur Wright, *Myron Holley: and
What He Did for Liberty and True Religion* (Boston, 1882), 256–57.

of the *Emancipator*, Tappan felt compelled to present a resolution censuring him in a stormy committee meeting—the first major break among the circle of friends.[40]

Leavitt could not brook his friend's bold move. At first he reacted to the mounting criticism by insisting that he expressed his own views, not those of the committee. Given his earlier condemnation of Garrison for supposedly using the *Liberator* (which was not the official organ of the national society) for similar ends on the nonresistance issue, this was a curious response. Leavitt, of course, considered Garrison's nonresistance philosophy not only wrong but dangerous, while he believed that third-party action was merely an expedient measure that held out some promise of success. This justification for his editorial stance, however, failed to appease his critics. Under fire from Tappan and others, he soon became irritated, warning his detractors: "Do not attempt to smother it by the authority of names or of official station. Do not assume that it is impossible for abolitionists to grow wiser than they were, or that their course of action may not be altered as circumstances change." With this defiant rebuke, Leavitt took up the gauntlet. Once more, hostile sentiment served merely to whet his appetite for combat and strengthen his conviction that he had chosen the correct and necessary course. He had committed himself on this issue and would defend his position with all the vigor he could muster. Indeed, as seemed to happen so often when Leavitt felt deeply about an issue and could not comprehend why others did not adopt his thinking, he resorted to questioning their motives and sincerity. In this case, in a fit of temper, he went so far as to imply that most abolitionists were not sufficiently committed to emancipation. "Is there not ground for the presumption," he asked, "that brothers Tappan, [Seth] Gates, Garrison, [Gamaliel] Bailey, and others, would not reason as they do, were not their minds unconsciously influenced by other interests, personal, social, political, or commercial, more than by the ONE IDEA of abolishing slavery?"[41]

Lewis Tappan was no less determined to oppose Leavitt's efforts to proselytize the executive committee and his readers. "We must," he warned Gerrit Smith, who had already defected to Leavitt's position,

40. Friedman, *Gregarious Saints*, 89–91; entries for November 7, December 11, 1839, in Minutes of Executive Committee of AASS; entry for November 7, 1839, in Tappan Diary; *Emancipator*, November 14, 1839.

41. *Emancipator*, November 14, December 12, 1839.

"stem the tide of evil, and not, after a few tugs of the oar, yield to the current." Exacerbating the tensions between these independent, proud, and sensitive men was the fact that they had been close friends for years and now felt deeply wounded and betrayed by each other. Neither man could separate the personal from the ideological and tactical dimensions of the conflict. Whittier, Stanton, and other committee members attempted to mediate between the combatants, but with little success. Furious with Leavitt, and disappointed with the committee's failure to rein him in, Tappan ceased to attend committee meetings. Despite some gestures toward compromise, Leavitt also remained defensive and angry. He believed that his prerogatives as editor had been challenged; this was a bitter pill to swallow. As he complained to Smith, "I am reminded, in a very tangible manner, that I am a hireling." [42] In the end, neither he nor Tappan received the support they desired from the committee.

The controversy surrounding antislavery nominations soon spread beyond the confines of the executive committee. Hoping to sweep to victory against Martin Van Buren and the Democrats in 1840 with a popular candidate, the Whigs nominated General William Henry Harrison, a military hero best known for his success in fighting Indians. Harrison's views on most subjects, including slavery, were not well known. Although the northern Whigs generally subordinated the slavery issue to party interests, they tended, more than other members of the major parties, to dislike slavery. Consequently, Whig loyalists naturally feared that an antislavery party might siphon enough votes from Harrison to doom their efforts to drive the Democrats from office. They worked to prevent this, and their labors bore fruit, as many abolitionists who had voted the National Republican and Whig tickets throughout the 1830s pledged to support Harrison, despite the fact that his running mate was John Tyler, a Virginia slaveholder. Even Gamaliel Bailey, the talented and shrewd editor of the Cincinnati *Philanthropist*, who was not a Whig partisan, assumed a position of benign neutrality toward Harrison, choosing to view him as a defender of free speech and, at the very least, not antiabolitionist. [43]

42. Lewis Tappan to Gerrit Smith, November 25, 1839, Joshua Leavitt to Gerrit Smith, March 10, 1840, in Smith Miller Collection; see also Joshua Leavitt to Elizur Wright, December 5, 1839, in Wright Papers; entries for December 19, 1839, February 20, 1840, in Minutes of Executive Committee of AASS; *Emancipator*, January 9, 16, 1840.
43. Lewis Tappan to Joseph Sturge, December 14, 1839, in Tappan Papers; Gamaliel

Because Leavitt believed that Harrison's nomination represented a concession to the slave interests, he ridiculed Bailey's stance as "Abolition made agreeable"—a label he also applied to Joshua Giddings, Seth Gates, and William Slade, antislavery Whig congressmen who had voted for R. M. T. Hunter, a Virginia Whig slaveholder, for speaker of the House. Giddings responded angrily to this harsh criticism, suggesting that Leavitt "deserves a straight jacket." As so often happened when he detected wrongdoing on the part of others, Leavitt stuck by his guns and refused to apologize to the congressmen. Instead, he attacked, demanding an explanation from Bailey and Gates for the "extraordinary satisfaction your views have afforded to the slaveholders, before you take me to task for having expressed in a phrase the substance of an essay showing that such is the true exposition of your views." Until he saw evidence to the contrary, he informed Gates, "I shall continue to believe that the election of *Harrison and Tyler*, by the *voting abolitionists*, would be a greater calamity than the reelection of Van Buren without them." Leavitt's belligerent tone and his questioning of their motives succeeded in doing little but infuriating these men, but his charge that the congressmen had voted for Hunter largely for partisan reasons was correct. Even such a staunch opponent of independent nominations as Tappan warned Bailey, Gates, and others that their partisan actions would only strengthen the hand of Leavitt and other like-minded abolitionists.[44]

As he moved far ahead of abolitionist opinion, Leavitt lost a number of subscribers to the *Emancipator* and helped further to divide the already fragmented movement. But even he proved more reluctant to call a nominating convention than did Holley, Smith, and Charles T. Torrey, an impetuous young leader of the anti-Garrison group in Massachusetts. Leavitt counseled Torrey to refrain from such action until a favorable southern Whig reaction to Harrison had convinced more abolitionists to abandon the Whig party and support independent nominations. Torrey deferred to his wishes, but Holley and Smith

---

Bailey to James Birney, February 21, March 31, 1840, in Dumond (ed.), *Birney Letters*, I, 532–33, 535–36.

44. *Emancipator*, January 16, 1840; Joshua Giddings to a constituent, December 28, 1839, in Joshua R. Giddings Papers, Ohio Historical Society; Joshua Leavitt to Seth Gates, March 2, 1840, in Smith Miller Collection; Lewis Tappan to Joshua Giddings, February 7, 1840, in Joshua R. Giddings–George W. Julian Collection, Library of Congress; Lewis Tappan to Seth Gates, January 31, March 11, April 24, 1840, in Tappan Papers.

pushed ahead, convincing a meeting held at Arcade, New York, in January 1840 to call a convention in Albany in April for the purpose of nominating candidates for president and vice president—a call that Leavitt endorsed.[45]

Traveling to Albany over snow-covered roads in late March, Leavitt could take comfort in the fact that several antislavery papers, including William Goodell's *Friend of Man*, had endorsed the call for the convention. They were a determined group. Elizur Wright, for example, warned that not to make nominations would be "not a *retreat*, but a rout—not a soldier like *counter-march*, but a dastardly desertion." Leavitt arrived in Albany tired but hopeful that a cause that recently had seemed moribund could be revitalized by bold action. Confronted by a vocal minority among the delegates who opposed making any nominations, he, Stewart, and Holley argued that nominations represented the only feasible course of action that remained. They carried the day by a vote of 54–33, with 44 delegates abstaining. The convention proceeded to nominate James Birney for president and Thomas Earle, a Democrat and Quaker from Pennsylvania, for vice president.[46]

For Leavitt, the step had been taken, and there could be no turning back if the cause was to be saved from perversion at the hands of the major parties and destruction by the Garrisonians and their non-resistance folly. Not surprisingly, however, the Albany nominations received criticism and derision from abolitionists and their foes alike. Garrison dubbed it the "April Fool's Convention," while the Boston *Courier*, a Whig paper, called it a "complete fiasco." In addition, many political abolitionists, including Whittier, Stanton, and Bailey, still considered the nominations premature and contrary to the wishes of most abolitionists. Nevertheless, Birney, after some hesitation, accepted the nomination and urged Earle to do the same.[47]

45. Charles T. Torrey to Edwin W. Clarke, March 2, 1840, in Slavery Manuscripts, Box II; Joshua Leavitt to Charles T. Torrey, January 24, 1840, Myron Holley to Charles T. Torrey, February, 1840, in Charles Turner Torrey Papers, Congregational Library; *Friend of Man*, February 12, 19, 1840.

46. *Friend of Man*, April 1, 1840; *Massachusetts Abolitionist*, March 5, April 9, 1840.

47. *Liberator*, April 10, 1840; Boston *Courier*, April 13, 1840; *Philanthropist*, April 21, 1840; John G. Whittier to James Birney, April 16, 1840, in Dumond (ed.), *Birney Letters*, I, 555; Betty Fladeland, *James Gillespie Birney, Slaveholder to Abolitionist* (Ithaca, N.Y., 1955), 187–88.

With the Albany nominations in place, Lewis Tappan's earlier observation that the antislavery movement had split into a political party, a church-oriented group, and the Garrisonian faction became a reality. Tappan placed part of the blame on Leavitt for the deep fissures that threatened the very existence of the national society. In truth, the American Anti-Slavery Society had long been experiencing serious difficulties, "limping along—restricted—slandered—impoverished," as Tappan complained to Birney in January 1840. The worsening financial situation caused by the continuing economic depression and the demands of the state antislavery societies for a larger degree of financial autonomy had proved especially debilitating. By late 1839, the prohibition on national agents collecting money in the states without the states' consent had placed the national society in such desperate straits that it could not pay Birney, Leavitt, or its agents and printers. With five sons and a wife to support and no reserves to fall back on, Leavitt warned that he might have to resign his post and look elsewhere for employment. To avoid bankruptcy, the executive committee severely limited its operations. All efforts to persuade the state organizations to rescind their ban on national agents failed.[48]

By January 1840, the deteriorating situation forced the executive committee to call an emergency meeting, but it did little good. Only a few people attended, and a resolution for the removal of restrictions on national agents passed by a mere two-vote margin. Only Leavitt and Gibbons voted against the resolution. Leavitt did so in part to avoid further exacerbating tensions between the national committee and the state organizations. Thus, while he often tended to be defensive and even combative when challenged, he could step forth as a conciliator when differences of opinion threatened to divide the movement. He of course had his own differences with the committee. Moreover, his overriding interest lay in the formation of an abolitionist ticket and the maintenance of the *Emancipator*, which he essentially viewed as his own paper. In April 1840 he made that point forcefully for all who cared to be reminded: "The editor has borne the responsibility, in precisely the same way that any other agent, a travelling

48. Lewis Tappan to James Birney, January 23, 1840, in Tappan Papers; Lewis Tappan to John Scoble, December 10, 1839, in Annie Heloise Abel and Frank J. Klingberg (eds.), *A Side-light on Anglo-American Relations, 1839–1858: Furnished by the Correspondence of Lewis Tappan and Others with the British and Foreign Anti-Slavery Society* (Lancaster, Pa., 1927), 62; *Seventh Annual Report of the American Anti-Slavery Society* (New York, 1840), 45–46.

lecturer for instance, bears the responsibility of his own arguments and modes of address."[49]

At an executive committee meeting in February Leavitt requested that the committee designate the paper as its first object of support, but his resolution was tabled and then rejected. Finally, in April he offered to assume control of the paper and pay the executive committee $100 in return for its financial support for the next month. At the same time, the executive committee assigned all of the society's property, except for the *Emancipator*, to Lewis Tappan and Seth Benedict, the publishing agent, as trustees in order to pay the arrears to the secretaries and Leavitt and to send Birney and Stanton to the World Anti-Slavery Convention in London. Shortly thereafter, the committee sold the *Emancipator*'s subscription lists to the New York City Young Men's Anti-Slavery Society, with the provision that Leavitt remain as editor for at least a year.[50]

The transfer of the *Emancipator* and Leavitt's role in the transaction remained the subject of bitter controversy for nearly a decade. As a full-fledged schism in the ranks fast approached, it was as if this "deal" became the issue that served as an outlet for the accumulated anger and frustration of the warring groups. In a lengthy defense of the transaction, which appeared in the *National Anti-Slavery Standard* in 1844, Leavitt charged Tappan and other members of the executive committee with transferring the *Emancipator* in order to rid themselves of his political views, "without a direct dismissal of the editor from his office."[51] Tappan and others indeed wished to dissociate the national society from an "official organ" that trumpeted the virtues of independent nominations. But Leavitt's portrayal of himself as an innocent victim of Tappan's machinations was both incorrect and self-serving. In fact, Leavitt had supported the resolution calling for the transfer of all the society's property and would loyally defend these transactions against the fury of the Garrisonians.

The outraged cry of robbery soon came. The Garrisonians were especially irate. James Gibbons, the only member of the executive

49. Proceedings of Special Meeting of American Anti-Slavery Society, January 15, 1840, in Anti-Slavery Papers; *Emancipator*, January 23, April 23, 1840.

50. Entries for February 20, March 5, April 2, 16, 24, 1840, in Minutes of Executive Committee of AASS. Leavitt's version of the transfer of the society's property is found in *Seventh Annual Report of the AASS*, 45–47.

51. *National Anti-Slavery Standard*, October 1, 1844.

committee to vote against the transfer, charged that the *Emancipator* was the property, not of the executive committee, but of all abolitionists who had sustained it; thus, no action should have been taken until the May meeting. Leavitt himself was naturally a prime target of the Garrisonians' fury. Above all, they believed that he had engineered the transfer and sold out his principles in order to draw a salary and maintain control of the paper. Writing several months after the transfer, Gibbons charged that "*the salary—the bread and butter*, was the moving power after all. . . . *Bread and Butter*—not principle!" Henry C. Wright went even further, calling the transfer a "dishonest transaction" undertaken "solely to get it into Leavitt's hand—that he may control it as he pleases." [52]

The charges of stealing for profit were unjustified. Tappan and other committee members had been forced to pay off some of the society's debts with their own money. They were also liable for the debts incurred and ultimately sold the property for considerably less than its worth. Yet this defense did not ring entirely true. Personal finances and control over the editorial policy of the paper, as Gibbons well knew, were indeed important considerations for Leavitt. Also, Leavitt and his colleagues effected the transfer of the *Emancipator* and the other property so quickly, with virtually no warning to, or consultation with, abolitionists outside the executive committee, that the committee was vulnerable to charges of impropriety and worse. Finally, the committee's decision to send Birney and Stanton to the World Anti-Slavery Convention weakened its argument that the society was bankrupt. The transfer can only be understood within the context of rising fears that the Garrisonians would soon take control of the American Anti-Slavery Society. The committee had some reason to believe that the Garrisonians would not pay off the society's debts, and Leavitt must have known that a Garrisonian takeover would end his tenure as editor of the *Emancipator*. Thus, the committee hoped, as Stanton confided to Amos Phelps, that when the Garrisonians came to control the national society, they would find it "a barren sceptic." [53]

As the antislavery movement approached a breaking point, Leavitt

52. *Ibid.*, November 12, 1840; Henry C. Wright to William Lloyd Garrison, May 6, 1840, in Garrison Papers.

53. Lewis Tappan, *Reply to Charges Brought Against the American and Foreign Anti-Slavery Society* (London, 1852), 9–12; Henry B. Stanton to Amos A. Phelps, April 17, 1840, in Phelps Papers.

was, according to Stanton, "verging toward" supporting the dissolution of the national society. Whereas he once had attempted to maintain a tenuous neutrality in the Clerical Controversy and, on occasion, had sought to act as a conciliator on financial and other matters, a succession of issues had drawn Leavitt and Garrison toward an angry confrontation. Even before the transfer of the *Emancipator*, Leavitt's advocacy of antislavery nominations in the columns of the *Emancipator* had so angered Garrison that he called for Leavitt's resignation. As much as he had appreciated Leavitt's "editorial tact and ability," Garrison now concluded that Leavitt exhibited such an "unfair, disingenuous, unlovely spirit" that he no longer had "that clearness of vision and freedom of soul" required of the paper's editor. If Garrison wished to arouse Leavitt's ire, he could not have calculated better. A proud and sensitive man, much like Garrison, he responded instinctively to what he considered a personal slight. Resentful of Garrison's presumption of leadership within the movement, infuriated by his vitriolic pen, and contemptuous of his nonresistance philosophy, Leavitt angrily labeled Garrison's *Liberator* "a self-constituted 'organ,' irresponsible, arbitrary, and allowing no appeal from its decrees." He, for one, would be guided by his own conscience and would never be Garrison's or anyone else's mouthpiece. "My soul," he remarked caustically, "has not a 'freedom' to plaster such gross and fulsome adulation upon a mortal worm, nor to worship an idiot that can be approached with such homage." [54]

By April 1840, Leavitt rapidly approached the view of Tappan, Birney, and Stanton that the national society should be dissolved. He warned that if an "accidental majority" placed the society under the control of the nonresistants, it would "amount to a dissolution." The Garrisonians, of course, had no intention of allowing the American Anti-Slavery Society to be dissolved. Instead, they hoped to control it and then unseat most of the present executive committee members. Fearful that Leavitt and other advocates of antislavery nominations planned to transform the society into a political party, the Garrisonians worked feverishly in the months before the annual meeting to mobilize supporters throughout New England. Their goal was clear: to make the movement safe, as James Gibbons stated, "from sectarianism—and every other *ism* that is dangerous." Their labors were suc-

54. *Liberator*, April 3, 1840; *Emancipator*, April 16, 23, 1840.

cessful: on May 11 approximately 450 men and women—most from Massachusetts and a majority of them women—arrived in New York on the steamer *Rhode Island*. Leavitt and other abolitionists bitterly denounced the Garrisonian forces for mobilizing for the annual meeting, but they also had not been idle in the weeks before the meeting. For his part, Leavitt had decided to fight to the bitter end, appealing at the last minute in the *Emancipator* for political abolitionists to defend their interests against the expected Garrisonian onslaught.[55]

When the meeting convened, it quickly became apparent that the Garrisonians had been more efficient in rallying their forces. With no clear rules stipulating the seating of delegates, and with the generally anti-Garrisonian western abolitionists significantly underrepresented, Garrison's close associate, Francis Jackson, was elected to preside, and Garrison's slate of candidates controlled the business committee. When the convention approved Abby Kelley, an outspoken feminist, as a member of the committee, Tappan, Phelps, Charles Denison, and nearly 300 other delegates walked out of both the meeting and the society.[56]

In the midst of this great upheaval Leavitt chose to remain at his post as secretary of the meeting and member of the executive committee "to discharge my duties and try to avoid division and perversion." This decision made some sense, for he did not agree with the seceding group on either the Kelley appointment or the issue of independent nominations. Garrison requested that Leavitt remain in the hall, primarily, as it turned out, in order to castigate him for the transfer of the *Emancipator* and other transgressions. Negotiations commenced with the New York City Young Men's Anti-Slavery Society for the return of the paper to the national society, and a resolution to that effect passed while Leavitt tended to business at the printer's office. When he returned to the hall, he became a convenient scapegoat for the angry and frustrated Garrisonian delegates, who accused him of stealing from the society, advocating a third party, and seeking to "undermine" the *Liberator*.[57]

55. *Emancipator*, March 26, May 8, 1840; James Gibbons to James Miller McKim, April 21, 1840, in James Miller McKim Papers, Cornell University.
56. *Seventh Annual Report of the AASS*, 9–10; *Pennsylvania Freeman*, June 11, 1840.
57. *Emancipator*, August 13, 1840; *National Anti-Slavery Standard*, August 20, 1840.

Leavitt categorically denied these charges and then dropped a bomb-shell on the assembled group by offering his services as editor of the *Emancipator* under the auspices of the national society—provided the new executive committee would allow him to "be FREE to conduct it" as he saw fit. A few of the delegates may have accepted Leavitt's version of his role in the transfer of the newspaper, but it was absurd to think that most abolitionists were, as he put it, "resigned to the event." Moreover, in view of many delegates' hostility toward him, and his increasingly bitter feud with Garrison, one wonders how he expected anyone to take seriously his offer to edit an organ of the American Anti-Slavery Society, with or without supervision.[58]

In making this offer, however, Leavitt was not as naïve or arrogant as it may appear at first glance. He had, after all, supported the election of Abby Kelley to the organization's business committee and at times had sought to restrain some of the more rabid anti-Garrison members of the national committee. This did not redeem Leavitt in the eyes of many Garrisonians, but a number of them seemed genuinely to respect his abilities. For example, even following the transfer of the *Emancipator,* James Gibbons confided to James Miller McKim, a Pennsylvania Garrisonian, that Leavitt "will serve you and the cause faithfully. You cannot do better than employ him." Leavitt possibly knew of Gibbons's (and others') favorable assessment. More probable as an explanation for Leavitt's offer is his feeling of isolation and vulnerability at this time. With the departure of many of his closest friends (including his father, who was among the first to walk out of the convention hall, not in response to the women's issue but because he believed that Garrison wished to make this matter a test of loyalty to the national society) who then formed the American and Foreign Anti-Slavery Society, he felt cut adrift. Like Smith and others, Leavitt did not agree with many of these men on the women's question and third-partyism.[59] In addition, he was in desperate financial straits. The nation's economy remained depressed, with no recovery in sight; he had enormous debts that must be paid; and the support provided the *Emancipator* by the New York Young Men's Anti-Slavery Society was minimal and very uncertain beyond the next few months. All of this served to deepen Leavitt's anxiety concerning his ability to support Sarah and the boys. Finally, he had endorsed third-party action in the

58. *National Anti-Slavery Standard*, August 20, 1840.

59. James Gibbons to James M. McKim, April 21, 1840, in James Miller McKim Papers; *Emancipator*, June 18, 1840.

face of widespread condemnation and ridicule from many of his close friends and associates, and the party, which he had so recently helped to create, faced an extremely uncertain future.

Not surprisingly, Leavitt received no response to his proposal. When the convention did not elect him to the new executive committee, he left the hall and the national society. Two weeks earlier he had warned that he would feel under no obligation to support the American Anti-Slavery Society "were it to become the tool of those who are seeking, in the name of abolition, to subvert the foundations of social order and peace." He now believed that nonresistants had accomplished this, though he never explained how he could have remained with them in the society under any conditions. Some Garrisonian abolitionists greeted his departure with a sigh of relief. Edmund Quincy remarked that they were fortunate that Leavitt had not been elected president of the national society in 1839, as some had contemplated, while David Lee Child, long an antagonist of Leavitt, responded in a more personal way, thanking God that Leavitt's friends "had not been able to inflict that heavy hypocrite" (an obvious reference to Leavitt's corpulent figure) on the society as its editor.[60]

Leavitt's departure from the national society rendered his break with Garrison irrevocable. Each man charged the other with being responsible for the schism in the antislavery ranks—Leavitt for his zealous advocacy of independent nominations; Garrison for his "determination to 'rule or ruin.'"[61] Both charges were grossly oversimplified. In truth, no individual or single issue created the rift. Substantive issues—including localism, the economic depression, and differences on tactics and principles—as well as petty personal disputes ultimately created an atmosphere of distrust and hostility that made cooperation and understanding virtually impossible. The need for a national society remained, but the state and local societies had become centers of activity in their own right; perhaps now they could act with greater efficiency. Likewise, the various factions in the movement could now go their own ways. The schism certainly freed Leavitt to pursue the approach to abolition that he considered most realistic and necessary, without having to defend his right to do so in an "official organ."

<hr/>

60. *Emancipator*, April 23, 1840; Edmund Quincy to Maria Weston Chapman, May 18, 1840, in Weston Family Papers; David Lee Child to Maria Weston Chapman, June 18, 1840, in Child Family Papers, Boston Public Library.

61. *Emancipator*, June 18, 1840.

9

THE LIBERTY PARTY AND
THE ANTISLAVERY LOBBY

When Leavitt walked out of the American Anti-Slavery Society and joined the newly formed American and Foreign Anti-Slavery Society's executive committee, the breach between him and most Garrisonians became complete. Garrison was not at all surprised by Leavitt's decision. "We are glad," he remarked dryly, "that he has now taken this stand, and openly placed his *name* where his heart has been for a long time." In fact, Leavitt made this move in spite of the new organization's ban on official participation in any "machinery of party political arrangements." His reasons for doing so are not altogether clear, though many of his friends as well as his father helped to found the society. Also, Leavitt was an inveterate joiner who, unlike Weld, was not comfortable standing apart from organizational structures. He fully agreed with the society's goal of fostering accord with European abolitionists and coordinating religious antislavery activity, and was not sufficiently committed to equality for women to reject the organization because it barred females from serving as delegates. Lewis Tappan, still furious about Leavitt's use of the *Emancipator* to advance the cause of third-party politics, insisted that Leavitt not serve as secretary of the new organization and that the paper not be connected with its executive committee. However, Leavitt seems not to have desired either position, and Tappan's fears that he wished to make the society an arm of the Abolitionist party were largely unfounded. Rather, Leavitt viewed his position on the executive committee as a means of recruiting individual members to the political movement.[1]

Throughout the remainder of 1840, Leavitt directed his energies primarily toward the arduous task of organizing the Abolitionist party. He threw himself into the campaign for James Birney and Thomas Earle, even organizing a political convention in New York at the time of the antislavery schism. Here, he succeeded in converting his father to the independent nominations; a week later he attended a convention in Boston that nominated Roger Leavitt as an elector for president and for the office of lieutenant-governor of Massachusetts on the Abolitionist party ticket. Unfortunately, a few days later Roger died suddenly at the age of 69. His father's death deeply saddened Joshua. They had enjoyed a close relationship over the years and shared the belief that all Christians must work for the betterment of mankind. Roger had served as a powerful example for his son, being active in the evangelical revivals and the temperance, moral reform, education, and antislavery causes. At the time of the antislavery schism, he prevailed upon Joshua to join the new organization. Yet it was Joshua who had converted his father to abolitionism in 1834, and, as he reminisced, both he and Roger had "experienced much obloquy" for their beliefs. Thus, his father had been a confidant, fellow reformer, supporter, and model, and a man whom Joshua loved and respected. "Let it be our care, my dear brothers and sisters," he wrote Roger Hooker Leavitt, "to follow him in all things wherein he followed Christ, to treasure up the bounty of his wisdom and to emulate the excellence of his example. . . . Thus let us endeavor to bring upon our own children, as far as possible, not to dishonor the good name which their departed grandfather has left as the best inheritance of his children."[2]

When the political campaign began, the Abolitionist party amounted to no more than the nominations of Birney and Earle. The Albany Convention had merely urged the delegates to return home and nominate presidential electors and candidates for local and state offices. Virtually no expertise or money was available for the task of constructing an organization, and most abolitionists planned either not to

1. *Liberator*, June 5, 1840; *American and Foreign Anti-Slavery Reporter*, I (June, 1840), 4–5; Lewis Tappan to Amos A. Phelps, May 19, 1840, in Phelps Papers; *Emancipator*, June 18, 1840.

2. *Emancipator*, May 22, June 18, 1840; Leavitt to Roger Hooker Leavitt, June 10, 1840, in Leavitt Papers.

vote or to cast their ballots for Harrison or Van Buren. Leavitt and other political abolitionists, of course, possessed tools for swaying public opinion. For example, throughout the campaign Leavitt devoted considerable space in the *Emancipator* to news of conventions, candidates, and the party's prospects. He also wrote a steady stream of editorials emphasizing the virtues of independent political action and reasons for abolitionists to abandon the major parties. In response to those who counseled delaying third-party action, he stated adamantly: "How long would it have taken the Apostles to 'Christianize the public mind,' had they continued to practice idolatry while preaching against it? Nothing neutralizes 'moral suasion' so effectively as inconsistent practice. A handful of men with their flag nailed to the mast can battle down the fortress of slavery. But we must *begin*." [3]

As it became inescapably clear that most abolitionists would not support Birney, Leavitt, who was convinced that he and like-minded men were struggling to uphold the integrity of the cause, frequently adopted a self-righteous and denunciatory tone. The fact that most abolitionists professed to desire emancipation yet planned to vote to perpetuate the Slave Power, he intoned at one point, was "not only incongruous and absurd, but presupposed either mental imbecility, a willful perversion of the understanding, or base hypocrisy." Antislavery Whigs received the brunt of his rage, for he viewed their promotion of Harrison's antislavery leanings as absolutely hypocritical. Nor did Leavitt spare the Garrisonians, calling them "irresponsible" and accusing them of "doing the dirty work of party and circulating groundless slanders and malignant personal abuse against Independent Abolitionists." They, in turn, made clear their contempt for him. By the summer of 1840, Garrison had begun to place pieces from the *Emancipator* in the "Refuge of Oppression" column of the *Liberator*. [4]

Although most Garrisonians would not have voted for Birney under any circumstances, Leavitt's shrill tone certainly alienated some potential recruits. His persistent efforts to rally support, however, did produce some results: The New York State Anti-Slavery Society endorsed Birney's candidacy; Gamaliel Bailey, Leavitt reported enthusiastically, was "coming over as fast as he can with decency"; Lewis Tappan seemed to assume a position of benign neutrality; and a few Garrison-

3. *Emancipator*, June 25, 1840.
4. *Ballot Box*, October 5, 1840; *Emancipator*, October 1, 1840; *Liberator*, June 19, 26, September 4, 1840.

ians even endorsed the party. These developments buoyed Leavitt's spirits, but he could not ignore the problems that confronted the party. Birney chose to remain in England until November, the existing anti-slavery societies generally remained neutral or hostile to Birney's candidacy, and the dearth of financial support severely limited the distribution of campaign literature.[5]

What little the Abolitionist party (soon to be named the Liberty party) accomplished during the 1840 campaign was due largely to the efforts of Leavitt, Alvan Stewart, Gerrit Smith, and a few other party stalwarts. If the Liberty party exemplified what James Brewer Stewart has termed "political antipolitics," Leavitt leaned more in the political direction. This is not to say that he thought or acted in a manner similar to Whig or Democratic activists. After all, he and most other Liberty men viewed themselves as a new breed of political activists who would fuse moral reform with politics and thereby purify the entire political process. Until the late 1840s he insisted that the party take an official stand only on the slavery question and avoid any coalition with antislavery Whigs and Democrats on a watered-down platform. In the early 1840s he even foresaw the dissolution of the party when slavery disappeared. In Massachusetts and other states, moreover, little coordination existed between the state and local levels, and party leaders paid little attention to organizational matters except during campaigns.[6]

Yet, perhaps no Liberty leader did more than Leavitt to build an organizational structure and to develop a strategy to strengthen the party. In his varied labors in behalf of the party, he stood squarely within the antebellum political culture. Although he repudiated the Whig and Democratic parties as hopelessly corrupt and proslavery, he (and many of his colleagues) borrowed numerous techniques those parties had developed for attracting voters. He helped to organize Liberty picnics, debates, rallies, and parades. He also dispensed a steady stream of practical advice to other party activists, urging them to organize at the grass-roots level, to visit prospective voters in their

5. Joshua Leavitt to Amos A. Phelps, July 20, 1840, in Phelps Papers; *American and Foreign Anti-Slavery Reporter*, I (August, 1840), 17; Sewell, *Ballots for Freedom*, 75; Fladeland, *James Gillespie Birney*, 188.

6. James Brewer Stewart, *Holy Warriors: The Abolitionists and American Slavery* (New York, 1976), 97; see Reinhard O. Johnson, "The Liberty Party in Massachusetts, 1840–1848: Antislavery Third Party Politics in the Bay State," *Civil War History*, XXVIII (September, 1982), 242–43.

homes, and to nominate humble men with whom voters could identify. In addition, he proved an indefatigable organizer and manager, serving for several years as a leading member of both the Massachusetts and the national Liberty committees—which arranged conventions, collected funds, and employed speakers—as well as on many party convention committees. Leavitt's forte was writing. He not only composed numerous convention addresses; more important, he edited two daily papers and the *Emancipator*, which served as the Massachusetts Liberty party's organ from 1841 until 1848 (following its removal to Boston) and circulated throughout much of the North. Until the founding of the *National Era* in 1847, the *Emancipator* was the leading Liberty paper in the nation. Finally, despite his busy schedule he found time to deliver stump speeches for Liberty candidates in several states—often traveling for weeks at a time during campaigns.[7]

The speeches Leavitt presented in Ohio in September 1840 had a particularly important impact on the party's fortunes and his own thinking regarding the relationship between slavery and the political economy of the United States. Although reluctant to leave his paper for three weeks to make the long journey to Ohio, his desire to visit an important wheat-growing region and to persuade Ohio abolitionists to support Birney eventually convinced him to make the trip. As he traveled by train through Maryland and Virginia and then by coach over the Cumberland road, his excitement mounted. By the time he reached Ohio, he was exuberant, detailing for his readers the "cultivated and populous country adorned with farms and neat dwellings, and handsome villages, and *old* and wealthy towns with . . . all the apparatus of the highest civilizations." An emotional meeting with Elijah Lovejoy's widow in Cincinnati further raised his spirits.[8]

As the featured speaker at the Ohio Anti-Slavery Convention in Hamilton, Leavitt charged that while slavery had never been acknowledged as a vital interest of the nation, southern domination of the national government, based on the three-fifths clause, shaped policies that created a "continual tax upon the products of free industry." In the existing political order, he argued, slave interests manipulated northern commercial allies, thereby preventing economic recovery in

7. Johnson, "The Liberty Party in Massachusetts," 241–42; Alan M. Kraut, "Partisanship and Principles: The Liberty Party in Antebellum Political Culture," in Alan M. Kraut (ed.), *Crusaders and Compromisers: Essays on the Relationship of the Antislavery Struggle to the Antebellum Party System* (Westport, Conn., 1983), 71–92.

8. *Emancipator*, September 24, 1840.

the North, sustaining a southern monopoly in Congress, and threatening republican government. His eloquence and personal magnetism, as well as his appeal to northern pride and pocketbook, had a powerful effect on the delegates, who—in the face of powerful opposition from Whig abolitionists—recommended that Ohio abolitionists support the Birney-Earle ticket. Gamaliel Bailey, editor of the Cincinnati *Philanthropist*, was among the converts to third-party action. Convinced that the speech would appeal to the "bread and butter" interests of Cincinnati workers, he subsequently had 1,000 copies printed.[9]

Following the convention, Leavitt delivered speeches in several other Ohio towns. Buoyed by the reception accorded the Hamilton speech, he increasingly emphasized the negative economic impact of slavery and a southern-dominated federal government on the northern economy. In 1835 William Goodell had appealed to the economic self-interest of Northerners in arguing that slavery had a degrading influence on all labor.[10] Leavitt now developed this theme much further and was the first abolitionist to realize fully its potential as a political issue. In speeches before Ohio and, later, eastern audiences, to which he gave the title "The Financial Power of Slavery," he blamed slavery for the continuing economic depression. Northern merchants, he declared, had extended credit to profligate slaveholders for investment in the internal slave trade and the cotton trade. The economic hardship that resulted from this drain of capital to the South, argued Leavitt, showed clearly that prosperity required the North to free itself from the control of the Slave Power. "In fine," he stated, "we trace the great severity, even of the financial evils of the country, the 'hard times,' more to slavery than to any or all of the other alleged causes. But for slavery, the pressure would not have been so great, nor its continuance so long."[11]

Although simplistic, his analysis of the depression helped to move

9. Joshua Leavitt, *Alarming Disclosures. Political Power of Slavery. Substance of Several Speeches by Rev. Joshua Leavitt in the Ohio Anti-Slavery Convention, and at Public Meetings in that State, in Oct. 1840, and Published in the "Emancipator"* (N.p., 1840), 4–7, 13–14; *Philanthropist*, September 8, November 18, 1840.

10. For an analysis of the growing emphasis of antislavery reformers on the relationship between slavery and American economic development, see Louis S. Gerteis, "Slavery and Hard Times: Morality and Utility in American Antislavery Reform," *Civil War History*, XXIX (December, 1983), 316–31.

11. Joshua Leavitt, *The Financial Power of Slavery. The Substance of an Address Delivered in Ohio, in September, 1840, by Joshua Leavitt, of New York* (N.p., 1841), 1, 3–4; *Emancipator*, October 8, 1840.

the antislavery argument in a new direction and held out the promise of attracting increasing numbers of Northerners to the Abolitionist party. Convinced of the issue's importance, he returned home determined to forge ahead. Despite his own precarious financial position, he established the *Ballot Box* as a daily paper in order to bring the party's message to the largest possible audience. In his papers and in numerous speeches he elaborated on his "Financial Power of Slavery" speech by hammering away at the connection between slavery, British and American tariff policies, and the economic interests of northern grain producers.

By the late 1830s, economic developments on both sides of the Atlantic had generated opposition to existing tariff policies. In Britain much of this agitation focused on the Corn Laws, which placed high duties on wheat, corn, and other grains. In 1838 Richard Cobden, John Bright, and other middle-class evangelical merchants and manufacturers founded the Anti-Corn Law League in Manchester. Arguing that repeal of the Corn Laws would stimulate British trade and industrial production by raising the standard of living of British workers and expanding American markets for British goods, these men injected into the cause a complex mix of humanitarianism, moralism, and economic self-interest.[12]

Some British manufacturers, disenchanted with their dependence on southern raw cotton and the southern market for their cotton cloth, turned more to northern markets, only to find that the Corn Laws limited this trade. Leavitt, who was engaged at the time in moving the antislavery cause toward independent political action, pounced on this antisouthern and antislavery dimension of the British league's message. In January 1840 he printed in the *Emancipator* a letter from "Senex," who denounced the British for importing products grown by slave labor, while refusing to admit corn and wheat produced by free labor. If the British wished to strike a blow against slavery, stated "Senex," they must radically alter their tariff policies.[13]

12. On the founding of the Anti-Corn Law League, see Thomas P. Martin, "The Upper Mississippi Valley in Anglo-American Anti-Slavery and Free Trade Relations: 1837–1842," *Mississippi Valley Historical Review*, XV (September, 1928), 208–10; Norman McCord, *The Anti-Corn Law League, 1838–1846* (London, 1958), 15–17; Frank Thistlethwaite, *America and the Atlantic Community: Anglo-American Aspects, 1790–1850* (New York, 1959), 157–58, 161–62.

13. Thistlethwaite, *America and the Atlantic Community*, 158–59, 161–63; *Emancipator*, January 23, 1840.

This letter deeply influenced Leavitt. In subsequent months he gave increasing attention to the Corn Laws, mapping out a broad strategy for repeal that he believed would benefit the manufacturing interests and workers in Britain and northern farmers in America, "while it will strike one of the heaviest blows at slavery, by relieving the free states of their dependence on cotton as the only means of paying their foreign debt." In his search for means of disseminating the message of anti-slavery and free trade, he urged Birney to pressure the World Anti-Slavery Convention in London to study the subject, and himself traveled to Ohio.[14]

Leavitt's observation of a major wheat-growing area further convinced him that only an antislavery American government would work for repeal of the Corn Laws and bring prosperity to the North. He now believed that "next to the abolition of slavery, this is the greatest question that can come before our government." Abolition, free trade, and cheap postage (which he also began to espouse in 1840) held the key, in his opinion, to moral progress and prosperity. While he carefully subordinated the free trade, cheap postage, and other issues to the primary goal of abolishing slavery, he now took the lead among abolitionists in emphasizing the integral relationship between moral reform and utilitarian values. He may also have recognized the potential for attracting additional support from the artisan class, which identified with the ideals of economic independence, democracy, liberty, and equality—all of which were antithetical to slavery. In doing so, Leavitt ran the risk of shifting the abolitionist focus from the damaging effects of slavery and racism on slaves and free blacks to the threat posed to northern whites by the Slave Power. He seemed scarcely cognizant of this risk. As he saw it, these reforms would strengthen the bonds between progressive elements in the United States and Britain, help to broaden the antislavery constituency and thus hasten the end of slavery, and ensure a stable, harmonious, and progressive society. These ends would be achieved by political means. As he pointed out confidently to Birney during the campaign, the free trade issue would bring all voting abolitionists to the party and "secure us the Democracy, and the corn movement will give us the West."[15]

14. *Emancipator*, May 1, 1840; Joshua Leavitt to James Birney, May 19, June 1, 1840, in Dumond (ed.), *Birney Letters*, I, 574, 580–81.

15. *Ballot Box*, October 7, 1840; Joshua Leavitt to James Birney, October 1, 1840,

Leavitt had voted the National Republican and Whig tickets until at least the mid-1830s. Historians have generally emphasized the Whig affiliation of most abolitionists and the support provided by the party's northern wing on the antislavery and black suffrage issues. But they have often ignored the fact that Leavitt, Bailey, Goodell, Smith, Stanton, Chase, and other leading political abolitionists came to express sympathy for the Democratic party philosophy.[16]

Both practical and ideological considerations led these men to identify with the stated ideals of the Democratic party. They realized that northern Whigs were their chief competitors for the loyalty of antislavery voters and that they might well absorb the developing Liberty organization. Thus, it was important to put as much distance as possible between themselves and the Whigs. Indeed, Leavitt later acknowledged that he had nominated Thomas Earle, a Pennsylvania Democrat, for vice-president on the Liberty ticket in 1840 in part because he wished to discourage Whig designs on the party and because he feared that the Democrats would seek to create the impression "that our independent party was a mere emanation of Whiggery, ingeniously contrived on purpose to distract 'the Democracy' with a new issue which they were badly prepared to meet, and destined, after they had done this job, to be absorbed into the Whig party, to swell the triumphs of Henry Clay."[17]

Leavitt and other political abolitionists also repudiated the Whig party because they viewed the Whigs' stand on slavery as hypocritical and deceptive, making empty gestures toward the abolitionists while standing behind the slave interests in supporting the gag laws in Congress and encouraging mob action against the abolitionists. Leavitt became thoroughly convinced of this during the 1840 campaign, and his suspicion and dislike only intensified in subsequent years. Goodell

---

in Dumond (ed.), *Birney Letters*, II, 604; see also Gerteis, "Slavery and Hard Times," 319–20; John B. Jentz, "The Antislavery Constituency in Jacksonian New York City," 101–22.

16. *Signal of Liberty*, May 27, 1844. On the antislavery posture of many northern Whigs, see Stewart, *Holy Warriors*, 99–101; James Brewer Stewart, "Abolitionists, Insurgents, and Third Parties: Sectionalism and Partisan Politics in Northern Whiggery, 1836–1844," in Kraut (ed.), *Crusaders and Compromisers*, 25–39; Lee Benson, *The Concept of Jacksonian Democracy: New York as a Test Case* (Princeton, N.J., 1961), 14–39, 208–12.

17. *Emancipator*, August 5, 1848.

fully agreed with his assessment. "The half and half gradualism of the Whigs," he charged, "has been more deceptive, and we confess it has cost us more pain and trouble than the undisguised and thorough pro-slaveryism of their opponents." These men seemed to credit the Democrats with being at least forthright in their opposition to abolition, in contrast to the Whigs' duplicitous and opportunistic stance. In addition, they accepted the widely held view of the time that the Whigs were the conservative party; they therefore tended to conclude, as Goodell told Birney in 1840, that the Whigs "never can get the ascendancy enough to accomplish the work of Emancipation; that our hope must be in the Democracy, whose principles will ensure them ultimate triumph in the government."[18]

Yet there were also important ideological reasons for the tendency to gravitate toward the Democratic party philosophy. Leavitt believed that in the process of espousing freedom and equal rights, abolitionists must logically move away from what he called the "anti-democratic or Conservative" party. These principles, he informed his readers, included "the practice of dwelling upon human rights as paramount to pecuniary interests; the effort to bring back government to its true objects, the protection of persons in the enjoyment first of life and liberty, and then of property, instead of making it the means of creating property; the very idea of employing our political power first and chiefly for the good of others."[19] While Leavitt and his colleagues had a decidedly mixed record on making racial equality an important part of the Liberty party agenda, they generally remained committed to human equality in the 1840s. Beyond that, growing affinity to democratic ideals helped Leavitt move away from his overt nativism of the 1830s—a development perhaps influenced as much by his desire to attract Democrats to the Liberty ranks as by the fact that most Whigs harbored nativist sentiments. In condemning the nativists in 1844 for harassing Irish Catholics and other immigrants, he remarked: "Beginning with the wrong, unconstitutional, un-American assumption that a naturalized American is therefore less an American than one who had the good luck to be born here, they soon come to regard them not

18. Joshua Leavitt to Amos A. Phelps, December 7, 1840, in Phelps Papers; *Friend of Man*, March 3, 1840; entry for June 10, 1840, in James G. Birney Diary, Library of Congress.

19. *Emancipator*, August 5, 1846.

as citizens but as aliens." His editorials denouncing the nativists led John Duffy, an Ohio Catholic and Liberty man, to declare to Salmon P. Chase that the *Emancipator* was the only Liberty paper to "pursue a wise, a charitable and Christian course" toward Catholics.[20]

These Democratic-oriented political abolitionists severely criticized the Democrats for failing to live up to their lofty principles, especially in their policies regarding slavery and free blacks. Gamaliel Bailey asserted in 1842, "True Democracy recognizes nothing that is exclusive in the application of principles, that it metes out equal justice to all mankind, irrespectively of sex, color, class or condition; and that no man is a democrat who denies to his fellow man an equality of rights with himself." Leavitt echoed these sentiments in pointedly reminding Orestes Brownson that in many states where the Democrats were in power, they spent the taxpayers' money extravagantly, permitted the "Bank power" to subjugate the government to its will, and, above all, consistently denied blacks fundamental political rights. Yet he, like Bailey and others, believed that northern Democrats could be recruited to political abolitionism. He editorialized in the *Ballot Box* in 1840:

> Northern Democrats have never been able to set forth their fundamental principles of 'Equal Rights, Equal Laws, and Equal Justice,' without using the very language of abolition. They cannot say a word about man AS MAN, about the superior value of human rights over mere property, about the duty of government to protect the weak and elevate the humble, about the rights of the laboring man to his just wages, about the obligation resting upon every citizen to succor those first that are most needy, about the injustice of monopolies and exclusive privileges—they cannot move a step without using the language of abolition.[21]

Leavitt and other like-minded political abolitionists tended to confuse the terms *democratic* and *Democratic*. Moreover, given the fact that most Democrats refused to condemn slavery, remained overtly racist, and refused to abandon their party for any of the antislavery parties, these men probably were naïve in hoping that they could convert the Democrats to the cause. But, in their defense, it should be noted that they endorsed many of the Democrats' stated ideals, and

20. *Ibid.*, July 17, 1844; John Duffy to Salmon P. Chase, August 24, 1842, in Salmon P. Chase Papers, Library of Congress (Chase Papers located in the Library of Congress hereinafter cited as LC).

21. *Philanthropist*, June 15, 1842; *Ballot Box*, October 31, 1840.

that the odds of converting many Whigs to the party seemed little better and less palatable. Also, viewing themselves as moral, principled men who had right on their side, they believed they could, as Leavitt stated, convince Democrats that their "anti-democratic actions have been founded on false opinions." Indeed, in Massachusetts, where Leavitt would edit the *Emancipator* during much of the 1840s, large numbers of Democrats, reacting against the proslavery stance of their party, moved into the Liberty ranks after 1843.[22]

At the party's inception Leavitt, of course, realized that most abolitionists remained committed to the Whig party. In order not to alienate these Whigs and destroy his effectiveness as a spokesman for the Abolitionist party, during the 1840 campaign he confided his political inclinations only to a few trusted confidants. "The great problem," he wrote Phelps, "is while our democratic tendencies are so rapidly developing, how far we ought to go in making democratic professions." For the time being, he resolved to "steer the via media between concealment and prematurity."[23]

As the 1840 campaign neared an end, it became painfully clear to Leavitt that nothing could be done to convince most abolitionists to abandon the major parties. Party attachments were so strong, he complained, that "it is almost like plucking out a right eye, or off a right arm, for one who has mingled much in party strife, and enjoyed the confidence of political associates, to cut loose and pronounce his party corrupt." The determination of many abolitionists to vote the Whig ticket "once more" in order to defeat Van Buren compounded the problems posed by the virtual absence of a grass-roots organization. In all, Birney and Earle garnered a mere 7,054 of more than 2,400,000 votes cast in the election (less than one-tenth of the abolitionists eligible to vote).[24]

Garrison could not resist the temptation to ridicule the party for its dismal showing, terming the results "equally ludicrous and melancholy." He added, however, that Leavitt and other party leaders "seem determined to keep it up." Garrison was certainly correct on the

22. Boston *Morning Chronicle*, April 1, 1844; Johnson, "The Liberty Party in Massachusetts," 253–55; Joel H. Silbey, "'There Are Other Questions Beside That of Slavery Merely': The Democratic Party and Antislavery Politics," in Kraut (ed.), *Crusaders and Compromisers*, 143–69.

23. Joshua Leavitt to Amos A. Phelps, December 7, 1840, in Phelps Papers.

24. *Ballot Box*, October 20, 1840; Sewell, *Ballots for Freedom*, 74–79.

175

second count. Like many of his fellow party activists, Leavitt was troubled by the rout but determined to emphasize the long-term positive effects of the nominations. The Birney-Earle ticket, he declared defiantly, "had more effect in preparing the way for the abolition of slavery, yes, tenfold more than all the rest [of the abolitionists] put together." He continued to dispense advice to the party faithful and in December 1840 addressed meetings and rallies in Fall River, Lowell, Worcester, and several other Massachusetts towns. The farther he traveled, the more discouraged he became with the lack of party organization. Notices of his speeches were posted only the day before he arrived in most towns, thus severely limiting attendance. Frustrated and angry, he advised Phelps that in any future campaign a person should be brought into the state for a week or two to organize the campaign, and agents should be hired to present lectures in every town. Discouraged, facing yet another financial crisis with the *Emancipator*, and eager to prepare for his upcoming trip to Washington, on Christmas eve Leavitt abruptly cut short his tour of the state and returned home.[25]

Leavitt's decision to move to Washington for a few weeks to lobby for the antislavery cause was not without precedent. The petitions controversy had convinced many abolitionists of the strategic importance of Washington, and in 1838 Stanton had spent a few weeks in the nation's capital overseeing the petitions drive. The growing financial crisis and deepening divisions within the movement, however, caused the idea of an antislavery agency in Washington to be shelved until Leavitt revived it in 1840.[26] In establishing an agency in Washington he sought to add yet another weapon to the antislavery arsenal. Extending over a period of five years, his agency represents one of his most important contributions to the cause. His lobbying efforts provided party members and other abolitionists with valuable informa-

25. William Lloyd Garrison to John A. Collins, December 1, 1840, in Garrison Papers; *Emancipator*, November 12, 1840; Leavitt to Phelps, November 27, December 7, 24, 1840, in Phelps Papers; W.C.C. to Deborah Weston, January 1, 1841, in Weston Family Papers; Joshua Leavitt to Roger Hooker Leavitt, December 15, 1840, in Leavitt Papers.

26. James M. McPherson, "The Fight Against the Gag Rule: Joshua Leavitt and the Antislavery Insurgency in the Whig Party, 1839–1842," *Journal of Negro History*, XLVIII (July, 1963), 179–80; Henry B. Stanton, *Random Recollections* (3rd ed.; New York, 1887), 60.

tion concerning congressional actions on matters relating to slavery. He also helped to mobilize an antislavery insurgency in the House of Representatives, which ultimately succeeded in breaking through the wall of silence surrounding the slavery question in Congress and pointed toward an irreparable breach in the Whig party.

Upon arriving in Washington in mid-January 1841, Leavitt moved into Mrs. Sprigg's boardinghouse across from the Capitol, where Giddings and Slade resided while Congress was in session. (Sarah and the boys remained at home in Bloomfield.) During the next few weeks, other pressing matters prevented him from devoting much energy to mobilizing congressional opposition to slavery. He had timed his arrival to coincide with the expected rendering of the decision by the U.S. Supreme Court in the *Amistad* case. He had been involved in the case from the moment that fifty-four Mendi Africans, having risen up against their Cuban captors and killed all but two of them, were intercepted by a U.S. Navy cutter near the tip of Long Island and brought to New London and then New Haven to stand trial for murder on the high seas. Upon receiving word of the Africans' detention, he and Lewis Tappan visited them in New Haven, where Leavitt used his contacts among the Yale faculty to procure an interpreter. Shortly thereafter, a meeting held in New York appointed Leavitt, Tappan, and Simeon S. Jocelyn, a New Haven minister, as a committee and authorized them to employ legal counsel, raise funds, and publicize the plight of the unfortunate captives. At the same time, they hoped to provide the captives with extensive religious instruction and to convert them as a means of Christianizing Africa.[27]

During the two years that the case moved slowly through the court system, much of the committee's work fell to Tappan. Leavitt often visited the prisoners in Hartford, but his editorial and other responsibilities occupied most of his time. Not until he came to Washington in January 1841 to attend the presentation of arguments before the Supreme Court and to consult with John Quincy Adams did he again become actively involved in the case. In the days before the hearing he met several times with Adams, whom Tappan had hired as legal counsel in the fall of 1840. Leavitt fully supported the hiring of Adams, whom he had admired for years as a defender of liberty. Adams

27. *Emancipator*, January 14, 1841; Wyatt-Brown, *Lewis Tappan*, 205–20; Warner, *New Haven Negroes*, 66–68.

fulfilled this expectation. Throughout the hearing in late February, Leavitt listened intently to both the government's arguments and those of Adams and Roger Sherman Baldwin, a New Haven attorney whom the *Amistad* Committee had hired in 1839, taking extensive notes, which he later expanded for publication in the *Emancipator*. He considered Baldwin's legal brief "one of the most complete, finished, conclusive legal arguments ever made before that Court," but he was most moved by Adams's eloquent and lengthy defense of the rights of the accused and the obligations of the courts to uphold justice.[28]

With the case in the hands of the Court, Leavitt, Adams, and Baldwin could only anxiously await the decision. During the following week, Leavitt's mind never strayed far from the case. A cold, blustery Inauguration Day found him ensconced in the front room of Adams's house on F Street, where the inaugural parade for Harrison was slated to pass. Adams had chosen to pass up the Inauguration to sit with Leavitt and pore over legal precedents as a contingency for what the Supreme Court might rule. From their lofty perch they looked down on the bands as they passed by. Neither man was impressed—Adams referred to it as "showy-shabby," while Leavitt sniffed that it was a "small affair" compared with many parades in New York.[29]

Immediately following his visit with Adams, Leavitt returned to New York. A few days later the news came that the Supreme Court had declared the captives free. After eighteen months of labor and many anxious moments, Leavitt was overjoyed by the news. The Court's decision, he exulted to Adams, represented "a glorious triumph of *justice*—of liberty, and of law, over *sympathy*, and slavery, and Executive power."[30]

The *Amistad* Committee, which would suffer setbacks during the next few months, set out to raise funds by holding mass meetings in

28. Joshua Leavitt to Roger Sherman Baldwin, September 6, 15, 1839, Lewis Tappan to Baldwin, September 2, 1839, in Baldwin Family Papers, Sterling Library, Yale University; Christopher Martin, *The Amistad Affair* (New York, 1970), 139–66; entries for September 23, October 1–2, 1839, February 10, March 10, 23, May 25, 1840, in Charles Francis Adams (ed.) *Memoirs of John Quincy Adams* (Philadelphia, 1876), X, 131–35, 216, 233, 241, 296; *Emancipator*, March 4, 11, 1841; Joshua Leavitt to John Quincy Adams, March 11, 1841, in Adams Family Papers, Massachusetts Historical Society.

29. Entry for March 4, 1841, in John Quincy Adams Diary, Massachusetts Historical Society; *Emancipator*, March 11, 1841.

30. Joshua Leavitt to John Quincy Adams, May 18, 1841, in Adams Family Papers.

several cities and asking friends for contributions. Pressured by the Africans' growing restiveness under the strict supervision of their white benefactors, the committee decided to return their charges to their homeland by the fall of 1841. Finally, having raised sufficient money to send the Africans and two missionaries to Mendi country, the committee prepared to see them off, hoping, as Leavitt informed the British governor of Sierra Leone, "to make them also the bearers of all the blessings of Christianity to their benighted and injured countrymen."[31]

In December 1841 Leavitt, Tappan, Jocelyn, and two other abolitionists boarded a ferry in New York harbor that carried the Africans to their waiting ship. In a moving farewell, they prayed with the Mendis and presented each of them with a memento of their stay in America. As he returned home, Leavitt could be justly proud of the yeoman work he, Tappan, and Jocelyn had performed in behalf of the captives. They had fought the good fight in support of the Africans and against the illegal slave trade. Basking in the afterglow of their triumph—one of the few that the abolitionists achieved within the legal system—Leavitt was gracious toward Tappan, acknowledging that the committee's success had been due largely to his "untiring vigilance, his immovable decision of character, and his facility in the despatch of business."[32]

Leavitt had also come to Washington to agitate the Corn Law issue. In an attempt to educate Congress to the beneficial effects of a lower tariff, in February 1841 he submitted to the Senate Committee on Agriculture his *Memorial . . . Praying the Adoption of Measures to Secure an Equitable Market for American Wheat*, which Congress accepted and ordered to be printed. In this memorial Leavitt reiterated what had become a standard theme in his editorials: that of a productive Northwest suffering grievously as a result of the "unjust and ungenerous" Corn Laws. Repeal, or at least modification, of the Corn Laws, he argued, would stimulate both British manufacturing and northwestern agriculture, increase public land sales and bring more revenue into the federal treasury, improve relations between the two nations, and stimulate moral progress.[33]

31. *Emancipator*, July 1, 1841; Joshua Leavitt for *Amistad* Committee to Sir John Jerome, March 2, 1841, in Tappan Papers.
32. *Emancipator*, December 3, 10, 1841.
33. *Memorial of Joshua Leavitt Praying the Adoption of Measures to Secure an*

In addition, Leavitt helped to strengthen ties between northern advocates of free trade and abolition and leaders of the British anti–Corn Laws movement. In correspondence with English friends, published in the *Anti-Corn Law Circular* in Britain, he employed the carrot-and-stick approach in an attempt to persuade British abolitionists and free traders to consider America's economic interests. He warned that if the British would not accept grains, Americans would turn more toward producing their own manufactured goods. But he also noted that increased levels of trade would enhance the value of northwestern state bonds held by British capitalists. This correspondence convinced him of the need for an anti–Corn Laws mission to take the American free trade message directly to the British public. He arranged for John Curtis, an Ohio abolitionist and free trader, to travel to England as an emissary of the Liberty party; Curtis spoke before numerous league meetings during an eight-month tour of Britain in 1841. At the same time, Leavitt, an inveterate organizer, threw himself into establishing anti–Corn Laws societies in New York and the Northwest for the purpose of collecting and diffusing statistics, holding meetings, disseminating information to journals, and pressuring the federal government to reform its tariff policies. Not all political abolitionists supported his organizing efforts. Many Whig-oriented abolitionists favored a protectionist policy, and even Elizur Wright, a free trade advocate, feared that Leavitt's editorial stance on the free trade issue might be viewed as the official position of the party—an ironic twist in light of Leavitt's recent criticism of Garrison on the women's question and nonresistance.[34] But such considerations did not particularly concern him. He always denied that he wished to make free trade a test of membership in the party; perhaps more important, he believed that his stand on the issue was correct and that it held enormous promise for growth within the Liberty party.

The party's ranks were indeed beginning to swell with new members, especially Whigs. With the sudden elevation of John Tyler, a Virginia slaveholder, to the presidency following Harrison's death one

---

Equitable Market for American Wheat, Senate Documents, 26th Cong., 2nd Sess., No. 222, pp. 1–8.

34. Thistlethwaite, *America and the Atlantic Community*, 163–64; *Emancipator*, December 24, 1840, May 6, 1841; Joseph Sturge, *A Visit to the United States in 1841* (London, 1842), 110–11; *Massachusetts Abolitionist*, January 21, 1841.

month after assuming office, many Whigs found their hopes of an antislavery influence in the White House dashed. This dramatic development strengthened the Liberty leadership's determination to choose a standardbearer as soon as possible to facilitate party recruiting efforts. Leavitt had long pushed for Birney to be selected again, and at a convention held in May 1841 he and other Liberty stalwarts—most of them Easterners—nominated Birney by a nearly unanimous vote and chose former senator Thomas Morris of Ohio as their candidate for vice-president. Both the nomination of Morris, a western Democrat, and the publication of an address that urged repeal of the Corn Laws and passage of fiscal and land policies favorable to the free states demonstrated Leavitt's influence on the proceedings.[35]

Buoyed by the convention's action, Leavitt traveled to Albany, where he lobbied successfully for repeal of the state's slavery statutes and, at the invitation of Governor William Seward and other New York officials, presented a revised version of his *Memorial on Wheat* to the legislature's Committee on Trade and Manufactures. He carefully tailored his earlier memorial to a New York audience by appealing to sectional pride and economic interest. Realizing that far more wheat farmers and grain merchants than cotton factors lived in the state, he attacked the federal government for giving preference to cotton over wheat in its foreign trade. His argument proved so popular that the legislature printed an unusually large number of copies.[36]

Leavitt derived immense satisfaction from the outcome of the *Amistad* case, the nomination of Birney, and the reception accorded his memorials on the wheat trade. But the financial crisis that occurred at the same time diminished his joy. The 1840 agreement by the New York City Young Men's Anti-Slavery Society to publish the *Emancipator* had never provided adequately for his salary or for the paper's operation. By February 1841, the situation had deteriorated to the point that he seriously considered moving the paper to Boston; two

35. Joshua Leavitt to James Birney, October 1, 1840, Committee on Nominations to James Birney, May 12, 1841, in Dumond (ed.), *Birney Letters*, II, 603, 627; *Emancipator*, November 12, December 17, 1840, May 20, 1841; Liberty Party Notebook, 16–17, in Theodore Foster Papers, William L. Clements Library, University of Michigan.

36. *Memorial of Joshua Leavitt, Setting Forth the Importance of an Equitable and Adequate Market for American Wheat*, New York Assembly, 64th Sess., Doc. 295, pp. 1–12; Joshua Leavitt to Roger Hooker Leavitt, May 17, 1841, in Leavitt Papers.

months later he became sole proprietor of the paper. He remained in the city only because the American and Foreign Anti-Slavery Society appointed him corresponding secretary at a salary of $1,500. This proved a mixed blessing, for the society was struggling badly, the position added time-consuming responsibilities to his already busy work schedule, and the appointment raised the specter of another confrontation with Tappan over party politics. For months Leavitt had bided his time, quietly cultivating a generally friendly executive committee and avoiding any action that might arouse Tappan's suspicion. By the spring of 1841, however, the committee had moved close to an open endorsement of the Liberty party, proclaiming independent nominations to be "a permanent and integral part of the great movements by which slavery is to be overthrown."[37]

It was only a matter of time until these two stubborn and sensitive men clashed again. In this confrontation neither man seemed able either to distinguish clearly between fundamental principles and the pithy details of logistics or to find a satisfactory compromise. Outmaneuvered, outmanned, and convinced that the committee wished to make the *Emancipator* the organ of the society and the society an arm of the Liberty party, Tappan—who had edited the society's organ, the *Reporter*, from its inception—resigned from the organization. Although Leavitt did not wish to achieve either of the objectives that Tappan feared, he knew that he had much of the committee behind him and therefore refused to agree with Tappan as to who should edit the *Reporter*. Indeed, he seemed rather indifferent about Tappan's resignation. "We are going on, as you will see," he nonchalantly informed Gerrit Smith, "and hope to do something for the cause." Cooler heads ultimately prevailed among those who hoped not to lose Tappan's valuable services. John Greenleaf Whittier and Joseph Sturge, a British friend of both men who was then touring the United States, soon prevailed upon Leavitt to accept Whittier as editor of the *Reporter*, with both Leavitt and Tappan as contributors. Whatever triumph Leavitt achieved was more symbolic than real, for the *Reporter* had few subscribers and the society was little more than a shell. When he returned to Washington for the special session of Congress called by the Whigs

37. *Emancipator*, February 4, 11, 25, March 11, 1841; Fladeland, *James Gillespie Birney*, 210; Joshua Leavitt to Luther Bradish, June 10, 1841, Luther Bradish Papers; *American and Foreign Anti-Slavery Reporter*, I (April, 1841), 152; *British and Foreign Anti-Slavery Reporter*, July 14, 1841.

for the purpose of pushing through a broad economic program to lift the nation out of a protracted depression, he ceased to have any sustained contact with the *Reporter*.[38] In some respects this confrontation was merely a continuation of their bitter feud a year and a half earlier. At that time Leavitt had believed his professional integrity and his commitment to the cause were called into question; by forcing Tappan's hand, he now appears to have sought to gain a measure of revenge and to prove once again that Tappan's money and influence could not silence or control him.

As events proved, Leavitt also had not laid to rest his earlier dispute with the antislavery Whigs in Congress, who continued to reject his call to leave the party. Thus, it was perhaps inevitable that their 1840 confrontation would be repeated. His inability to unite the "practical anti-moonshine abolitionists"—as he termed the anti-Garrisonians— or to wean the antislavery Whigs from their partisan ways frustrated him enormously. The fireworks between him and these Whigs began in June 1841 when he accused them of doing nothing to prevent the election of a slaveholder as speaker of the House and of supporting the gag on reception of antislavery petitions during the special session in order to push through the Whig economic program. He was wrong on both counts: These men had in fact made an important symbolic gesture in defiance of party regularity by voting for a northern Whig for speaker and had not specifically supported a gag on antislavery petitions. Yet, once again, in the heat of battle Leavitt found it extremely difficult to apologize unreservedly. He refused to retract the first charge and, after recanting the second, essentially negated his apology by insisting that the Whigs' replacement of "the gag superseding it with a rule that does all that a gag did, is not to be boasted of among freemen."[39]

The antislavery Whigs' reaction to his charges was nearly as predictable. Seth Gates thought his accusations to be exceedingly unfair. "We get curses enough here for obstinacy, and bolting party," he la-

38. Lewis Tappan to William Jay, June 11, 28, 1841, Tappan Papers; entries for June 9, 11, 12, 1841, Tappan Diary; Joshua Leavitt to Gerrit Smith, June 10, July 29, 1841, in Smith Miller Collection; Lewis Tappan to John G. Whittier, June 18, 1841, in John Greenleaf Whittier Papers, Essex Institute; *American and Foreign Anti-Slavery Reporter*, II (July, 1841), 1.

39. Leavitt to Smith, July 29, 1841, in Smith Miller Collection; *Emancipator*, June 17, July 1, 8, 1841.

mented to Birney, "without getting it from him." Joshua Giddings, seething with anger, informed Leavitt that his "sympathies and feelings are too strongly identified with the Locofoco party for you to do exact justice to those who belong to the opposite political faith."[40] Giddings's assessment of Leavitt's political sympathies was not far from the mark, but the fact remains that the antislavery Whigs continued to be guided by partisan motives on many occasions. Yet Leavitt could take little comfort in calling them to task, for his shrill tone and blunt accusations had alienated them. When he left Washington in mid-July, he could look back on no accomplishments of note during the session.

An equally unpleasant situation faced him at home. With both the *Emancipator* and the American and Foreign Anti-Slavery Society in dire financial straits, and with mounting obligations to his creditors and his family, he admitted to Amos Phelps, a close confidant in the early 1840s, that he was forced to "live from hand to hand, and quite up to my means, this is very embarrassing." He even felt compelled to pressure his brothers to settle their father's estate so that he could pay off some of his debts.[41] Above all, he was frustrated and angry that he had sacrificed so much for the cause while so many had contributed so little. "I confess," he lamented to Phelps, "with all the kind considerations my poor labors receive, it weighs heavily on my spirits that so few are willing to *do* any thing for my support, and with my very burdensome family, not to know from week to week where I am to get the means of support, or whether I can get it at all, is rather trying, and then to have the whole burden, including the pecuniary responsibility of the National Society thrown upon my shoulders alone, is sometimes more than I can bear."[42]

When he dealt with public issues, antislavery tactics, and organizational concerns, Leavitt generally was able to appear in command and to project a brave exterior. But on financial matters his sense of vulnerability allowed him to express, at least to friends, his deepest fears and anxieties. He constantly worried about the material privations his family had to endure. Some of this concern manifested itself

40. Seth Gates to James Birney, June 7, 1841, in Dumond (ed.), *Birney Letters*, II, 630–31; Joshua Giddings to Joshua Leavitt, July 19, 1841, in Giddings Papers.

41. Joshua Leavitt to Amos A. Phelps, November 27, 1840, in Phelps Papers; Joshua Leavitt to Roger Hooker Leavitt, May 17, 1841, in Leavitt Papers.

42. Joshua Leavitt to Amos A. Phelps, October 7, 1840, in Phelps Papers.

in resentment that he alone must support the entire family. In 1840 he expressed to Phelps the hope that his son William, a recent graduate of Yale, could find a teaching job "in order to relieve me of some of my financial troubles"; four years later he grumbled to Gerrit Smith about the need to support the family—"not one of them earning a cent." Occasionally his complaints about money assumed a self-pitying tone, and his feelings of guilt—perhaps intensified by his failure to provide for his family in the manner his father had for his—led him compulsively to deny that he was extravagant in his spending habits. In 1845, for example, he plaintively informed his readers that he still used the watch his father had given him thirty years earlier, that he had not owned a horse since 1828 and walked two miles to his office each day, and that he had heavily mortgaged his modest home. But in fairness to him, his salary was often uncertain or far in arrears and his financial plight was real.[43]

By November 1841, the situation had become so grave that Leavitt confessed to his brother: "It may be I shall be driven back to the old hive, with all my helpless brood, but not if I can help it. I will work harder than I have yet, i.e., if I can find any thing to do." But, with his salary $600 in arrears and the national organization "but a broken reed," he ultimately chose to resign his position with the American and Foreign Anti-Slavery Society and move the *Emancipator* to Boston, where he merged it with the *Free American* under the auspices of the Massachusetts Abolition Society. His Garrisonian antagonists could not resist the temptation to gloat about his misfortune. "I am sorry," a Groton, Massachusetts, abolitionist informed Anne Warren Weston, "I would prefer that the wretch starve where he is. . . . He is an expensive dog, and [the] new org[anization] will have to work hard to raise the where with all to feed him—there is some consolation in that."[44]

The *Free American*, previously edited by Elizur Wright, was mired in debt, but Leavitt still chose to view the merger as a new lease on life. He also was pleased that the transfer to Boston would permit him to see his mother, toward whom he was very protective after his fa-

43. *Ibid.*; Joshua Leavitt to Gerrit Smith, January 7, 1844, in Smith Miller Collection; Joshua Leavitt to Roger Hooker Leavitt, December 12, 17, 1842, in Leavitt Papers; *Emancipator*, October 8, 1845.

44. Joshua Leavitt to Roger Hooker Leavitt, November 9, 1841, in Leavitt Papers; A. Farnsworth to Anne Warren Weston, November 22, 1841, in Weston Family Papers.

ther's death, as well as his many other Massachusetts relatives.[45] The merger, however, also meant that he had to uproot his family from their home in Bloomfield, where they had lived since the mid-1830s. Sarah and the boys enjoyed the town and their home and made it clear that they did not wish to move. As Leavitt reported to his brother Roger Hooker, "It will be harder to wean them from that place, than any other we have lived in." He tended to be philosophical about the move, conceding that "it is a world of change, and we must not show affections in things earthly." But Sarah, a strong-willed woman, did not share his thinking on the proposed move. She, after all, had been at home and a part of the community while Joshua was in Washington or at the newspaper office in the city. She refused for nearly a year to move to Boston and vigorously protested his plans to return to Washington in December.[46]

In this battle of wills, Leavitt with his sense of duty to the cause prevailed. Nevertheless, Sarah's decision to remain in Bloomfield indicates that Joshua could not, and probably did not wish to, dictate to her on such a matter. Their roles within the marriage were certainly quite traditional, with Sarah being largely responsible for the household chores and child rearing, while Johsua was away from home working for the cause. Even when he came home from trips to Washington, speaking tours, meetings, and other ventures, he often worked at the office fourteen or sixteen hours a day, where he wrote most of the columns himself. He admitted that he frequently could not find the time even to store the potatoes in the cellar or to complete other chores. Yet he and Sarah seem to have had a companionate marriage. She was devoted to and involved in the same causes he was and shared his sense of the mission upon which they had embarked. They clearly cared about each other. He was a devoted and loving family man and often complained about being forced to be away from home for extended periods of time. Whenever he returned home for a few days, he thoroughly enjoyed himself. As he wrote Giddings in 1842, "I find it so pleasant that I shall not be ready to leave it until imperiously called

45. Joshua Leavitt to Roger Hooker Leavitt, November 9, 1841, in Leavitt Papers; Leavitt to Smith, November 11, 1841, in Smith Miller Collection; Joshua Leavitt to Salmon P. Chase, December 6, 1841, Salmon P. Chase Papers, Historical Society of Pennsylvania (Chase Papers located in Historical Society of Pennsylvania hereinafter cited as HSP).

46. Joshua Leavitt to Roger Hooker Leavitt, December 8, 1841, in Leavitt Papers.

away. My family were much pleased to see me home again, and wish me to stay as long as I can."[47]

The painful separations from Sarah and the boys grew more and more intolerable as the years passed and would ultimately play a role in Leavitt's decision to end the antislavery lobby. But in December 1841 he seemed determined, even eager, to return to the nation's capital. An important factor drawing him back was the fact that both he and his Whig antagonists seemed to have set aside their rancor and were seeking constructive ways to cooperate in a common cause. Their bitter rejoinders in the summer may have served as a catharsis, allowing them to blow off steam and move to a point where they could see clearly that they needed each other. As early as July a decided thaw in their relations had become evident, with Giddings telling Leavitt sympathetically: "While on my part it shall at all times be my greatest pleasure to aid you in the discharge of your high duties in every way in my power. If you suffer the cause in which we are both engaged suffers." Giddings and his antislavery colleagues in the House realized, however imperfectly, that Leavitt served their purposes well, for in comparison to his demands for immediate action and total abolition, their views on slavery appeared to many voters to be rather moderate. Thus, as James Brewer Stewart has noted, they enjoyed the luxury of speaking out aggressively on the slavery issue, while remaining Whigs in good standing. A few months later, in an obvious attempt to mend fences with Giddings, Leavitt credited him with being "as sincerely opposed to the domination of the slave power" as he was, despite their obvious differences. In a rare display of introspective thought, he even sought to explain why he often seemed so abrasive and combative to others. "I feel so sure I am right," he admitted to Giddings, "that I cannot be satisfied without doing all in my power to bring people to this view." This confession seemed to break the ice between them. When he asked Giddings to reserve a room for him at Mrs. Sprigg's boardinghouse, he added warmly: "If you think it would be agreeable to the wife to have so unreasonable and troublesome a person in it."[48] He realized that it made good sense to patch up his relationship with Giddings if he hoped to influence him further. But his gestures of

47. Joshua Leavitt to Roger Hooker Leavitt, November 9, 1841, February 26, 1842, in Leavitt Papers; Joshua Leavitt to Joshua Giddings, July 27, 1842, in Giddings Papers.

48. Stewart, *Holy Warriors*, 101; Joshua Giddings to Joshua Leavitt, July 19, 1841, Leavitt to Giddings, October 29, 1841, in Giddings Papers.

friendship were sincere. After all, Leavitt was capable of warmth and tenderness—even toward some of those with whom he disagreed.

These conciliatory gestures helped immensely to move Giddings and Leavitt from discord to harmony and to encourage the antislavery Whigs to go much further in the direction of forcing congressional debate on slavery. In fact, by the time Leavitt arrived in Washington, Giddings, Gates, William Slade, Sherlock Andrews of Ohio, and a handful of other Whig congressmen, with Adams standing near the periphery, had begun to coalesce into an antislavery insurgency group in defiance of their party's wishes. Leavitt invited his old friend Theodore Weld, an indefatigable researcher, to Washington in late December to assist this "select committee." Ensconced on his New Jersey farm, located near Leavitt's home in Bloomfield, and unwilling to support the Liberty party, Weld nevertheless came to Washington as a favor to Leavitt and Tappan and to help further the cause. He immediately moved into Leavitt's room on the third floor of Mrs. Sprigg's house. They spent evenings together writing and studying, and on Sundays attended black churches in the vicinity, where Leavitt said he felt "as much at home as any where, because their religion seems so sincere and hearty." At one point he, Gates, and Weld also took time out to attend an open house hosted by President Tyler, but, as Weld reported to his wife with a hint of smugness, they "took care *not* to shake hands with him." In fact, they stayed only fifteen minutes, and then went to visit John Quincy Adams.[49]

Long-time friends and kindred spirits, Leavitt and Weld admired each other's abilities and forthrightness and genuinely enjoyed each other's company. As Weld wrote his wife, it was "mutual consultation between us on points constantly occurring" that "seemed to make it best." They essentially agreed to disagree on the issue of third-party action, with each man respecting the other's views. Weld appears to have been one of few non-Garrisonian abolitionists whom Leavitt did not attempt to proselytize, and Weld was rather philosophical about the fact that friends such as Leavitt and Birney were committed to political abolitionism. He conceded to Birney that it was "one of those

49. Theodore Weld to James Birney, May 23, 1842, in Dumond (ed.), *Birney Letters*, II, 693; James Brewer Stewart, *Joshua R. Giddings and the Tactics of Radical Politics* (Cleveland, 1970), 69; Joshua Leavitt to mother, May 18, 1842, in Leavitt Papers; Theodore Weld to Angelina G. Weld, January 1, 2, 1842, in Barnes and Dumond (eds.), *Weld-Grimké Letters*, II, 883–84.

mysteries which I can dispose of in no way but by depositing it in my heap of *unaccountables*; where I doubt not you deposited long ago my *Anti Third Partyism.*"[50]

Weld and Leavitt lived with twenty other boarders at Mrs. Sprigg's. Mrs. Sprigg, a Virginian, hired slaves to work in her boardinghouse but seemed to be essentially apolitical; most of her boarders were Northerners and several were openly antislavery. Relations among the boarders were friendly and open. As Weld reported, the other boarders treated him and Leavitt "exactly as though we were not fanatics, and we talk over with them at the table and elsewhere abolition just as we should at home." Leavitt and Weld found themselves in the somewhat awkward position of being served by slaves, but did not consider moving out of the boardinghouse because of this situation. In fact, Leavitt thought it might be considered indiscreet to talk to the slaves too much, though he did wonder what effect the talk of fugitive slaves and other matters at the dinner table had on the slaves.[51]

Weld's and Leavitt's relationship with the Whig insurgents differed in important respects. Weld came to Washington at the request of the antislavery Whigs (and Leavitt) to work for them as a researcher. He belonged to no party and therefore brought no political agenda with him. Leavitt occupied a more independent and, at times, adversarial position. He respected Adams, Giddings, Gates, Slade, and others for opposing slavery and seeking to force discussion of the slavery question in Congress, and he constantly prodded them to do more. Even when most critical of the insurgents, he seemed to sense that they stood very close to the abolitionist position. Yet he consciously sought to stand somewhat apart from them. He had established the antislavery lobby to serve as a sentinel for the antislavery movement, and he hoped somehow to persuade the insurgents to place antislavery above Whig party considerations—to attack slavery and to leave the Whig ranks and join the Liberty party.

During the session Leavitt alternately consulted with the Whig insurgents, criticized them, and encouraged them to force debate on such matters as the Florida war, constitutional rights of free blacks,

50. Theodore Weld to Angelina G. Weld, January 1, 1842, in Barnes and Dumond (eds.), *Weld-Grimké Letters*, II, 883; Weld to Birney, May 23, 1842, in Dumond (ed.), *Birney Letters*, II, 693.

51. Theodore Weld to Angelina G. Weld, January 1, 2, 1842, in Barnes and Dumond (eds.), *Weld-Grimké Letters*, II, 883–84; Leavitt to mother, May 18, 1842, in Leavitt Papers.

diplomatic recognition of Haiti, and the domestic slave trade. Always searching for ways to probe the defenses surrounding the slave system and to keep the issue before the American public, he also lobbied for an ingenious plan for ending slavery in the District of Columbia. His faith in the judicial system, revived by the courts' rulings in the *Amistad* case, led him to consider testing the constitutionality of slavery in the District of Columbia by finding a slave willing to sue for his freedom and having either Birney or Chase argue the case. This approach, he reasoned to Chase, was far superior to the petitions method and would force the Supreme Court to render a "clear-cut" decision. But, despite Leavitt's assiduous efforts to drum up support for the project, the lukewarm response by Chase, Gates, and others—grounded in their belief that it had little chance of succeeding—ultimately forced him to shelve the plan.[52]

Throughout the session, he sat in the reporters' section of the House, where he closely scrutinized the actions and speeches of the members. Every day that Congress met in session he was there, pen and writing pad in hand, taking notes and making comments in the margins; he then returned to his room, where he fleshed out certain of the speeches and composed editorial comments for the next issue of the *Emancipator*. All of this kept him very busy. At one point during the session he confided to his mother the fear that he might fall "into the lazy habits of the place and of everything around it and the government under the stupefying influence of slavery."[53] He need not have worried, for he drove himself hard during his stay.

If anything, the censure trial of John Quincy Adams only quickened the hectic pace of his work schedule. For weeks in February and March 1842, Leavitt thought of little else, exploiting every miscalculation by the enemy and standing by Adams in his hour of need. He and the antislavery Whigs had long anticipated Adams's censure, and they could not have written a better script for their antagonists. Adams and other Whig insurgents frequently had aroused the ire of southern representatives by reading antislavery petitions in violation of House rules. In late January Leavitt observed that the southern House members had become "very anxious," but erroneously predicted that they

---

52. See Leavitt to Chase, December 6, 1841, January 23, 1842, in Chase Papers, HSP; Seth Gates to James Birney, December 11, 1841, in Dumond (ed.), *Birney Letters*, II, 642; *Emancipator*, December 10, 1841.

53. Joshua Leavitt to mother, January 23, 1842, in Leavitt Papers.

would not risk "any *great* deed of wickedness." Only one day later Adams gave his opponents the opening they had long awaited but had been reluctant to pursue because of his prestige. When he read a petition from constituents in Haverhill, Massachusetts, praying for the immediate dissolution of the Union on the grounds that the slave system drained northern resources—a plea that Adams did not personally favor—his adversaries, fearing that he might ultimately succeed in creating an aggressive antislavery movement in Congress, presented a resolution of censure. Leavitt was almost beside himself with glee as he observed the Southerners' fury: "A hen with her head cut off is but a faint picture of their gyrations at this moment." [54]

In some ways it is ironic that the House censured Adams, for he consistently had sought to steer the Whig insurgents away from an emphasis on abolition and toward the right of petition. Yet Adams realized that the other members' collaboration was crucial to his efforts, and Leavitt and the others knew that if the censure motion passed the very fabric of antislavery insurgency might well be destroyed; conversely, its defeat would represent a major step toward meaningful congressional debate on slavery. Thus, they rushed to Adams's defense. Within hours of the censure resolution, Leavitt, Weld, and the antislavery Whigs met and appointed the two abolitionists as a committee to offer Adams whatever assistance he desired. Even though it was late at night, Leavitt and Weld walked to Adams's house and presented him the offer, which Adams accepted with gratitude. [55]

Adams's censure trial lasted for more than a week, riveting the attention of the House and much of the Washington community on the confrontation. Led by Representative Henry Wise of Virginia, southern representatives accused Adams of needlessly endangering the unity of the nation and violating the established rules of the House. In response to these charges, Adams accused the slaveholders of seeking to destroy basic constitutional rights. Throughout the trial, Leavitt stood in the thick of the battle, assisting Weld in gathering materials for the defense and attending strategy meetings with Weld at Adams's house. He spent much of each day taking extensive notes on Adams's

54. *Ibid.*; entry for January 23–26, 1842, in Adams (ed.), *Memoirs of John Quincy Adams*, XI, 71–73; *Emancipator*, February 11, 1842.
55. Joshua R. Giddings, *History of the Rebellion, Its Authors and Causes* (New York, 1864), 161–62.

speeches—an important task because the *National Intelligencer* and most other papers refused to print what Adams said. Leavitt sat at a reporter's desk located directly behind Adams's seat. Unable to hear much of what Adams said, he moved to an open area where he could hear better. When the doorkeeper asked him to leave, he then sat on a box behind a screen near Adams. Even here he was rebuked and forced to return to his regular seat. Predictably, in this first of several confrontations with House members, he charged that the situation was part of a grand conspiracy to crush Adams and suppress freedom of the press.[56]

When debate on the censure motion ended, Adams emerged victorious, receiving the support of most northern House members and even a few from the South. His opponents had overreacted and had failed either to discredit or to silence him. Leavitt was delighted, crowing to his brother that the slaveholders "feel as if they had been to Waterloo or Bunker Hill." Although he and Adams never agreed on the primacy of immediate abolition as a practical object to be strived for, Adams's courage, integrity, and plain-spoken honesty in his trial and in the *Amistad* case deeply moved him. While seated near Adams day after day during the session, Leavitt drew a portrait of the old man, which he sent to his mother, noting that nowhere could one see such a marvelous sight as "when the lightning gleams over that marble countenance and the bolts of burning vituperation dart thick and inevitable, putting to flight the armies of the aliens." He genuinely admired Adams, declaring to his readers that this "extraordinary man" deserved the title of "Champion of the rights of personal liberty in the 19th Century." The admiration was mutual. Having spent considerable time with him during the past year, Adams confided in his diary that he only wished he could do more to assist Leavitt, "this excellent man, who is the salt of the earth."[57]

Adams's victory by no means ruled out another southern move to silence the antislavery insurgents. Leavitt himself sensed that the Southerners "feel as if they could not live very long in their present

---

56. *Emancipator*, February 10, 17, 24, March 3, 10, 17, 24, 1842; Theodore Weld to Angelina G. Weld, January 30, February 6, 1842, in Barnes and Dumond (eds.), *Weld-Grimké Letters*, I, 905, 911.

57. Joshua Leavitt to Roger Hooker Leavitt, February 9, 1842, Leavitt to mother, May 18, 1842, in Leavitt Papers; *Emancipator*, March 10, 1842; entry for July 20, 1842, in John Quincy Adams Diary.

condition." The dust had scarcely settled from the Adams trial when Joshua Giddings presented the "Creole" resolutions, which affirmed the right of slaves to rebel within territorial waters and condemned the federal government for fostering the slave trade. Slavery, Giddings argued, was an abridgment of natural rights and a local institution with which the federal government could have no connection. The House summarily censured Giddings for violating the prohibition on discussion of slavery. Far more vulnerable than Adams, he was not even given the chance to defend himself. He immediately resigned his seat, bade Leavitt and other friends farewell, and left for Ohio to seek reelection and vindication. Leavitt condemned the censure as "the greatest outrage on the cause of Liberty that has yet been committed," but he worried that the Whig establishment might well succeed in preventing Giddings's reelection. This would deal the insurgents a devastating blow, he told Giddings, to whom he frequently offered advice and encouragement; he also informed him that he would "greatly miss your society and help—but I hope only for a brief period."[58]

While awaiting the special election in Ohio, Leavitt clashed with some of the same southern representatives who had censured Giddings. For months he had caustically denounced House members in the columns of his paper, which he sent gratis to each congressman. An editorial that strongly implied that one-half of the members were overseers and the other half slaves was especially provocative, and Leavitt's rather lame explanation that he had merely said the southern members acted like overseers and Northerners should act like freemen did little to cool tempers. Representative John Minor Botts of Virginia obviously read the *Emancipator*, for he stood before the House, enraged, waving a copy of the paper in his hand. Leavitt, he shouted, should be banished from the House for making defamatory remarks. Leavitt maintained his composure and assiduously continued to take notes while Botts angrily pointed his finger at him.[59]

In the little drama that unfolded, Leavitt denied having "the smallest ambition for any degree of martyrdom." But, notwithstanding this disclaimer, he recognized the propaganda value that would accrue

58. Joshua Leavitt to editor, February 7, 1842, in Boston *Courier*, February 14, 1842; Stewart, *Joshua R. Giddings and the Tactics of Radical Politics*, 71–74; *Emancipator*, April 7, 1842; Joshua Leavitt to Joshua Giddings, April 4, 1842, Seth Gates to Joshua Giddings, April 2, 1842, in Giddings-Julian Papers.

59. *Emancipator*, May 5, 1842.

from his banishment. He not only predicted to his readers that his expulsion would bring him 1,000 new subscribers but also saw a glorious opportunity to further expose the slavocracy's dangerous encroachment on the rights of free people. "It is plain," he warned his readers, "that if they assume the right to expel a reporter from the desk and from the floor, because his representations do not suit them, they may also expel him from the gallery, and from the capital, and from the Federal District. . . . It is, in fact, the question whether a reporter shall be allowed to represent the conduct of members *as it is*, when the picture happens not to be creditable to the character or flattering to the pride of honorable members." None of this happened, for Botts ultimately did nothing. It was almost as if Leavitt had manufactured the entire episode to taunt and further humiliate the southern "bullies" following the Adams trial. He even managed to have the last word in the confrontation, stating with tongue in cheek that he no longer would send free copies of the *Emancipator* to Botts.[60]

Botts chose not to pursue his threat of expulsion in part because Giddings's overwhelming reelection victory and triumphant return to Washington dispirited Botts and other southern representatives. Giddings's triumph and Adams's vindication represented major turning points in the struggle to breach the wall of silence surrounding the slavery question in Congress. The gag rule remained in force, but it was now essentially a dead letter, and its repeal was virtually assured. The Whigs could no longer effectively make silence on slavery a test of party regularity. With the insurgent group beginning to serve as a rallying point for antislavery sentiment in the North, the party moved slowly toward a process of dissolution, which culminated in its collapse in the 1850s.

When Leavitt joined Adams and other antislavery Whigs in greeting Giddings on his return to Washington in early May, he felt a mixture of pride and disappointment. The Whig insurgents' refusal to abandon their party thoroughly disgusted him. "I am fully convinced," he complained bitterly to Birney, "that we must hold on until a new set of politicians have grown up, men not accustomed to yield to overseeism but always on the watch for the deceptions and overreaching and encroachments of the slave power. We shall get no members of Congress to join us—their attachment to proslavery parties is irresistible, a

60. *Ibid.*, May 12, 1842; also May 5, 1842.

thousand failures, a thousand kicks in the back do not weary them, but they cling firm to their oppressors with enduring fondness."[61]

Because he simply could not understand how anyone who professed to hate slavery could remain within what he considered a proslavery party, Leavitt summarily rejected the antislavery Whigs' contention that they could more effectively change the party from within than in a third party. In his frustration and anger Leavitt once again went on the attack, insinuating that William Slade and other Whig abolitionists supported slavery, or at least slaveholders. "He is among those," he editorialized, "who think that the best way to abolish slavery is to vote for it. If this is too strong, or the King's English, I will state it another way. William Slade goes for the Whig party, and the Whig party goes for Henry Clay, and Henry Clay goes for slavery. This is precisely the position of multitudes who call themselves abolitionists."[62] Thus, for all their common labors, their shared triumphs and joys, and their growing sense of camaraderie, Leavitt and the antislavery Whig congressmen remained quite far apart on the matter of political means to destroy slavery. Yet he could also justifiably take pride in his role in recent developments. Through a blend of dogged determination, principled action, criticism, and encouragement, he had gained the respect of the antislavery Whigs and helped to move them toward unified action in defiance of their party's leaders.

Leavitt's work continued, however, during this long and eventful session of Congress. Even though he had seen his family for only two or three weeks during the previous seven months, he decided to remain in Washington into the summer to present his *Memorial on the Tariff* to Congress. While reporting on Congress during the winter and spring of 1842, he had spoken to a number of leading Democrats and Whigs on the tariff issue, and they at times had solicited his views on the subject. With the assistance of Senator Benjamin Tappan of Ohio, a Democrat and brother of Lewis and Arthur, his memorial was referred to the Senate Committee on Agriculture. Leavitt testified before that committee several times to explain the contents and purpose of his 150-page manuscript. His reputation as an abolitionist seems to have had little bearing on the memorial's reception; even he believed

61. Joshua Leavitt to James Birney, June 19, 1842, in Dumond (ed.), *Birney Letters*, I, 699.

62. *Emancipator*, October 6, 1842.

that he was treated with "much politeness." This may have been so because he did not attack southern interests but rather argued in the name of American prosperity and criticized British tariff policies as they affected the United States. The only objection to the printing of the memorial came from a senator who believed that it offered little new evidence of the need for repeal of the Corn Laws and would be too expensive to print.[63]

In his memorial Leavitt insisted that a tariff for revenue only, which would take into account the greater bulk and higher freight costs of American grains, as opposed to British finished products, should replace protectionism. In addition, he reiterated his earlier arguments concerning the Corn Laws' damaging effects on British industry and northern agriculture. But he now clearly exhibited his democratic sympathies in appealing directly to the social conscience of his readers. Above all, he attacked the British political system for excluding from the political process the working class and the poor, who he believed suffered most as a result of the artificially high price of bread created by the Corn Laws. He therefore urged the British to pursue the twin goals of political suffrage and repeal in the name of democracy and prosperity. "It is at least not inconsistent with decorum," he declared, "for republicans to desire that the period may be hastened, as rapidly as is consistent with the state of things, when so great an advancement of popular rights may be peacefully established in that kingdom. But whatever may be the result in regard to suffrage, your memorialist believes that this movement will hasten the repeal of the corn laws, as a matter of policy on the part of the landowners, to pacify discontent by concession, when other means have failed. The two agitations will move on in harmony."[64]

Although Leavitt's attempts to mobilize American public opinion behind the repeal movement provided valuable moral support for the British Anti-Corn Law League, his drive for tariff reform for the benefit of northern agricultural interests met an uncertain fate in the 1840s. If anything, the position occupied by cotton in American trade became more entrenched as new lands were opened for cultivation and wheat

63. *Memorial of Joshua Leavitt, Praying That, in the Revision of the Tariff Laws, the Principle of Discrimination May be Inserted in Favor of Those Countries in Which American Grain, Flour, and Salted Meat, Are Admitted Duty Free, Senate Documents*, 27th Cong., 2nd Sess., No. 339, pp. 117–24; *Emancipator*, July 7, 1842.

64. *Memorial on the Tarriff*, 83; also 7–11, 44–45, 83, 88.

prices in England declined in the early 1840s. In fact, the Whigs raised tariff rates in 1842, and in later years Democratic administrations lowered rates primarily to assist southern cotton producers. Only in the 1860s did American wheat begin to flood British markets on a scale envisioned by Leavitt and other antislavery free traders.[65]

As Leavitt prepared to return home in July 1842, he could look back on the past several months with some satisfaction. Both the triumphs of the antislavery insurgents and the publication of his memorial seemed to bode well for the Liberty party by further exposing the true nature of the Whig party and by creating a rallying point for those who wished to advance northern economic interests. Yet there was little time for celebration. Already Liberty men differed on the basic questions of what the party stood for and where it should move.

65. Thistlethwaite, *America and the Atlantic Community*, 164.

10

THE EXPANDING SCOPE
OF POLITICAL ABOLITIONISM

Following an absence of eight months from Sarah and the boys, Leavitt hoped to return to Bloomfield and spend a few weeks relaxing with his family. He thoroughly enjoyed his stay at home, finding it "so pleasant that I shall not be ready to leave it until imperiously called away." There, he doted on his four youngest boys—Thomas, James, Samuel, and Joshua, ranging in age from fourteen to two—used his scythe and hoe to "make havoc among the weeds and bushes that have encroached upon my premises during my absence," visited his friend Weld, and, with Sarah, held antislavery prayer meetings at their home, as they had for the past six years. But he had scarcely become settled at home when his editorial chores and his responsibilities as corresponding secretary of the Massachusetts Abolition Society called him to Boston in August 1842.[1]

During much of the next several months, he threw himself into the political campaign, feverishly organizing the party at the local and state levels and speaking before the party faithful in the Northeast. He had agreed to attend several Liberty conventions and speak in a number of towns in Maine in late August. Traveling by coach through Maine with Alvan Stewart, he admired the "flourishing farms, decorated with buildings and comforts to which nine-tenths of the lordly planters of the South were utter strangers." These were his kind of people—"as true Yankees as ever whittled a shingle." Not surpris-

1. Joshua Leavitt to Joshua Giddings, July 27, 1842, in Giddings Papers.

ingly, after lecturing in churches and meetinghouses in Somerset, Portland, and several other Maine towns, he returned to Boston convinced that the state would lead the way to abolition.[2]

Leavitt devoted much of his attention to the Liberty campaign in Massachusetts. As a leading member of the state Liberty Committee, he helped to plan a series of county nominating conventions throughout the state. With Henry B. Stanton and other party leaders, he attended many of these conventions, serving on committees and delivering speeches. From early September until late October he was on the road much of the time, speaking in all corners of the state, from Fall River to Charlemont, where he witnessed the nomination of his brother Roger Hooker for the state senate. He implored his listeners to organize the party at the grass-roots level. Slavery, he repeatedly argued, would be destroyed only if its members adopted the tactics of their political opponents and formed local committees, visited their neighbors at their homes and in small social gatherings, and systematically distributed party literature.[3]

During the campaign he bought a house in Cambridgeport, a small town located a few miles from Boston. Sarah and the boys soon moved up from New Jersey. Now reunited with his family following another lengthy separation, Leavitt dreaded the thought of returning to his post in Washington, complaining to his readers that "I have seen enough, and I have a home, as pleasant and dear as others, where I should love to stay." As usual, however, once December arrived and his friends raised enough money to sustain him while in Washington, he heeded the call to duty.[4]

Joshua Giddings, Seth Gates, and William Slade were waiting to welcome him to Mrs. Sprigg's boardinghouse. Twenty-four boarders now lived at the house, several of them abolitionists; the others, according to Weld, who arrived in late December for a five-week stay, were "favorably inclined." Weld and other boarders seemed protective of Mrs. Sprigg's interests, fearing that the house's reputation as the "Abolition house" would hurt her business. But in fact during the 1842–1843 session it was the only one in town filled to capacity.

2. *Emancipator*, September 1, 8, 1842.
3. See *ibid.*, September 29, October 6, 13, 20, 27, December 8, 1842.
4. *Ibid.*, December 1, 1842; Joshua Leavitt to Roger Hooker Leavitt, December 12, 17, 1842, in Leavitt Papers; Joshua Leavitt to James Birney, February 19, 1843, in Dumond (ed.), *Birney Letters*, II, 716.

The only major change from the previous year at Mrs. Sprigg's was that the slaves who worked there had run away, to be replaced by free black servants. The discussions among the boarders were intense but generally friendly, with Weld noting at one point that Leavitt and Giddings were seated on either side of him, "both battling a point with all their lungs."[5]

Even though the 1842–1843 session of Congress witnessed no *cause célèbre* such as the Adams and Giddings trials, Leavitt remained in Washington for the entire session to monitor Congress' disturbing move toward the annexation of Texas. As early as 1837 abolitionists had sounded the alarm on Texas annexation. This crisis had passed when President Van Buren rejected the request by Texas for annexation; it did not emerge again until President Tyler, a southern slaveholder who hoped to use the annexation issue as a means of gaining political support outside the Whig party, began to make moves in that direction. Alarmed by these developments, Leavitt held a series of strategy meetings with Gates and Adams in 1841. He arrived in Washington in December 1842, convinced that the goal of annexation "will never be abandoned, until the leading politicians of the South abandon slavery itself."[6]

A few weeks later Adams, Gates, Giddings, Slade, and the other antislavery Whig congressmen set forth a strongly worded joint statement, which warned that Texas annexation would constitute such a flagrant violation of the national compact as to lead the North to dissolve the Union. At the same time that he urged his friends in Congress to resist any move toward annexation, Leavitt also joined Lewis Tappan and other abolitionists in asking their friends in the British and Foreign Anti-Slavery Society to exert pressure on the British government to recognize the independence of Texas and to provide substantial loans to the infant Texas Republic on the condition that it abolish slavery.[7]

Leavitt's desire to impress upon the English public and government

5. Theodore Weld to Angelina G. Weld, December 27, 1842, in Barnes and Dumond (eds.), *Weld-Grimké Letters*, II, 947; Joshua Giddings to Laura Waters Giddings, January 1, 1843, in Giddings Papers.

6. *Emancipator*, February 9, 1843; see also December 24, 1841.

7. *Emancipator*, May 18, 1843; Madeleine Stern, "Stephen Pearl Andrews, Abolitionist, and the Annexation of Texas," *Southwestern Historical Quarterly*, LXVI (April, 1964), 491–523.

the importance of the Texas issue underlay his decision to attend Joseph Sturge's second World Anti-Slavery Convention in June 1843. The Massachusetts Abolition Society chose Leavitt to represent it, but because the society provided no funds he had to scramble until the last minute for the $500 required to cover his expenses. Lewis Tappan's generosity ultimately made it possible for Leavitt to go to England. Tappan still believed, as he informed Gamaliel Bailey, that "Br. Leavitt's *manner* is sometimes arrogant, and his temper hasty," and he continued to differ with him "on some points of policy," especially third-party politics. Yet he considered Leavitt a friend and thought his attendance at the World Anti-Slavery Convention to be "a matter of great importance to the anti-slavery cause in this country and throughout the world." Indeed, he even praised Leavitt for having served the Liberty party "so ably." Thus, he gave Leavitt $100 for the trip—an act that stands somewhat in contrast to Gerrit Smith's continued efforts to collect the debt Leavitt owed him from 1837.[8] Leavitt respected Smith for his warmth, his dependability, and his sacrifices for the cause, but he never felt as close to him as he did to Tappan, Weld, and other members of the old inner circle of stewards.

With sufficient funds in hand and Elizur Wright installed as interim editor of the *Emancipator* in May, Leavitt bade farewell to his family and friends and boarded the steamer *Hibernia* bound for Liverpool. He arrived in England at a time when Anglo-American relations were strained. The Texas issue had produced friction between Great Britain, which had abolished slavery in the empire, and the Tyler administration, which was committed to annexation and the protection of slavery in the Texas Republic. Moreover, groups in both countries had become increasingly critical of the other nation's trade barriers. Several provisions of the Webster-Ashburton Treaty of 1842, including those relating to the extradition of American fugitive slaves, also remained unresolved. Finally, the repudiation of debts by several American states had angered the British business community. Eager to strengthen the ties of friendship with British reformers such as John

8. Joshua Leavitt to John Scoble, July 22, 1841, January 29, 1843, in Abel and Klingberg (eds.), *Side-light on Anglo-American Relations*, 97n, 110; Lewis Tappan to Joshua Leavitt, March 28, May 3, 1843, Lewis Tappan to Gamaliel Bailey, March 6, 20, 1843, in Tappan Papers; Joshua Leavitt to John G. Whittier, April 21, 1843, in Whittier Papers; Joshua Leavitt to Gerrit Smith, April 1, 1843, in Smith Miller Collection.

Scoble, Joseph Sturge, Richard Cobden, and John Bright, Leavitt especially looked forward to the antislavery convention, which he hoped would "exert an effective influence upon the destiny of mankind, in regard to Liberty and Slavery."[9]

On June 13 he joined 400 delegates—including Amos Phelps, Tappan, the Reverend James Pennington, a black minister from Hartford, and several other American abolitionists—at the convention held in Freemason's Hall in London. The convention, which met in lengthy daily sessions for ten days, proceeded smoothly under the leadership of Sturge and Scoble, with the cream of the British reform galaxy in attendance and the spirit, if not the physical presence, of the aging Thomas Clarkson to provide inspiration and a link with the early years of the British antislavery movement.[10]

Leavitt quickly emerged as one of the leading American voices at the convention, chairing one of the sessions and speaking at length on a broad range of issues. Introducing himself to the assemblage—not immodestly—as "a sort of sentinel on the walls, carrying my firelock over my shoulder, and watching to see what were the signs of the times," he castigated the American government for its racist and proslavery policies. One of his targets was the government's "war of extermination" against the Seminoles in Florida, which he believed it pursued for the benefit of the Slave Power. To underscore his point, he persuaded a British acquaintance to bring the son of a Seminole chief before the packed convention. This dramatic gesture had the desired effect: the boy, dressed in his native garb, standing majestically before the convention with his arms crossed, while Leavitt read extracts from Giddings's "Creole" speech to thunderous applause.[11]

Leavitt and the other American delegates came to England determined above all to arouse British abolitionists to action on the Texas issue. They repeatedly warned that the South desired annexation and urged the British to grant a loan to Texas on the condition that it abolish slavery. In a speech before the convention Leavitt declared: "The annexation of Texas to the United States is deemed by us to be the *articulum stantis vel cadentis*; it is that by which slavery is to stand

9. *Emancipator*, May 18, 1843.
10. *British and Foreign Anti-Slavery Reporter*, June 14, 1843.
11. *Proceedings of the General Anti-Slavery Convention in London, 1843* (London, 1843), 28, 62, 121, 322; *Emancipator*, July 27, 1843.

or fall in our country. . . . I know the slaveholders; I know their necessities; I know their desperation; I know that if by any means they can obtain Texas, they will do it." The convention's response to their impassioned speeches, however, was vague and noncommittal. It merely called upon the British government to use its influence to achieve abolition in Texas, without specifying the means to be employed. Although Leavitt himself seriously doubted whether the British government would spend any money to persuade Texans to outlaw slavery, following the convention's adjournment he, Stephen Pearl Andrews, and George Stacey, a British abolitionist, persisted in their attempts to pressure the British to inject themselves into the Texas situation. In an interview with Lords Brougham and Morpeth, both members of the House of Lords, they succeeded only in extracting an assurance that the British government wished to see Mexico allow Texas to be independent in return for abolishing slavery. This was a slim reed to hang on to. Indeed, in pursuing the Texas question so diligently, American and British abolitionists may inadvertently have strengthened the hand of the Tyler administration on the annexation issue. Duff Green, who was then in London to negotiate a reciprocal lowering of the tariff, duly reported to the administration the existence of a British plot to prevent annexation and free the slaves in Texas—thereby increasing the sense of urgency felt by pro-annexationists. While there is little evidence of an official British plot, those who supported annexation used this argument effectively in the debates on this issue.[12]

Abolitionists achieved more success in their efforts to elicit assurances from British officials concerning the enforcement of Article X of the Webster-Ashburton Treaty, in which both nations agreed to extradite persons charged with crimes. Both American and British abolitionists feared that this clause might be used by the United States to demand the return of fugitive slaves who had escaped to Canada. In two interviews with Charles Buller and Vernon Smith, both members of Parliament, Leavitt, Scoble, and Stacey received assurances that various protections against fraud in extradition demands would be inserted in the treaty. These efforts were rewarded in the fall of 1843, when British officials in Nassau refused to hand over to the American government seven slaves who had escaped from Florida, thus ensuring

12. *Proceedings of 1843 General Anti-Slavery Convention*, 302–303; see Frederick Merk, *Slavery and the Annexation of Texas* (New York, 1972), 11–13, 73, 221–22.

that British territory would continue to be a haven for American fugitive slaves.[13]

Following the World Anti-Slavery Convention, Leavitt received so many invitations to address reform meetings that he postponed his departure for America until early August. But he did not devote all of his time to reform business; during July, he found time to visit Oxford University, Windsor Castle, and other requisite historical sites for tourists. Often traveling in the company of Sturge and Cobden, he confessed to having "a glorious time." One of the high points of his travels was a social visit in the company of Tappan with Thomas Clarkson, the patriarch of the British antislavery movement, at his home, Playford Hall. Here, he spent a "most delightful and instructive" evening with the old man, whom he found feeble but with a keen mind and an awe-inspiring presence.[14] He devoted much of his time, however, to attending numerous reform gatherings—including the annual meeting of the British and Foreign Anti-Slavery Society; a mass peace convention held at Freemason's Hall, which proposed the establishment of a Court of Nations and a mechanism for the arbitration of international treaties; and a temperance and peace festival at Hartwell Park, the residence of the Honorable John Lee, a prominent jurist, where he represented American abolitionists.[15]

Leavitt was duly impressed by the majestic splendor of Lee's mansion and the homes of other members of the British aristocracy, describing many of them in detail to his readers. But in his travels through England he frequently noted the "sad contrast" between the wealth and splendor of the nobility and comfort and refinement of the middle class, and the misery and squalor that characterized the lives of the poor and the working class. He came to Britain as a self-proclaimed "spokesman for humanity" and democratic principles, determined to "exercise a manly and conscientious freedom" in speaking out on controversial issues, including popular suffrage.[16]

13. British and Foreign Anti-Slavery Society, *Minute Books*, II, 90; *Emancipator*, July 27, 1843. On the British abolitionists and the American fugitive slave issue, see David M. Turley, "'Free Air' and Fugitive Slaves: British Abolitionists Versus Government over American Fugitives," in Bolt and Drescher (eds.), *Antislavery, Religion, and Reform*, 163–82.

14. Joshua Leavitt to Amos A. Phelps, July 4, 1843, in Phelps Papers; *Emancipator*, August 10, 31, 1843; entry for July 11–12, 1843, in Tappan Journal.

15. *Emancipator*, August 10, 31, 1843.

16. *Ibid.*, September 28, 1843.

At a soirée sponsored by the Complete Suffrage Union, headed by Joseph Sturge, whom he had come to know during Sturge's visit to America in 1841, Leavitt praised the Chartist cause, a working-class movement that called for universal manhood suffrage, annual Parliaments, equal electoral districts, vote by ballot, and other reforms. Convinced that the Chartists wanted no more than the political rights that most American males already enjoyed, he declared the movement worthy of support. His endorsement of the Chartists' goals disturbed some of his English friends, whom he identified as people "who dread the suffrage movement as much as the abolitionist movement is dreaded in America." These men—probably Anti-Corn Law Leaguers who remained hostile toward the workers—"expressed some regret" that he "should thus publicly identify" himself with the Chartists, not because he was a foreigner but because they disliked the movement. Yet, as Betty Fladeland has argued, many British abolitionists and free traders such as Sturge applauded Leavitt's endorsement of Chartism. Even the more conservative Richard Cobden had come to favor an extended franchise and hoped that the middle class would support free suffrage, while the workers, in turn, would assist in repealing the Corn Laws.[17]

Several scholars, however, have emphasized the differences that separated many British middle-class reformers from the Chartists. British abolitionists, like their American counterparts, according to these historians, tended to view slaves as far more oppressed than workers. Moreover, many manufacturers involved in the Anti-Corn Law League favored cheap labor, opposed factory reforms and trade unions, and feared the masses. Even Sturge, who attempted against great odds to reconcile the classes, sought to work with a selected group of workers.[18] Leavitt stood with Sturge, who adopted the most radical stance taken by British middle-class reformers. But Leavitt,

17. *Ibid.*, August 10, September 28, 1843; Betty Fladeland, "'Our Cause being One and the Same': Abolitionists and Chartism," in James Walvin (ed.), *Slavery and British Society 1776–1846* (Baton Rouge, 1982), 69–70, 80–92.

18. See Dorothy Thompson, *The Chartists, Popular Politics in the Industrial Revolution* (New York, 1984), 237–40, 251–53, 274–75; Edward Royle and James Walvin, *English Radicals and Reformers, 1760–1848* (Brighton, England, 1982), 175–77; Patricia Hollis, "Anti-Slavery and British Working-Class Radicalism in the Years of Reform," in Bolt and Drescher (eds.), *Antislavery, Religion, and Reform*, 294–315; Donald Read, *Cobden and Bright: A Victorian Political Partnership* (New York, 1968), 29–38.

too, gave somewhat qualified support to the Chartists. He would continue to embrace Chartism, he told his English audiences, so long as the movement remained sufficiently Christian in its orientation.[19]

For most Anti-Corn Law Leaguers, repeal remained the all-important issue. They tended to see society as divided between the landlords and the people, whereas the Chartists emphasized the struggle between capital and labor. For his part Leavitt gave little attention to the relationship between the workers' low wages and their hunger and misery. Rather, he, like Cobden, often argued that the high cost and limited supply of bread was largely responsible for the workers' plight. His explanation for the workers' problems was shaped in part by the fact that he viewed himself more as a crusader for free trade than for political democracy. Perhaps more important, he was first and foremost an abolitionist and therefore grimly determined to see the landed aristocracy and American slaveholders acting in collusion to the detriment of British workers. As he told a meeting honoring John Bright, a supporter of both suffrage and repeal with whom Leavitt traveled during much of his stay in England, these rapacious interests refused to listen to the cries of the poor "but stuff your mouths with cotton, and then give you for your starving children what the sailor calls 'a little more baccy.'"[20]

Although simplistic and strained, this conspiracy theory appealed to many Leaguers and Chartists and—in light of the Tyler administration's attempts to persuade the British government to lower duties on cotton and tobacco—contained an element of truth. Moreover, what little Leavitt saw of poverty in London and other cities shocked him and evoked a genuine sympathy. He overstated the case in asserting that no reform would truly aid the masses until universal manhood suffrage became a reality, but he did discern that policies promulgated by the privileged classes had an important bearing on the conditions that afflicted the lower classes and that political rights might generate stronger pressures for social and economic reforms. Leavitt may also be faulted for showing more sympathy for the poor of Britain than of America. Notwithstanding his inability to understand the problems confronting growing numbers of American workers, the fact remains

19. *Emancipator*, August 31, September 28, 1843.
20. *Ibid.*, August 10, 1843; Royle and Walvin, *English Radicals and Reformers*, 175–77.

206

that the Industrial Revolution had carried much further, class lines were more sharply drawn, and political rights more limited in Britain than in America.[21]

All too soon it was time to depart for home. Although reluctant to leave his English friends, Leavitt had been away from his family and his paper for nearly three months and wished to get back into the thick of Liberty politics. Following a pleasant voyage of twelve days, he arrived in Boston, thankful to be once more in his "sweet, sweet home" with his family.[22]

Two weeks after his arrival, the Liberty party held its national nominating convention in Buffalo. This convention—which Leavitt chose not to attend in order to remain with his family and to oversee the *Emancipator*—was an important event in the history of the party. During the past three years, a party infrastructure had developed, with several newspapers, local and state party committees, and a growing body of party literature to inform and mobilize the faithful. This had helped to attract many Whigs and a few Democrats into the Liberty ranks.[23]

Yet, notwithstanding its growing vote totals, the Liberty party remained a small third party able to influence the outcome of only a few state and local elections. This fact convinced some Liberty men—especially Salmon P. Chase, Samuel Lewis, and Gamaliel Bailey of Ohio—that James Birney was neither popular nor experienced enough to attract broad support and that the party's dogmatic stance on immediate emancipation would prevent it from ever achieving electoral success. Thus, they began to lecture Easterners in the party on the problems inherent in attempts to distinguish clearly between moral and political goals. They also urged that the party nominate William Jay, John Quincy Adams, or William Seward and adopt a platform that emphasized objectives that could be achieved politically—i.e., the denationalization of slavery and condemnation of the Slave Power. Gerrit Smith and Henry B. Stanton also cast about briefly for a more acceptable candidate than Birney, but the Ohio Liberty men were most

21. *Emancipator*, August 10, 17, 1843.

22. *Ibid.*, August 24, 1843.

23. See *ibid.*, August 10, 1843; Ray M. Shortridge, "Voting for Minor Parties in the Antebellum Midwest," *Indiana Magazine of History*, LXXIV (June, 1978), 124–26; Benjamin Quarles, *Black Abolitionists* (New York, 1969), 183–85.

persistent and outspoken in their demands. Their machinations inevitably infuriated those within the party who rejected any thought of watering down principles for electoral gain.[24]

Leavitt, like Chase, Bailey, and Lewis, disagreed with Birney's pessimistic pronouncements concerning the future of America and the state of democracy. Since 1842 Birney, who was aristocratic in his upbringing and increasingly dubious of the people's ability to utilize their political rights wisely, had urged that immigrants not be permitted to vote immediately and that those who violated others' civil liberties forfeit their elective franchise. Leavitt sympathized with Birney's assessment of the iniquities of the past, but he shared neither Birney's concerns about the "ultrademocratic tendencies" of the Liberty party nor his "strong apprehensions respecting the impracticability of a popular government, nor respecting the reformability of our own."[25]

Leavitt, however, admired Birney as a person, respected his counsel on many matters, and believed that the 1841 nominations should stand. Anyway, he argued, Seward was too ambitious, Adams too old, and Jay too hostile toward the Liberty party to accept its nomination. The Ohio group's apparent desire to disavow the abolitionist label and have Liberty men "buy up some old political trash on whom to throw away our votes" in order to "prove that we care more for office than we do for principle" deeply disturbed him. But for all his protests Leavitt was not entirely consistent in demanding that only Liberty men be supported for office. At times, personal feelings and practical considerations prevailed. In 1842, for example, he had supported John Quincy Adams's candidacy for the House. In response to a reader's complaint that this was tantamount to supporting Henry Clay and opposing abolition in the District of Columbia—charges that Leavitt had often hurled at antislavery Whigs—he explained that Adams ran unopposed and that his great services to the cause of freedom over-

24. See Salmon P. Chase to James Birney, January 21, 1842, Gamaliel Bailey to James Birney, March 31, 1843, in Dumond (ed.), *Birney Letters*, II, 661–62, 726–27; Salmon P. Chase to Lewis Tappan, May 26, September 15, 24, February 15, 1843, in Chase Papers, LC; Salmon P. Chase to Gerrit Smith, May 14, 1842, in Smith Miller Collection; Stanley Harrold, *Gamaliel Bailey and Antislavery Union* (Kent, Ohio, 1986), 57–69.

25. James Birney to Joshua Leavitt *et al.*, January 10, 1842, Joshua Leavitt to James Birney, January 18, 1842, James Birney to Gamaliel Bailey, April 16, 1843, Joshua Leavitt to James Birney, February 14, 1842, in Dumond (ed.), *Birney Letters*, II, 645–46, 733–34, 674.

shadowed his inconsistency. Yet he in fact allowed his personal feelings for Adams to stand in the way of urging that a Liberty man contest Adams in his district. In addition, when some Massachusetts Liberty legislators ultimately supported an antislavery Whig for speaker of the deadlocked Massachusetts lower house in 1843, he supported the action on the questionable grounds that it was acceptable in an internal legislative election if a party member was not available.[26]

These inconsistencies did not temper Leavitt's anger toward the Ohio Liberty men, for he believed that they had indiscriminately shopped for the most available candidate. He directed much of his rage toward Chase, an ambitious and pragmatic Cincinnati lawyer whom he viewed as "a raw recruit . . . much impressed with the idea that there is very little practical wisdom among those who raised the Liberty standard while he was worshipping the Log Cabin." In the midst of this confrontation Lewis Tappan cautioned Gamaliel Bailey that Leavitt had "a very good opinion of himself, and does not like to be put in the wrong." He knew Leavitt well—once challenged, Leavitt was determined to stand his ground, come what may. When Birney considered resigning his nomination in early 1843, Leavitt stated defiantly: "They have treated us with entire disregard, approaching to insolence, and I am not in favor of yielding a hair's breadth to such bald dictation."[27]

Until well into 1843 Leavitt continued to lecture Chase, Bailey, and Lewis in private correspondence on "decency in political movements" and to warn them that their efforts could well bring "irreparable calamity" to the cause. Leavitt ultimately had his way, though his attempt to take credit for the outcome was somewhat misplaced. In fact, neither Seward, nor Adams, nor Jay desired the nomination, and the Ohio faction eventually realized that success in replacing Birney might thoroughly divide the party. By early 1843, only the date of a new Liberty national convention remained unresolved. Throughout 1842 Leavitt had opposed holding such a convention, fearing that it might dump Birney's candidacy. But once he concluded that no formidable challenge to Birney would materialize, he endorsed the call for the

26. Joshua Leavitt to James Birney, February 19, 1843, *ibid.*, II, 714–16; *Emancipator*, September 29, 1842, February 2, 16, 23, 1843.

27. Leavitt to Birney, February 14, 19, 1842, in Dumond (ed.), *Birney Letters*, II, 673, 714; Tappan to Bailey, March 20, 1843, in Tappan Papers.

nominating convention and advised Birney, in a calculating manner, to open the nominating process so as not to appear to take the outcome for granted.[28]

The convention held in Buffalo in late August 1843 nominated Birney and Ohio Senator Thomas Morris, who earlier in the year had resigned his nomination for vice-president in the face of criticism from Bailey and others. The Morris situation created a serious dilemma for Leavitt. Although Bailey's allegations that Morris had opposed suffrage for free blacks troubled him, he conceded to Birney that he would have supported Morris "zealously, because I respect him and believe him honest, and because he took a bold stand in the Senate, and I would like to see him preside there." He also, of course, placed great stock in the fact that Morris was a Democrat. Yet, in the final analysis, his continuing struggle with the Ohio Liberty leaders, more than his admiration for Morris, seems to have influenced his reaction to Bailey, whom he believed was seeking to sabotage the 1841 nominations that he had worked so hard to achieve. This tended to distract him from the fact that Morris had opposed black suffrage in the 1830s.[29]

Many Liberty men continued to condemn racial prejudice. Leavitt, for example, editorialized in 1844: "All prejudice is injurious to its votary as well as its victim; but the habitual indignity and ill treatment to which persons wholly or partially, of African descent, are subjected in this country, is so flagrantly inconsistent with our political axioms and our religious faith, that persistence in it would seem not merely a gross wrong but a shameful hypocrisy." Many northern blacks recognized that the Liberty party was the only party that supported their interests, and consequently voted for its candidates. Yet the fact that white Liberty leaders such as Leavitt seemed to attach more importance to Morris's opposition to slavery than to his racial views did not bode well for the party's concern for racial equality in the years ahead.[30]

28. Joshua Leavitt to Salmon P. Chase, February 16, 1843, in Chase Papers, HSP; Joshua Leavitt to Charles H. Stewart, February 9, 1843, Leavitt to Birney, February 19, 28, 1843, James Birney to Joshua Leavitt, August 17, 1843, in Dumond (ed.), *Birney Letters*, II, 715, 718–19, 754, 756, 758; *Emancipator*, March 23, 1843.

29. *Emancipator*, September 7, 1843; Leavitt to Birney, February 19, 1843, in Dumond (ed.), *Birney Letters*, II, 714–15; Leavitt to Whittier, April 21, 1843, in Whittier Papers.

30. *Morning Chronicle*, April 1, 1844; *Minutes of the National Convention of Ne-*

Chase greeted Birney's nomination rather coldly, informing Tappan, "So the thing is as it is and we must make the best of it." But most Liberty leaders responded favorably. Leavitt naturally viewed it as a vindication of his stand during the past eighteen months. The convention, he exulted, was "highly honorable to our cause, and full of hope for the future." During the fall campaign, in which he delivered several speeches in Massachusetts, the party increased its vote total to approximately 60,000.[31]

Soon after the 1843 elections, Leavitt again had to depart for Washington. He had increasingly come to dread the lengthy separations from his family which the Washington vigil entailed; this time he went so far as to attempt to convince another man to replace him. Failing this, he left hurriedly for the nation's capital in early December. Upon moving into his old room at Mrs. Sprigg's boardinghouse, it became apparent that the ranks of the old insurgency group were depleted. William Slade had retired earlier in the year, as had Seth Gates, who soon joined the Liberty party. Despite his earlier confrontations with Leavitt, Gates confided to Giddings how much he missed discussing important matters with Leavitt, "that most inveterate upandicular Liberty party man, with his iron pen, invincible zeal and indomitable labors, who is after all partly by nature and partly from circumstances the safest and strongest Liberty party man in America." Nor was Weld there, despite repeated efforts by Leavitt, Tappan, and Giddings to convince him to leave his New Jersey farm. Adams continued to stand outside the insurgency group. This left Giddings as the only member of the original group; his continued attachment to the Whig party helps to explain Giddings's feeling that Leavitt did not appear "as friendly and social as formerly."[32]

Leavitt's foul mood was in part due to the fact that he came to Washington extremely short of funds. As the only representative of the

---

gro Citizens held at Buffalo, on the 15th, 16th, 17th, 18th, and 19th of August, 1843, for the purpose of considering their moral and political conditions as American citizens (New York, 1843), 28.

31. Salmon P. Chase to Lewis Tappan, September 12, 1843, in Chase Papers, LC; *Emancipator*, September 7, 1843; Joshua Leavitt to John Scoble, September 1, 1843, Joshua Leavitt to John Beaumont, November 15, 1843, in Abel and Klingberg (eds.), *Side-light on Anglo-American Relations*, 144, 157.

32. *Emancipator*, December 14, 1843; Seth Gates to Joshua Giddings, December 6, 1843, Joshua Giddings to Laura Waters Giddings, December 10, 1843, in Giddings Papers.

abolitionist press in Washington for the fourth consecutive year, he also felt weighed down by onerous responsibilities. Many abolitionists, including those with whom he had clashed over the years, greatly appreciated his contributions to the cause. For example, despite his differences with Leavitt, Bailey declared that Leavitt had "done more to expose the aggressions of the Slave Power, the evil influence of slavery upon the welfare of the nation, and servility of the political parties, than any other single person." Lewis Tappan, who considered Leavitt "the watchman at headquarters," once again generously offered to pay many of his expenses and to hire an assistant for Leavitt to enable him to devote more attention to lobbying members of Congress. "Just write me what is needed," he stated, "to enable you to carry on the *Emancipator* and do the needful at W[ashington] this winter, and the expense, and I will try to raise the money." [33]

Despite Tappan's efforts, the money raised permitted Leavitt to remain in Washington for only two months. Even if additional funds had been forthcoming, he might not have stayed through the session, for he wished to return to his family, no action was expected on the Texas issue, and, perhaps more important, he was eager to launch a daily paper as soon as possible. Thus, he departed for home one month before Congress adjourned. For several months he, Stanton, Elizur Wright, and John Alden had discussed the possibility of establishing a daily paper that would include news of the antislavery cause and other reforms, as well as commercial information for the business community. Despite the presence of several well-established commercial newspapers in Boston and the precarious financial position of the *Emancipator*, in late March Leavitt, hoping to expand his readership among those connected with the mercantile community and bring in much-needed revenue, established the *Morning Chronicle*. With extremely hard work and long hours at the office, their own printing office and press, two columns of articles contributed each week by Wright, and teetotal employees who worked for low wages, Leavitt and his associates made the paper a paying proposition by the summer of 1844. The task of editing both a daily and a weekly paper was exhausting. "Well, by the time the morning mails are disposed of," he wrote to Birney, "along comes the noon mails, and the clamor for

33. *Philanthropist*, November 15, 1843; Lewis Tappan to Joshua Leavitt, December 29, 1843, January 9, 16, 1844, in Tappan Papers.

copy grows louder, and as evening draws on, more mails come in, and every thing portends a crisis at hand, to wit, the closing of the account on which the character and standing of the *Morning Chronicle* is to be determined for tomorrow. The history of one day is the history of all days, with the exception only, that about half of them are seriously burdened with calls of company, from Mr. Adams down."[34]

While some of the news pieces and editorials in the *Emancipator* also appeared in the columns of the *Morning Chronicle*, the daily paper focused largely on matters of interest to the commercial classes. The cause of free trade, which Leavitt hoped would help to free northern merchants from the influence of the slaveholders, received considerable attention. He also strongly espoused the cause of cheap postage, calling for the adoption of the British postal reforms, which in 1840, as a result of Rowland Hill's efforts, had drastically lowered rates in order to increase volume and revenue.[35]

The American postal system desperately needed reform. In contrast to the reformed British system, in which a half-ounce letter cost two American cents to send, in the United States rates ranged from six cents for three sheets sent less than 30 miles to twenty-five cents for a letter sent more than 400 miles. These high rates produced declining per capita revenue and large annual deficits in the system. Consequently, by the time Hill's writings and Leavitt's correspondence with Cobden and other British cheap postage advocates had converted him to the cause, pressures for reform of the American system had already begun to mount.[36]

Convinced that cheap postage was a worthy cause that would advance the welfare of all Americans, Leavitt threw himself into the crusade with his usual vigor. If the principle of free trade were applied to

34. Joshua Leavitt to Joseph Soul, January 12, 1844, in Abel and Klingberg (eds.), *Side-Light on Anglo-American Relations*, 168–69; *Emancipator*, December 21, 1843, January 25, February 29, June 12, 1844; Elizur Wright to Salmon P. Chase, February 3, 1844, Henry B. Stanton to Salmon P. Chase, February 6, 1844, in Chase Papers, LC; Joshua Leavitt to Roger Hooker Leavitt, July 13, 1844, in Leavitt Papers; Joshua Leavitt to James Birney, September 11, 1844, in Dumond (ed.), *Birney Letters*, II, 839.

35. *Morning Chronicle*, March 22, 1844; Joshua Leavitt, "Post-Office Reform," *New Englander*, VI (January, 1848), 113–14; "The British System of Postage," *New Englander*, VI (April, 1848), 154–65.

36. Daniel C. Roper, *The United States Post Office: Its Past Record, Present Condition, and the Potential Relation to the New World Era* (New York, 1917), 60–62; Read, *Cobden and Bright*, 19.

American and English letters, newspapers, pamphlets, and books, he argued, the free exchange of ideas within each society and across the Atlantic would strengthen the forces of reform, enhance moral progress, and lead to the intellectual and material enrichment of both nations. By the mid-1840s, Leavitt was recognized as one of the leading American advocates of cheap postage. He took pride in the fact that, among the daily papers in America, only the *Morning Chronicle* advocated a specific system of postal reform—i.e., two cents postage prepaid for all domestic deliveries weighing less than two ounces. Many politicians considered such a proposal preposterous, but he believed that once the public understood the benefits that would accrue from significantly reducing rates, discontinuing all routes that were not self-sustaining, and abolishing the franking system, its representatives would be forced to discard the existing system.[37]

Cheap postage, Leavitt believed, would strengthen the forces of reform in Europe and America and would strike a blow at the Slave Power by ending northern subsidies to rural postal routes in the South. Yet he always clearly subordinated the cheap postage issue to the slavery question and continued to focus much of his attention on abolition. In the mid-1840s the Torrey case, which provoked heated debate among abolitionists on tactics, constituted part of that focus. In 1844 he became actively involved in the defense of Charles Torrey, an impulsive and irascible abolitionist whom Maryland and Virginia authorities accused of aiding slaves to escape. Content neither with agitation directed toward the northern public nor with verbal assaults on slaveholders, between 1842 and 1844 Torrey assisted numerous slaves in Maryland, Delaware, and Virginia to escape to the North. In 1844 his luck ran out when Maryland authorities captured him. In his appeal to fellow abolitionists for support, Torrey argued that his efforts constituted an act of humanity and not a crime under the laws of God, the common law, the U. S. Constitution, or the laws of Maryland and Virginia.[38]

Leavitt fully agreed with Torrey's position. Following the Supreme

37. See *Ballot Box*, October 12, 1840; *Emancipator*, August 31, November 16, 1843; *Morning Chronicle*, March 21, 22, April 9, 18, May 16, 25, October 9, December 18, 1844, January 23, 1845.

38. *Emancipator*, November 16, 1843; Joseph C. Lovejoy, *Memoir of Rev. Charles T. Torrey, Who Died in the Penitentiary of Maryland, Where He Was Confined for Showing Mercy to the Poor* (Boston, 1847), 99–125.

Court's ruling in *Prigg v. Pennsylvania* in 1842, which strengthened slaveholders' claims to fugitives, Leavitt had heartily applauded the resolution of the 1843 Liberty party's national convention declaring the fugitive slave clause of the U.S. Constitution "utterly null and void." At the time, this resolution stood as the most advanced position assumed by the party. Following Torrey's arrest, Leavitt, most black abolitionists, Gerrit Smith, and a few others acknowledged that Torrey had been imprudent, but they insisted that since it could not be a crime for a slave to escape from bondage, assisting slaves to escape likewise was not a crime. "It is, and *can be* no 'crime' for a slave to flee from bondage," Leavitt editorialized, "nor, consequently, can it be made a crime, by local statutes, to aid any slave in escaping." He was hopeful that if the lower courts ruled against Torrey, the case could be taken to the Supreme Court, "where, from precedents already established in several great trials, there is good reason to hope that a correct decision may be secured." In defending Torrey's actions, he even went so far as to ask whether "the good of society requires that law, as law, should be sustained, good or bad, till it is regularly repealed." His answer was no: "*The greatest possible damage which can be done to law, as the protection of society, is to observe or pay deference to a law which sanctions the violation of right.*"[39] Although he ultimately did not advocate outright noncompliance with laws which he deemed wrong, he firmly believed that Torrey had not committed a crime.

Many abolitionists called for Torrey's release as a humanitarian gesture and helped to raise thousands of dollars for his legal defense, but they tended to be either unsupportive or critical of his actions. Garrisonians tended to believe that assisting fugitive slaves to escape was peripheral to the essential task of moral agitation against slavery. Some abolitionists even feared that such efforts might have the effect of easing the glutted slave market, while others had more fundamental misgivings about Torrey's endeavors. For instance, Lewis Tappan declared that "no abolitionist has a right to go into a Slave State with the avowed design of trampling upon its laws. If he does we are not bound to sustain him." To encourage such actions, Tappan added,

39. *Emancipator*, September 14, 1843; Howard P. Nash, Jr., *Third Parties in American Politics* (Washington, D.C., 1959), 31; *Morning Chronicle*, August 2, December 9, 1844. For a discussion of abolitionists' attitudes toward aiding slaves to escape, see Larry Gara, *The Liberty Line: The Legend of the Underground Railroad* (Lexington, Ky., 1961), 72–92.

would injure the cause by further exasperating slaveholders and thus preventing them from reading antislavery documents. Since slaveholders appeared unwilling to listen to antislavery arguments under any circumstances, Tappan's position seems unrealistic. But, in fact, few abolitionists explored or adopted a policy of direct action against the slave system—whether in the form of civil disobedience in the North or guerrilla action directed against slaveholders or proslavery spokesmen—either because they considered it morally repugnant or contrary to a strict legalism.[40]

Torrey's quick temper and uneven disposition certainly did not endear him to many abolitionists. He even subjected Leavitt, one of his staunchest defenders, to his wrath when Leavitt published in the *Emancipator* a letter from a subscriber that condemned Torrey's actions. Nevertheless, Leavitt persisted in his efforts to gain Torrey's release, hiring Stephen Pearl Andrews as legal counsel in the summer of 1844. Numerous difficulties plagued Torrey's defense—the most important being his abortive attempt to escape from jail, which shattered any hope of having bond posted for his release. Thoroughly exasperated by Torrey's erratic behavior, Tappan complained to Leavitt: "I almost wish they had got a better man." Leavitt, however, insisted that Torrey had as much right to escape from illegal imprisonment as did a slave to flee from bondage. During the fall of 1844, he worked diligently to raise funds for Torrey at numerous public meetings and was instrumental in hiring Reverdy Johnson, a prominent Baltimore lawyer and politician, to defend Torrey. Johnson proved less than committed to Torrey's defense, but Torrey's conviction and sentence of six years of hard labor was probably a foregone conclusion.[41]

Throughout Torrey's imprisonment and trial Leavitt stood by him, comforting him, assuring him that he had done no wrong, cautioning him to be patient, and promising that he would do everything in his power to help Torrey gain his freedom. Much as he had several years earlier with John McDowall, Leavitt remained a loyal friend

40. Lewis Tappan to John W. Alden, July 8, 1844, Lewis Tappan to Joshua Leavitt, January 25, 1845, in Tappan Papers; Gara, *The Liberty Line*, 69–78; Bertram Wyatt-Brown, "William Lloyd Garrison and Antislavery Unity: A Reappraisal," *Civil War History*, XIII (March, 1967), 5–24.

41. Lewis Tappan to Joshua Leavitt, October 1, 1844, in Tappan Papers; *Emancipator*, July 17, December 4, 1844; Lovejoy, *Memoir of Rev. Charles T. Torrey*, 148–49, 173–202, 282–85.

throughout Torrey's ordeal, despite Torrey's aberrant behavior and limited abolitionist support for assisting slaves to escape. In both the McDowall and Torrey cases Leavitt showed a warm and caring side and a deep compassion for those whom he believed to be victims of injustice and forsaken by their friends. Leavitt identified with these men in part because he himself had at times felt ridiculed and castigated by friends and foes alike for taking an unpopular stand. In an attempt to cheer up Torrey following his conviction, he expressed the hope that Torrey would regard his letters and visits to the prison as "a token of my brotherly kindness, and a pledge that I shall leave nothing untried, which is within my power, to hasten the period when the prison door shall open again to let you out into the world, to participate in the destinies of the age, and to enjoy the sweets of friends and home." [42]

During the following year Leavitt lived up to his promise, but all pleas to Maryland officials fell on deaf ears. In declining health and without hope of freedom, Torrey died in prison in May 1846. All of the efforts of Leavitt and other friends had come to naught; all that they could do in the end was to give Torrey's widow and children the nearly $3,000 they had collected for his defense. At a memorial service attended by hundreds of abolitionists at Faneuil Hall in Boston in June 1846, Leavitt praised Torrey in a moving speech for being a true Christian martyr and a humanitarian. [43]

Notwithstanding the attention he gave to Torrey's defense in 1844, Leavitt was increasingly forced to concentrate on the presidential campaign. The burdensome task of editing both the *Emancipator* and the *Morning Chronicle* prevented him from making many political speeches during the campaign and forced him to delegate to Beriah Green the responsibility of writing a campaign biography of Birney. But he played a major role in the Liberty campaign as an influential member of the national Liberty Central Committee and the party's leading editor. Throughout the campaign, he vigorously argued the

42. Lovejoy, *Memoir of Rev. Charles T. Torrey*, 238–39.
43. *Ibid.*, 238, 282–84; *Emancipator*, May 13, 1846. Likewise, Leavitt's efforts in 1844 to gain the release of Jonathan Walker, a Massachussetts sea captain arrested and imprisoned by Florida authorities for allegedly aiding slaves to escape to the Bahamas, were unsuccessful. *Morning Chronicle*, September 24, 1844; *Emancipator*, October 23, 1844, February 4, 1845; *Trial and Imprisonment of Jonathan Walker of Pensacola, Florida. . .* (Boston, 1845).

Liberty case in his papers, trumpeting the virtues of Birney and the party and condemning both major parties as hopelessly proslavery.[44]

Most issues of Leavitt's papers contained at least one editorial or news story critical of James K. Polk and the Democrats. He repeatedly insisted that because the Liberty party rejected racism and was beholden to neither the northern autocracy nor the southern aristocracy, "it is the true Democratic party, and the only Democratic party in the country." The Democrats, he charged, were "hypocrisy incarnate," for the "whole history of that party, and every individual act of the party itself, and even of all its principal sections, goes to prove that the Democratic party confirms its regard for the rights of men as strictly within the limits of class or caste."[45]

But Leavitt saved his sharpest barbs for the Whigs, and they returned the favor. Because northern Whigs feared defections from their antislavery wing, they strongly encouraged Giddings, Slade, and others to campaign for Clay and pushed the wasted vote theory extremely hard. For their part Leavitt and other Liberty spokesmen emphasized their long-standing theme of the Whigs as unprincipled opportunists who could not be trusted on the slavery issue. They viewed Clay as the quintessential Whig, especially on the crucial issue of Texas annexation. Antislavery Whigs often argued that if the Liberty party really wished to prevent annexation, they should vote for Clay. With Polk irrevocably committed to annexation, Clay indeed sought to straddle the fence, at first acknowledging certain objections to annexation (though many antislavery Whigs conveniently overlooked his use of the phrase "at this time" to describe his position), then later stating that he had no objections. This waffling on the issue naturally convinced Leavitt and other Liberty men, already deeply skeptical of Clay's intentions, that if elected he would achieve annexation, as Leavitt stated, "by indirection and compromise, and in a way to silence much of the northern opposition."[46]

Many political abolitionists also vigorously opposed Clay on moral grounds, viewing him as a degenerate and disreputable gambler and duelist. In the heat of the campaign Leavitt hurriedly pasted together *The Great Duellist*, a scurrilous attack on Clay that characterized him

44. Joshua Leavitt to James Birney, September 11, 1844, in Dumond (ed.), *Birney Letters*, II, 839; *Morning Chronicle*, September 19, 1844.

45. *Morning Chronicle*, April 1, November 19, 1844.

46. *Ibid.*, August 30, 1844; Clement Eaton, *Henry Clay and the Art of American Politics* (Boston, 1957), 173–75; Fladeland, *James Gillespie Birney*, 234–37.

as "overbearing, quick, implacable, intolerant, reckless of human rights, careless of life." Many Liberty men preferred Polk to Clay, not because they had any great love for Polk but rather because they believed Clay to be both proslavery and immoral. They also tended to follow the rather questionable dictum that it was best to know your enemy. As Leavitt reasoned, the election of Polk, an outspoken supporter of annexation, would "insure a powerful revulsion at the North against slavery." Finally, they chose to view Polk as a man incapable of imposing his will on the northern wing of his party, whereas they feared that the wily and popular Clay would bring most Whigs with him on the annexation issue.[47]

Given the rather obvious tilt of many Liberty leaders against Clay, it is not surprising that Whig papers, such as the Boston *Daily Atlas*, accused them of being Locofocos intent upon "firing six pounders at the Whigs, and pop guns at the Democrats." Birney, a naive and inexperienced politician, gave the Whigs even more ammunition when he accepted the nomination for the Michigan legislature by a group of Saginaw Democrats. Birney lamely sought to reassure the agonized and astonished Liberty faithful that the nomination was merely a local matter and bore no relation to party measures. Leavitt, though completely caught off guard, refused to criticize Birney. "It only shows," he explained rather lamely, "that those who made the nomination, had rather elect, in that instance, a Liberty man, than see a Democrat elected." Others, however, were not so charitable and insisted that he decline the nomination immediately.[48]

The Whigs lost no time in taking advantage of Birney's foolish move. On the eve of the election they published a letter purportedly written by Birney to Jerome Garland, a Liberty man, in which Birney declared his sympathy for Locofoco principles and admitted his support for Polk. Reeling from this damaging development, Leavitt and other Liberty men could do little more than denounce it as a "basely forged letter"—which, in fact, it was.[49]

47. Joshua Leavitt, *The Great Duellist* (Utica, 1844), 175; *Morning Chronicle*, August 30, November 13, 1844; Lewis Tappan to Joseph Sturge, November 15, 1844, in Abel and Klingberg (eds.), *Side-light on Anglo-American Relations*, 199.

48. Boston *Daily Atlas*, July 22, 1844; *Signal of Liberty*, October 14, 28, 1844; Joshua Leavitt to James Birney, October 8, 1844, James Birney to Liberty party, October 15, 1844, in Dumond (ed.), *Birney Letters*, II, 848, 856; *Morning Chronicle*, October 10, 1844.

49. *Morning Chronicle*, November 6, 25, 1844; Fladeland, *James Gillespie Birney*, 244–45, 247, 250–51.

It is impossible to calculate how many abolitionists voted for Clay rather than Birney because of the Garland forgery. But, while some Liberty leaders had predicted as many as 100,000 votes in 1844, Birney received only 62,300—a small increase over the 1843 total. The election, however, produced some satisfaction. The concerted efforts of Leavitt, Stanton, and other Massachusetts abolitionists enabled the party to increase its vote total to 10,000 in the state, and Birney's 15,000 votes in the hotly contested New York election allowed Polk to carry the state and probably denied Clay the presidency. The Whigs were outraged. As the Boston *Daily Atlas* fulminated, "downright robbery" lay at the door of the Liberty party. But in view of Clay's public statements regarding slavery, colonization, and the abolitionists during the past two decades, it is difficult to see how Leavitt and other Liberty men could have supported his candidacy. Most Liberty leaders rejoiced in Clay's defeat. Leavitt, for one, chose to lecture the Whigs on the art of conducting a political campaign. "Had their discretion equalled their zeal," he noted smugly, "a far different result might have been reasonably expected. Their fatal error was, in devoting so much of their time, money, speeches, and papers, in a vain attempt to break up the Liberty party, and induce abolitionists to give the lie to professions by voting for a slaveholder." He had no sympathy whatsoever for the Whigs. "Let, then, the Whig party reap the reward of its own doings," he intoned. "We waste none of our sympathies upon it. Let it perish. Humanity loses nothing by its downfall."[50]

Leavitt had little reason, however, to view the Liberty vote total as a harbinger of a brighter future. Not only was the party's showing in the 1844 election disappointing, but disquieting rumblings beneath the surface would rend the party asunder within little more than two years of the election.

50. Boston *Daily Atlas*, November 15, 1844; Fladeland, *James Gillespie Birney*, 246; *Morning Chronicle*, November 16, 1844. For similar sentiments, see *Christian Citizen*, November 16, 1844; *Christian Freeman*, November 14, 1844.

11

MEANS AND ENDS
AND THE CRISIS OF
POLITICAL ABOLITIONISM

Looking back on the past four years, Liberty men could take heart in the ten-fold increase in the party's vote total and the fact that it had supporters in nearly 80 percent of the counties in the free states. At the same time, however, the party's declining rate of growth and the continued resistance to its appeal by nearly all Democrats and most Whigs did not bode well for the party's future. Leavitt, as usual, directed much of his anger and frustration toward the northern Whigs. The Liberty party had succeeded in forcing them to adopt a more vocal defense of northern rights, but, as he realized, the Whig strategy of neutralizing the effects of political abolitionism while maintaining intersectional party unity—which he contemptuously termed "pure fraud—intentional fraud"—had proved quite effective.[1]

These developments led Gerrit Smith and other New York Liberty leaders to organize a meeting in Albany one month after the 1844 elections for the purpose of analyzing the party's goals and prospects. Leavitt considered the meeting so important that he postponed his departure for Washington in order to attend. In a major address to the convention he pointed to the recent campaign in underscoring the need to remain absolutely apart from the major parties. He also

1. *Emancipator*, March 16, 1843, August 12, 1846. For an analysis of Whig strategy, see Stewart, "Abolitionists, Insurgents, and Third Parties," in Kraut (ed.), *Crusaders and Compromisers*, 25–39.

sought to clear up any doubts in people's minds regarding the Garland forgery. By his own account he succeeded admirably, bringing the delegates to tears by reading a letter he had just received from James Birney. He had another, larger purpose in reading Birney's letter: He wanted Birney to be the candidate once again in 1848. Hearing disquieting rumors that the Ohio Liberty leaders once more had sent out feelers to Seward, he insisted that any such move "be checked, killed, and if it cannot be done any other way, there must be a nomination." To ensure Birney's nomination, Leavitt urged him to come East, where he could more easily mingle with the party faithful and maintain his power base within the party. But his offer of a $1,000 salary to live in Boston and write articles for the *Morning Chronicle* came to naught. Citing personal responsibilities, failing health, and the fear that his nomination would revive intraparty conflict, Birney declared in January 1845 that he would not head the ticket in 1848; two months later he suffered a stroke, which shattered any hopes Leavitt may have had that he would reconsider his decision.[2]

Yet even if Birney had agreed to come East it is doubtful that Leavitt could have hired him to write for his papers. Due to the failure to collect money owed by subscribers, as well as stiff competition from other commercial papers in the city, by the end of 1844 both papers were losing money. Forced to release Elizur Wright, who wrote half time for the *Morning Chronicle*, from his position and to mortgage the printing office to pay his debts, in late 1845 Leavitt suspended publication of the daily paper.[3]

Even with the *Morning Chronicle* in dire financial straits, Leavitt left Wright in the editorial chair and departed for Washington in December 1844. When he moved into his old room at Mrs. Sprigg's boardinghouse—the last time he would reside in Washington for any extended period of time—he found most Whigs "exceedingly bitter"; even Joshua Giddings was cool toward him because of his harsh at-

2. *Morning Chronicle*, November 28, 1844; Joshua Leavitt to Salmon P. Chase, December 13, 1844, in Chase Papers, HSP; Joshua Leavitt to James Birney, January 25, 1845, James Birney to editor of Albany *Patriot*, January 31, 1845, in Dumond (ed.), *Birney Letters*, II, 922–23; Joshua Leavitt to James Birney, April 26, 1845, in James G. Birney Papers, William Clements Library, University of Michigan.

3. Henry B. Stanton to James Birney, August 11, 1845, in Dumond (ed.), *Birney Letters*, II, 958; *Morning Chronicle*, May 6, September 19, 1845; Elizur Wright to Beriah Green, July 1, 1845, in Wright Papers.

tacks on Clay during the recent campaign. Leavitt welcomed their anger, believing that "it keeps the public attention awake . . . and is rapidly glazing the fissure between us and the Whig party, so as to secure us against all future danger of coalition or absorption." He indeed had nothing but contempt for the Whig party. "I have reason daily," he told his readers, "to thank Providence that the world does not belong to the Whig party. I am equally glad that I owe them nothing." [4]

It was not long before several southern Whigs exhibited their hostility toward Leavitt by forcing him to vacate his assigned desk on the House floor. Once more he made the most of the situation, perching himself on the railing overlooking the House chamber, with a makeshift desk balanced on his knees so that he could take notes. Having experienced a similar situation three years earlier, he was able to react with a touch of sardonic humor: "I am entitled to the badge of sovereignty; I sit with my hat on! I can look down upon the 'servants of the people' below me, every man of whom must doff his beaver before taking his chair, while I sit as a 'sovereign' in covered dignity, overlooking them to see that they mind their business, and occasionally thrashing them with the knot of my lash, if they do not go right. In a word, I am promoted to oversee the overseers." Yet he could not resist the temptation to denounce the Whigs for violating his constitutional rights and to appeal to his readers for sympathy for one who was "prepared, as I always have been in this cause, to take what comes, while I am in the path of duty, whether from friends or foe." Thus, in almost ritual fashion he again had baited the Whigs, who had then risen to the occasion, thereby allowing him to raise the specter of the Whig party, dominated by the slavocracy, seeking to destroy freedom of the press. [5]

Leavitt did not consider returning home following his removal from the floor of the House, for he wished to observe the debate on Texas. Many of Polk's supporters considered his election a mandate for annexation and proceeded to plan for its consummation. Yet other Americans, especially northern Whigs, feared that annexation would add to the political strength of the South in national affairs and would lead to war with Mexico and perhaps England. Leavitt, Lewis Tappan,

4. Joshua Leavitt to James Birney, December 18, 1844, in Dumond (ed.), *Birney Letters*, II, 890; *Morning Chronicle*, January 9, 1845.

5. *Morning Chronicle*, January 13, February 3, 1845.

and other abolitionists hoped that many Whigs, as well as some Democrats, whom they believed Polk could not control, would block annexation. When a "prominent and influential" northern Democrat (whom he never identified) approached Leavitt in December, inquiring whether the Liberty party would join forces with the Democrats if they succeeded in blocking annexation, their conviction seemingly was confirmed. Leavitt informed Birney that he immediately rejected the offer, and he reiterated his determination to let the anti-Texas Whigs and Democrats "act on their own responsibility and take care of themselves—that we had deliberately formed our party for permanent and entire success and for nothing short, and having resisted the instances of the Whigs, we could not listen to any proposals from the Democrats." Yet he also feared that Tyler, having nothing to lose and southern support to gain, would seek to annex Texas by means of a joint resolution in Congress.[6]

As events soon proved, while Leavitt's assessment of Tyler's designs was accurate, he exaggerated the strength of northern Democratic opposition and mistakenly assumed that no action would be taken during the present session. Thus, he was understandably shocked when, en route home to Boston, he learned that annexation had been effected. He wrote angrily, "We have no English expressive of marked meanness which is too strong to characterize such an act." In some ways his Whig fixation deepened his sense of betrayal. Notwithstanding widespread Democratic support for annexation, Leavitt had automatically assumed that it would be the Whigs who would consummate that act. Consequently, he seemed particularly disappointed with the northern Democrats, whom he never suspected "would so cheaply yield their objections, and allow their constitutional or other scruples to be lulled to sleep by the merest show of concession." He also charged that many of these Democrats had foolishly based their opposition to annexation on such a "mere pettifogging technicality" as the right of Congress to obtain foreign land, rather than on the negative effects of the Slave Power spreading slavery farther afield.[7]

Annexation represented a major setback for the abolitionists. All of

6. Lewis Tappan to John Scoble, November 9, 1844, in Abel and Klingberg (eds.), *Side-light on Anglo-American Relations*, 195–96; Leavitt to Birney, December 18, 1844, in Dumond (ed.), *Birney Letters*, II, 890–91; Joshua Leavitt to John Jay, Jr., December 14, 1844, in Jay Collection.

7. *Morning Chronicle*, March 4, 5, 1845.

their efforts during the past decade had failed to generate sufficient opposition to prevent a number of Whigs from joining hands with the Democrats to consummate the "foul deed." Leavitt and other Liberty men hoped that the act would focus public attention on the slavery question and would further steel the abolitionists to continue the struggle. As he warned in the summer of 1845: "The opposition that has been made, and the discussion which they [slaveholders] have themselves called forth, in their zeal to obtain Texas, have permanently directed the attention of the people of the North, of all parties, to the bearing of public measures for or against slavery. . . . And the strict silence which northern politicians have maintained, for party ends, is now effectively broken. Now slavery cannot stand this."[8] Their optimism was not entirely unfounded. The Whigs' and Democrats' collusion would, they hoped, lend credence to the Liberty charge that both major parties were beholden to the slave interests. Moreover, they believed that disaffected Whigs and Democrats would defect to the Liberty ranks and help to reverse the party's seeming decline in vitality. Consequently, some Liberty men increasingly sought to make the party attractive to antislavery elements in the major parties; in response to these pressures, others, who viewed the party as a permanent entity, attempted to maintain its separate identity. Ultimately, the debate over what the party was and what it should stand for rent the fabric of the Liberty organization.

The Great Southern and Western Liberty Convention, held in Cincinnati in June 1845, was a portent of both the promise and the problems that would confront the party during the next three years. The convention attracted nearly 2,000 delegates and elicited sympathetic letters from such Whig stalwarts as William Seward and Cassius Clay—all of which seemed to reflect the party's vitality and the possibility of expanding its base of support.[9] Several issues injected into the proceedings, however, would soon come to threaten the very existence of the party. The convention debated whether to stand completely apart from the major parties or to attempt to coalesce with antislavery Whigs and Democrats. Salmon P. Chase and other Democratic-oriented coalitionists made their point in the convention's ad-

8. *Ibid.*, July 1, 1845.
9. *Address of the Southern and Western Liberty Convention, to the People of the United States* . . . (Cincinnati, 1845), 13, 18–22.

dress, referring to the Liberty party as "the true Democratic party of the country." A second issue concerned the content of the Liberty platform: whether the party should remain a "one-idea" party or become a broad reform party that declared itself on various issues of national concern. While the convention's address stated categorically that until emancipation was achieved the party would take an official stand only on the slavery question, William Goodell and others urged the party to state its opposition to class legislation, monopolies, and protectionist trade policies. Finally, sharp differences on the nature of the U. S. Constitution as it related to slavery surfaced at the convention. The address included the party's familiar demand that the federal government be separated from slavery, but Goodell stated that because slavery was illegal Congress must abolish the institution wherever it existed in the nation.[10]

The Liberty coalitionists who wished to forge an alliance with antislavery Whigs and Democrats enjoyed little support among the party faithful until the impact of the Mexican War and the Wilmot Proviso began to be felt. Although Leavitt had become increasingly sympathetic toward the principles espoused by the Democrats, he resisted any moves toward an alliance with, or absorption by, either one of the major parties. The Great Southern and Western Convention, he argued, should have pledged never to compromise the party's fundamental principles. Even in early 1847 he remained sharply critical of any hint of coalition, telling his readers that it would be "inconsistent, suicidal, treacherous, to abandon our organization, and dissolve, and merge into other parties, even temporarily, for the sake of defeating the election of a slaveholder, or hindering the extension of slavery, in any case, or even to carry such a favorite measure as the abolition of the slave trade, or of slavery itself in the District of Columbia."[11]

The issue of whether to seek a party's basic objectives through balance-of-power politics, thereby forcing one or both major parties to adopt much or all of the minor party's demands, or to stand as a permanent party whose goal is to replace one of the major parties and eventually achieve electoral success, has confronted third parties in America throughout the past 150 years. During 1845 and 1846, an

10. *Address of Southern and Western Liberty Convention*, 8–9, 22–23. For an analysis of the issues that divided the Liberty party, see Hugh Davis, "The Failure of Political Abolitionism," *Connecticut Review*, VI (April, 1973), 76–86.

11. *Emancipator*, February 24, 1847; see also *Morning Chronicle*, June 26, 1845; Joshua Leavitt to Salmon P. Chase, March 26, 1846, in Chase Papers, HSP.

increasing number of Liberty men concluded that to prevent absorption by another party the Liberty organization must become a broad reform party that would take a stand on a variety of issues that concerned the American people. Birney, Goodell, Beriah Green, Gerrit Smith, Wright, and several other party leaders came to argue that if the party clung to "one-ideaism" it would remain, as Guy Beckley and Theodore Foster stated in a widely circulated letter, "a *mere* Temporary *party*, shortlived in existence, few in numbers and accomplishing no other good than to prepare the way for the coming of another that shall succeed it." [12]

Leavitt's perception of how the party would achieve its objectives did not differ radically from that of these men. If anything, he had moved inexorably from viewing the party as a temporary instrument that would disappear, "cheerfully and triumphantly," the moment politicians in the major parties moved to destroy slavery, to speculating on the agenda of a Liberty administration once it had swept into office. He also had no quarrel with those who wished to speak out on various questions of public policy not related to slavery. In the columns of his papers and in numerous speeches he had, after all, long advocated reforms in tariff, land, postal, suffrage, and fiscal policies; indeed, his agitation in behalf of free trade had encouraged some of those who now called for an expanded Liberty platform to see important connections between the slavery issue and other matters of public policy. Leavitt and most other Liberty men, however, remained steadfastly opposed to any departure from the party's one-idea policy. They warned that the abandonment of one-ideaism might well splinter the party, attract people more interested in "extraneous" issues than in abolition, and drive from its ranks sound abolitionists who could not agree with the party's positions on such issues. "In theory," Leavitt reminded Goodell and others, "it costs not much more to reform the planet than it does one's own chimney nook. . . . [But] when we come to practice, things have to be done one at a time." [13]

Many Liberty men who wished to create a permanent liberal re-

12. *New Jersey Freeman*, March 1846. For similar sentiments, see James Birney to Lewis Tappan, September 12, 1845, Theodore Foster to James Birney, July 7, October 16, 1845, Beriah Green to James Birney, September 23, 1846, in Dumond (ed.), *Birney Letters*, II, 950–52, 970, 980, 1011; Liberty Party Notebook, 78–80, 83–84, in Foster Papers.

13. *Emancipator*, August 27, 1840, March 30, 1843, August 13, 1845, March 18, 7, 1846.

form party also came to subscribe to the radical constitutional theory espoused by Alvan Stewart in 1838. In the early 1840s only a handful of political abolitionists had challenged the standard Liberty position that the U.S. Constitution, though an imperfect document, required the separation of the national government from slavery; this in turn, the party asserted confidently, would compel the southern states to abolish slavery within their boundaries. But a growing number of Liberty men questioned whether the party's strategy for total abolition was feasible. During the 1844 campaign, even Birney could only express the vague hope that once the party came to power "a method as simple as it is constitutional . . . would doubtless be adopted for the abolition of slavery."[14] By the mid-1840s, a minority of Liberty men, including Birney and Smith, as well as several party conventions, endorsed the constitutional arguments of Goodell and Lysander Spooner, a Massachusetts abolitionist who never joined the Liberty party. In their works, published in 1844 and 1845, respectively, Goodell and Spooner insisted that the constitutional guarantees of a republican form of government and due process and the fact that slavery violated man's natural rights obligated the federal government to abolish slavery in the southern states.[15]

Most abolitionists remained extremely skeptical of Goodell's and Spooner's arguments, pointing out that they were based on a misreading of the historical record and tended to focus on either grand moral precepts or petty legal technicalities. In addition, though many Liberty men did not know exactly how the southern states could be compelled or persuaded to abolish slavery, their conviction that the slave interests controlled the federal government naturally made them wary of a constitutional theory that so forcefully proclaimed national supremacy. They, like the Garrisonians, also feared that any direct assault on the states' rights barrier would destroy the Union and precipitate a bloody

14. James Birney to Hartford Central Committee, August 15, 1844, in Dumond (ed.), *Birney Letters*, II, 834–35. For statements of the standard Liberty position on the Constitution, see Richard Hildreth, *Despotism in America; or an Inquiry into the Nature and Results of the Slave-Holding System in the United States* (Boston, 1840), 170–71; *Signal of Liberty*, April 6, 1842; Salmon P. Chase to Gerrit Smith, May 14, 1842, in Smith Miller Collection.

15. William Goodell, *View of American Constitutional Law, In Its Bearing Upon American Slavery* (Utica, N.Y., 1844); Lysander Spooner, *The Unconstitutionality of Slavery* (Boston, 1845); see also William M. Wiecek, *The Sources of Antislavery Constitutionalism in America, 1760–1848* (Ithaca, N.Y., 1977), 253–59.

civil war. Finally, from an eminently practical standpoint, many political abolitionists concluded that endorsement of the theory would sabotage any hope of attracting antislavery allies.[16]

Although Leavitt never explicitly endorsed Goodell's and Spooner's arguments, they profoundly impressed him. After reading Goodell's work, he concluded that the federal government should use its power "in the most direct way" to abolish slavery in the southern states. He saved his highest accolades for Spooner's book, terming it an "unanswerable" argument and the greatest work ever written by an abolitionist.[17]

There is no single explanation as to why a constitutional theory so at odds with the considered judgment of jurists, constitutional theorists, and even most abolitionists had such a favorable impact on Leavitt, who himself had been a lawyer in his earlier years. He and other political abolitionists certainly found themselves in a difficult position. They demanded total abolition and, as Leavitt noted, had "always held that the Constitution, as a whole, is anti-slavery, and would destroy slavery, if rightfully administered, by men who love liberty and hate slavery."[18] Thus, he had frequently scolded Chase for seeking to jettison the rhetoric of abolition. Yet, so long as he and other Liberty men accepted the prevailing view of the Constitution as giving the states exclusive control over slavery within their boundaries, the only *political* objective of the Liberty party could be federal abolition on the periphery of the slave system. Even if successful in electoral politics, the party would be left with the enormous task of persuading Southerners to effect emancipation within their states. The likelihood of this happening in the foreseeable future seemed extremely remote, as the South appeared determined to resist emancipation in any form. It is also difficult to imagine Leavitt or other abolitionists being satisfied merely with ending slavery where it existed under federal jurisdiction. As simplistic and illogical as it may have been, the radical constitutional theory at least seemed to offer hope by establishing a legal foundation for the exercise of national power to effect total abolition.

16. For abolitionist sentiment opposed to the radical constitutional theory, see *National Era*, January 7, May 6, 1847; *Christian Citizen*, August 7, 1847; *Pennsylvania Freeman*, July 8, 1847; Wendell Phillips, *Review of Lysander Spooner's Essay on the Unconstitutionality of Slavery* (Boston, 1847).

17. *Morning Chronicle*, April 26, 1845; *Emancipator*, October 1, 1845.

18. *Emancipator*, October 15, 1845.

On at least two occasions during the 1840s Leavitt had hoped to take cases to the Supreme Court that he believed would produce definitive rulings on the legality of slavery. He confessed that the Somerset decision, which had outlawed slavery in England in 1773, was "our star of hope." However, a lack of enthusiasm among abolitionists to test slavery in the courts had thwarted his designs, and several northern state court decisions that had recently implied that blacks were not citizens deserving of rights, as well as the Supreme Court's decision in *Prigg v. Pennsylvania*, shattered his "sanguine expectations of absolute justice from the courts." He thus concluded that he no longer could hope that the courts would rule on the basis of legal rather than political grounds on matters relating to slavery and equal rights. His feeling that the Liberty party must dissociate itself from the stigma of disunionism, which many Garrisonians had begun to advocate in the early 1840s, also helped to push him toward the radical constitutional position. Influenced especially by the appearance in 1840 of James Madison's notes on the convention of 1787, disunionists declared that Southerners were correct in viewing the Constitution as a proslavery document that protected the interests of the slaveholding class. They concluded that agitation for dissolution of the Union between the free and slave states would present the South with two alternatives—end slavery or end the Union, which the slaveholders depended upon for their own protection.[19]

Most political abolitionists, whatever their constitutional persuasion, viewed the disunionist theory with alarm. They mistakenly tended to link disunionism with the nonresistance philosophy and to view it not as a form of moral agitation but as a plan for literally dividing the Union along geographical lines. Yet, while disunionists may have grasped the essential nature of the Constitution better than did other abolitionists, critics such as Leavitt effectively argued that, by telling the northern public what it already suspected about the nature of the Constitution, disunionists negated much of the effect of their agitation. Also, if Leavitt stood on shaky legal ground in asserting that Liberty men were justified in rejecting "whatever of iniquitous

19. *Ibid.*, October 1, 8, 1845. For treatments of disunionism, see Kraditor, *Means and Ends in American Abolitionism*, 158–66, 196–207, 211–17; Walters, *Antislavery Appeal*, 129–33; Thomas, *The Liberator*, 247–63; Staughton Lynd, "The Abolitionist Critique of the United States Constitution," in Duberman (ed.), *The Antislavery Vanguard*, 209–39.

contract there is in the constitution, without rejecting it altogether as a system of government," disunionists tended to ignore or minimize those portions of the Constitution which could be construed as anti-slavery in meaning.[20]

Yet, in the end, Leavitt could not bring himself to endorse without reservation the radical constitutional theory. He was sufficiently alarmed and frustrated by recent developments to grasp at virtually any plan that seemed capable of circumventing the states' rights barrier. In 1845 he went so far as to express the chimerical hope that a refusal by all slaves to harvest the crops would end slavery on the spot. "We have often thought," he wrote in the *Morning Chronicle*, "how easy it would be for the slaves to free themselves, peaceably and lawfully, if they could train themselves and confide in one another, to cease work simultaneously, on a given day, just at the commencement of the gathering of the crops. Let every man stop in the field, and firmly demand fair wages or no work, and then let them signify that they are resolved no longer to be coerced with stripes. Slavery would thus come to an end in a single day." Although many abolitionists must at some point have fantasized about such a scenario, it was an unrealistic hope. In all, Leavitt's rhetoric tended to mask his true position on the constitutional question. When it came to stipulating specific means for effecting total abolition, he did not deviate far from the standard Liberty proposals—effecting abolition in the District of Columbia, ending the domestic slave trade, and building a truly national party with support among southern nonslaveholders, who would eventually destroy the slave oligarchy that oppressed them.[21] This scarcely constituted "direct action" by the federal government.

As late as 1846 the divisions within the Liberty party were not irreparable. The Mexican War and especially the promulgation of the Wilmot Proviso, however, hardened the lines of division to the point of threatening the party's very existence. The annexation of Texas and Polk's efforts to force Mexico to cede New Mexico and California precipitated armed conflict in the spring of 1846; Congress then declared war, with only sixteen members dissenting.[22]

20. *Morning Chronicle*, June 9, 1845. For the political abolitionists' rejection of disunionism, see *Philanthropist*, March 9, 1842; *Emancipator*, March 24, 1842; *Signal of Liberty*, April 6, 1842.

21. *Morning Chronicle*, July 29, 1845; *Emancipator*, October 8, 1845.

22. For discussions of Polk's policies, see John H. Schroeder, *Mr. Polk's War: Ameri-*

Many Whigs, as well as a minority of Democrats, criticized the Polk administration's actions and called for a just settlement. But, as John Schroeder has pointed out, they also consistently voted for war appropriations once the fighting began. Only the antislavery Whigs and the abolitionists condemned the war on the basis of moral convictions and antislavery principles, charging that the Slave Power waged it to extend slavery and to increase its control over the national government. Leavitt was one of the most persistent critics of the war. He placed the blame for the war squarely on Polk's shoulders, but he did not let the northern Whigs off the hook and even accused them of voting for war appropriations in order to justify a protective tariff. Although this charge seems to have had little substance, he did capture the essence of the Whig dilemma in Massachusetts and other parts of the Northeast: to preserve unity within their party, which generally supported war appropriations, while seeking to represent many of their constituents who opposed the war. As he noted with obvious glee: "So they keep saying 'Good Lord' and 'Good Devil,' according as local or general contingencies may require one or the other to be most earnestly concentrated." [23]

Leavitt faced no such quandary. Believing it to be his patriotic duty to denounce a war he considered "a crime against the world and the gospel and God," he joined many American pacifists in condemning the killing of Mexicans as "murder" and those who supported the war effort as accessories to murder. In early 1847 he joined the Boston branch of the League of Universal Brotherhood, founded a year earlier by Elihu Burritt, the "Learned Blacksmith," whom he had converted to abolitionism in 1841. The league, which was active in both the United States and England, declared all war, whether offensive or defensive, to be inconsistent with the spirit of Christianity and destructive to the best interests of mankind. It pledged its members never to "yield any voluntary support or sanction to the preparation or prose-

can Opposition and Dissent, 1846–1848 (Madison, Wis., 1973), 8–19; Charles G. Sellers, *James K. Polk, Continentalist, 1843–1846* (New York, 1966), 215–34, 259–66; Frederick Merk, "Dissent in the Mexican War," in Samuel Eliot Morison, Frederick Merk, and Frank Friedel, *Dissent in Three American Wars* (Cambridge, Mass., 1970), 35–46.

23. Schroeder, *Mr. Polk's War*, 20–32, 99–106; *Morning Chronicle*, May 27, 1846.

cution of any war, by whomsoever, for whatsoever purpose, declared or waged."[24]

Never a radical pacifist, Leavitt chose, as did many other members of the league, to interpret its ill-defined pledge not as a denial of the right of self-defense but as a protest against war and all forms of oppression. He fully agreed with Burritt that free trade and cheap postage would facilitate trade and communication among the peoples of the world and advance the cause of peace. But his antiwar stance did not far transcend his hatred for what he viewed as an unjust war. He believed that the Mexican people had every right to defend themselves against the American aggressors with all the means at their disposal. It was, he editorialized in early 1847, legitimate for the Mexican people "to cause every American now in arms in that Republic to be baptized in his own blood, either on the battle field in open conflict, or by private assassination by the road side or under cover of the night."[25]

Many Americans considered such sentiments highly unpatriotic, but by 1847 many others had grown weary of the war. Increasing numbers of Northerners feared that the war would lead to the acquisition of a vast area into which slavery would be extended. The Wilmot Proviso, the most significant protest generated by the war, registered the discontent of many northern Democrats with what they considered the Polk administration's proslavery record. By injecting the issue of slavery extension fully into the debate and redirecting the controversy surrounding the war in a sectional direction, the Wilmot Proviso was an ominous portent for the future.[26]

The outpouring of northern public support for the Wilmot Proviso during the months following its promulgation appeared to augur well for the Liberty party's future. Sectionalism indeed gained ground in American politics in the mid-1840s, especially within the northern Whig party, which contained antislavery constituencies and which, in

24. *Emancipator*, January 13, 27, 1847; *Christian Citizen*, June 5, 1847; see also Peter Brock, *Pacifism in the United States: From the Colonial Era to the First World War* (Princeton, N.J., 1968), 640–52.

25. *Emancipator*, May 26, 1847; Brock, *Pacifism in the United States*, 652–66.

26. For treatments of the origins of the Wilmot Proviso, see Eric Foner, "The Wilmot Proviso Revisited," *Journal of American History*, LXI (September, 1969), 269–79; Chaplain Morrison, *Democratic Politics and Sectionalism: The Wilmot Proviso Controversy* (Chapel Hill, 1967), 3–19.

opposition to "doughface" northern Democrats, often stood before the northern electorate as defenders of northern rights. Thus, as some historians have argued, the definition of party loyalty adopted by growing numbers of Whigs in the North jeopardized party unity. This also held true, in some degree, for Democrats in a state such as Ohio, where the war and the Wilmot Proviso tapped a reservoir of anti-southern and antislavery sentiment.[27]

But, despite the fact that Texas annexation, the Mexican War, and the Wilmot Proviso intensified the sectional debate within both parties, these developments did not seriously weaken the second party system. Both the Democrats and Whigs found ways to offer party alternatives on the volatile issue of slavery extension. In response to the enthusiastic Democratic support for annexation, many northern and southern Whigs, fearful of war with Mexico and opposed to further expansion, rejected Tyler's efforts. Thus, as Michael F. Holt concludes, for most voters Texas was a party issue and not a sectional one. Even though sectional tensions mounted during the Mexican War, Polk's insistence that Democrats support the war effort helped to make it a party issue. Even the Wilmot Proviso, which widened the gulf between the sections and posed a grave threat to the unity of both parties, did not prevent most state parties from providing clear party alternatives on the issue of slavery extension during the war.[28]

It was not clear whether the Liberty party could take advantage of these developments. By 1847 a growing minority of Liberty men, convinced that the party had compromised its principles to facilitate its absorption in a moderate antislavery alliance, doubted whether the party could—or even should—continue to exist. As James C. Jackson, a New York Liberty man, complained to Birney: "Practically the Liberty Party is defunct. Its leading men are divided and distracted. There is no coherence in its ranks, only semblance." When Jackson, Smith, Goodell, Wright, and other Liberty men concluded that the bulk of the party members would not support a broad reform platform that

27. See Stewart, "Abolitionists, Insurgents, and Third Parties," in Kraut (ed.), *Crusaders and Compromisers*, 25–39; Stephen E. Maizlish, *The Triumph of Sectionalism: The Transformation of Ohio Politics, 1844–1856* (Kent, Oh., 1983), 38–39, 52–66, 73–74.

28. Holt, *The Political Crisis of the 1850s*, 41–43, 49–61; Stewart, "Abolitionists, Insurgents, and Third Parties," in Kraut (ed.), *Crusaders and Compromisers*, 35.

endorsed the radical constitutional theory, they formed the Liberty League in June 1847 and nominated Gerrit Smith as its candidate.[29]

Leavitt could not ignore the fact that several influential party members openly supported the Liberty League at a time when the Liberty party was experiencing difficulty in merely holding its own in many states. Nevertheless, he attempted to minimize the potential damage of the revolt, ridiculing its program as "wholly impracticable" and predicting that few Liberty men would defect to the League.[30] He did not care to isolate himself from the mainstream of politics to the extent that the Liberty Leaguers seemed willing to do, with little or no chance of ever achieving electoral success. His strategy of maintaining a delicate balance between principles and votes was, as the Garrisonians and many church-based abolitionists had long warned, fraught with risks. As northern public opinion increasingly moved toward the antislavery position, the constant temptation existed to accept, however reluctantly, a program that seemed capable of attracting the broadest possible antislavery support. Leavitt of course shared with other abolitionists the belief that the weight of their principles would convert Northerners to their moral position. Moreover, in the 1840s neither the church-based antislavery activists nor the Garrisonian disunionists developed a large following or appeared to have much influence on northern public opinion. Yet, unlike the Liberty men, who needed to attract antislavery Democrats and Whigs to the party if it was to achieve its political objectives, these groups (and the Liberty Leaguers) enjoyed the freedom to insist that Northerners adopt their undiluted principles of immediate emancipation and racial equality.

At the same time that the party approached a critical juncture, Leavitt himself came to a crossroads in his long and varied reform career. After ten years as editor of the *Emancipator*, he suddenly announced in early 1847 that Joseph C. Lovejoy, brother of the martyred Elijah, would join him as co-editor of the paper, and Henry B. Stanton and Samuel E. Sewall, a Massachusetts Liberty leader, would serve as contributing editors. These changes, he informed his readers, would make the paper "stronger and more attractive and useful."

29. James C. Jackson to James Birney, April 23, 1847, in Dumond (ed.), *Birney Letters*, II, 1060; *Address to the Macedon Convention, by William Goodell; and Letters of Gerrit Smith* (Albany, 1847), esp. 3, 13–14.

30. *Emancipator*, July 21, 1847.

However, his decision involved more than simply his desire to improve the quality of the *Emancipator*. In truth, Leavitt had been dealt a serious personal and professional setback in 1846 when, despite Birney's strong endorsement of him as "the most decided abolitionist," Lewis Tappan passed over Leavitt and chose Gamaliel Bailey to edit the *National Era*, an abolitionist paper soon to be established in Washington, D.C.[31]

Given Leavitt's bitter feud with Tappan from 1839 to 1843, the decision was perhaps a foregone conclusion. Tappan later told him that "if you had possessed the amenity of Dr. Bailey—his gentlemanly style—no editor in the Anti-Slavery ranks would have had so much popularity or been so useful."[32] It is doubtful whether Leavitt appreciated Tappan's patronizing critique of his personality. But, worn down by the heavy workload, the absences from his family, and the succession of financial crises during his editorship of the *Emancipator*, he accepted the decision with some equanimity, even to the point of wishing Bailey success in his undertaking. Yet he fully realized that his already faltering paper would lose subscribers to the *National Era* and would no longer be the preeminent Liberty organ. Already saddled with debts from the now defunct *Morning Chronicle*, Leavitt felt the need to look elsewhere for means of providing for his sons and for his and Sarah's old age. Once more in his reform career, he felt as though he was living on the edge of financial disaster and was unable to provide adequately for his wife and children. Leavitt resigned as co-editor in August 1847 and ended his connection with the *Emancipator* in March 1848. His departure from the editorial chair of the *Emancipator* elicited a mixture of contempt and qualified praise from the *Liberator*: "The downfall of the Emancipator must be indicative, further, of the downfall of the party. What must be the vitality of that party which cannot maintain its ablest editor in the field? . . . It would be but a questionable compliment to say that he is equal to all the other editors of his party put together. . . . He has given himself, for several years, with all his ability and industry, and certainly with no excess of

31. *Emancipator*, February 24, 1847; James Birney to Lewis Tappan, May 10, 1847, in Dumond (ed.), *Birney Letters*, II, 1073.

32. Lewis Tappan to Joshua Leavitt, January 14, 1848, in Tappan Papers. Birney and Beriah Green agreed that while Bailey may have been more discreet than Leavitt, what was really needed was "a little *bravery*." Beriah Green to James Birney, August 2, 1847, in Dumond (ed.), *Birney Letters*, II, 1078.

scrupulosity, to the service of his party, and as a reward they let him starve!"[33]

Leavitt achieved only limited success in his efforts to compensate for the loss of income from the *Emancipator*, though it was not for the lack of trying. The editorship of the *Philanthropist* in Cincinnati, vacated by Bailey, was not offered to him, and he did not wish to depend for his livelihood once more on the position of corresponding secretary of the American and Foreign Anti-Slavery Society. He managed to earn some money by preaching in two Boston churches two Sundays a month, by serving as the Boston correspondent for the New York *Evangelist*, and by editing the *Liberty Almanac* for the American and Foreign Anti-Slavery Society. Four reading books for school children, which he wrote in 1847, however, did little to ease the financial burden.[34]

Hoping to earn a steady income, he accepted an offer in November 1847 to serve as interim minister of the Second Congregational Church in South Weymouth, Massachusetts. Serving for the first time in nineteen years as a settled minister, he remained with the church for seven months, but his stay was less than pleasant. The problem appears to have been not so much his abolitionist views or his abrasive personality as the fact that his old adversaries, the conservative Calvinists, objected to his theological views. The people were, he informed his brother, "Hopkinsians of the deepest dye, so that it is quite uncertain whether I shall pass for orthodox enough to suit them." His premonition was correct; when a faction of the congregation, which had been seriously divided on doctrinal matters for fifteen years, sought to have him installed as permanent pastor in February 1848, the more conservative group in the church defeated the move. Forced to look elsewhere for employment once the church hired a new pastor, he confided to Chase that he was scarcely "able to keep the wolf at a good distance from the door."[35]

33. *Emancipator*, December 2, 1846, August 18, 1847, August 22, 1847, March 25, 1848; Joshua Leavitt to Salmon P. Chase, November 24, 1846, in Chase Papers, HSP; *Liberator*, September 24, 1847.
34. Leavitt to Chase, November 24, 1846, in Chase Papers, HSP; Joshua Leavitt to Oliver Dyer, June 10, 1847, in Simon Gratz Autograph Collection, Historical Society of Pennsylvania; Joshua Leavitt to Gerrit Smith, July 26, 1847, in Smith Miller Collection.
35. Joshua Leavitt to Roger Hooker Leavitt, December 7, 1847, in Leavitt Papers;

Leavitt's acceptance of a pastorate in South Weymouth shows clearly that, while he had come in the 1840s to subordinate church-based antislavery to political abolitionism and had been instrumental in developing a secular theme such as the relationship between anti-slavery and free trade, he remained a devoted Christian committed to the evangelization of the world. From the Liberty party's inception he had reminded Lewis Tappan and other critics that third-party action represented an expedient measure, not a rejection of church-based efforts. There was in fact, as John McKivigan has pointed out, considerable cooperation between political abolitionists and those who concentrated their energies on converting the churches to the cause.[36]

Liberty men viewed their party as an instrument of Bible politics and never completely subsumed the moral and ethical dimension to economic considerations. Leavitt continued to be affiliated with the American and Foreign Anti-Slavery Society throughout the 1840s and participated in a number of Christian Anti-Slavery Conventions. He also held to the conviction that the clergy was indispensable to the success of the cause. "It is *impossible*," he declared in 1848, "to abolish slavery without having the concurrent will and purpose of the whole country to do it. And it is equally *impossible* to carry the public mind of the country in favor of emancipation without the active and earnest co-operation of the ministers." This did not mean that he held out much hope that the clergy would soon be converted to abolitionism. Indeed, he remained extremely bitter toward the churches, even charging that they were largely responsible for Garrison's attacks on the religious community. In addition, while he had no official connection with Tappan's American Missionary Association, founded in 1846 to advance the cause of free missions, he also continued to denounce the Bible, tract, and foreign missionary societies for their connections with the slave interests and their failure to direct their energies toward the goal of emancipation.[37]

Joshua Leavitt to Salmon P. Chase, April 1, 24, 1848, in Chase Papers, HSP; Gilbert Nash (comp.), "Historical Sketch of the Town of Weymouth, Massachusetts, from 1622–1884," *Publications of Weymouth Historical Society*, II (1885), 110.

36. John R. McKivigan, "Vote as You Pray and Pray as You Vote: Church-Oriented Abolitionism and Antislavery Politics," in Kraut (ed.), *Crusaders and Compromisers*, 180–83.

37. *Emancipator*, January 19, 1848; see also *Morning Chronicle*, May 26, 27, June 2, 4, 18, 1845, September 2, 1846.

Leavitt concentrated especially on the American Bible Society, which for ten years had rejected the abolitionists' demands that it consecrate its overflowing coffers to the cause of freedom, claiming that it could not force its southern auxiliaries to distribute Bibles to slaves. Leavitt and other critics scoffed at these arguments and continued to insist that the society live up to its moral obligations. As a devoted evangelical he believed that the Bible would remove all moral evils. In fact, he argued before the 1847 annual meeting of the American and Foreign Anti-Slavery Society that if slaves had had Bibles in their hands they would have gained the respect and sympathy of mankind and created a groundswell of support for abolition. He was enthusiastic about the prospects of this cause. "Why the very idea of giving the Bible to the slave . . . ," he declared, "is electrical. The time is not distant when it will thrill through the whole of these free States, ay, and run largely into the slave states, like a voice from Heaven." [38]

In 1846 Leavitt launched an ambitious "Bible for Slaves" campaign to solicit pledges totaling $40,000, to be earmarked for the American Bible Society's treasury. In response to his pamphlet *Shall We Give Bibles to Three Millions of American Slaves?*, his editorials, a whirlwind lecture tour, and widespread publicity in the religious press, several northern congregations and ministerial associations endorsed the campaign and a flood of money poured into the society's coffers. But Leavitt's conviction that the society could not resist these mounting pressures came to naught. While its leaders accepted and recorded these donations "for the slaves," they again pleaded inability to force the society's southern auxiliaries to distribute Bibles to slaves. [39]

It is difficult to imagine how Leavitt's scheme could have succeeded. The Garrisonians ridiculed the project from its inception. Frederick Douglass, for example, warned that "as a means of abolishing the Slave system in America, it seems to me a sham, a delusion, and a snare, and cannot be too soon exposed before all the people." Douglass logically questioned whether southern masters would ever permit Bibles to be placed in their slaves' hands by American Bible Society

38. *Emancipator*, June 9, 1848.
39. (New York, n.d.), 8; *Emancipator*, May 19, 1847; *Liberty Bell* (1848), 121–22. The American Missionary Association experienced no more success in its efforts to supply slaves with Bibles. John R. McKivigan, "The Gospel Will Burst the Bonds of the Slave: The Abolitionists' Bible for Slaves Campaign," *Negro History Bulletin*, XLV (July–September, 1982), 62–64.

agents, even if the society agreed to undertake the task. Yet, despite the American Bible Society's intransigence and Douglass' denunciations, Leavitt, Lewis Tappan, and other abolitionists continued well into the 1850s to solicit contributions for the distribution of Bibles to slaves. In doing so, they hoped at the very least to expose the venality of slaveholders who denied the Scriptures to their slaves and to enlist northern churchmen in the effort to purge the benevolent societies of the corrupting influence of slavery.[40]

Even in the midst of his Bible crusade Leavitt never doubted the efficacy of political abolitionism or seriously considered returning to a focus on church-based action. Events moved rapidly in this period of mounting sectional controversy. Chase, Bailey, and other western Liberty men, heartened by the growing support for the Wilmot Proviso and by the Liberty Leaguers' defection, redoubled their efforts to move the party toward a broad antislavery alliance headed by a popular candidate. In New Hampshire, antislavery Democrats and Whigs, with Liberty support, combined forces to elect several candidates to state offices, as well as John P. Hale, a young Democratic congressman, to the Senate. Chase and others insisted that the Liberty party could achieve its objectives only by working within an antislavery union. As Chase wrote Hale in the spring of 1847, "I see no prospect of greater future progress, but rather of less. As fast as we can bring public sentiment right the other parties will approach our ground, and keep sufficiently close to it, to prevent any great accession to our ranks." Supported by the *National Era* and several other Liberty newspapers, the coalitionists urged postponement of the party's nominating convention until the spring of 1848 in order to facilitate the creation of an antislavery alliance.[41]

Leavitt had very different ideas. He believed the Wilmot Proviso to be a totally inadequate measure. "As in 1833, and in 1840, as now in

40. *Liberty Bell* (1848), 121–26; McKivigan, "The Gospel Will Burst the Bonds of the Slave," 63–64.

41. Salmon P. Chase to John P. Hale, May 12, 1847, in John P. Hale Papers, New Hampshire Historical Society; Richard H. Sewell, *John P. Hale and the Politics of Abolition* (Cambridge, Mass., 1965), 52–85; *National Era*, April 15, 22, 29, 1847; Salmon P. Chase to Joshua Leavitt, June 16, 1847, in Edward G. Bourne (ed.), *Annual Report of the American Historical Association for the Year 1902* (Washington, D.C., 1903), II, 116–17.

1847," he lectured his readers, "Liberty men are abolishers. Hence, though they may regard the Wilmot Proviso with favor, and treat its advocates with respect, and may look upon it as an important measure, tending (so far as it goes) in the right direction, the Liberty party treat it as a subordinate measure, totally insufficient to meet the issue which the Slave Power tenders to the country. The Proviso aims merely to prevent the extension of slavery—the Liberty party at its complete extinction." Equally important, he could not bring himself to trust the motives of its adherents. They would support the Wilmot Proviso, he warned, "just enough to make it appear as if they were in earnest, and just enough to fail of carrying it." Thus, he beseeched Liberty men to have "nothing—nothing at all" to do with the designs of the Wilmot Proviso's supporters. Seeking to head off any broad antislavery alliance, he and a majority of the Liberty National Committee decided to hold the national convention in Buffalo in October 1847.[42]

Yet inexorable pressures that pointed toward a broad antislavery coalition severely tested Leavitt's genuine desire to remain aloof from the Wilmot Proviso forces. He favored Samuel Fessenden of Maine, a long-time Liberty activist, as the party's candidate, but other Liberty men wished to consider Hale, even though he had never endorsed the party and did not acknowledge the constitutionality and propriety of abolishing the domestic slave trade or slavery in the District of Columbia. With support for Hale's nomination mounting rapidly within the Liberty ranks, Leavitt soon relented; in July he joined Stanton, John Greenleaf Whittier, Joseph Lovejoy, and others in inviting Hale to meet with them in Boston to determine what they had in common and to sound him out as a possible candidate. Leavitt's new-found conviction that a man who did not support the Liberty party would nevertheless be an attractive candidate stood in sharp contrast to his earlier lectures to Chase and Bailey on the impropriety of their designs. The rush of events, his fear that the party would be left in the backwash of an emerging moderate antislavery movement, and his hope that the *Emancipator* could hold its own in this difficult time largely explain the rather sudden shift in his thinking. Although he emerged from the July meeting with Hale still concerned that the senator was not a Liberty man, he now believed that Hale's acceptance of the party's nomi-

42. *Emancipator*, October 13, June 16, 1847.

nation would signal his attachment to the party; he even recommended that Chase, the leading coalitionist, be the vice-presidential candidate.[43]

Not all political abolitionists or friends of Hale agreed with Leavitt's position. For instance, Chase, hoping to attract an even more popular antislavery candidate than Hale, continued to urge postponement of any nomination until the spring of 1848; whereas L. P. Noble, a Liberty Leaguer, considered Leavitt's acceptance of Hale "inexplicable." In addition, George G. Fogg, a close political associate of Hale, warned him against accepting the Liberty nomination. "I am confident," he told Hale, "you must not commit your fate unreservedly to Joshua Leavitt." At the party's convention held in Buffalo on October 20–21, however, Leavitt and other "moderate" Liberty men beat back the efforts of both the Chase faction and the Liberty Leaguers. In the end, this group—primarily from the East—carried the day, nominating Hale over Smith by a vote of 103–43 and adopting a platform that contained standard Liberty demands.[44] Unwilling to adopt the league's platform or to remain a small independent party with no chance of adding to its electoral strength, yet at this time opposed to joining an antislavery coalition based primarily upon the Wilmot Proviso, they adopted a tenuous middle ground fraught with manifold temptations and problems. The selection of Hale was in fact merely one more step in the party's move toward an antislavery coalition—a process that Leavitt increasingly appeared to endorse. As he remarked to Hale following the convention, the party would be well served by a man who "had already marked his banners with the emblems of success."[45]

Developments within the major parties in the first half of 1848 pushed the Liberty party rapidly toward an antislavery coalition. Both the Democrats and Whigs approached the 1848 election determined to maintain intraparty unity by minimizing sectional disagreements on the issue of slavery extension. Consequently, the Democrats nomi-

43. *Ibid.*, March 31, 1847; Sewell, *John P. Hale*, 87–90; Joshua Leavit to John P. Hale, June 22, 1847, in Hale Papers; Henry B. Stanton to Salmon P. Chase, July 1, 1847, Joshua Leavitt to Salmon P. Chase, September 27, 1847, in Chase Papers, HSP.

44. Salmon P. Chase to Charles Sumner, September 22, 1847, in Bourne, *Annual Report of the AHA, 1902*, II, 123; L. P. Noble to Gerrit Smith, September 1847, in Smith Miller Collection; George C. Fogg to John P. Hale, August 3, 1847, in Hale Papers; Liberty Party Notebook, 92–94, in Foster Papers.

45. Joshua Leavitt to John P. Hale, November 9, 1847, in Hale Papers.

nated Lewis Cass, who had condemned the Wilmot Proviso as unconstitutional and advocated popular sovereignty as a means of taking the
territorial issue out of the hands of Congress; while the Whigs nominated Zachary Taylor, a Louisiana slaveholder whose views on the
issue were so vague that the party could run him in a different way in
each section. These efforts to avoid sectional divisions generated serious protest within both major parties. In Ohio and Massachusetts
antislavery Whigs, such as Giddings, Charles Francis Adams, and
Charles Sumner, who strongly backed the Wilmot Proviso, found
themselves at odds with their party and willing to consider overtures
for a broad free soil coalition. At the same time, in New York the
Barnburners—followers of Van Buren who deeply resented southern
domination of their party—split with the party regulars.[46]

Many Liberty men watched with a mixture of hope and anxiety as
these dramatic developments unfolded. They were determined to say
to dissident Whigs and Democrats that, as Lewis Tappan stated, "our
principle is the correct one and you should sacrifice your pride on the
altar of principle and your Country." Leavitt fully agreed with Tappan's sentiment. At the Massachusetts Liberty Convention in early
1848, which Hale regaled with a bitter attack on the war, he helped
to write resolutions that declared the Wilmot Proviso to be only the
first step toward a truly abolitionist position. Leavitt probably sincerely wished to stand by Hale and Liberty principles. Yet, when
Chase and other Ohio Liberty men, supported by Bailey and Stanton,
issued a call at the Ohio Free Territory Convention for a free soil convention to be held at Buffalo in August, they placed him in a very
difficult position (though certainly one partly of his own making). The
pressures grew stronger when the Barnburners and Conscience Whigs,
in separate conventions, issued similar calls.[47]

46. On developments within the major parties during the first several months of
1848, see Holt, *The Political Crisis of the 1850's*, 60–64; Maizlish, *The Triumph of
Sectionalism*, 73, 80, 94, 99; Martin B. Duberman, *Charles Francis Adams, 1807–1886*
(Boston, 1961), 110–38; David Donald, *Charles Sumner and the Coming of the Civil
War* (New York, 1960), 130–59; Kinley J. Brauer, *Cotton Versus Conscience: Massachusetts Whig Politics and Southwestern Expansion, 1843–1848* (Lexington, Ky.,
1967); Joseph G. Rayback, "Martin Van Buren's Break with James K. Polk: The Record," *New York History*, XXXVI (January, 1955), 51–62.

47. Lewis Tappan to John Scoble, November 14, 1847, in Abel and Klingberg (eds.),
Side-light on Anglo-American Relations, 227; *Massachusetts Liberty Convention and*

Leavitt followed much the same tortuous path as did many Liberty men in deciding whether to attend the Buffalo Free Soil Convention. Having warned Chase in April that any antislavery alliance would be either a "Whig trick" or would "run itself into contemptible imbecility," by July he had come to argue that while the party must not do anything that would "embarrass or cripple or divide us," it should send a delegation to Buffalo and stand by Hale. Above all, he, like most Liberty men, could not stomach the thought of supporting Van Buren as the candidate of a free soil coalition—not only because Van Buren had committed himself to veto any bill abolishing slavery in the District of Columbia, but also because his nomination would be a "re-endorsement of the mobs, gags, robberies, murders, and outrages against liberty, which marked the period from 1833 to 1840."[48] Leavitt would find this position extremely difficult to uphold, given the fact that Hale, a reluctant candidate, was willing to have his name withdrawn from consideration; that many Barnburners, committed to little more than the exclusion of slavery from the territories (often on racist grounds) and determined to support no one but Van Buren, constituted the largest group going to Buffalo; and that negotiations with experienced politicians would take place in a chaotic and charged atmosphere. In the final analysis, the assurances given by several leading Barnburners and Conscience Whigs that they favored the denationalization of slavery, as well as the fear that if the party sat out the convention it could not hope to influence the emerging antislavery coalition (and, even worse, might be relegated to total obscurity), convinced most Liberty men that, whatever the risks, they must go to Buffalo.

While en route to the convention, Leavitt still feared "that under the pressure of a deep desire to stay the spread of slavery, and amid the excitement of an immense assembly, our members would be hurried away to abandon our platform of principles, and basely desert" Hale. When he arrived in Buffalo a circus atmosphere prevailed, with vast crowds packing the hot, dusty streets and overflowing the few

---

Speech of Hon. John P. Hale, Together with his Letter Accepting his Nomination for the Presidency (Boston, 1848), 1, 4–7; Salmon P. Chase to [?], May 31, 1848, in Salmon P. Chase Papers, Ohio Historical Society; Henry B. Stanton to Salmon P. Chase, June 6, 1848, in Chase Papers, LC; *National Era*, July 6, 13, 1848.

48. Joshua Leavitt to Salmon P. Chase, April 1, July 7, 1848, in Chase Papers, HSP.

available hotels. In all, 465 delegates, equally apportioned among the Barnburners and other free soil Democrats, Conscience Whigs, and Liberty men, along with nearly 20,000 spectators from every northern state and three slave states, attended the convention. Because of the vast numbers present, the convention created a Committee on Resolutions, on which Leavitt and Chase served, and a Committee of Conferees, which conducted the essential business of the convention. The mass of delegates met periodically in a huge tent to listen to speeches by Chase, Charles Francis Adams, Preston King, and others. At the same time Leavitt, Chase, and Benjamin Butler, a New York Barnburner, played major roles in piecing together a series of planks that condemned slavery expansion, called for the denationalization of slavery, and supported a tariff for revenue only, cheap postage, free homesteads, efficient government, and river and harbor improvements. The delegates enthusiastically endorsed all of these planks.[49]

The Committee of Conferees then turned its attention to the selection of a candidate for President. When John McLean withdrew from the contest and Hale granted Leavitt, Stanton, and others authority to withdraw his name if the convention appeared to desire Van Buren, Van Buren's nomination became quite likely; Butler's vague pledge that Van Buren would sign any bill outlawing slavery in the District of Columbia virtually assured the outcome. In a straw ballot Leavitt, Stanton, Chase, and perhaps a few other Liberty men joined the Barnburners and a number of Conscience Whigs to give Van Buren a total of 244 votes, to 183 for Hale, 23 for Giddings, 13 for Adams, and 4 scattered.[50]

In keeping with a pledge that he, Stanton, and Chase had made to the Barnburners to support Van Buren in exchange for a "thoroughly Liberty platform," Leavitt stood before the vast throng—an imposing figure, well over six feet tall, with a large frame and flowing white

49. Horace Mann, *The Right of Congress to Legislate for the Territories of the United States, and Its Duty to Exclude Slavery Therefrom: Delivered in the House of Representatives, in the Committee of the Whole, June 30, 1848, to Which is Added, A Letter from Hon. Martin Van Buren and Rev. Joshua Leavitt* (Boston, 1848), 43–44; *National Era*, August 17, 24, 1848; *Emancipator*, August 16, 1848.

50. Mann, *The Right of Congress*, 42, 45–46; Martin Van Buren to New York delegates to the Buffalo Convention, August 2, 1848, in Martin Van Buren Papers, Library of Congress; Salmon P. Chase to John McLean, August 12, 1848, in John McLean Papers, Library of Congress.

beard—to move that the nomination be made unanimous. It was a dramatic moment—so much so that at first he could scarcely speak. In what he termed "one of the most solemn acts of my life," he traced the history, principles, and sacrifices of the Liberty party over the past eight years and insisted that he had acted honorably toward Hale. The party, he declared with obvious emotion, must now surrender its identity to the free soil movement and nominate Van Buren by acclamation. His speech, which Richard Henry Dana, Jr., believed had "never been surpassed for effect," produced tears and shouts of joy among the spectators.[51]

Before departing for home, the Liberty leaders present gave Leavitt the responsibility of preparing a statement explaining their actions at the convention. In his "Address to the Members of the Liberty Party of the United States," written while his train was held over in Rochester, he emphasized the enthusiasm and spirit of conciliation that had prevailed in Buffalo and the unanimous acceptance of the outcome by the Liberty men present. Then, in the most emotional passage of his plea, he stated: "The Liberty party of 1840 is not dead. It has been expanded into the great Union party, or Free Democracy of 1848. What have we lost? Not one of our principles—not one of our aims—not one of our men. . . . We have gained everything, lost nothing. . . . By this movement, our cause is advanced, in a day, to a higher position, than we could have achieved by the labor of seven years, at our former state of progress."[52]

Notwithstanding Leavitt's usual zeal for a new-found cause, not all Liberty men greeted his performance with enthusiasm. The criticism ranged from Beriah Green's denunciation of the deal as "wholesale apostasy" to Tappan's bitter complaint that Leavitt and Stanton had acted without Hale's authorization in withdrawing his candidacy. Tappan's charge was unfounded; indeed, Hale publicly upheld Leavitt's account.[53] In some respects Leavitt's actions were not only logical but defensible. The party, after all, had recently experienced a decline in enthusiasm and a defection by its radical wing—developments that

51. Mann, *The Right of Congress*, 47; Richard Henry Dana, Jr., *Speeches in Stirring Times and Letters to a Son*, ed. Richard Henry Dana III (Boston, 1910), 158.

52. Mann, *The Right of Congress*, 47–48.

53. Beriah Green to Gerrit Smith, August 28, 1848, in Smith Miller Collection; Lewis Tappan to Joshua Leavitt, October 30, 1848, in Tappan Papers; Joshua Leavitt to John P. Hale, August 22, 23, 1848, in Hale Papers.

did not bode well for the future of the Liberty cause. In addition, he believed that the platform, which many Liberty men considered the key to any antislavery alliance, embodied the party's "essential principles and our policy." Perhaps most important, it transcended the mere demand for exclusion of slavery from the territories by insisting upon denationalization—an article of faith for years among western Liberty men, who viewed this as the only legitimate political objective of the party. Many delegates interpreted Butler's assurances regarding abolition in the federal district as an important step in that direction. Finally, Leavitt had long been an outspoken proponent of several of the planks not directly related to slavery. He therefore felt fully justified in giving the Barnburners their part of the bargain.

Leavitt had come to Buffalo extremely suspicious of the Barnburners' motives and disdainful of Van Buren's record. But on the way to the convention he had spoken with several of them; their "tone of candor and respect" toward Hale and the Liberty party and their stated belief that a union must be effected only on an honorable basis impressed him. In spite of Van Buren's tarnished record, it now seemed that the former president was fully prepared to join the struggle against slavery and would attract a large vote. Perhaps the northern Democratic party at last had begun to apply its principles to the slavery question.[54]

Yet Leavitt's actions raise serious questions about his judgment. Van Buren may have been "the best we could get at the time," as he confided to Chase fifteen years later. But Leavitt's sudden shift to a person whom he had detested for so many years certainly smacked of expediency, especially since most other Liberty delegates had remained with Hale on the first ballot. Subsequent events showed that Butler's assurances had little substance; in accepting the nomination Van Buren merely stated that once the territories were truly safe from slavery, the institution in the District of Columbia "will fall of itself." Beyond this, after years of defending one-ideaism against its detractors, Leavitt now applauded a platform that contained ten planks that bore no direct relationship to slavery. The platform also included no condemnation of the Fugitive Slave Act or the three-fifths clause and failed to mention racial discrimination or equal rights for blacks—the first time an antislavery party ignored these matters. He now found himself

54. Mann, *Right of Congress*, 44.

aligned with the Barnburners, some of whom subscribed to the racist belief that the territories should be kept free of both slaves and free blacks.[55]

The Garrisonians remarked sarcastically that the Buffalo convention gave Leavitt and other Liberty men "an opportunity to obtain a respectable political status—to get into good company again." Leavitt had indeed been deeply moved by the vast crowds and the warm reception accorded his counsel by men who had been in the political limelight for years. Speaking before a Free Soil convention in Worcester a few weeks later, he termed the Buffalo gathering "the dearest day of my life." Yet one need not create a scenario in which seasoned, scheming politicians seduce a naïve reformer who yearns for political respectability, to conclude that in some important respects Leavitt departed from positions he had maintained for years. In truth, he had been retreating by half steps from his original principles—for instance, by supporting Thomas Morris in the early 1840s despite Morris's opposition to black suffrage and by pushing Hale as a candidate in 1847 even though he was not a Liberty man. Now, seemingly without the energy to continue wandering in the political wilderness and desperately hoping that, in the words of Stanton, they could "knock in pieces the main prop of slavery, *the Northern democratic party*," he grabbed at this opportunity and hoped for the best. Unlike Stanton, he did not do so to further his political ambition. But, contrary to the views of some historians, he nonetheless ended up settling for a party and a candidate that did not come up to the standards of the Liberty party.[56]

Most Liberty men ultimately came to support the Free Soil party. No one, however, threw himself into the campaign with more enthusiasm than did Leavitt. On his way to New York for consultations with

55. Joshua Leavitt to Salmon P. Chase, September 30, 1863, in Chase Papers, LC; Martin Van Buren to Benjamin Butler *et al.*, August 22, 1848, in Van Buren Papers. For discussions of the Free Soilers and the race issue, see Eric Foner, "Politics and Prejudice: The Free Soil Party and the Negro, 1849–1852," *Journal of Negro History*, L (October, 1956), 239–56; Eric Foner, "Racial Attitudes of the New York Free Soilers," *New York History*, XLVI (October, 1965), 311–29.

56. *Seventeenth Annual Report of the Massachusetts Anti-Slavery Society* (Boston, 1849), 24; *Emancipator*, August 30, 1848; Henry B. Stanton to John P. Hale, August 20, 1848, in Hale Papers. For works that emphasize the continuity between the Liberty and Free Soil parties, see, for example, Sewell, *Ballots for Freedom*, 159–62; Dwight L. Dumond, *Antislavery: The Crusade for Freedom in America* (Ann Arbor, Mich., 1961), 304.

Butler and other leading Barnburners following the convention, he visited Van Buren at his home in Lindenwald. He emerged from the meeting with "our glorious old man"—as he now termed Van Buren—entirely satisfied that "he is with us, heart and soul, and will be with us to the last battle against the Slave Power." Leavitt was prepared to do whatever he could for the ticket. "I am getting my steam up to the highest pitch (below the bursting point), in favor of *Van Buren and Adams*," he informed Chase.[57]

In spite of meager financial resources, Leavitt campaigned aggressively for the ticket by serving as secretary of the party's State Central Committee in Massachusetts, by helping to found Free Soil Clubs throughout the state, and by delivering numerous speeches. He constantly urged Liberty men to work for the Van Buren–Adams ticket. In a circular that he sent to his old colleagues, he once more called them to battle in the cause of righteousness: "Let us have no half-way work; let us infuse into this new movement the whole of that fearless firmness, that indomitable adherence to principle, and that ever-hopeful energy, which has hiterto characterized the Liberty Party."[58]

Many Conscience Whigs and Liberty men, however, found it difficult to throw themselves into the fray for Van Buren. Leavitt, too, had his doubts about Van Buren, especially in relation to the *Amistad* case. Yet he was so committed to the new-found cause that, in a blatantly expedient move, he asked Senator Benjamin Tappan of Ohio to forward any available evidence that might clear Van Buren of charges that Leavitt and other abolitionists had made in connection with the case several years earlier. Leavitt claimed to Tappan that he did not wish "to make Van Buren a god when he is only a man," but merely "to write so that honest men will feel that I write honestly." At best, that would have been a difficult undertaking; Van Buren made it even more difficult by refusing to place any responsibility on other people for his actions in the case.[59]

57. Joshua Leavitt to Salmon P. Chase, August 21, 1848, in Chase Papers, HSP.

58. Enclosed in Joshua Leavitt to John P. Hale, August 2, 1848, in Hale Papers; also Leavitt to Chase, August 21, 1848, in Chase Papers, HSP; *Emancipator*, August 30, September 13, 1848; Samuel May, Jr., to Anne W. Weston, September 14, 1848, in Weston Family Papers; Joshua Leavitt to Roger Hooker Leavitt, October 19, 1848, in Leavitt Papers; Joshua Leavitt to George G. Fogg, September 7, 1848, in George G. Fogg Papers, New Hampshire Historical Society.

59. Joshua Leavitt to Benjamin Tappan, September 25, 1848, in Benjamin Tappan

In the final analysis, the Free Soil party failed to attract much support—aside from Liberty voters—outside of Massachusetts, New York, and Ohio. The Democratic vote declined by nearly 25 percent from 1844 in the Northeast, but 80 percent of that came with the Barnburner defection in New York. The Whig vote registered 97 percent of the 1844 total in the free states. There were, however, some bright spots for the Free Soilers: Van Buren attracted 14 percent of the votes cast in the North; most Liberty men ended up voting for the ticket; the efforts of Leavitt and other Massachusetts Free Soilers gave Van Buren 28 percent of the votes in that state; and, though most Whigs in Ohio remained loyal, with the loss of Giddings and other leading antislavery men to the Free Soilers the party would never again be a serious contender in a state election. Even some Ohio Democrats, feeling betrayed by southern party members who voted for Taylor as a sectional candidate, became increasingly antisouthern and inclined toward an alliance with Free Soilers in the state. Contrary to the expectations of many Free Soilers, the 1848 election was not the beginning of the end of the second party system. But it created growing fissures within the national parties that did not bode well for the vitality of the system.[60]

An important chapter in Leavitt's varied reform career now came to a close. Notwithstanding his claim that the Liberty party had merely been translated and enlarged, it was in fact dead. Its demise, combined with his retirement from the *Emancipator* and his failure to be appointed editor of the *National Era*, set the stage for a less productive period of his life.

Papers, Library of Congress; Martin Van Buren to Lewis Tappan, October 2, 1848, in Lewis Tappan Papers.

60. Holt, *The Political Crisis of the 1850's*, 64; Joseph G. Rayback, *Free Soil: The Election of 1848* (Lexington, Ky., 1970), 279–87.

12

THE *INDEPENDENT* AND
ANTISLAVERY POLITICS

Without funds or regular employment and eager to serve the antislavery cause in some capacity, in late 1848 Leavitt accepted a subordinate position on the staff of the *Independent*, a paper established in New York City in December of that year. In part the product of the fertile mind of Lewis Tappan, who had proposed in 1846 that Leavitt edit an independent paper "advocating Congregationalism, Bible Missions, Temperance, the Sabbath, and antislavery principles," the *Independent* was ultimately founded by Tappan's son-in-law, Henry Bowen, and several other New York merchants. These men subscribed to the evangelical theology of Nathaniel Taylor and wished to strengthen the Congregational Church in New York and the West. They viewed the *Independent* as a useful forum, free of sectarian pressures and apart from the pulpit, in which the major moral and social issues, including antislavery, could be discussed. As Leonard Bacon, one of its original editors, later recalled: "The proposed journal was not to be identified with the anti-slavery societies, nor with any society for special reforms, nor with any political party, nor even with Congregationalism, any further than as its conductors should be known as Congregationalists." [1]

Given the proprietors' rather conservative antislavery views, their selection of Bacon, Joseph P. Thompson, and Richard S. Storrs as editors—none of whom had been associated with the abolitionists—

1. Lewis Tappan to Joshua Leavitt, December 9, 1846, in Tappan Papers; *Independent*, February 13, 1873.

made eminent sense. Moreover, Bacon and Thompson had editorial experience, and all three men were prominent Congregational ministers—the older and better-known Bacon at the First Church in New Haven and Thompson and Storrs at the Broadway Tabernacle and the Church of the Pilgrims in New York and Brooklyn, respectively. Leavitt was naturally disappointed at being passed over for the editorship and thus reluctant to accept the offer of the position of managing editor. Since 1828 he had edited several newspapers—a task he enjoyed despite the financial sacrifice and labor involved. He was now asked to be a silent, lesser partner, subject to the decisions of men who had less journalistic experience and had never been abolitionists. Nevertheless, at the urging of Bacon and Thompson, who visited him in Boston and argued that his wealth of experience as a journalist, his stature among Congregationalists, and his contacts with abolitionists and other reformers would be invaluable to the paper's success, he accepted the offer.[2]

In truth, Leavitt soon overcame his initial reluctance to join the *Independent* staff. There were no other job offers at the moment, and he still had to pay off debts incurred with the *Morning Chronicle*. The salary of $1,000, to be raised by contributions, appeared sufficient to support his family and allow him to travel and speak in behalf of various causes. Perhaps most important, having recently ended his lengthy tenure as editor of the *Emancipator* and engineered the absorption of the Liberty party, he now seemed conscious of his advancing age and reluctant to assume the responsibilities associated with editing his own paper. He was only in his mid-fifties—not old by the standards of the romantic writers of the time—but the endless hours devoted to editing his papers, the constant anxiety about his ability to provide for Sarah and the boys, and the long absences from his family, which he calculated to have amounted to half of each year from the late 1830s until the mid-1840s, had worn him down. As he informed his mother in 1849, he had borne his share of such responsibility and felt old—his eyes being "a little dim, and I wear false teeth and false hair." Consequently, he heeded the advice of his old friend John Greenleaf Whittier,

2. Louis Filler, "Liberalism, Anti-Slavery, and the Founders of the *Independent*," *New England Quarterly*, XXVII (September, 1954), 294–95, 298–99; Donald David Housley, "The *Independent*: A Study in Religious and Social Opinion, 1848–1870" (Ph.D. dissertation, Pennsylvania State University, 1971), 18–20; *Independent*, February 13, March 6, 1873.

who said to him, "Not all that thee might wish, Joshua, but a good harbor for thy old age."[3]

From 1848 until 1861, when Bacon, Storrs, and Thompson resigned their posts, Leavitt maintained a cordial relationship with the editors. Bacon, who essentially served as the senior editor, remained in New Haven and seldom appeared at the *Independent* office. Storrs, too, devoted much of his time to his pastorate and civic responsibilities in Brooklyn. Thus, Leavitt and Thompson directed the day-to-day operations of the office. They came to admire and respect each other during their time in the office, which often extended from dawn to dusk six days a week.[4] Leavitt's daily routine in the office was quite varied. During a typical morning, he read through numerous letters and articles from correspondents and from regular contributors, such as Henry Ward Beecher and George B. Cheever. According to Thompson, he would also "make his clippings, condense their contents, and prepare three columns of clear, concise, readable intelligence, classified according to topics or relations." Moreover, as the elder statesman of the staff, he "made friends for the paper and its policy, smoothed asperities, healed alienations, and, above all, protected the editors from bores."[5]

During the pre–Civil War years, Leavitt clearly played an important role on the *Independent* staff. In the course of advising Bacon on editorial problems, selecting articles for inclusion in its columns, editing news reports, reading Thompson's editorial comments before they were published, and helping to move Henry Ward Beecher—who often came to the office in the 1850s to write his "Star Paper" column for the paper—toward a more coherent and forceful stand against slavery, he influenced the tenor of the paper. The editors appreciated the value of his contributions. "This is work," Thompson later remarked, "that makes the paper and makes it tell, and in such work Dr. Leavitt had no superior."[6] But historians have tended to exaggerate his role in developing the paper's policies. His influence did not in

3. Leavitt to mother, March 10, 1849, in Leavitt Papers; *Independent*, March 6, 1873.

4. *Independent*, January 2, 1851, July 15, 1852, August 17, 1854, March 6, 1873; Housley, "The *Independent*," 13, 19, 21–22.

5. *Independent*, March 13, 1873.

6. Joshua Leavitt to Leonard Bacon, March 21, May 14, July 7, 1849, July 25, 1850, January 19, February 2, 1852, April 13, August 4, 1853, in Bacon Family Collection, Sterling Library, Yale University; *Independent*, March 13, 1873.

fact extend in any formal way to editorial policy or to final decisions regarding the general character of the paper. The editors, fearful that Leavitt's abolitionism might alienate the clergy and other potential subscribers, even went so far as to periodically assure their readers that he did not write the paper's editorials.[7]

In some respects Leavitt found his working and living situations satisfying. The editors treated him with respect; and, while he probably agreed in principle with Tappan's desire that the editors take a stronger stand against slavery, he generally agreed with their stance on such issues as temperance, cheap postage, the denominational interests of Congregationalism, and the benevolent societies' obligation to condemn slavery.[8]

When Leavitt came to the *Independent* staff he moved to Brooklyn, where he joined Storrs's Church of the Pilgrims. Sarah and the younger boys remained in Cambridgeport until the early 1850s. Thus, once more Joshua's work kept him from his family, and Sarah was left at home to care for the boys. Neither Joshua nor Sarah desired this separation, but they believed the arrangement to be the most economical under the circumstances; his frequent train trips to Boston helped to make the separation bearable. By the early 1850s, most of their five sons had begun to strike out on their own. William, the eldest, who had graduated from Yale and then received his theological degree, served as a pastor in Newton Corner, Massachusetts, and later in Hudson, New York, where Joshua and Sarah proudly witnessed his installation. Although Leavitt was not often able to parent his boys on a day-to-day basis, he was a caring father who paid close attention to their physical and emotional well-being. As an evangelical Christian he worried especially about his sons' spiritual state. In 1853, for example, he expressed to his brother the hope that "all the dear youth, the grandchildren of our honored father and mother, would set themselves early and with our consent in the right way." He was pleased that both James, then a college student, and Samuel, who worked in Boston, had turned to God and associated themselves with a church. Another son, Thomas, an ambitious young merchant, moved with his

7. See Housley, "The *Independent*," 23; Filler, "Liberalism, Anti-Slavery, and the Founders of the *Independent*," 299–300. For the editors' assurances, see *Independent*, December 7, 1848, August 17, 1854, March 13, 1873.

8. For discussions of the *Independent*'s stand on the slavery question in the 1850s, see Housley, "The *Independent*," 114–43.

father's blessing to Melbourne, Australia, in the early 1850s as a partner in Cobb & Co., an exporting firm. By the mid-1850s, only Joshua, the youngest boy, still lived at home. Leavitt could then express a sense of relief that nearly all his sons had come "to the point of self-maintenance," thus relieving him of some of his anxieties regarding money.[9]

After Leavitt's death in 1873, both Bacon and Thompson would remark that he had never complained about his subordinate position on the editorial staff. However, he confided his true feelings only to his old antislavery associates and his brother. Over the years he expressed a number of grievances about the job, including the salary, which required the "closest economy" to make ends meet, as well as the fact that he was a "mere employee" who, he informed Birney in 1855, had "no will, no power, no control, and therefore no responsibility to the public or to the contributors in any form." In the mid-1850s he complained to his brother that he found the position of managing editor "more engrossing and confining from year to year."[10] He often thought about embracing "the first opportunity of rushing into the risks and toils of the political encounter, at whatever sacrifice or hazard," but when Salmon P. Chase suggested in 1856 that Leavitt could perhaps be hired to manage the *National Era*, he declined the offer—again citing old age and a natural affinity for financial disaster. In the final analysis, he tended to view the managing editorship as tolerable employment that provided steady work and income. He simply did not have the energy to return to the fray and to cope with the uncertainties that came with editing an antislavery paper. A steady income also seemed especially important at a time when his sons were in college and launching their careers and as he looked toward sustaining himself and Sarah in their old age.[11]

Leavitt's preoccupation with financial security led him to search for additional sources of income. Even while working long hours at the *Independent* office, he preached periodically at his old church in Strat-

9. *Independent*, February 13, 1873; Leavitt to mother, March 10, 1849, Joshua Leavitt to Roger Hooker Leavitt, November 19, 1853, November 5, 12, 1852, April 15, 1856, in Leavitt Papers; Joshua Leavitt to James Birney, January 23, 1855, in Dumond (ed.), *Birney Letters*, II, 1168.

10. Joshua Leavitt to Salmon P. Chase, February 2, 1850, in Chase Papers, HSP; Joshua Leavitt to James Birney, April 10, 1855, in Dumond (ed.), *Birney Letters*, II, 1172; Joshua Leavitt to Roger Hooker Leavitt, April 26, 1855, in Leavitt Papers.

11. Joshua Leavitt to Salmon P. Chase, July 4, 1856, in Chase Papers, HSP.

ford, Connecticut, in the mid-1850s. His need for income, combined with the absence of a forum from which he could seek to influence public opinion on a regular basis, explain in part the limited role that he played in various reform causes during the 1850s. He retained a keen interest in the antislavery, cheap postage, and free trade causes and was prepared to do what he could to advance them. Especially in the late 1840s and early 1850s he focused considerable attention on cheap postage, an issue that he generally had subordinated to other concerns in earlier years. Indeed, in 1849 he became so carried away by his enthusiasm for the cause that he wrote Samuel Gridley Howe: "If I was not too poor to live a week without wages, I would drop everything and devote the ensuing three or six months to this 'one idea' until it has carried." [12]

Leavitt and other cheap postage advocates had won a minor victory in 1845 when Congress lowered rates slightly, thereby generating an increased flow of mail and making the system self-supporting. Leavitt, however, believed that the bill did not change enough to "cure the evils of the old system" and thus continued to press for further reform. In the late 1840s he wrote several articles on the subject for the *New Englander*, a Congregational magazine, as well as a lengthy pamphlet for the Boston Cheap Postage Association, a lobbying group that he, Howe, Elizur Wright, and other activists founded in 1848 for the purpose of petitioning Congress and presenting lectures to lyceum groups. [13]

When Leavitt moved to New York, he retained his post as secretary of the Boston organization. He resorted to tactics that he had employed effectively in the antislavery movement: writing several additional pamphlets; urging Chase, Charles Sumner, John Gorham Palfrey, and other Free Soil congressmen to act on the cheap postage plank in the 1848 platform; and spending two weeks in Washington

12. *Ibid*; Leavitt to Samuel G. Howe, November 27, 1849, in Samuel Gridley Howe Papers, Houghton Library, Harvard University.

13. Joshua Leavitt, *The Moral and Social Benefits of Cheap Postage* (New York, 1849), 3; Joshua Leavitt to Salmon P. Chase, April 1, 2, 4, May 17, 1848, in Chase Papers, HSP; Joshua Leavitt to John M. Niles, April 20, 1848, in John Milton Niles Papers, Connecticut Historical Society; *Independent*, March 27, 1851. For Leavitt's articles on cheap postage published in the *New Englander* in 1848, see "Post-Office Reform," VI (January, 1848), 111–20; "The British System of Postage," VI (April, 1848), 153–65; "Our Post Office," VI (July, 1848), 393–404.

in early 1850 to lobby for the cause.[14] He threw himself into the fray with his usual enthusiasm, and his efforts and those of other cheap postage advocates met with some success. In 1851 Congress reduced rates for most letters to three cents and increased the volume of newspapers carried at less than cost; in 1852 it further reduced newspaper rates. By this time Leavitt had endorsed Howe's call for one-cent letter postage. But he accepted the positive features of the 1851 bill and hoped that its "blunders and crudities"—especially the complicated rate schedules and provisions for increased franking privileges—would be changed.[15]

In 1852 an English postal official credited Leavitt with having contributed more than any other American to the cause of cheap postage in the United States during the previous decade. Yet, except for a few pieces he later wrote for the *Independent* and the New York *Evening Post*, Leavitt devoted little energy to the cheap postage cause after 1852. This may be explained in part by his resignation from the Boston Cheap Postage Association in 1851 in a dispute over compensation for a pamphlet he had devoted months to writing, as well as the fact that neither that group nor its counterpart in New York offered much institutional support for him and other activists. He also sensed that Congress would not consider lowering postal rates further in the foreseeable future. (In fact, rates did not decline during the last half of the century, partly because the increase in franking privileges produced a deficit in the system.)[16] Such formidable obstacles had not deterred him in his quest for abolition during the 1830s and 1840s. But he appears not to have had sufficient energy or depth of commitment to sustain a concerted effort for postal reform.

At the time Leavitt went to Washington to lobby for postal reform

14. Leavitt's most important treatments of the subject in 1849 and 1850 were *The Finance of Cheap Postage* (New York, 1849); *The Moral and Social Benefits of Cheap Postage* (New York, 1849); *The Practical Working of Cheap Postage* (New York, 1850). For Leavitt's correspondence with members of Congress and others on the subject, see, for example, Joshua Leavitt to John G. Palfrey, May 1, 4, 1849, in John Gorham Palfrey Papers, Houghton Library, Harvard University; Leavitt to Chase, August 2, 1849, January 30, February 2, 1850, in Chase Papers, HSP; Joshua Leavitt to Elizur Wright, February 10, 1850, in Wright Papers.

15. Joshua Leavitt to Samuel G. Howe, September 19, 1851, in Howe Papers; Leavitt to Charles Sumner, June 11, 1852, in Sumner Papers; *Independent*, October 9, 1851.

16. *Independent*, January 8, 1852; Roper, *The United States Post Office*, 68.

in 1850, he realized that most members of Congress were focusing their attention on the slavery issue, which threatened to engulf the nation in civil war. It is instructive that in the midst of this profound national crisis he chose to lobby in Washington, not for the admission of California to the Union as a free state or against a stricter fugitive slave law, but for a cheap postage bill. This decision, however, did not so much signal a loss of interest in the antislavery struggle as it did the fact that he now considered himself more an observer than an active participant and leader in the movement.

Until 1847 Leavitt had been the leading Liberty party editor, an influential party strategist, and a tireless organizer and speaker. The 1848 Free Soil Convention and his departure from the editor's chair effectively marked the end of his role as a central figure in antislavery politics. He now seemed willing to step aside for the more pragmatic and experienced former Whigs and Democrats who had helped to establish the Free Soil party, as well as old Liberty men such as the politically ambitious Chase. It was these men, and not himself, who Leavitt believed would take the principles he had articulated and carry them to victory. He would, he reasoned, proffer advice and encouragement and would speak and write in behalf of the cause as time permitted. In some respects his subordinate role was not entirely of his own making. The more pragmatic political antislavery activists gave little indication of desiring to thrust him into the limelight. In 1850 Chase did urge Charles Sumner to float a trial balloon to determine whether Democrats and cheap postage advocates might join Free Soilers in Massachusetts to support Leavitt as a candidate for the House of Representatives, but nothing came of this. Yet, in the final analysis, Leavitt gave clear signals to his friends in the movement that he would not (and could not) accept major responsibilities in behalf of the cause. Leavitt—like James Birney, Theodore Weld, Elizur Wright, and many other pioneer abolitionists—increasingly appeared to view antislavery more as an important part of their past than as an integral aspect of their present lives. As Leavitt noted nostalgically in reminiscing with his old friend Birney in 1855, his days as a leading light of the cause were "old experiences of mine, belonging to a period of life that has long passed away, never to return." [17]

17. Salmon P. Chase to Charles Sumner, April 13, 1850, in Bourne, *Annual Report of the AHA, 1902*, II, 209; Leavitt to Birney, April 10, 1855, in Dumond (ed.), *Birney Letters*, II, 1172.

Leavitt continued to emphasize the need to convert the churches and benevolent societies to the antislavery cause, and he remained critical of the American Bible Society and missionary organizations for failing to condemn slavery. In 1852 he joined Bacon, Henry Ward Beecher, Lewis Tappan, and other leading Congregational clergy and laymen as a delegate to the church's national convention in Albany—one of the most important meetings of the Congregational Church since the seventeenth century. The move by the Congregationalists and New School Presbyterians toward a denominational consciousness during the previous fifteen years had weakened their sense of unity. At the Albany Convention the delegates repudiated the Plan of Union, affirmed the superiority of the Congregational system, and pledged $50,000 for the construction of churches in the West. Equally important, the New School's refusal to denounce slavery in unequivocal terms angered many Congregationalists. Leavitt and most other delegates condemned slavery as an individual and social sin and held the New School morally responsible for refusing to discipline members who held slaves.[18]

Leavitt remained convinced, however, that slavery must be destroyed by political action and that the Free Soil party was the most feasible instrument for achieving that end. The party achieved a degree of success that the Liberty party had never enjoyed, sending a dozen men to the House in 1848, and Chase—with significant assistance from Ohio Democrats—to the Senate in 1849. Ever distrustful of the Whigs, Leavitt welcomed Chase's election, believing that it would secure "our glorious movement forever from being sponged by the Clay and Webster Whigs." Yet all was not well with the party. Serious differences arose between the coalitionists and those Free Soilers— especially former Whigs—who feared that, in the end, the party would lose its sense of identity. In addition, the return of most New York Barnburners to the Democratic ranks between 1849 and 1851 for reasons of office and power dealt a severe blow to the Free Soilers. Their exodus was especially embarrassing to Leavitt, who had helped to engineer the 1848 alliance at Buffalo. "I am a little amazed," he

18. *Eleventh Annual Report of the American and Foreign Anti-Slavery Society* (New York, 1851), 106, 113; Leavitt to Bacon, March 13, April 19, May 1, July 7, 1849, in Bacon Papers; *Proceedings of the General Convention of Congregational Ministers and Delegates in the United States, Held at Albany, N.Y., on the 5th, 6th, 7th, and 8th of October, 1852* (New York, 1852), 13–14, 16, 19–21, 26, 90; *Independent*, October 14, 1852.

259

remarked sheepishly to Sumner after the dust had settled, "at the completeness of the surrender which our old friends of 1848 in New York have made of themselves." [19]

The party suffered its most severe setback when it (and antislavery Whigs and Democrats) failed to prevent the passage of congressional bills that organized the Utah and New Mexico territories with no restrictions on slavery and enacted a stronger fugitive slave law. The latter bill particularly shocked and angered Leavitt and other antislavery Northerners. With its "effects on our juridical administration in destroying all the safeguards of personal freedom, the *animus* which its authors show in carrying it into effect—the diabolical inhumanity it proclaims," he complained bitterly to Richard Henry Dana, Jr., the Fugitive Slave Act represented a devastating blow to liberty. Attempting, as he so often did, to find a silver lining in the clouds, he wanly expressed the hope that Americans would now be shocked into action against the Slave Power. Most Americans, however, welcomed a resolution of the sectional crisis, thus leaving many Free Soilers and old abolitionists feeling demoralized and isolated. These developments so discouraged Birney that he concluded that any further efforts by him in the struggle would be "unnecessary or futile." While by no means prepared to give up the struggle, even Leavitt confided to his friend Chase that "the times look dark for liberty." "Of late I have been rather despondent," he confessed, "and often could see nothing but darkness in any human resource. 'The Lord reigns' would sometimes cheer me—but then I was made sad by asking—How do we know he will take the trouble to reform and save a nation so guilty—so carnal—so base?" [20]

With the party in disarray and coalition politics a mixed success at best, most Free Soilers concluded that the party must pursue a rigorously independent antislavery course and nominate Hale. Leavitt was prepared to support the mercurial Hale, who again proved a reluctant

19. Joshua Leavitt to Salmon P. Chase, March 2, 1849, in Chase Papers; HSP; Frederick J. Blue, *The Free Soilers: Third Party Politics, 1848–1854* (Urbana, Ill., 1973), 154–60, 162–71; Joshua Leavitt to Charles Sumner, July 11, 1852, in Sumner Papers.

20. Joshua Leavitt to Richard Henry Dana, Jr., March 12, 1851, in Richard Henry Dana Papers, Massachusetts Historical Society; entry for February 1, 1851, in James G. Birney Diary, Library of Congress; Joshua Leavitt to Salmon P. Chase, March 11, 1851, in Chase Papers, HSP.

candidate, but he did so primarily out of a sense of obligation "to repair the (apparent, but certainly unintended, and probably unavoidable) slight given" to Hale in 1848. In the end, the party, hoping to draw votes away from Franklin Pierce and the Democrats, changed its name to Free Democratic, wrote a platform filled with Democratic doctrines, and nominated Hale. Although Hale received only 156,000 votes and the Democrats swept to victory, Leavitt optimistically believed a fundamental restructuring of the party system to be imminent. The crushing Whig defeat, he reasoned, was "hopeful to the cause of freedom," for the Democrats would now assume the position of "general conservation and panic-making." The Free Democracy, he predicted with some accuracy, would thus stand as the radical party and "carry the country in eight years, if not in four."[21]

When Leavitt made this prediction, he could not know that within months of the 1852 election Senator Stephen A. Douglas and other "cowardly and impudent bullies" would attempt to push through Congress a bill to organize the Nebraska Territory, or that debate on this matter would help to destroy a second party system already seriously weakened by a number of social, economic, and political developments—including the declining intensity of interparty debate on constitutional and economic issues and the growing sense among voters that both major parties were corrupt and unresponsive to the needs of the people. Ironically, as Michael F. Holt has pointed out, Douglas's effort to provide an issue that would unify the Democratic party in fact severed the northern and southern wings of the Whig party—already dealt a severe blow by massive defections to the Know-Nothing movement—and produced a significant voter realignment. This process culminated in the formation of the Republican party, which argued effectively that it alone would protect northern interests against the Slave Power. Leavitt played only a minor role in these events. But, as he informed Birney in 1855, he was pleased to be able "to do something, at least indirectly, for the cause we all love." His contribution generally took the form of writing a few pieces for newspapers and journals, editing news reports for the columns of the *Independent*, and, perhaps most gratifying of all, holding long talks with

21. Joshua Leavitt to Charles Sumner, June 11, 1852, in Sumner Papers; Joshua Leavitt to Roger Hooker Leavitt, November 12, 1852, in Leavitt Papers; see also Blue, *The Free Soilers*, 232–68.

Sumner and other antislavery congressmen when they stopped by the paper's office to share information and solicit his views on a broad range of issues.[22]

By 1856, former Democrats constituted a small but influential minority of the Republican party's supporters. Leavitt clearly aligned himself with this faction of the party. He believed that the new party must be a thoroughgoing antislavery party and espouse democratic principles, which he continued essentially to equate with the principles endorsed by the Democratic party.

In a series of articles that appeared in the *New Englander* in 1856, he agreed with Senator Thomas Hart Benton, whose book on democracy he reviewed, that whatever its defects, democracy was "productive of more good and less evil, than any method of government which can be brought into comparison with it." The popular will, he argued, must therefore be given free application in the control of the government, with a minimum of checks imposed on it. The human rights and egalitarian implications of the antislavery philosophy clearly had moved him far from his emphasis a quarter century earlier on the need to impose controls on humanity's baser instincts. Yet his experience with antiabolitionist mobs and gag rules also had convinced him that, at times, the popular will could be the instrument of oppression and serve to place the government beyond the reach of the people. The nativists, he believed, were a case in point. He still harbored some of the anti-Catholic sentiment that he had expressed so vocally in the 1830s. Now, following the massive influx of Catholic immigrants and growing evidence that they voted overwhelmingly Democratic, he became more openly anti-Catholic. There was, he wrote in the *New Englander*, "evidence of a design on the part of a foreign priesthood to exert an undue control over the measures of government." In pointing to the "general rally of the people" which had "warned the foreign party to keep their place," he showed a degree of sympathy for the nativist movement. But in the final analysis he condemned the Know-Nothings for their undemocratic means. It would be "a sad day for democracy," he said, "if bigoted alarmists are allowed to seize upon the opportunity, and trample down the great democratic principle,

22. Joshua Leavitt to Charles Sumner, July 7, 1854, in Sumner Papers; Leavitt to Birney, April 10, 1855, in Dumond (ed.), *Birney Letters*, II, 1172. On the disintegration of the second party system and the rise of the Republican party, see Holt, *The Political Crisis of the 1850s*, 101–81.

that the government of the state belongs to the people of the state, as a whole, and not to a favored class, by whatever mark or accident distinguished."[23]

Leavitt also could not bring himself to support the Know-Nothings because they sought to subordinate the slavery question to the Catholic issue. At the same time, he remained thoroughly convinced that the Democrats could not translate their basic principles into action, whether with slavery, the tariff, or other issues. A Republican administration, he wrote in 1856, "shall be Democratic without being subservient to the dictation of a sectional or class interest." He continued to be pulled by the force of the Democrats' stated ideals, even to the point of confiding to Chase, who shared his strong attachment to Democratic doctrines: "In looking to the future, I am driven again and again to consider the question, which I have so many times examined and re-examined, whether in a contingency I would not rather vote for the old rotten and corrupt Democratic hierarchy, with all its abominations." It is difficult to imagine how he could have supported the party of Pierce, Buchanan, and Douglas. But he quickly added that he could not do this "unless it were a case of speedy life or death to the country itself—a crisis which I have no expectation of living to see."[24]

When Leavitt looked at the political landscape in the mid-1850s, he saw only one choice that made any sense: the Republican party. The Know-Nothings were "reactionary Protestant Jesuits," the Democrats hopelessly corrupt and proslavery, and the Whigs—what remained of the party—"the chief cause of *all* the political evils of the last thirty years—including the dominancy of the slave power." From the Republican party's inception he feared that the "Whig stupidity," as he termed it, would pervert the party's principles. As a political outsider he could do little but complain bitterly to Chase and other Democratic-oriented Republicans. He took some comfort, however, in the conviction that the principles he had espoused in the columns of the *Emancipator* would become the foundation of the Republican philosophy. "That labor," he wrote to Chase with a sense of pride, "was not lost. Those sound Democratic principles were good seed sown in

23. Leavitt, "American Democracy," *New Englander*, XIV (February, 1856), 52–53, 59, 71; also (August, 1856), 385–409.

24. *Ibid.*, 397; Joshua Leavitt to Salmon P. Chase, March 13, 1855, in Chase Papers, HSP.

good ground, and it grew while State Street slept, and it will bring forth fruit an hundred fold. My old readers are being scattered all over the country—the boys have become men, and they understand principles, and they know their rights, and knowing, dare maintain them." He also believed that only a "true Democrat" from the West such as Chase could free the party from the suspicion that it was "a Whig trick in disguise," successfully combat the "Proslavery Know-Nothings," defeat the Democrats, and save the nation. If Chase, who was governor of Ohio, should win the 1856 election, Leavitt informed him, "I should consider the salvation of my country as secured for the next hundred years, and the greatest danger it has to apprehend as already passed. . . . It would turn back the tide of slavery, and with that the flood of official corruption which now threatens destruction almost as much as slavery itself."[25]

No other prospective candidate interested Leavitt. Throughout 1855 and the first months of 1856, he threw himself into the drive to effect Chase's nomination, writing pieces for newspapers and sending a circular to all of the Republican delegates on the eve of the nominating convention. He was prepared to "go wherever that may call me" if Chase was elected. However, even before the convention, Chase, though certain that his leadership qualities and the principles he stood for would attract mass support, had been outmaneuvered and outorganized by the followers of John C. Frémont. Seemingly bothered more by "too many signs of the old Whig cats in the meal" than by Frémont's vague antislavery views, Leavitt went so far as to warn that if an old-line conservative Whig joined the Frémont ticket, he would become "one of any number, large or small, to hoist anew the flag of our old faithful and true seven thousand [1840]." Once Frémont was nominated, however, Leavitt quickly expressed admiration for him as the only man who could unite the party and support his candidacy, which carried all but five nonslaveholding states and polled more than 1,300,000 votes.[26]

It is extremely doubtful whether Leavitt had either the energy or the will to begin the antislavery struggle anew; or, if he had, whether he could have found more than a few political abolitionists willing to

25. Leavitt to Chase, March 13, 14, 1855, May 2, 1856, in Chase Papers, HSP; also Joshua Leavitt to Roger Hooker Leavitt, March 2, 1855, in Leavitt Papers.

26. Joshua Leavitt to Salmon P. Chase, June 2, 1856, in Chase Papers; Frederick J. Blue, *Salmon P. Chase: A Life in Politics* (Kent, Oh., 1987), 103–15.

join him in such an undertaking. Having ultimately supported Hale rather than Fessenden in 1847, and then Van Buren rather than Hale in 1848, he was not now inclined to stand apart from the Republican party at a time when it was rapidly becoming a major force in northern politics. Unable—and in many ways unwilling—to alter the course of antislavery politics, he had come to the point of accepting virtually any candidate for president who professed to dislike slavery and seemed electable. In the late 1850s he did not even consider supporting the Radical Abolitionist party—an extension of the old Liberty League headed by Gerrit Smith, William Goodell, and Frederick Douglass—in part because it called for federal abolition in the states but more so because he believed that it had no chance to win. While at times tempted to move back toward a more uncompromising abolitionist stance, he concluded that, given the limits of northern public opinion, this would be fruitless. As he noted to Birney in explaining why he would not consider editing an antislavery paper in New York with which both men could be satisfied: "There is no demand, so far as I can see, for our labors in carrying forward these investigations to higher points and more profound principles."[27]

Now in his early sixties, Leavitt was increasingly conscious of his advancing age. He noted, for example, that few in his mother's or father's family had lived longer than he; the death of Birney in 1857, William Jay in 1858, and Gamaliel Bailey in 1859 made him even more keenly aware of his age. Moreover, his position with the *Independent* provided tolerable employment and a measure of financial security for him and Sarah. Recurring illness, which ultimately forced him to take a leave of absence from the paper for several months in 1858, intensified his preoccupation with stability and security. He managed to make the long journey to Columbus, Ohio, in the spring of 1857 to visit his friend Chase, then governor, and to talk about antislavery politics.[28] He also frequently visited his brothers in Massachusetts and his sons, who were now scattered throughout the Northeast. But, in all, these were rather uneventful years for him.

Leavitt's interest in politics revived as the 1860 presidential election

27. Leavitt to Birney, April 10, 1855, in Dumond (ed.), *Birney Letters*, II, 1173; see also Benjamin Quarles, *Frederick Douglass* (New York, 1968), 156–62.

28. Joshua Leavitt to Roger Hooker Leavitt, May 21, 22, 1857, in Leavitt Papers. In 1854 he received an honorary doctorate from Wabash College, a Congregational school in Indiana. *Independent*, May 30, 1854.

drew near. Despite his Democratic sympathies, he continued to give his wholehearted support to the Republican party, believing it to be the repository of antislavery sentiment in the North. He had enthusiastically supported Chase in 1856 and would have done so again, but Chase's failure to organize in the East and even to persuade many Ohio Republicans to back him had forced him out of the race by 1859. For Leavitt and many other radical Republicans this left William Seward as the logical candidate. Although Seward was a former Whig and, in Leavitt's opinion, "no favorite of mine," his "Irrepressible Conflict" speech of 1858 and the Democrats' and conservative Republicans' subsequent attacks on him made Seward appear to be one of the Radicals. Even after Seward had begun to make conciliatory gestures to the South and to conservatives in the party, Leavitt felt that he would "now rather be defeated with him than succeed with a Southern Man," such as Abraham Lincoln. Yet, following Lincoln's nomination Leavitt (and most blacks and other abolitionists) supported him. Whatever reservations they had concerning his views on race and slavery were offset by the fact that he represented, as Leavitt saw it, the "nature, object and spirit of the party" and, perhaps most important, would sweep to victory. Upon hearing the news of Lincoln's election in November 1860, he was elated. "Thank God! Lincoln is chosen," he wrote to Chase. "It is a joy to have lived to this day." [29]

Lincoln's election thrust the nation into a crisis that threatened its existence. South Carolina's secession from the Union a month later infuriated Leavitt and most other Republicans. He insisted to Sumner that "there is no such thing as lawful secession from the Union, and the first *overt act* in that direction is simply treason, and must be held and treated as such." In addition, because President James Buchanan had provided aid and comfort to the secessionists, he must resign or be impeached. [30]

But like many radical Republicans, Leavitt feared that Lincoln would not stand firm in the deepening crisis. The Whig factor again loomed large, as it had since 1840. Long after Clay's death, Leavitt still saw evidence of his insidious influence. "The idea of uncommittalism, timidity, lack of definite political belief, and irresoluteness," he

29. Joshua Leavitt to Roger Hooker Leavitt, April 3, May 25, 1860, in Leavitt Papers; Joshua Leavitt to Salmon P. Chase, November 7, 1860, in Chase Papers, LC.

30. Joshua Leavitt to Charles Sumner, December 17, 1860, in Sumner Papers.

complained to Chase, might well guide the actions of Lincoln, Seward, and other old Clay Whigs in the secession crisis. If Lincoln in fact wished to move the party "over the same trash that Henry Clay marked out for the Whig party—to the same end," he warned, the Republicans would suffer the same fate as had the Whigs. Thus, he urged that young Benton Democrats be given prominent Cabinet positions and that Chase become secretary of the treasury, where he could help to move the tariff in the direction of free trade. Yet, notwithstanding his serious reservations about Lincoln's decisiveness and fortitude, he became increasingly exuberant as the inauguration approached. "12 1/2 O'clock P.M.," he wrote his brother on March 2. "Only 47 1/2 hours—and then! Hurrah for President Lincoln! The above slipped from my pen spontaneously." [31]

To Leavitt, the Republican triumph was a most auspicious signpost along the path on which he and a few others had embarked more than twenty years earlier. All too soon, a terrible, bloody war would engulf the nation, plunging it into the horrors of fratricide; yet it would also move the nation inexorably toward the long-awaited destruction of slavery. In the midst of this great struggle—and even into the postwar years—Leavitt would regain some of his old vivacity and energy, espousing some old causes and discovering new ones that he believed worthy of public concern and support.

31. Joshua Leavitt to Salmon P. Chase, January 19, 1861, in Chase Papers, LC; Joshua Leavitt to Roger Hooker Leavitt, March 2, 1861, in Leavitt Papers.

13

CIVIL WAR DIPLOMACY AND
THE FINAL YEARS

When the Civil War began in April 1861 most abolitionists, including many Garrisonians, closed ranks in support of the war effort. The gulf that had separated Leavitt and Garrison for twenty years remained, but they could agree that the war must be vigorously prosecuted and that emancipation must stand with the preservation of the Union as twin goals of the struggle. Unlike many of the Garrisonians, Leavitt had never doubted whether the Union was worth preserving; even in the darkest hours of the nation's travail he remained certain that the great sacrifices made in behalf of the Union were worthwhile. In early 1864, when the outcome of the war still hung in the balance, Leavitt confided to Chase that while the state was "bound to bear true allegiance to God, to honor his government, and to obey his laws," it was also "a sacred thing, entitled to the most intense loyalty, the most ardent love, and the greatest possible efforts and sacrifices for its protection and advancement." He and many other northern evangelical Protestants viewed the war as a necessary if terrible means by which the American people would purge themselves and their nation of "the false maxims and unsound doctrines with which Slavery had poisoned the whole social constitution of this country through all the channels of thought and sentiment."[1]

---

1. Joshua Leavitt to Salmon P. Chase, February 12, 1864, in Chase Papers, LC. On the northern churches and the war effort, see James H. Moorhead, *American Apocalypse: Yankee Protestants and the Civil War* (New Haven, Conn., 1978).

Leavitt never wavered in his belief that all Northerners must contribute to the war effort in whatever way they could. While a seminary student in the 1820s, he had counseled his younger brother Roger Hooker, who had declined to serve in the militia, that military service was "an important duty, which every militia man owes to his country." Now that the nation faced the ultimate test of survival, he immediately sprang to its defense. In May 1861 he asked Chase to assist in obtaining commissions for his son William and other men who wished to form a volunteer cavalry regiment. During the war Leavitt was disturbed by news of inadequate provisions and incompetent officers and often worried about the safety of William and Thomas, both of whom saw considerable action in the Virginia theater during their enlistments. But he never wavered in his commitment to the Union cause and was immensely proud of his sons' service in defense of the country. As he wrote his sister Chloe, who questioned whether they should send their boys off to war: "It seems to me, not only a duty but a privilege, and with many benefits as well as dangers. . . . There is hardly one of our boys who has not already *doubled* his manhood."[2]

Throughout the war Leavitt continued to work for the *Independent*, but personnel changes in the office significantly altered his position. Some of these changes resulted from the paper's chronic financial troubles. The *Independent*'s subscription list had reached 45,000 by the end of the 1850s, but high production costs and low subscription rates caused the paper to continue to lose money. In an attempt to improve the paper's position Henry Bowen, who was the sole proprietor by the late 1850s, placed more advertising in its columns and hired Theodore Tilton, a brash young journalist with ties to the Garrisonian camp, as Leavitt's assistant in the office. With his heavy work load, Leavitt no doubt needed some assistance. But it soon became clear that Tilton was being groomed to replace him. During Leavitt's illness in 1858, Bowen gave Tilton $500 of Leavitt's salary, which was not returned when he came back to the office. Angered and hurt, he nevertheless felt compelled to suffer in silence and prove that he could perform his duties.[3]

2. Joshua Leavitt to Roger Hooker Leavitt, April 16, 1824, Joshua Leavitt to Chloe Leavitt, January 3, 1862, in Leavitt Papers.

3. Leonard Bacon to Henry C. Bowen, December 18, 1858, in Bacon Papers; *Independent*, September 2, 1851, January 5, 1854, December 13, 1855; Joshua Leavitt to Roger Hooker Leavitt, October 15, 1858, in Leavitt Papers.

Leavitt chose to remain with the paper, but Leonard Bacon, Joseph Thompson, and Richard Storrs—resentful of undue interference with editorial policy and Bowen's failure to consult them on important matters—resigned their posts in 1861. In the wake of these resignations Bowen appointed Henry Ward Beecher as editor-in-chief and Tilton as managing editor. Leavitt reacted with ambivalence to these dramatic changes, which made Tilton his superior in the office. "It leaves me," he informed his sister Chloe, "with more freedom to work, more responsibility, more care and labor, and more apprehension for the future, but cheerful in my work." He got along well with Beecher, who respected him as a "patriarch among journalists and second to none in experience and sound judgment." While he regretted the way in which the original editors had been forced out, under the leadership of Beecher, and especially Tilton, the *Independent* became more outspoken in its support of abolition than it had been in the 1850s. Further, Beecher's busy schedule until his resignation in 1863 left much of the decision making in the hands of the energetic and innovative Tilton, who presided over the meteoric rise of the paper's subscription level to 100,000 by 1865.[4]

The resignation of Bacon, Thompson, and Storrs also worked to Leavitt's disadvantage. Tilton viewed him as an old man who added relatively little to the efficiency of the operation. He was determined to bring new blood to the staff, hiring Fred Perkins as Leavitt's assistant and Oliver Johnson as office manager in 1863, and then relegating Leavitt to the Office of Religious Intelligence. Whether these changes resulted from a personality clash with Leavitt or from the desire to develop a more youthful staff is not clear, but Tilton seemed essentially indifferent to the old man's presence. In 1863 he reported to Beecher: "The office goes on as smoothly as a Prayer Meeting. The Doctor [Leavitt] takes it very easy, doing almost nothing, but is growing good natured, which is all I ask." Leavitt was obviously unhappy with this state of affairs. He did not agree with some of Tilton's and Bowen's policies and was furious that his salary of $1,500 fell far below the range of $3,000 to $5,000 paid to others in the office. This situation, he remarked bitterly to Salmon P. Chase in 1864, could be attributed

4. Joshua Leavitt to Chloe Leavitt, January 3, 1862, in Leavitt Papers; *Independent*, December 19, 1861; Filler, "Liberalism, Anti-Slavery, and the Founders of the *Independent*," 303–304.

to the fact that he was "69 years old—too old to seek another situation, and too poor to give up what I get." [5]

The war years, however, were also a time of some contentment and satisfaction for Leavitt. His son James, a prosperous merchant in New York, married in the summer of 1863, and both William and Thomas served with distinction in the army and came home safely. In addition, he maintained an abiding interest in the affairs of Yale College, advising Bacon and college officials on such matters as the expansion of the physical plant and conferring of honorary degrees. In 1864 he helped to plan his fiftieth reunion. This was a time to look back over a half century and gain some perspective on the passage of time since his days as an undergraduate. Writing to Samuel B. Ruggles, a classmate from 1814, he remarked: "If you reckon back 50 years from 1814, it goes to 1764, the year before the Stamp Act, and just after the French War, which then looked to us like an event of ancient history, it was so remote. It is different now to realize that, to the old men we were then conversant with, these events were as familiar as the War of 1812 is to us." [6]

In these years Leavitt's normal daily routine moved at a more relaxed pace, with fewer responsibilities in the office and fewer obligations outside the workplace. He no longer worked fourteen-hour days at the office but left at tea time in mid-afternoon. He then spent quiet evenings with Sarah, reading and writing. "And so," he wrote Chase in 1864, "with a few good friends around, and occasional attendance at public meetings, I am spending my seventieth year, with a good degree of satisfaction, and very little to give me discomfort." [7]

Yet Leavitt did not plan to live out the remaining years of his life in domestic ease. In fact, the free time that his subordinate post at the *Independent* afforded him, as well as the important domestic and international developments generated by the Civil War, combined to energize him. Once more he threw himself into the task of shaping public

5. Theodore Tilton to Henry Ward Beecher, August 23, 1863, in Beecher Family Papers, Sterling Library, Yale University; Joshua Leavitt to Salmon P. Chase, February 6, 1864, in Chase Papers, LC.

6. Joshua Leavitt to S. B. Ruggles, enclosed in circular to Class of 1814 of Yale College, June 30, 1864, in Stokes Autograph Collection, Sterling Library, Yale University.

7. Leavitt to Chase, February 12, 1864, in Chase Papers, LC.

opinion on matters he believed to be of paramount importance to the welfare of the American people. Perhaps more than at any other time in his life, he now knew that men such as Chase and Charles Sumner, who wielded power in the highest levels of government, valued his opinions on a broad range of issues, and that he could influence the thinking of Henry Ward Beecher, Francis Lieber, George Bancroft, and other prominent men outside the government.

During the war years Leavitt devoted much of his attention to foreign policy matters, especially America's relations with the Latin American republics and the need to uphold the nation's honor and prestige in the world. In this effort he did not ignore the aspirations of blacks in the United States and the rest of the hemisphere. He firmly believed that the Lincoln administration must move against slavery at home in the course of prosecuting the war, as well as advance the interests of blacks and the nation by recognizing Haiti. Such diplomatic recognition, he wrote in the *Independent* at the time debate on recognition raged in Congress in early 1862, would be a "simple act of justice" toward a much wronged people as well as a means of strengthening American interests in the Caribbean. Even as this debate progressed, some of his friends, with his consent, had begun to recommend him for the post of commissioner to Haiti. With passage of the Haitian recognition bill in April 1862, which he viewed as a "final blow to the slave power," he joined a small army of office seekers who beseeched public officials to assist them in obtaining a government job. He launched a vigorous campaign to obtain the post, asking Chase, Sumner, and even William Seward to work in his behalf to enlist Lincoln's support, and forwarding recommendations from Lieber, Joseph Thompson, Bancroft, and a host of other friends and acquaintances. At one point he even contemplated visiting Washington to plead his case.[8]

Leavitt's reasons for seeking the post were quite varied. He sincerely believed that a sympathetic American presence in Haiti would do much to improve relations between the two peoples and would assist blacks throughout the Western Hemisphere. While he advanced the

8. *Independent*, March 20, 1862; Joshua Leavitt to Charles Sumner, April 25, May 10, 1862, in Sumner Papers; Joshua Leavitt to Joshua Giddings, February 25, 1862, in Giddings Papers; Joshua Leavitt to George Bancroft, April 28, 1862, in Bancroft Papers; Joshua Leavitt to Salmon P. Chase, April 22, 1862, in Chase Papers, LC.

paternalistic theory that the Haitian people would benefit greatly from their contact with American Protestantism and republicanism, he also understood, however imperfectly, that Haiti logically would be in the vanguard of an emerging black consciousness in the Americas. As he remarked to Chase, there were 12 million blacks in the Western Hemisphere "and Haiti is the center, and ought to take the lead in gradually nationalizing this mass." Having read widely on the region, he fashioned himself as something of an expert on Latin American and Caribbean affairs and believed that he could "serve my country—and humanity—if it is not too late." Yet, perhaps above all, he believed that he should be supported for the post "for old times' sake" in light of his lengthy service to the antislavery cause.[9]

All of his lobbying, however, came to naught. Following the appointment of B. F. Whidden of New Hampshire as ambassador, Leavitt accused Senator Hale of simply desiring additional "diplomatic plunder" for his constituents and claimed, probably on the basis of inside information from Chase, that Lincoln himself was "both disappointed and mortified at being peremptorily reined up" by Hale. When it became known that Whidden might not be able to accept the post, Leavitt regained hope and suggested to Seward, Chase, and others that Whidden be given another government position. After all, he reiterated to Joshua Giddings, who had also expressed interest in the position, the Haitian post should be given to "one of the old abolitionists, and not to a mere political jobber, of no special qualification." He received assurances from Hale that he would recommend Whidden for another slot, but to Leavitt's disappointment Whidden ultimately decided to accept the ambassadorship to Haiti.[10]

Leavitt's assumption that the post should be his because of his years of service to the cause of abolition was not so much incorrect as essentially irrelevant. Sumner, Chase, and other friends—and perhaps Lincoln himself—recognized the symbolic importance of appointing an abolitionist to the Haitian post. But Leavitt failed to realize sufficiently

9. Leavitt to Chase, April 22, July 18, 30, 1862, in Chase Papers, LC; Leavitt to Giddings, February 25, 1862, in Giddings Papers.

10. Joshua Leavitt to Joshua Giddings, June 26, 1862, in Giddings Papers; Joshua Leavitt to Charles Sumner, June 25, August 18, 1862, in Sumner Papers; Joshua Leavitt to William Seward, July 18, 1862, in William Henry Seward Papers, University of Rochester; Leavitt to Chase, June 6, July 18, 29, 30, August 12, 1862, in Chase Papers, LC.

that patronage was an important means of generating and maintaining broad support for the party. In the appointment of diplomatic representatives and other government officials, political influence often carried more weight than did ability or experience. Leavitt, of course, lacked diplomatic experience, and his political influence had been limited largely to Liberty party circles in the 1840s.

After the dust had settled Leavitt attempted to hide his disappointment, informing Chase that it was probably too late in life "to learn a new trade" and that Sarah was pleased "once more by learning that I am to stay at home." His failure to receive the Haitian appointment did not lessen his interest in America's foreign policy. Though nearly seventy years old, he threw himself, with an energy and zeal he had not displayed since the 1840s, into the effort to educate government officials and the public to the dangers and opportunities confronting the United States in the world order. He wrote numerous articles for the *Independent*, the *New Englander*, and other newspapers and magazines; presented scores of speeches; and frequently argued his case to Chase, Sumner, and other government leaders. Throughout the war he argued vigorously for closer relations with the nations of the Western Hemisphere and for an aggressive policy in defense of America's prerogatives and the entire hemisphere's interests in the face of encroachments by the European powers. He did not ignore the nation's gradual movement toward the cherished goal of emancipation, but he focused much of his attention on foreign policy. The affairs of America's neighbors, he wrote to Chase in 1864, were so important to America's future that he had dropped most other projects, including writing a history of the Liberty party.[11]

An intense nationalism, which stemmed from his belief that the United States must not only crush the rebel insurgents and preserve the beloved Union but also stand before the world as a great power in the face of European aggression, goes far to explain Leavitt's concentration on foreign policy issues. More specifically, the invasion of Mexico in 1861 by the combined forces of France, England, and Spain for the purpose of forcing payment of foreign debts, and the subsequent French establishment of a puppet government in Mexico, sparked his interest in America's Latin American policy. These actions, as much as "the apathy and inaction with which our own Government

11. Leavitt to Chase, August 12, 1862, February 12, 1864, in Chase Papers, LC.

apparently regards these threatening inroads upon the independence of all American nations," angered him. The Lincoln administration must, he declared, take bold and immediate action—by relieving Thomas Corwin, whom he regarded as excessively pro-British, of his duties as minister to Mexico; by appointing respected plenipotentiaries, including John C. Frémont, to argue the American case before the French government; and, above all, as he argued as early as 1862, by invoking the Monroe Doctrine, thereby forcing the European powers out of Mexico and the Western Hemisphere. "We only dissent," he wrote in the *Independent*, "from the idea that we will wait *till after* the rebellion before we take our stand once more alongside of our glorious fathers of the golden period of American politics. The European powers understand too well the value of their present opportunity. The time to assert our Doctrine, and thus recover our honor, is *now*, in the very day of our fiery trial."[12]

In an article on the Monroe Doctrine, which first appeared in the *New Englander* and was then printed in pamphlet form and sent to every member of the U.S. Senate, he argued that when the Monroe Doctrine was promulgated in the 1820s the Holy Alliance seriously threatened the independence of the United States, the English played a very minor role in preventing the alliance from intervening in the Western Hemisphere, and the doctrine was intended as a timeless statement of American foreign policy—"an axiomatic truth in political science."[13] This made for bad history. But Leavitt was far less interested in carefully analyzing the complex process that had produced the Monroe Doctrine than in arousing the patriotic feelings of his readers and mobilizing the public and government officials behind an aggressive foreign policy designed to throw the French out of Mexico.

Some members of the State Department and the Senate shared Leavitt's concerns about the French presence in Mexico. For example, in 1863 Senator James A. McDougall of California called for war with France if it did not withdraw its troops immediately. But most senators, including Leavitt's friend Sumner, who served as chairman of the Committee on Foreign Relations, opposed such a drastic measure. Even Chase, though disturbed by the European presence in the Ameri-

12. Joshua Leavitt to Salmon P. Chase, October 23, 1862, in Chase Papers, LC; *Independent*, April 23, 1862.
13. Joshua Leavitt, *The Monroe Doctrine* (New York, 1863), 7–12, 18, 20–25, 48.

cas, reminded Leavitt that for the government to insist that France leave Mexico immediately might precipitate France's recognition of the Confederacy and, perhaps, war. Leavitt, however, believed that such an ultimatum would result in neither war nor recognition. In any event, he concluded that war with France was preferable to being forced to "crawl at the feet of European absolutism." [14] To say that Americans could not assert their honor because they were engaged in a civil war, he stated fervently to Chase, "was simply to invite indignity by proclaiming that we can neither resist injury nor assert our self-respect." Most Americans shared Chase's reservations about risking a war with France in the midst of a desperate struggle to save the Union, but this did not deter Leavitt from his course. As so often happened in his life, he believed that he was right, that he must speak out, and that his work was extremely important to the future of the country. [15]

In 1864 Leavitt's preoccupation with the need for the government to stand firm against the designs of the European powers and to hire competent men in the field prompted him once more to seek a diplomatic post—this time as minister to Ecuador. He had long considered the minister, Frederick Hassurek, to be typical of those officials who were "either purchasable or reactionary in their personal feelings, or else are careful for nothing but their schemes." When he learned that Hassurek would soon resign his post, Leavitt again turned to Thompson, Beecher, Sumner, and other friends for recommendations. He cited as reasons why he should receive the appointment his interest in and knowledge of Latin America, his failure to receive the Haitian post in 1862, and his desire to leave his children "some evidence of recognition." He even attempted to learn Spanish in preparation for the position. But once more he failed in his quest. [16]

Although Leavitt sought no other diplomatic position, his interest in Latin American affairs continued unabated. In addition, he increas-

14. David Donald, *Charles Sumner and the Rights of Man* (New York, 1970), 101–102, 142–43; Joshua Leavitt to Salmon P. Chase, November 12, 1863, in Chase Papers, LC; Salmon P. Chase to Joshua Leavitt, January 24, 1864, in Robert B. Warden, *An Account of the Private Life and Public Services of Salmon Portland Chase* (Cincinnati, 1874), 562.

15. Joshua Leavitt to Salmon P. Chase, February 12, 1864, in Chase Papers, LC.

16. Joshua Leavitt to Charles Sumner, January 15, March 1, June 27, September 17, 30, 1864, in Sumner Papers.

ingly argued the relevance of the Monroe Doctrine to the existing European situation. Obviously influenced by the French presence in Mexico and by the South's secession from the Union, he denounced the German Confederation and its Danish sympathizers for attempting to foment secession in Denmark's territory and for intervening in the internal affairs of a sovereign nation. He urged Sumner to press the Russian government to declare in favor of the rights of the weaker European nations, just as the United States had done in the Western Hemisphere in 1823.[17]

Yet, in stark contrast to his expressed hope that the European powers would adopt the principles of the Monroe Doctrine, Leavitt insisted that Russia had been justified in carving up Poland in the past and in suppressing the recent Polish rebellion. "For the extinction of Poland," he stated coldly, "there need not be even the passing cloud of national sorrow." Here, as in his other writings on international relations, he showed far more interest in shaping public opinion than in presenting a balanced analysis. Thus, he conveniently viewed both the Polish and the southern American rebellions as "unwarranted, reckless, and hopeless" and strongly defended the actions of Russia, the Union's strongest ally in Europe and then engaged in emancipating the serfs—an undertaking that he considered "as much an act of simple justice" as was Lincoln's Emancipation Proclamation.[18]

Leavitt's belief that Catholicism was a reactionary and dangerous force in the world and that the Church of Rome and the French government were part of an enormous conspiracy to destroy religious liberty and self-determination among the peoples of both Latin America and Europe also explains his lack of sympathy for the Polish people and his vociferous denunciation of the French occupation of Mexico. Even while criticizing the nativists in the 1850s for their undemocratic measures and their attempts to subordinate the slavery issue to the anti-Catholic crusade, he had feared that a "foreign priesthood" threatened to subvert cherished American values and institutions. Now, perhaps because he considered the French to be allies of the Confederates, he leaped to the improbable conclusion that a vast Catholic conspiracy existed on the world stage. A sinister papacy and

17. Joshua Leavitt to Charles Sumner, March 14, April 23, 1864, in Sumner Papers; Joshua Leavitt, *Denmark, and Its Relations* (New York, 1864), 7, 11–13, 16–17.

18. Joshua Leavitt, *Poland* (New York, 1864), 12; *Independent*, June 1, 1864.

the French, with the Jesuits as their shock troops and the Protestant English as unwitting accomplices, he charged, sought to advance the forces of "priestcraft, popular ignorance, and barbarism" at the expense of "liberty and law, public improvement, and general educational progress." In seeking to explain the American government's inaction in the face of these threats, he even blamed Secretary of State Seward's friendship with Archbishop John Hughes of New York.[19]

Leavitt conceded to Chase in 1864 that in advancing his views on the Monroe Doctrine, "my vanity may run me into some ludicrous extravagance, but I hope not." It appears that he reached that point. His harangues about the dangers of an international Catholic conspiracy and his call for a massive Protestant missionary effort in Latin America to destroy the supposed conspiracy and raise the people of Latin America "to a much higher level of intelligence, liberty, and civilization" seem rather absurd. Moreover, his scheme appealed to few Americans in the midst of the Civil War.[20]

In all of his publications and correspondence relating to America's foreign policy Leavitt criticized, either directly or by implication, the course pursued by the Lincoln administration. "And we share in the prevalent wonder," he exclaimed in the *Independent*, "at the apathy and inaction with which our own Government apparently regards these threatening inroads upon the independence of all American nations." Similarly, he and many other radical Republicans believed that the government should prosecute the war more vigorously and immediately deal slavery a death blow. "We are solemnly waiting for the army of the Potomac to win *one* victory that it can use and follow up," he complained to his brother in 1862. While hoping that "God pities us enough to give us time to work it out in this slipshod way," he clearly blamed Lincoln for failing to provide the necessary leadership. By 1863, he had concluded that Lincoln could not meet "the exigencies that will inevitably arise in our domestic *and* foreign affairs the next four years." A growing number of Republicans who shared

19. Joshua Leavitt to Charles Sumner, January 30, 1863, in Sumner Papers. For an excellent treatment of the pervasive theme of conspiracy in nineteenth-century America, see David B. Davis, "Some Themes of Counter-Subversion: An Analysis of Anti-Masonic, Anti-Catholic, and Anti-Mormon Literature," *Mississippi Valley Historical Review*, XLVII (September, 1960), 205–24.

20. Leavitt to Chase, February 12, 1864, in Chase Papers, LC; Joshua Leavitt to Charles Sumner, January 15, 16, 1864, in Sumner Papers.

his dissatisfaction with Lincoln's performance looked to Chase as the man who could best achieve the Radicals' objectives. Just as in 1856 and 1860, Chase wanted the presidency; in late 1863, while expressing his admiration for Lincoln, he declared himself a candidate.[21]

Leavitt feared that Lincoln would lose the election and thus ensure "the elevation of probably the most injurious ticket that shall be up." Consequently, he fully supported Chase, whose performance in the Treasury Department he considered "truly brilliant." He announced that if Chase were nominated he would "hoist again the Old Liberty Party flag of uncompromising and pure principles, and nail it to the mast with the name on it of the most worthy and stand by it, let who will succeed in gaining the election." He stuck with Chase to the bitter end. He not only objected to the Lincoln administration's failure to act decisively on foreign policy matters and on the home front but also remained convinced that the Whig factor was responsible for these shortcomings. In early 1864 he even went so far as to argue to Sumner that it would be preferable to lose with Chase than to support the "Blair-Seward-Lincoln Administration." "It is possible," he added ominously, "that if the Union party have two candidates, a Copperhead may succeed. If so, let those bear the responsibility who are resolved to stick by Lincoln in order to preserve slavery."[22]

When the Chase boom collapsed following the premature appearance of the Pomeroy Circular in February 1864, in which Chase's principal supporters proposed him for the nomination, Leavitt felt cut adrift, with no viable options left. He seems not to have supported the hastily organized Radical Democracy party, which nominated Frémont and drew up a platform that contained many planks Leavitt certainly favored—including economy in government, passage of a constitutional amendment forever banning slavery, and a strong Reconstruction program under the aegis of Congress. He failed to support this movement more because he believed that it could not succeed

21. *Independent*, October 23, 1862; Joshua Leavitt to Roger Hooker Leavitt, December 6, 1862, in Leavitt Papers; Joshua Leavitt to Salmon P. Chase, September 30, 1863, in Chase Papers, LC. For contrasting treatments of Chase's political ambitions in 1864, see Albert Bushnell Hart, *Salmon Portland Chase* (Boston, 1899), 307–11; William Frank Zornow, *Lincoln and the Party Divided* (Norman. Okla., 1954), 24–27; Blue, *Salmon P. Chase*, 214–23.

22. Leavitt to Chase, September 30, 1863, February 12, 1864, in Chase Papers, LC; Joshua Leavitt to Charles Sumner, November 18, 1863, in Sumner Papers.

than because of any sudden interest in Lincoln's candidacy. The fact that he joined Tilton, George Cheever, Sumner, David Dudley Field, and other friends and associates in an ill-fated effort to persuade both Lincoln and Frémont to withdraw from the race in favor of Chase may be attributed largely to his strong attachment to Chase and his political philosophy. When this feeble effort went nowhere, Leavitt was despondent. "What are we poor radicals to do," he asked Sumner plaintively, "who dare not take the responsibility of prolonging the Seward-Weed Dynasty by voting for re-election?"[23]

In the final analysis, despite his Whig fixation and his fear that the Lincoln campaign might leave the party "without any basis of principle, a mere party of expediency," Leavitt reluctantly voted for Lincoln. The difficult dilemma that he faced in 1864 remained with him for the rest of his life: He subscribed to what he termed "democratic-republican ideas"—i.e., the exercise of national authority in times of crisis and war, and states' rights, "now free of the disturbing influence of slavery," in times of peace and stability—but could not bring himself to support the Democratic party so long as it remained committed to racist policies and the *status quo antebellum* in the South.[24] Thus, he found himself with little choice but to adopt the label "Independent Democrat" while consistently voting Republican.

Other Northerners, including William Cullen Bryant, editor of the New York *Evening Post*, shared his quandary. Beginning in 1864 Leavitt split his time between the *Independent*, where he reported weekly on religious conventions and personnel changes, and Bryant's *Evening Post*. This arrangement allowed for steady work, increased his salary in an inflationary period, and enabled him to serve as contributing editor for a newspaper whose stand on most major issues he generally supported. Bryant had carried the Democratic *Evening Post* into the Republican ranks in the mid-1850s, where it remained throughout the war. As the great issues of reconcilation and reconstruction loomed before the nation, he was a voice of moderation in the Republican party, initially supporting Andrew Johnson's call for a rapid restoration of self-government in the South. The South's fierce resistance to congressional Reconstruction, as well as Andrew John-

23. Blue, *Salmon P. Chase*, 222–39; Joshua Leavitt to Charles Sumner, July 6, 1864, in Sumner Papers.

24. New York *Evening Post*, January 17, 1865.

son's rigidity and negativism, however, moved him steadily toward the Radical position in support of black civil rights and suffrage.[25]

Bryant later stated that Leavitt's "politics were the politics of the *Evening Post*." In fact, from the Republican party's inception Leavitt had more consistently stood with the Radicals than had Bryant. He remained strongly committed to abolition and freedmen's rights. During the war, he and Beecher, Tilton, and other Radicals urged Lincoln to allow blacks to enlist in the army. He also argued in 1862 that the military must directly assist the freedmen and that blacks must be given fair wages, adequate tools, and some of the best of the confiscated lands. Only by these means, he pointed out to Chase, could the validity of the free labor ideal be confirmed and the nation be purged of the "false maxims and unsound doctrines with which Slavery had poisoned the whole social constitution."[26]

During the postwar era Leavitt continued to endorse efforts to bring millions of freedmen into the mainstream of American society and to protect their basic rights, believing that the government must be "one of the whole people regardless of race or class." Yet, unlike Wendell Phillips and a few other old abolitionists who continued to agitate for the protection of the freedmen's newly gained rights, he appears to have brought little of the crusading zeal to the cause of black civil rights that he once had directed toward abolition.[27]

At times, Leavitt seemed more interested in the spiritual state of blacks than in improving their social and economic conditions. For instance, when he and other Congregational leaders met in Boston for the National Council of Congregational Churches—one of the most important Congregational conventions of the nineteenth century—only a few weeks after the war ended, they sought primarily to extend the "benign measures of true Christian evangelization" to whites mov-

25. *Independent*, December 3, 1908; Joshua Leavitt to Roger Hooker Leavitt, July 24, 1866, in Leavitt Papers; New York *Evening Post*, May 25, June 17, September 25, 1865, February 20, March 30, 1866, July 16, 20, 25, 1867; Charles H. Brown, *William Cullen Bryant* (New York, 1971), 473–75.

26. *Independent*, January 20, 1873; Joshua Leavitt *et al.* to Abraham Lincoln, [August 1862], in Robert Todd Lincoln Collection, Library of Congress; Leavitt to Chase, February 27, 1863, February 12, 1864, in Chase Papers, LC.

27. New York *Evening Post*, September 27, 1865. Most of the pieces that appeared in the columns of the *Evening Post* were unsigned, thus making it extremely difficult to determine the authorship of much that Leavitt wrote for the paper.

ing into the West and to freedmen in the South. They viewed this endeavor as a Christian obligation as well as an important means of strengthening the church and making it a truly national denomination. The debate focused on how Congregationalists could best achieve these objectives, not on the future of race relations in America or the Reconstruction proposals then being debated by Congress. Leavitt led the convention's minority in calling upon the church to be both innovative and ecumenical in its efforts to evangelize whites and blacks. In a strongly worded minority report he emphasized the need for Christian unity and denounced the majority's attempt to equate Congregationalism with Calvinism as both unnecessary and divisive. After heated debate, he succeeded in forcing a compromise that deleted the term "Calvinism" from the convention's report.[28]

Following the ratification of the Thirteenth Amendment, Leavitt also devoted more attention to the tariff issue than to Reconstruction. In pamphlets, lectures, articles in the *Evening Post*, and from 1864 to 1868 as an active member of the executive committee of the American Free Trade League (a lobbying group headed by Bryant that sought to promote "an unrestricted commmercial intercourse" between the United States and all other nations), he called for the emancipation of Americans from the burden of class legislation promoted by selfish interests. He and other league members—including Parke Godwin, David Dudley Field, David Ames Wells, and Gerrit Smith—borrowed heavily from abolitionist rhetoric, branding protectionism as "injustice, fraud, robbery, the twin sister of slavery, the foe of truth, and the corrupter of good morals." Leavitt saw the two movements as fundamentally related. Both causes, he believed, sought to enable people to exercise their natural rights to make their own contracts in relation to the products of their labor. Free trade, he declared to Timothy Dwight Woolsey, a league member, "is therefore the proper complement of Free Labor."[29] Yet at times the league seemed to resent the fact that debate on the Reconstruction question had pushed aside most other public issues. As *The League*, the organization's journal, argued in 1867, the public must be prepared for the battle between "privilege

28. See *Debates and Proceedings of the National Council of Congregational Churches, 1865* (Boston, 1866), 430–37, 445–55.

29. *The League*, II (January, 1869), 182; Joshua Leavitt to Timothy D. Woolsey, May 16, 1868, in Woolsey Family Collection, Sterling Library, Yale University.

and freedom, the tariff and free trade," in spite of the "present obsession" with the Reconstruction question.[30]

Many of the league's leaders, including Leavitt, however, could not accept the Democrats' stance on the Reconstruction issue. Likewise, while their preference for an economy in which government largely left business alone closely paralleled that of many Democrats, these liberal reformers did not entirely trust the Democratic party's commitment to free trade. Leavitt remained extremely skeptical of the Democrats' rhetoric on this issue, noting to Woolsey in 1868 that they had "never once carried out their own theory to anything like a consistent conclusion."[31] But if the Democrats were untrustworthy on the tariff issue and unpalatable on the race issue, the Republicans—who during the war had boosted tariff rates to 57 percent, the highest in the nation's history to that date—occupied an intolerable position in relation to trade policy.

With the Republicans firmly entrenched in power, many league members realized that free trade in any pure form could not be enacted. Leavitt therefore urged the league to lobby for a tariff for revenue only, which he had first advocated in the 1840s. This "happy middleground," on which all opponents of protectionism could unite, he wrote Woolsey, would "produce required revenue, with the surest results, at the smallest expense, in a way the least burdensome to the people, and affording the fewest opportunities for fraud and evasion." The league adopted his compromise proposal in the late 1860s. Although in his early seventies, he remained active in the cause until the end of the decade, organizing league-sponsored conferences for the purpose of mobilizing scholars and students behind the concept of a tariff for revenue only, and in 1868 he even spent two weeks in Washington lobbying for congressional support.[32]

It was perhaps fitting that, as one of the American free trade movement's elder statesmen, Leavitt received recognition for his three decades of labor in behalf of the cause. At a gala dinner in 1868 honoring Bryant on his retirement as president of the American Free

30. *The League*, I (June, 1867), 1; also *Address to the American People, by the American Free Trade League* (New York, 1867), 2.

31. Leavitt to Woolsey, May 16, 1868, in Woolsey Family Collection.

32. Joshua Leavitt to Timothy D. Woolsey, May 6, April 9, 1868, in Woolsey Family Collection; Joshua Leavitt to Gerrit Smith, April 27, 1868, in Smith Miller Collection.

Trade League, Parke Godwin, Bryant's son-in-law and a leading liberal reformer, saluted Leavitt as the one who had "carried the torch of free trade through many dangers and difficulties." In an emotional speech Leavitt reminded the distinguished audience, which included Ralph Waldo Emerson, Walt Whitman, and Samuel J. Tilden, that the cause was grounded in the "law of God, which He has imposed on human progress, in our favor, and we shall succeed." He received a greater honor in 1869, when the prestigious Cobden Club of London, founded in 1866 to advance the cause of free trade in the Western world, awarded him the first Cobden Prize for the best essay on a public question with which Cobden's political career had been identified. In his essay Leavitt attacked the protective tariff and restrictive copyright laws as injurious obstacles to the free flow of ideas and goods: "The interferences of power to restrict trade are, like the interpositions of force in opposition to free will, mechanical and obstructive in their nature and oppressive in their operation, except where justified by some higher extraneous reason." By raising prices and wages, he declared, protectionism more than offset any of the positive effects its advocates promised the American people.[33]

During the last few years of his life, ill health and old age made Leavitt, as he informed Chase, little more than an "interested observer" of the political scene. In 1868 he again favored Chase for the presidency, believing that his election would be "the greatest blessing the country has received since the 'Rising of the Great Nation' in 1861." He, as well as Tilton, Wendell Phillips, and other Radicals regarded Grant as too conservative on the Reconstruction question and too closely associated with President Johnson. They persisted in their support of Chase, even though he differed with most Republicans on the issues of impeachment and military reconstruction and most party members believed Grant to be the man most likely to win the election. In the end, Leavitt voted for Grant because he could not bring himself to support the "unreconstructed" Democratic party.[34]

Leavitt's aversion to that party, though not its stated principles, persisted to the end of his life. In 1872 he refused to join his old friends

33. *The League*, I (March, 1868), 111; *England and America: The Cobden Prize Essay on Improved Political and Commercial Relations between Great Britain and the United States* (New York, 1869), 9–10.

34. Joshua Leavitt to Salmon P. Chase, June 16, 1868, in Chase Papers, LC; Joshua Leavitt to Gerrit Smith, July 11, 1872, in Smith Miller Collection.

Sumner and Chase as well as other Republicans who supported Horace Greeley on the Liberal Republican ticket, which the Democrats then absorbed. Not only did he heartily dislike Greeley for his Whig past, but the fact that Greeley accepted the nomination of the "unchanged Democracy" confirmed his long-held view that Greeley was "void of any principle except hatred to the law of God." Despite the mounting scandals that had begun to rock the Grant administration, Leavitt and most other old abolitionists stood by Grant. Leavitt acknowledged that Sumner and others might well be correct in charging Grant with stupidity, selfishness, and moral blindness. But he feared that the Liberal Republicans' emphasis on "conciliation" seriously endangered black civil rights. Leavitt certainly grasped for straws in asserting that a more flexible man than Grant would have permitted even more corruption and venality. Yet, to the end of his life he seemed able to penetrate to the core of an issue in a reasonable and insightful manner. "I think," he reminded Gerrit Smith, "we ought not forget that *we made* Grant President against his own wishes and interests. If it was a mistake, it was not his but ours."[35]

In these twilight years of their lives Joshua and Sarah lived with their son James in Brooklyn. In 1870 they celebrated their fiftieth wedding anniversary, surrounded by family and friends and eulogized in the columns of the *Independent*. The kindness of his old friends deeply touched Leavitt. "Indeed, it is pleasant," he wrote to Bacon, "to find that one is not forgotten, after being so long comparatively absent from public view." Yet advancing age had taken its toll. Failing health forced him in 1868 to cease writing on a regular basis for the *Evening Post*, and he now attended few meetings. Also, his speech-making ability, as he informed his brother in 1871, was "mostly gone." He considered writing a history of the antislavery struggle (which Garrison suspected would be "a very jaundiced one"), but he never completed it.[36]

35. Leavitt to Smith, July 11, 1872, in Smith Miller Collection. For treatments of the Liberal Republicans, see James M. McPherson, "Grant or Greeley? The Abolitionist Dilemma in the Election of 1872," *American Historical Review*, LXXI (October, 1965), 43, 44, 49, 51–56; John G. Sproat, *"The Best Men": Liberal Reformers in the Gilded Age* (New York, 1968), 81–87.

36. Joshua Leavitt to Leonard Bacon, December 29, 1870, in Bacon Family Collection; *Independent*, October 24, 1870; Joshua Leavitt to Roger Hooker Leavitt, January 17, July 11, 1871, in Leavitt Papers; William Lloyd Garrison to Samuel J. May, December 7, 1870, in Garrison Papers.

Leavitt remained somewhat active until his death. In 1872 he attended the fifty-year anniversary of his Yale Theological Seminary class, where he listened to speeches and visited the grave sites of several of his former professors. He also continued to walk to the *Independent* office frequently, where he sat at his desk in the back room with his young assistant, William Ward, chatting about the events of the day, compiling religious intelligence, and occasionally writing pieces on assorted topics. He wrote his last piece—an article advocating cheap postage—on the same day that he died of a stroke, January 16, 1873, at the home of his son. At the funeral held at Plymouth Church, Henry Ward Beecher eulogized Leavitt as "not a man of one idea, but one who had that seeking and gathering intent, giving himself up" to the task of advancing the welfare of mankind. Other old associates and friends, including Bacon, Charles G. Finney, Bryant, and Thompson, noted his achievements as a reformer, journalist, and religious activist during the previous half century. Perhaps Leavitt would have been most pleased with the tribute accorded him by Parke Godwin, who praised his "genuine and ostentatious philanthropy, an absolute love of justice and a sincere and reverent regard for truth."[37] It is instructive that most of those who attended his funeral had been part of his life from the 1850s on. Few if any of his old abolitionist comrades from the 1830s and 1840s were there—most of them having died or retired from public life. Except for a few Congregational leaders and the small circle of liberal reformers with whom he had recently been associated, few Americans noted his passing or remembered his significant contributions to antebellum reform.

37. Joshua Leavitt to Roger Hooker Leavitt, January 17, 1871, in Leavitt Papers; *Independent*, January 23, 1873, December 3, 1908; *The Semi-Centennial Anniversary of the Divinity School of Yale College, May 15th and 16th, 1872* (New Haven, Conn., 1872), 31–32; New York *Evening Post*, January 17, 20, 1873.

BIBLIOGRAPHY

Primary Sources

MANUSCRIPTS

American Antiquarian Society, Worcester, Mass.
  Cheever Family Papers, 1835–1836.
Boston Public Library, Boston
  Chapman Family Papers, 1836.
  Child Family Papers, 1840.
  Garrison, William Lloyd. Papers, 1838–1870.
  May, Samuel J. Papers, 1837–1841.
  "Minutes of the Committee on Agencies of the American Anti-Slavery Society, 1833–1840."
  "Minutes of the Executive Committee of the American Anti-Slavery Society, 1837–1841."
  Phelps, Amos A. Papers, 1833–1846.
  Spooner, Lysander. Papers, 1844–1848.
  Weston Family Papers, 1838–1848.
Columbia University (Baker Library), New York
  Jay, John. Collection, 1838–1844.
Congregational Library, Boston
  Torrey, Charles Turner. Papers, 1840.
Connecticut Historical Society, Hartford
  Niles, John Milton. Papers, 1848.
Cornell University, Ithaca, N.Y.
  McKim, James Miller. Papers, 1837–1844.
Essex Institute, Salem, Mass.
  Whittier, John Greenleaf. Papers, 1841–1848.
First Congregational Church, Stratford, Conn.
  "Church Record Book, 1813–1833."
Harvard University (Houghton Library), Cambridge, Mass.
  Howe, Samuel Gridley. Papers, 1849–1851.

Palfrey, John Gorham. Papers, 1849–1850.
Sumner, Charles. Papers, 1848–1864.
Heath Historical Society, Heath, Mass.
Leavitt Family Scrapbook.
Historical Society of Pennsylvania, Philadelphia
Chase, Salmon P. Papers, 1841–1857.
Gratz, Simon. Autograph Collection, 1864–1865.
Library of Congress, Washington, D.C.
American Colonization Society. Papers, 1829–1833.
Anti-Slavery Papers, 1833–1840.
Birney, James G. Diary, 1840–1851.
Chase, Salmon P. Papers, 1842–1868.
Giddings, Joshua R.–George W. Julian. Papers, 1840–1842.
Leavitt, Joshua. Papers, 1812–1872.
Lincoln, Robert Todd. Collection, 1862–1863.
McLean, John. Papers, 1848.
Tappan, Benjamin. Papers, 1848.
Tappan, Lewis. Diary, 1839–1841.
Tappan, Lewis. Journal, 1829–1843.
Tappan, Lewis. Papers, 1829–1848.
Van Buren, Martin. Papers, 1848.
Wright, Elizur. Papers, 1834–1850.
Massachusetts Historical Society, Boston
Adams, John Quincy. Diary, 1841–1842.
Adams Family Papers, 1841–1842.
Bancroft, George. Papers, 1839–1862.
Dana, Richard Henry. Papers, 1848–1851.
New Hampshire Historical Society, Concord
Fogg, George G. Papers, 1848.
Hale, John P. Papers, 1847–1848.
New-York Historical Society, New York
Bradish, Luther. Papers, 1838–1841.
Holley, Myron. Papers, 1839–1841.
Miscellaneous Manuscripts, 1839–1865.
Slavery Manuscripts, Box II, 1839–1840.
Stewart, Alvan. Papers, 1838–1839.
New York Public Library, New York
McKim, James Miller. Papers, 1840.
"Minutes of Proceedings of the Executive Committee of the New-York City
Temperance Society, 1829–1842."
New York State Historical Society, Cooperstown
Stewart, Alvan. Papers, 1838–1840.

Oberlin College, Oberlin, Ohio
   Finney, Charles Grandison. Papers, 1827–1832.
Ohio Historical Society, Columbus
   Chase, Salmon P. Papers, 1848.
   Giddings, Joshua R. Papers, 1839–1862.
Putney Historical Society, Putney, Vt.
   "Records of the Church of Christ in Putney, Beginning June 25th, 1807."
   "Records of the Putney Musical Society, 1820–1840."
   "Town Meeting Records, Vol. II (1796–1833)."
Stratford Town Hall, Stratford, Conn.
   "Town Acts, Town of Stratford."
Syracuse University, Syracuse, N.Y.
   Smith Miller, Gerrit. Collection, 1834–1872.
University of Michigan (Clements Library), Ann Arbor
   Birney, James G. Papers, 1840–1845.
   Foster, Theodore. Liberty Party Notebook.
University of Rochester, Rochester, N.Y.
   Seward, William Henry. Papers, 1862–1863.
Yale University (Beinecke Library), New Haven, Conn.
   Day, Jeremiah. Papers, 1837.
Yale University (Sterling Library), New Haven, Conn.
   Bacon Family Collection, 1849–1870.
   Baldwin Family Papers, 1839–1849.
   Beecher Family Papers, 1863.
   "Constitution of the Benevolent Society of Yale College."
   "Notes from the instruction given by Dr. Dwight to the Senior Class in
      Yale College, 1812–1813."
   Stokes Autograph Collection, 1864.
   Woolsey Family Collection, 1864–1868.

NEWSPAPERS AND MAGAZINES

African Repository and Colonial Journal, August, 1825.
American and Foreign Anti-Slavery Reporter, 1840–1844.
American Quarterly Register, February, 1838.
Ballot Box, 1840.
Biblical Repertory and Theological Review, January, 1835.
Boston *Courier*, April 13, 1840; February 7, 1842.
Boston *Daily Atlas*, 1841, 1844.
Boston *Morning Chronicle*, 1844–1845.
British and Foreign Anti-Slavery Reporter, 1841–1844.
Christian Citizen, November 16, 1844; June 15, 1847.

Christian Freeman, November 14, December 12, 1844.
Christian Spectator (also *Quarterly Christian Spectator*), 1823–1831.
Congregational Quarterly, July, October, 1865.
Emancipator, 1833–1848.
Friend of Man, 1836–1841.
Hampshire Gazette and Public Advertiser, 1819.
Independent, 1848–1873, 1908.
Journal of Public Morals, 1836–1837.
The League, 1867–1868.
Liberator, 1831–1849.
McDowall's Journal, 1833–1834.
Massachusetts Abolitionist, 1840–1841.
National Anti-Slavery Standard, 1840–1848.
National Era, 1847–1849.
National Preacher, 1830–1831.
New Englander, 1848–1865.
New Jersey Freeman, March, 1844.
New York *Evangelist*, 1830–1837, 1847–1849.
New York *Evening Post*, 1834, 1865–1868, 1873.
New York *Observer*, July 19, 1834.
Pennsylvania Freeman, 1838–1840, 1846–1848.
Philanthropist, 1837–1846.
Sailor's Magazine and Naval Journal, 1828–1836.
Signal of Liberty, 1841–1847.

GOVERNMENT PUBLICATIONS

Harrison, James L., comp. *Biographical Directory of the American Congress, 1774–1949*. Washington, D.C., 1950.
Richardson, James D., comp. *A Compilation of the Messages and Papers of the Presidents, 1789–1908*. 11 vols. Washington, D.C., 1910.

LEAVITT'S WRITINGS

Alarming Disclosures. Political Power of Slavery. Substance of Several Speeches by Rev. Joshua Leavitt in the Ohio Anti-Slavery Convention, and at Public Meetings in that State, in Oct. 1840, and Published in the "Emancipator." N.p., 1840.
"American Democracy." *New Englander*, XIV (February and August, 1856), 52–74, 385–409.
"The British System of Postage." *New Englander*, VI (April, 1848), 153–65.
Cheap Postage: Remarks and Statistics on the Subject of Cheap Postage and Postal Reform in Great Britain and the United States. Boston, 1850.

The Christian Lyre. New York, 1830.
"Common Schools." *Christian Spectator,* VII (November, 1825), 582–83.
Companion to the Christian Lyre. New York, 1833.
Denmark, and Its Relations. New York, 1864.
Easy Lessons in Reading. For the Use of the Younger Classes in Common Schools. 2nd ed. Keene, N.H., 1825.
Easy Lessons in Reading. For the Younger Classes in Common Schools. Boston, 1847.
England and America: The Cobden Prize on Improved Political and Commercial Relations between Great Britain and the United States. New York, 1869.
The Finance of Cheap Postage. New York, 1849.
The Financial Power of Slavery. The Substance of an Address Delivered in Ohio, in September, 1840, by Joshua Leavitt, of New York. N.p., 1841.
"God Helps Them That Help Themselves." *Christian Spectator,* n.s., I (November, 1827), 584–85.
The Great Duellist. Utica, N.Y., 1844.
"The Key of the Continent." *New Englander,* XXIII (July, 1864), 517–39.
The Liberty Almanac for 1848. New York, 1848.
"The Living Epistle." *National Preacher,* V (December, 1830), 106–12.
Memorial of Joshua Leavitt, Praying the Adoption of Measures to Secure an Equitable Market for American Wheat. Senate Documents, 26th Cong., 2nd Sess., No. 222.
Memorial of Joshua Leavitt, Praying That, in the Revision of the Tariff Laws, the Principle of Discrimination May be Inserted in Favor of Those Countries in Which American Grain, Flour, and Salted Meat, Are Admitted Duty Free. Senate Documents, 27th Cong., 2nd Sess., No. 339.
Memorial of Joshua Leavitt, Setting Forth the Importance of an Equitable and Adequate Market for American Wheat. New York Assembly, 64th Sess., Doc. 295.
The Monroe Doctrine. New York, 1863.
The Moral and Social Benefits of Cheap Postage. New York, 1849.
"On the Office and Duty of Deacons." *Christian Spectator,* n.s., I (June, 1827), 281–88.
"Our Post-Office." *New Englander,* VI (July, 1848), 393–404.
"People of Colour." *Christian Spectator,* VII (March and May, 1825), 130–38, 239–46.
Poland. New York, 1864.
"Post-Office Reform." *New Englander,* VI (January, 1848), 111–20.
The Practical Working of Cheap Postage. New York, 1850.
Primer: or, Little Lessons for Little Learners. Boston, 1847.
Reading Lessons. For the Use of the Middle Classes in Common Schools. Boston, 1847.

291

"Review of Hawes' Tribute to the Memory of the Pilgrims." *Quarterly Christian Spectator*, III (September, 1831), 358–93.

"Review on Missions to China." *Quarterly Christian Spectator*, II (June, 1830), 299–321.

Seamen's Devotional Assistant, and Mariners' Hymns. New York, 1830.

"Seamen's Friend Society." *Quarterly Christian Spectator*, III (June, 1831), 253–67.

Selections for Reading and Speaking. Boston, 1847.

Shall We Give Bibles to Three Millions of American Slaves? New York, n.d.

"Sunday School Magazine." *Christian Spectator*, VII (November, 1825), 583–84.

"Systematic Charity." *Christian Spectator*, VII (December, 1825), 645.

"Thoughts on the Revival under Whitefield." *Christian Spectator*, n.s., II (April, 1828), 174–78.

"To the Trustees and Directors of those Institutions which hold grants or charters for Lotteries." *Christian Spectator*, n.s., II (August, 1828), 402–403.

"The Use and Abuse of Ardent Spirits." *Christian Spectator*, VIII (June, 1826), 300–304.

PUBLISHED PRIMARY SOURCES

Abel, Annie Heloise, and Frank J. Klingberg, eds. *A Side-light on Anglo-American Relations, 1839–1858: Furnished by the Correspondence of Lewis Tappan and Others with the British and Foreign Anti-Slavery Society*. Lancaster, Pa., 1927.

Adams, Charles Francis, ed. *Memoirs of John Quincy Adams*. 12 vols. Philadelphia, 1874–1877.

Address of the New-York City Anti-Slavery Society, to the People of the City of New-York. New York, 1833.

The Address of the Southern and Western Liberty Convention, to the People of the United States; the Proceedings and Resolutions of the Convention . . . . Cincinnati, 1845.

Address to the American People, by the American Free Trade League. New York, 1867.

An Address to Grocers and Vendors of Ardent Spirits, by the Board of Managers of the New-York City Temperance Society. New York, 1829.

An Address to the Inhabitants of the City of New-York, by the Board of Managers of the New-York City Temperance Society. New York, 1829.

Address to the Inhabitants of New Mexico and California, on the Omission by Congress to Provide Them With Territorial Governments and on the Social and Political Evils of Slavery. New York, 1849.

Address to the Macedon Convention, by William Goodell; and Letters of Gerrit Smith. Albany, 1847.

Address to the People of Color, in the City of New York, by the Members of the Executive Committee of the American Anti-Slavery Society. New York, 1834.

An Address to Physicians, by the Executive Committee of the Board of Managers of the New-York City Temperance Society. New York, 1829.

Address to the Public, by the Executive Committee of the American Anti-Slavery Society. New York, 1835.

An Address to the Young Men of the United States, on the Subject of Temperance, by the New York Young Men's Society for the Promotion of Temperance. New York, 1830.

The African Captives. Trial of the Prisoners of the Amistad . . . . New York, 1839.

Ames, Nathaniel. *Nautical Reminiscences.* Providence, R.I., 1832.

Annual Report of the American Society for Colonizing the Free People of Colour of the United States. Washington, D.C., 1831.

Annual Report of the Female Benevolent Society of the City of New York. New York, 1834.

Annual Report of the Massachusetts Anti-Slavery Society. Boston, 1849.

Annual Report of the New England Anti-Slavery Society. Boston, 1833.

Annual Report of the New-York City Magdalen Society. New York, 1831.

Annual Report of the New-York City Temperance Society. New York, 1830.

Annual Report of the New York State Anti-Slavery Society. Utica, 1835.

Annual Report of the Society for Promoting Manual Labor in Literary Institutions. New York, 1833.

Annual Reports of the American Anti-Slavery Society. New York, 1834–1840.

Annual Reports of the American and Foreign Anti-Slavery Society. New York, 1849–1851.

Annual Reports of the American Moral Reform Society. New York, 1836–1838.

Annual Reports of the American Seamen's Friend Society. New York, 1829–1837.

Annual Reports of the American Society for the Promotion of Temperance. Boston, 1828–1829.

Annual Reports of the Connecticut Sunday School Union. New Haven, 1825–1828.

Armstrong, Rev. Lebbeus. *The Temperance Reformation: Its History from the Organization of the First Temperance Society to the Adoption of the Liquor Law of Maine, 1851.* New York, 1853.

Bacon, Leonard. *Slavery Discussed in Occasional Essays, From 1833 to 1846.* New York, 1846.

Barbar, John W. *A History of the Amistad Captives* . . . . New Haven, Conn., 1840.

Barnes, Gilbert H., and Dwight L. Dumond, eds. *Letters of Theodore Dwight Weld and Angelina Grimké Weld and Sarah Grimké, 1822–1844.* 2 vols. New York, 1934.

Beecher, Charles, ed. *Autobiography, Correspondence, etc. of Lyman Beecher.* Vol. II of 2 vols. New York, 1864.

Beecher, Lyman. *Six Sermons on the Nature, Occasions, Signs, Evils, and Remedy of Intemperance.* Boston, 1827.

Belden, Ezekiel Porter. *Sketches of Yale College.* New York, 1843.

Birney, James G. *A Letter on the Political Obligations of Abolitionists, With a Reply by William Lloyd Garrison.* Boston, 1839.

Bourne, Edward G., ed. *Annual Report of the American Historical Association for the Year 1902.* Vol. II of 2 vols. Washington, D.C., 1903.

British and Foreign Anti-Slavery Society. *Minute Books.* Vol. II of 2 vols.

Buffum, Arnold. *Lecture Showing the Necessity for a Liberty Party.* Cincinnati, 1844.

Catalogus Collegii Yalensis. Newport, R.I., 1835.

Chapman, Maria Weston. *Right and Wrong in Massachusetts.* Boston, 1839.

Cheeseman, Rev. Lewis. *Differences between Old and New School Presbyterians.* Rochester, N.Y., 1848.

The Church Book of the First Church of Christ in Northampton, 1860. Northampton, Mass., 1860.

"Clerical Convention." *Christian Spectator,* n.s., I (September, 1827), 499–501.

A Collection of Valuable Documents. Boston, 1836.

"The Congregational Convention." *New Englander,* XI (February, 1853), 72–92.

Constitution of the American Free Trade League and List of Officers. N.p., n.d.

Contributions to the Ecclesiastical History of Connecticut. New Haven, 1861.

Crocker, Zebulon. *The Catastrophe of the Presbyterian Church, 1837, Including a Full View of the Recent Theological Controversies in New England.* New Haven, Conn., 1838.

Dana, Richard Henry, Jr. *Speeches in Stirring Times and Letters to a Son.* Edited by Richard Henry Dana III. Boston, 1910.

Davis, Emerson. *The Half Century.* Boston, 1851.

Debates and Proceedings of the National Council of Congregational Churches, 1865. Boston, 1866.

Dumond, Dwight L., ed. *Letters of James Gillespie Birney, 1831–1857.* 2 vols. New York, 1938.

Dutton, S. W. S. *A Sermon Preached in the North Church, March 14, 1858, the First Sabbath after the Death of Rev. Nathaniel W. Taylor, D.D.* New Haven, Conn., 1858.

Dwight, Timothy, Jr. *Memories of Yale Life and Men, 1845–1899.* New York, 1903.

Dwight, Timothy, Jr., ed. *President Dwight's Decision of Questions Discussed by the Senior Class in Yale College, in 1813 and 1814.* New York, 1833.

An Expose of the Circumstances Which Led to the Resignation by the Hon. Joshua R. Giddings, of His Office of Representative in the Congress of the United States. Painesville, Ohio, 1842.

Finney, Charles Grandison. *Lectures on Revivals of Religion.* Edited by William G. McLoughlin. Cambridge, Mass., 1960.

———. *Memoirs.* New York, 1876.

Fisher, George P. *A Sermon Preached in the Chapel of Yale College, March 14, 1858, the First Sunday After the Death of Rev. Nathaniel Taylor.* New Haven, Conn., 1858.

A General Catalogue of the Theological Department in Yale College. New Haven, Conn., n.d.

Giddings, Joshua R. *History of the Rebellion, Its Authors and Causes.* New York, 1864.

Gillette, Rev. E. H. *History of the Presbyterian Church in the United States of America.* Vol. II of 2 vols. Philadelphia, 1864.

Goodell, William. *Slavery and Anti-Slavery: A History of the Great Struggle in Both Hemispheres; With a View of the Slavery Question in the United States.* New York, 1853.

———. *View of American Constitutional Law, In Its Bearing Upon American Slavery.* Utica, N.Y., 1844.

Green, Beriah. *Sketches of the Life and Writings of James Gillespie Birney.* Utica, N.Y., 1844.

Hastings, Thomas, and Lowell Mason. *Spiritual Songs for Social Worship.* Utica, N.Y., 1832.

Hildreth, Richard. *Despotism in America; or an Inquiry into the Nature and Results of the Slave-Holding System in the United States.* Boston, 1840.

A Historical Discourse Delivered by Rev. Moses Miller, October 13, 1852. Shelburne Falls, Mass., 1853.

Jay, William. *A View of the Action of the Federal Government, in Behalf of Slavery, with Appendix by Joshua Leavitt on the Amistad Case and the Creole Case.* Utica, N.Y., 1839.

Julian, George W. *Political Recollections, 1840–1872,* Chicago, 1884.

Leonard Bacon: Pastor of the First Church in New Haven. New Haven, Conn., 1882.

Letter of Gerrit Smith to Hon. Henry Clay. New York, 1839.

Letter of Gerrit Smith to S.P. Chase on the Unconstitutionality of Every Part of American Slavery. Albany, 1847.

Letters of the Rev. Dr. Beecher and Rev. Mr. Nettleton on the "New Measures" in Conducting Revivals of Religion. New York, 1828.

Liberty Bell. N.p., 1848.

Lovejoy, Joseph C. *Memoir of Rev. Charles T. Torrey, Who Died in the Peni-*

tentiary of Maryland, Where He Was Confined for Showing Mercy to the Poor. Boston, 1847.

McDowall's Defence. N.p., 1836.

McNally, William. *Evils and Abuses in the Naval and Merchant Service Exposed; With Proposals for their Remedy and Redress.* Boston, 1839.

Madden, R. R. *The Island of Cuba: Its Resources, Programs, and Prospects.* London, 1849.

Madden, Thomas More, ed. *The Memoirs (Chiefly Autobiographical) from 1798 to 1886, of Richard Robert Madden.* London, 1891.

Mann, Horace. *The Right of Congress to Legislate for the Territories of the United States, and Its Duty to Exclude Slavery Therefrom: Delivered in the House of Representatives, in the Committee of the Whole, June 30, 1848, to Which is Added, a Letter from Hon. Martin Van Buren and Rev. Joshua Leavitt.* Boston, 1848.

Marsh, John. *Temperance Recollections. Labors, Defeats, Triumphs.* New York, 1867.

Marsh, Luther Rawson, ed. *Writings and Speeches of Alvan Stewart on Slavery.* New York, 1860.

Massachusetts Anti-Slavery Society. *An Address to the Abolitionists of Massachusetts on the Subject of Political Action.* Boston, 1838.

Massachusetts Liberty Convention and Speech of Hon. John P. Hale, Together with his Letter Accepting his Nomination for the Presidency. Boston, 1848.

May, Samuel J. *Some Recollections of our Antislavery Conflict.* Boston, 1869.

Memoir and Select Remains of the Late Rev. John R. McDowall. New York, 1838.

Memoir of Jonathan Leavitt, A Member of the Junior Class in Yale College, Who Died at New Haven the 10th of May, 1821, Aged Eighteen Years and One Month. New Haven, Conn., 1822.

Minutes of the General Assembly of the Presbyterian Church in the United States of America; With an Appendix, A.D. 1835. Philadelphia, 1835.

Minutes of the National Convention of Negro Citizens held at Buffalo, on the 15th, 16th, 17th, 18th, and 19th of August, 1843, for the purpose of considering their moral and political conditions as American citizens. New York, 1843.

Minutes of the Philadelphia Convention of Ministers and Ruling Elders in the Presbyterian Church. Philadelphia, 1837.

Nevins, Allan, ed. *The Diary of Philip Hone, 1828–1851.* Vol. I of 2 vols. New York, 1927.

Olmsted, Denison. *Timothy Dwight as a Teacher.* N.p., 1857.

Parker, H. E. *A Discourse, preached in the First Congregational Church in Keene, N.H., Thursday, March 6, 1873, at the Funeral of the Rev.*

Zedakiah Smith, D.D., for fifty years pastor of the First Church in Keene. Hanover, N.H., 1873.

Permanent Temperance Documents of the American Temperance Society. Boston, 1835.

Phelps, Amos A. *Lectures on Slavery and Its Remedy.* Boston, 1834.

Phillips, Wendell. *Review of Lysander Spooner's Essay on the Unconstitutionality of Slavery.* Boston, 1847.

Pierce, Edward L., ed. *Memoir and Letters of Charles Sumner.* Vol. III of 4 vols. Boston, 1877–1893.

Presbyterian Reunion. A Memorial Volume. 1837–1871. New York, 1870.

Proceedings of the Anti-Slavery Convention, Assembled at Philadelphia. December 4, 5, and 6, 1833. New York, 1833.

Proceedings of a Convention of Delegates from the Counties of Hampshire, Franklin, and Hampden, Holden at Northampton, the 14th and 15th of July, 1812. Northampton, Mass., 1812.

Proceedings of the General Anti-Slavery Convention in London, 1843. London, 1843.

Proceedings of the General Association of Connecticut, 1825–1828. Hartford, 1825–1828.

Proceedings of the General Convention of Congregational Ministers and Delegates in the United States, Held at Albany, N.Y., on the 5th, 6th, 7th and 8th of October, 1852. New York, 1852.

Proceedings of the National Liberty Convention, Held at Buffalo, N.Y., June 14th and 15th, 1848 . . . . Utica, N.Y., 1848.

Report of the Society for Promoting the Gospel Among Seamen in the Port of New-York. New York, 1821.

Reunion of the Free-Soilers of 1848, at Downer Landing, Hingham, Mass., August 9, 1877. Boston, 1877.

Reunion of the Free Soilers of 1848–1852 at the Parker House, Boston, Massachusetts, June 28, 1888. Cambridge, Mass., 1888.

The Semi-Centennial Anniversary of the Divinity School of Yale College, May 15th and 16th, 1872. New Haven, Conn., 1872.

Sermons; by Timothy Dwight, D.D., L.L.D., Late President of Yale College. Vol. I of 2 vols. New Haven, Conn., 1828.

Silliman, Benjamin. *A Sketch of the Life and Character of President Dwight, Delivered as a Eulogium, in New Haven, February 12th, 1817, Before the Academic Body of Yale College . . . .* New Haven, Conn., 1817.

Smith, George C. *Intemperance . . . with An Appendix, Containing the Chief Pamphlets That Have Appeared in the City of New York on the Subject of Intemperance, by Joshua Leavitt.* New York, 1829.

Spooner, Lysander. *The Unconstitutionality of Slavery.* Boston, 1845.

Stanton, Henry B. *Random Recollections.* 3rd ed. New York, 1887.

Sturge, Joseph. *A Visit to the United States in 1841.* London, 1842.

Tappan, Lewis. *The Life of Arthur Tappan.* New York, 1870.

———. *Reply to Charges Brought Against the American and Foreign Anti-Slavery Society.* London, 1852.

Theology, Explained and Defended, in a Series of Sermons, by Timothy Dwight, S.T.D., L.L.D., Late President of Yale College. With a Memoir of the Life of the Author. Vol. I of 2 vols. Glasgow, 1821.

Todd, Joseph E. *In Memoriam: Rev. Joseph P. Thompson, D.D.* New Haven, Conn., 1879.

Trial and Imprisonment of Jonathan Walker of Pensacola, Florida . . . . Boston, 1845.

Truair, John. *Call from the Ocean, or An Appeal to the Patriot and the Christian in Behalf of Seamen.* New York, 1826.

Tyler, Bennet. *Memoir of the Life and Character of Rev. Asahel Nettleton.* Hartford, 1844.

Vital Records of Heath, Massachusetts, to the Year 1850. Boston, 1915.

White, Joseph. *Charlemont as a Plantation: An Historical Discourse at the Centennial Anniversary of the Death of Moses Rice, the First Settler of the Town, Delivered at Charlemont, Mass., June 11, 1855.* Boston, 1858.

Wilson, Henry. *History of the Rise and Fall of the Slave Power in America.* 2 vols. Boston, 1872.

Wright, Elizur. *Myron Holley: and What He Did for Liberty and True Religion.* Boston, 1882.

The Year-Book of the American Congregational Union, for the Year 1854. New York, 1854.

Secondary Sources

ARTICLES

Abzug, Robert H. "The Influence of Garrisonian Abolitionists' Fears of Slave Violence on the Antislavery Argument, 1829–1840." *Journal of Negro History,* LV (January, 1970), 15–28.

Ahlstrom, Sydney E. "The Scottish Philosophy and American Theology." *Church History,* XXIV (1955), 257–72.

Anderson, L. F. "The Manual Labor School Movement." *Educational Review,* XLVI (November, 1913), 369–86.

Banner, Lois. "Religious Benevolence as Social Control: A Critique of an Interpretation." *Journal of American History,* LX (June, 1973), 23–41.

Bidwell, Percy Wells. "Rural Economy in New England at the Beginning of the Nineteenth Century." *Transactions of the Connecticut Academy of the Arts and Sciences,* XX (1916), 241–89.

Birdsall, Richard D. "The Second Great Awakening and the New England Social Order." *Church History*, XXXIX (September, 1970), 345–64.

Boylan, Ann M. "Sunday Schools and Changing Evangelical Views of Children in the 1820's." *Church History*, XLVIII (September, 1979), 320–33.

Bretz, Julian P. "The Economic Background of the Liberty Party." *American Historical Review*, XXXIV (January, 1929), 250–64.

Cole, Charles C., Jr. "The Free Church Movement in New York City." *New York History*, XXXIV (July, 1953), 284–97.

———. "The New Lebanon Convention." *New York History*, XXXI (October, 1950), 385–97.

Curti, Merle E. "Non-Resistance in New England." *New England Quarterly*, II (January, 1929), 34–57.

Davis, David B. "The Emergence of Immediatism in British and American Antislavery Thought." *Mississippi Valley Historical Review*, XLIX (September, 1962), 209–30.

———. "Some Themes of Counter-Subversion: An Analysis of Anti-Masonic, Anti-Catholic, and Anti-Mormon Literature." *Mississippi Valley Historical Review*, XLVII (September, 1960), 205–24.

Davis, Hugh. "The American Seamen's Friend Society and the American Sailor, 1828–1838." *American Neptune*, XXXIX (January, 1979), 45–57.

———. "The Failure of Political Abolitionism." *Connecticut Review*, VI (April, 1973), 76–86.

Doherty, Robert W. "Social Bases for the Presbyterian Schism of 1837–1838: The Philadelphia Case." *Journal of Social History*, II (Fall, 1968), 69–79.

———. "Status Anxiety and American Reform: Some Alternatives." *American Quarterly*, XIX (Summer, 1967), 329–37.

Duberman, Martin B. "The Abolitionists and Psychology." *Journal of Negro History*, XLVII (July, 1962), 183–91.

Dudley, Harold M. "The Election of 1864." *Mississippi Valley Historical Review*, XVIII (March, 1932), 500–519.

Duncan, C. Rice. "The Anti-Slavery Mission of George Thompson to the United States, 1834–1835." *Journal of American Studies*, II (April, 1968), 13–31.

Eaton, Clement. "Censorship of the Southern Mails." *American Historical Review*, XLVIII (January, 1943), 266–80.

Ellsworth, Clayton Sumner. "The American Churches and the Mexican War." *American Historical Review*, XLV (January, 1940), 301–26.

Elsbree, Oliver Wendell. "Samuel Hopkins and His Doctrine of Benevolence." *New England Quarterly*, VIII (December, 1935), 534–50.

Elson, Ruth Miller, "American Schoolbooks and 'Culture' in the Nineteenth Century." *Mississippi Valley Historical Review*, XLVI (December, 1959), 411–34.

Filler, Louis. "Liberalism, Anti-Slavery, and the Founders of the *Independent*." *New England Quarterly*, XXVII (September, 1954), 291–306.

Finnie, Gordon E. "The Antislavery Movement in the Upper South Before 1840." *Journal of Southern History*, XXXV (August, 1969), 319–42.

Fladeland, Betty. "Who Were the Abolitionists?" *Journal of Negro History*, XLIX (April, 1964), 99–115.

Foner, Eric. "Politics and Prejudice: The Free Soil Party and the Negro, 1849–1852." *Journal of Negro History*, L (October, 1965), 239–56.

———. "Racial Attitudes of the New York Free Soilers." *New York History*, XLVI (October, 1965), 311–29.

———. "The Wilmot Proviso Revisited." *Journal of American History*, LXI (September, 1969), 269–79.

French, David. "Puritan Conservatism and the Frontier: The Elizur Wright Family on the Connecticut Western Reserve." *Old Northwest*, I (March, 1975), 85–95.

Gara, Larry. "Slavery and the Slave Power: A Crucial Distinction." *Civil War History*, XV (March, 1969), 5–18.

Gerteis, Louis S. "Slavery and Hard Times: Morality and Utility in American Antislavery Reform." *Civil War History*, XXIX (December, 1983), 316–31.

Graham, Howard Jay. "The Early Background of the Fourteenth Amendment, II: Systematization, 1835–1837." *Wisconsin Law Review* (July, 1950), 638–45.

Griffin, Clifford S. "The Abolitionists and the Benevolent Societies, 1831–1861." *Journal of Negro History*, XLIV (July, 1959), 195–216.

Gross, Robert A. "Culture and Cultivation: Agriculture and Society in Thoreau's Concord." *Journal of American History*, LXIX (June, 1982), 42–61.

Harwood, Thomas F. "British Evangelical Abolitionism and American Churches in the 1830's." *Journal of Southern History*, XXVIII (August, 1962), 287–306.

Hastings, Robert. "The Plan of Union in New York." *Church History*, V (March, 1936), 29–41.

Hubbell, John. "The National Free Soil Convention of '48.'" *Publications of the Buffalo Historical Society*, IV (1896).

Jentz, John B. "The Antislavery Constituency in Jacksonian New York City." *Civil War History*, XXVII (June, 1981), 101–22.

Johnson, James E. "Charles G. Finney and a Theology of Revivalism." *Church History*, XXXVIII (September, 1969), 338–58.

Johnson, Reinhard O. "The Liberty Party in Massachusetts, 1840–1848: Antislavery Third Party Politics in the Bay State." *Civil War History*, XXVIII (September, 1982), 237–64.

300

Jones, William Devereux. "The Influence of Slavery on the Webster-Ashburton Negotiations." *Journal of Southern History*, XXII (February, 1956), 48–58.

Kerber, Linda K. "Abolitionists and Amalgamators: The New York City Race Riots of 1834." *New York History*, XLVIII (January, 1967), 28–39.

Kirkland, Edward C. "The Hoosac Tunnel Route: The Great Bore." *New England Quarterly*, XX (March, 1947), 88–113.

Kuhns, Frederick. "New Light on the Plan of Union." *Journal of the Presbyterian Historical Society*, XXVI (March, 1948), 19–43.

Kull, Irving Stoddard. "Presbyterian Attitudes Toward Slavery." *Church History*, VII (1938), 101–14.

Loetscher, Lefferts A. "The Problem of Christian Unity in Early Nineteenth-Century America." *Church History*, XXXII (March, 1963), 3–15.

Lofton, Williston H. "Abolition and Labor." *Journal of Negro History*, XXXIII (October, 1949), 249–83.

Loveland, Anne C. "Evangelicalism and 'Immediate Emancipation' in American Antislavery Thought." *Journal of Southern History*, XXXII (May, 1966), 172–88.

Lull, Herbert G. "The Manual Labor Movement in the United States." *Manual Training*, XV (June, 1914), 375–88.

MacCormac, Earl R. "Missions and the Presbyterian Schism of 1837." *Church History*, XXXII (March, 1963), 32–45.

McKivigan, John R. "The Gospel Will Burst the Bonds of the Slave: The Abolitionists' Bible for Slaves Campaign." *Negro History Bulletin*, XLV (July–September, 1982), 62–64.

McLoughlin, William G. "Evangelical Childrearing in the Age of Jackson: Francis Wayland's Views on When and How to Subdue the Willfulness of Children." *Journal of Social History*, IX (Fall, 1975), 21–34.

McPherson, James M. "The Fight Against the Gag Rule: Joshua Leavitt and Antislavery Insurgency in the Whig Party, 1839–1842." *Journal of Negro History*, XLVIII (July, 1963), 177–95.

———. "Grant or Greeley? The Abolitionist Dilemma in the Election of 1872." *American Historical Review*, LXXI (October, 1965), 43–61.

Martin, Thomas P. "The Upper Mississippi Valley in Anglo-American Anti-Slavery and Free Trade Relations: 1837–1842." *Mississippi Valley Historical Review*, XV (September, 1928), 204–20.

Mathews, Donald G. "The Abolitionists on Slavery: The Critique Behind the Social Movement." *Journal of Southern History*, XXXIII (May, 1967), 163–82.

———. "The Second Great Awakening as an Organizing Process, 1780–1830: An Hypothesis." *American Quarterly*, XXI (Spring, 1969), 23–43.

Maynard, Douglas H. "The World's Anti-Slavery Convention of 1840." *Mis-*

sissippi *Valley Historical Review*, XLVII (December, 1960), 452–71.

Melder, Keith E. "Forerunners of Freedom: The Grimké Sisters in Massachusetts, 1837–38." *Essex Institute Historical Collections*, CIII (July, 1967), 223–49.

Moorhead, James H. "Social Reform and the Divided Conscience of Antebellum Protestantism." *Church History*, XLVIII (December, 1979), 416–30.

Morrow, R. L. "The Liberty Party in Vermont." *New England Quarterly*, II (April, 1929), 234–48.

Myers, John L. "The Beginning of Anti-Slavery Agencies in New York State, 1833–1836." *New York History*, XLIII (April, 1962), 149–81.

Nash, Gilbert, comp. "Historical Sketch of the Town of Weymouth, Massachusetts, from 1622–1884," *Publications of Weymouth Historical Society*, II (1885), 106–14.

Oliphant, J. Orin. "The American Missionary Spirit, 1828–1835." *Church History*, VII (1938), 125–37.

Pearson, Samuel C. "From Church to Denomination: American Congregationalism in the Nineteenth Century." *Church History*, XXXVIII (March, 1969), 67–87.

Pease, William H., and Jane H. Pease. "Antislavery Ambivalence: Immediatism, Expediency, Race." *American Quarterly*, XVII (Winter, 1965), 682–95.

Pendleton, Othniel A. "Slavery and the Evangelical Churches." *Journal of the Presbyterian Historical Society*, XXV (September, 1947), 153–74.

Quarles, Benjamin. "Sources of Abolitionist Income." *Mississippi Valley Historical Review*, XXXII (June, 1945), 63–76.

Rayback, Joseph G. "The American Workingman and the Antislavery Crusade." *Journal of Economic History*, III (November, 1943), 152–63.

———. "Martin Van Buren's Break with James K. Polk: The Record." *New York History*, XXXVI (January, 1955), 51–62.

Schwab, John C. "The Yale College Curriculum, 1701–1901." *Educational Review*, XXII (1901), 1–11.

Sevitch, Benjamin. "The Well-Planned Riot of October 21, 1835: Utica's Answer to Abolitionism." *New York History*, L (July, 1969), 251–63.

Shortridge, Ray M. "Voting for Minor Parties in the Antebellum Midwest." *Indiana Magazine of History*, LXXIV (June, 1978), 117–34.

Skotheim, Robert Allen. "A Note on Historical Method: David Donald's 'Toward A Reconsideration of Abolitionists.' " *Journal of Southern History*, XXV (August, 1959), 356–65.

Smith, Elwyn A. "The Role of the South in the Presbyterian Schism of 1837–38." *Church History*, XXIX (1960), 44–63.

Smith-Rosenberg, Carroll. "Beauty, the Beast and the Militant Woman: A Case Study in Sex Roles and Social Stress in Jacksonian America." *American Quarterly*, XXIII (October, 1971), 562–84.

————. "Protestants and Five Pointers: The Five Points House of Industry." *New-York Historical Society Quarterly*, XLVIII (October, 1964), 327–47.

Staiger, C. Bruce. "Abolitionism and the Presbyterian Schism of 1837–1838." *Mississippi Valley Historical Review*, XXXVI (December, 1949), 391–414.

Stearns, Bertha-Monica. "Reform Periodicals and Female Reformers, 1830–1860." *American Historical Review*, XXXVII (July, 1932), 678–99.

Stern, Madeleine. "Stephen Pearl Andrews, Abolitionist, and the Annexation of Texas." *Southwestern Historical Quarterly*, LXVI (April, 1964), 491–523.

Stewart, James Brewer. "Politics and Beliefs in Abolitionism: Stanley Elkins' Concept of Antiinstitutionalism and Recent Interpretations of American Antislavery." *South Atlantic Quarterly*, LXXV (Winter, 1976), 74–97.

Streifford, David M. "The American Colonization Society: An Application of Republican Ideology to Early Antebellum Reform." *Journal of Southern History*, XLV (May, 1979), 201–20.

Sweet, Leonard I. "The View of Man Inherent in New Measures Revivalism." *Church History*, XLV (June, 1976), 206–21.

Sweet, William Warren. "The Rise of Theological Schools in America." *Church History*, VI (1937), 260–73.

Wyatt-Brown, Bertram. "The Abolitionists' Postal Campaign of 1835." *Journal of Negro History*, L (October, 1965), 227–38.

————. "Prelude to Abolitionism: Sabbatarian Politics and the Rise of the Second Party System." *Journal of American History*, LVIII (September, 1971), 316–41.

————. "William Lloyd Garrison and Antislavery Unity: A Reappraisal." *Civil War History*, XIII (March, 1967), 5–24.

BOOKS

Abzug, Robert H. *Passionate Liberator: Theodore Dwight Weld and the Dilemma of Reform.* New York, 1980.

The Acts of the Apostles of the Sea: An Eighty Years' Record of the Work of the American Seamen's Friend Society. New York, 1909.

Adams, Alice Dana. *The Neglected Period of Anti-Slavery in America, 1808–1831.* Boston, 1908.

Ahlstrom, Sydney E. *A Religious History of the American People.* New Haven, Conn., 1972.

Albion, Robert. *The Rise of New York Port, 1815–1860.* New York, 1939.

Alexander, Samuel D. *The Presbytery of New York, 1738–1888.* New York, 1888.

Almendinger, David F., Jr. *Paupers and Scholars: The Transformation of Student Life in Nineteenth-Century New England.* New York, 1977.

Andrew, John A. *Rebuilding the Christian Commonwealth: New England*

Congregationalism and Foreign Missions, 1800–1830. Lexington, Ky., 1976.

Atkins, Gaius Glenn, and Frederick L. Fagley. *History of American Congregationalism.* Boston, 1942.

Bacon, Theodore Davenport. *Leonard Bacon: A Statesman in the Church.* New Haven, Conn., 1931.

Bainton, Roland H. *Yale and the Ministry: A History of Education for the Christian Ministry at Yale from the Founding in 1701.* New York, 1957.

Banner, James M., Jr. *To the Hartford Convention: The Federalists and the Origins of Party Politics in Massachusetts, 1789–1815.* New York, 1970.

Barnes, Gilbert Hobbes. *The Antislavery Impulse, 1830–1844.* New York, 1933.

Beardsley, Frank G. *A Mighty Winner of Souls, Charles G. Finney: A Study in Evangelism.* New York, 1937.

Bell, Marion L. *Crusade in the City: Revivalism in Nineteenth-Century Philadelphia.* Lewisburg, Pa., 1977.

Bemis, Samuel Flagg. *John Quincy Adams and the Union.* New York, 1965.

Bennett, Charles Alpheus. *History of Manual and Industrial Education Up to 1870.* Peoria, Ill., 1926.

Bennett, Whitman. *Whittier: Bard of Freedom.* Chapel Hill, 1941.

Benson, Lee. *The Concept of Jacksonian Democracy: New York as a Test Case.* Princeton, N.J., 1961.

Benson, Louis F. *The English Hymn: Its Development and Use in Worship.* New York, 1915.

Billington, Ray Allen. *The Protestant Crusade, 1800–1860: A Study of the Origins of American Nativism.* Chicago, 1964.

Bloomfield, Maxwell. *American Lawyers in a Changing Society, 1776–1876.* Cambridge, Mass., 1976.

Blue, Frederick J. *The Free Soilers: Third Party Politics, 1848–1854.* Urbana, Ill., 1973.

———. *Salmon P. Chase: A Life in Politics.* Kent, Ohio, 1987.

Bodo, John R. *The Protestant Clergy and Public Issues, 1812–1848.* Princeton, N.J., 1954.

Bolt, Christine, and Seymour Drescher, eds. *Anti-Slavery, Religion, and Reform: Essays in Memory of Roger Anstey.* Folkestone, England, 1980.

Bonner, Edwin B. *Thomas Earle as a Reformer.* Philadelphia, 1948.

Boyer, Paul. *Urban Masses and Moral Order in America, 1820–1920.* Cambridge, Mass., 1978.

Brauer, Kinley J. *Cotton versus Conscience: Massachusetts Whig Politics and Southwestern Expansion, 1843–1848.* Lexington, Ky., 1967.

Brock, Peter. *Pacifism in the United States: From the Colonial Era to the First World War.* Princeton, N.J., 1968.

Brown, Charles H. *William Cullen Bryant*. New York, 1971.

Bruchey, Stuart. *The Roots of American Economic Growth, 1607–1861: An Essay in Social Causation*. New York, 1965.

Calhoun, Daniel H. *Professional Lives in America: Structure and Aspiration, 1750–1850*. Cambridge, Mass., 1965.

Calver, Edward. *Heath, Massachusetts: A History and Guidebook*. Heath, Mass., 1979.

Carpenter, Charles. *History of American Schoolbooks*. Philadelphia, 1963.

Carwardine, Richard. *Transatlantic Revivalism: Popular Evangelicalism in Britain and America, 1790–1865*. Westport, Conn., 1978.

Caskey, Marie. *Chariot of Fire: Religion and the Beecher Family*. New Haven, 1978.

Chickering, Jesse. *A Statistical View of the Population of Massachusetts, from 1765–1840*. Boston, 1846.

Christie, John W., and Dwight Dumond. *George Bourne and the Book and Slavery Irreconcilable*. Wilmington, 1969.

Chroust, Anton-Hermann. *The Rise of the Legal Profession in America: Vol. II. The Revolution and the Post-Revolutionary Era*. Norman, Okla., 1965.

Clark, Clifford E. *Henry Ward Beecher: Spokesman for a Middle-Class America*. Urbana, Ill., 1978.

Clark, Rev. Solomon. *Historical Catalogue of Northampton First Church, 1661–1891*. Northampton, Mass., 1891.

Coben, Stanley, and Lorman Ratner, eds. *The Development of an American Culture*. Englewood Cliffs, N.J., 1970.

Cole, Charles C., Jr. *The Social Ideas of the Northern Evangelists, 1826–1860*. New York, 1954.

Cross, Whitney R. *The Burned-over District: The Social and Intellectual History of Enthusiastic Religion in Western New York, 1800–1850*. New York, 1950.

Cunningham, Charles E. *Timothy Dwight, 1752–1817: A Biography*. New York, 1942.

Davis, David B. *The Slave Power Conspiracy and the Paranoid Style*. Baton Rouge, 1969.

Dexter, Franklin Bowditch. *Biographical Sketches of the Graduates of Yale College . . . .* Vol. VI of 6 vols. New Haven, Conn., 1912.

———. *Student Life at Yale College Under the First President Dwight, 1795–1817*. Worcester, Mass., 1918.

Dillon, Merton L. *The Abolitionists: The Growth of a Dissenting Minority*. DeKalb, Ill., 1974.

———. *Benjamin Lundy and the Struggle for Negro Freedom*. Urbana, Ill., 1966.

———. *Elijah P. Lovejoy: Abolitionist Editor*. Urbana, Ill., 1961.

Doherty, Robert. *Society and Power: Five New England Towns, 1800–1860.* Amherst, Mass., 1977.

Donald, David. *Charles Sumner and the Coming of the Civil War.* New York, 1960.

―――. *Charles Sumner and the Rights of Man.* New York, 1970.

―――, ed. *Inside Lincoln's Cabinet: The Civil War Diaries of Salmon P. Chase.* New York, 1954.

―――. *Lincoln Reconsidered: Essays on the Civil War Era.* 2nd ed. New York, 1961.

Donovan, Herbert D. A. *The Barnburners: A Study of the Internal Movements in the Political History of New York State and the Resulting Changes in Political Affiliation, 1830–1852.* New York, 1925.

Duberman, Martin B., ed. *The Antislavery Vanguard: New Essays on the Abolitionists.* Princeton, N.J., 1965.

―――. *Charles Francis Adams, 1807–1886.* Boston, 1961.

Dumond, Dwight L. *Antislavery: The Crusade for Freedom in America.* Ann Arbor, 1961.

Eaton, Clement. *Henry Clay and the Art of American Politics.* Boston, 1957.

Elkins, Stanley M. *Slavery: A Problem in American Institutional and Intellectual Life.* Chicago, 1959.

Elson, Ruth Miller. *Guardians of Tradition: American Schoolbooks of the Nineteenth Century.* Lincoln, Neb., 1964.

Ernst, Robert. *Immigrant Life in New York City, 1825–1863.* New York, 1949.

Feldberg, Michael. *The Turbulent Era: Riot and Disorder in Jacksonian America.* New York, 1980.

Fennelly, Catherine. *The Country Lawyer in New England, 1790–1840.* Sturbridge, Mass., 1968.

―――. *Life in an Old New England Country Village.* New York, 1969.

Fischer, David Hackett. *The Revolution of American Conservatism: The Federalist Party in the Era of Jeffersonian Democracy.* New York, 1965.

Fladeland, Betty. *Abolitionists and Working-Class Problems in the Industrial Revolution.* New York, 1984.

―――. *James Gillespie Birney, Slaveholder to Abolitionist.* Ithaca, N.Y., 1955.

―――. *Men and Brothers: Anglo-American Antislavery Cooperation.* Urbana, Ill., 1972.

Foner, Eric. *Free Soil, Free Labor, Free Men: The Ideology of the Republican Party Before the Civil War.* New York, 1970.

Formisano, Ronald P. *The Transformation of Political Culture: Massachusetts Parties, 1790's–1840's.* New York, 1983.

Foster, Charles I. *An Errand of Mercy: The Evangelical United Front, 1790–1837.* Chapel Hill, 1960.

Foster, Frank H. *A Genetic History of the New England Theology.* Chicago, 1907.

Fowler, P. H. *Historical Sketch of Presbyterianism Within the Bounds of the Synod of Central New York.* Utica, N.Y., 1877.

Fowler, William Chauncey. *Essays: Historical, Literary, Educational.* Hartford, 1876.

Friedman, Lawrence J. *Gregarious Saints: Self and Community in American Abolitionism, 1830–1870.* Cambridge, England, 1982.

Gabriel, Ralph Henry. *Religion and Learning at Yale. The Church of Christ in the College and University, 1757–1957.* New Haven, Conn., 1958.

Galbreath, Charles Burleigh. *Samuel Lewis, Ohio's Militant Educator and Reformer.* Columbus, Ohio, 1904.

Gara, Larry. *The Liberty Line: The Legend of the Underground Railroad.* Lexington, Ky., 1961.

Gardiner, O.C. *The Great Issue: or, The Three Presidential Candidates; Being a Brief Historical Sketch of the Free Soil Question in the United States, From the Congresses of 1774 and '87 to the Present Time.* New York, 1848.

Garrison, Wendell Phillips, and Francis Jackson Garrison. *William Lloyd Garrison, 1805–1879: The Story of His Life Told by His Children.* Vol. II of 4 vols. New York, 1885–1889.

Gatell, Frank Otto. *John Gorham Palfrey and the New England Conscience.* Cambridge, Mass., 1963.

Gienapp, William E. "'Politics Seems to Enter into Everything': Political Culture in the North, 1840–1860." In *Essays on American Antebellum Politics, 1840–1860,* edited by Stephen E. Maizlish and John J. Kushma. College Station, Tex., 1982.

Goodykuntz, Colin B. *Home Missions on the American Frontier, with Particular Reference to the American Home Missionary Society.* Caldwell, Ida., 1939.

Greenleaf, Jonathan. *A History of All Denominations in the City of New York, From the First Settlement to the Year 1846.* New York, 1846.

Griffin, Clifford S. *Their Brothers' Keepers: Moral Stewardship in the United States, 1800–1865.* New Brunswick, N.J., 1960.

Guild, Edward P., ed. *Centennial Anniversary of the Town of Heath, Massachusetts, 1785–1885.* Boston, 1885.

Gusfield, Joseph R. *Symbolic Crusade: Status Politics and the American Temperance Movement.* Urbana, Ill., 1963.

Hammond, John L. *The Politics of Benevolence: Revival Religion and American Voting Behavior.* Norwood, N.J., 1979.

Hampel, Robert L. *Temperance and Prohibition in Massachusetts, 1813–1852.* Ann Arbor, 1982.

307

Harlow, Ralph Volney. *Gerrit Smith: Philanthropist and Reformer.* New York, 1939.

Haroutunian, Joseph. *Piety Versus Moralism: The Passing of the New England Theology.* New York, 1932.

Harrold, Stanley. *Gamaliel Bailey and Antislavery Union.* Kent, Ohio, 1986.

Hart, Albert Bushnell. *Salmon Portland Chase.* Boston, 1899.

Headley, Joel T. *The Great Riots of New York, 1712 to 1873.* New York, 1873.

Hersh, Blanche Glassman. *The Slavery of Sex: Feminist-Abolitionists in America.* Urbana, Ill., 1978.

Hibben, Paxton. *Henry Ward Beecher: An American Portrait.* New York, 1942.

History and Proceedings of the Pocumtuck Valley Memorial Association. Deerfield, Mass., 1905.

History of Weymouth, Massachusetts. Vol. I of 4 vols. Weymouth, 1923.

Hodge, Archibald A. *The Life of Charles Hodge, D.D., L.L.D.* New York, 1880.

Hohman, Elmo Paul. *The American Whaleman: A Study of Life and Labor in the Whaling Industry.* New York, 1928.

———. *History of American Merchant Seamen.* Hamden, Conn., 1956.

———. *Seamen Ashore: A Study of the United Seamen's Service and of Merchant Seamen in Port.* New Haven, Conn., 1952.

Holland, Josiah Gilbert. *History of Western Massachusetts.* Vol. I of 2 vols. Springfield, Mass., 1855.

Holt, Michael F. *The Political Crisis of the 1850s.* New York, 1978.

Hotchkin, Rev. James H. *A History of the Purchase and Settlement of Western New York, and of the Rise, Progress, and Present State of the Presbyterian Church in That Section.* New York, 1848.

Howe, Daniel Walker. *The Political Culture of the American Whigs.* Chicago, 1979.

Johnson, Curtiss S. *Politics and a Belly-full: The Journalistic Career of William Cullen Bryant, Civil War Editor of the New York Evening Post.* New York, 1962.

Johnson, Paul E. *A Shopkeeper's Millennium: Society and Revivals in Rochester, New York, 1815–1837.* New York, 1978.

Keller, Charles R. *The Second Great Awakening in Connecticut.* New Haven, Conn., 1942.

Kelley, Brooks Mather. *Yale: A History.* New York, 1974.

Kerber, Linda K. *Federalists in Dissent: Imagery and Ideology in Jeffersonian America.* Ithaca, N.Y., 1970.

Kett, Joseph F. *Rites of Passage: Adolescence in America, 1790 to the Present.* New York, 1977.

Klimm, Lester Earl. *The Relation Between Certain Population Changes and the Physical Environment in Hampden, Hampshire, and Franklin Counties, Massachusetts, 1790–1925.* Philadelphia, 1933.

Kraditor, Aileen S. *Means and Ends in American Abolitionism: Garrison and His Critics on Strategy and Tactics, 1834–1850.* New York, 1969.

Kraut, Alan M., ed. *Crusaders and Compromisers: Essays on the Relationship of the Antislavery Struggle to the Antebellum Party System.* Westport, Conn., 1983.

Krout, John Allen. *The Origins of Prohibition.* New York, 1925.

Langley, Harold D. *Social Reform in the United States Navy, 1798–1862.* Urbana, Ill., 1967.

Leavitt, William S. *First Parish, Northampton. Historical Sketch, 1653–1878.* Northampton, Mass., 1878.

———. *A Sketch of the Life and Character of Rev. Jonathan Leavitt: The First Minister of Charlemont, Mass.* N.p., 1903.

Lerner, Gerda. *The Grimké Sisters from South Carolina: Rebels Against Slavery.* Boston, 1967.

Locke, Mary S. *Anti-Slavery in America from the Introduction of African Slaves to the Prohibition of the Slave-Trade, 1619–1808.* Boston, 1901.

Lossing, Benson J. *History of New York City.* Vol. I of 2 vols. New York, 1884.

Mabee, Carleton. *Black Freedom: The Nonviolent Abolitionists from 1830 Through the Civil War.* New York, 1970.

McCord, Norman. *The Anti-Corn Law League, 1838–1846.* London, 1958.

McKivigan, John R. *The War Against Proslavery Religion: Abolitionism and the Northern Churches, 1830–1865.* Ithaca, N.Y., 1984.

McLoughlin, William G. *The Meaning of Henry Ward Beecher: An Essay on the Shifting Values of Mid-Victorian America, 1840–1870.* New York, 1970.

———. *Modern Revivalism: Charles Grandison Finney to Billy Graham.* New York, 1959.

———. *Revivals, Awakenings, and Reform: An Essay on Religion and Social Change in America, 1607–1977.* Chicago, 1978.

McPherson, James M. *The Struggle for Equality: Abolitionists and the Negro in the Civil War and Reconstruction.* Princeton, N.J., 1964.

Maizlish, Stephen E. *The Triumph of Sectionalism: The Transformation of Ohio Politics, 1844–1856.* Kent, Ohio, 1983.

Mandel, Bernard. *Labor: Free and Slave; Workingmen and the Anti-Slavery Movement in the United States.* New York, 1955.

Marsden, George M. *The Evangelical Mind and the New School Presbyterian Experience: A Case Study of Thought and Theology in Nineteenth-Century America..* New Haven, Conn., 1970.

Martin, Christopher. *The Amistad Affair*. New York, 1970.

Marty, Martin E. *Righteous Empire: The Protestant Experience in America*. New York, 1970.

Marvin, Winthrop L. *The American Merchant Marine: Its History and Romance from 1620 to 1902*. New York, 1910.

Mathews, Donald G. *Slavery and Methodism: A Chapter in American Morality, 1780–1845*. Princeton, N.J., 1965.

Mattingly, Paul H. *The Classless Profession: American Schoolmen in the Nineteenth Century*. New York, 1975.

Mead, Sidney E. *Nathaniel William Taylor, 1786–1858: A Connecticut Liberal*. Chicago, 1942.

Merk, Frederick. *Slavery and the Annexation of Texas*. New York, 1972.

Merrill, Walter M. *Against Wind and Tide: A Biography of Wm. Lloyd Garrison*. Cambridge, Mass., 1963.

Meyer, Jacob C. *Church and State in Massachusetts from 1740 to 1833: A Chapter in the History of the Development of Individual Freedom*. Cleveland, 1930.

Miller, Perry. *The Life of the Mind in America: From the Revolution to the Civil War*. New York, 1965.

Miller, Spencer, Jr. *Rev. Moses Miller of Heath, Mass., 1804–1840*. N.p., 1932.

Miyakawa, T. Scott. *Protestants and Pioneers: Individualism and Conformity on the American Frontier*. Chicago, 1964.

Mohl, Raymond A. *Poverty in New York, 1783–1825*. New York, 1971.

Moorhead, James H. *American Apocalypse: Yankee Protestants and the Civil War*. New Haven, Conn., 1978.

Morison, Samuel Eliot, Frederick Merk, and Frank Friedel. *Dissent in Three American Wars*. Cambridge, Mass., 1970.

Morris, Edward. *The Presbyterian Church New School, 1837–1869: An Historical Review*. Columbus, Ohio, 1905.

Morrison, Chaplain W. *Democratic Politics and Sectionalism: The Wilmot Proviso Controversy*. Chapel Hill, 1967.

Murray, Andrew E. *Presbyterians and the Negro—A History*. Philadelphia, 1966.

Nash, Howard P., Jr. *Third Parties in American Politics*. Washington, D.C., 1959.

Nevins, Allan. *The Evening Post: A Century of Journalism*. New York, 1922.

Nichols, L. Nelson. *History of the Broadway Tabernacle of New York City*. New Haven, Conn., 1940.

Nichols, Robert Hastings. *Presbyterianism in New York State*. Edited by James Hastings Nichols. Philadelphia, 1963.

Ninde, Edward S. *The Story of the American Hymn*. New York, 1921.

Northrup, Flora. *The Record of a Century, 1834–1934.* New York, 1934.

Novak, Steven J. *The Rights of Youth: American Colleges and Student Revolt, 1798–1815.* Cambridge, Mass., 1977.

Noyes, Emily Leavitt. *Leavitt: Descendants of John Leavitt, the Immigrant, Through his Son, Josiah, and Margaret Johnson.* Vol. III of 5 vols. Tilton, N.H., 1949.

Nye, Russell B. *Fettered Freedom: Civil Liberties and the Slavery Controversy, 1830–1860.* East Lansing, Mich., 1949.

———. *William Lloyd Garrison and the Humanitarian Reformers.* Boston, 1955.

Osterweis, Rollin G. *Three Centuries of New Haven, 1638–1938.* New Haven, Conn., 1953.

Owens, William A. *Slave Mutiny: The Revolt of the Schooner Amistad.* New York, 1953.

Packard, Rev. Theophilus, Jr. *A History of the Churches and Ministers and of the Franklin Association, in Franklin County, Mass.* Boston, 1854.

Pease, Jane H., and William H. Pease. *Bound with Them in Chains: A Biographical History of the Antislavery Movement.* Westport, Conn., 1972.

———. *They Who Would Be Free: Blacks' Search for Freedom, 1830–1861.* New York, 1974.

Perry, Lewis. *Radical Abolitionism: Anarchy and the Government of God in Antislavery Thought.* Ithaca, N.Y., 1973.

Perry, Lewis, and Michael Fellman, eds. *Antislavery Reconsidered: New Perspectives on the Abolitionists.* Baton Rouge, 1979.

Pessen, Edward. *Jacksonian America: Society, Personality, and Politics.* Homewood, Ill., 1978.

Phillips, Clifton Jackson. *Protestant America and the Pagan World: The First Half Century of the American Board of Commissioners for Foreign Missions, 1810–1860.* Cambridge, Mass., 1969.

Pickard, Samuel T. *Life and Letters of John Greenleaf Whittier.* Vol. I of 2 vols. Boston, 1894.

Quarles, Benjamin. *Black Abolitionists.* New York, 1969.

———. *Frederick Douglass.* New York, 1968.

The Quatro-Millennial Anniversary of the Congregational Church of Stratford, Connecticut, 1639–1889. Bridgeport, Conn., 1889.

Ratner, Lorman. *Powder Keg: Northern Opposition to the Antislavery Movement, 1831–1840.* New York, 1968.

Rayback, Joseph G. *Free Soil: The Election of 1848.* Lexington, Ky., 1970.

Read, Donald. *Cobden and Bright: A Victorian Political Partnership.* New York, 1968.

Reynolds, James B., Samuel H. Fisher, and Henry B. Wright, eds. *Two Centuries of Christian Activity at Yale.* New York, 1901.

Rice, Edwin Wilbur. *The Sunday-School Movement and the American Sunday-School Union.* 2nd ed. Philadelphia, 1927.

Richards, Leonard L. *"Gentlemen of Property and Standing": Anti-Abolition Mobs in Jacksonian America.* New York, 1970.

Robbins, Howard Chandler, ed. *1785–1935: Sesquicentennial Anniversary of the Town of Heath, Massachusetts, August 25–29, 1935.* Heath, Mass., 1935.

Robinson, Donald L. *Slavery in the Structure of American Politics, 1765–1820.* New York, 1971.

Robinson, Howard. *Britain's Post Office: A History of Development from the Beginnings to the Present Day.* London, 1953.

Roper, Daniel C. *The United States Post Office: Its Past Record, Present Condition, and the Potential Relation to the New World Era.* New York, 1917.

Rorabaugh, W. J. *The Alcoholic Republic: An American Tradition.* New York, 1979.

Royle, Edward, and James Walvin. *English Radicals and Reformers, 1760–1848.* Brighton, England, 1982.

Ryan, Mary P. *Cradle of the Middle Class: The Family in Oneida County, New York, 1790–1865.* Cambridge, England, 1981.

Savage, Theodore Fiske. *The Presbyterian Church in New York City.* New York, 1949.

Schroeder, John H. *Mr. Polk's War: American Opposition and Dissent, 1846–1848.* Madison, Wis., 1973.

Schuckers, J. W. *The Life and Public Services of Salmon Portland Chase, United States Senator and Governor of Ohio; Secretary of the Treasury, and Chief Justice of the United States.* New York, 1874.

Scott, Donald M. *From Office to Profession: The New England Ministry, 1750–1850.* Philadelphia, 1978.

The Seamen's Bank for Savings in the City of New York: One Hundred Fifteen Years of Service, 1829–1944. New York, 1944.

Sellers, Charles G. *James K. Polk, Continentalist, 1843–1846.* New York, 1966.

Sellick, F. Stanley. *The First Congregational Church of Stratford, Connecticut, 1639–1939.* Stratford, Conn., 1955.

Sewell, Richard H. *Ballots for Freedom: Antislavery Politics in the United States, 1837–1860.* New York, 1976.

———. *John P. Hale and the Politics of Abolition.* Cambridge, Mass., 1965.

Seymour, Jack M. *Ships, Sailors and Samaritans: The Woman's Seamen's Friend Society of Connecticut, 1859–1976.* New Haven, Conn., 1976.

Silverman, Kenneth. *Timothy Dwight.* New York, 1969.

Simms, Henry H. *Emotion at High Tide: Abolition as a Controversial Factor, 1830–1845.* Richmond, Va., 1960.

Sizer, Sandra S. *Gospel Hymns and Social Religion: The Rhetoric of Nineteenth-Century Revivalism.* Philadelphia, 1978.

Smith, H. Shelton. *Changing Conceptions of Original Sin: A Study in American Theology Since 1750.* New York, 1955.

Smith, Theodore Clarke. *The Liberty and Free Soil Parties in the Northwest.* New York, 1897.

Smith, Timothy. *Revivalism and Social Reform in Mid-Nineteenth-Century America.* New York, 1957.

Smith-Rosenberg, Carroll. *Religion and the Rise of the American City: The New-York City Missionary Movement, 1812–1870.* Ithaca, N.Y., 1971.

Sorin, Gerald. *The New York Abolitionists: A Case Study of Political Radicalism.* Westport, Conn., 1971.

Sproat, John G. *"The Best Men": Liberal Reformers in the Gilded Age.* New York, 1968.

Staff, Frank. *The Penny Post, 1680–1918.* London, 1964.

Staudenraus, P. J. *The African Colonization Movement, 1816–1865.* New York, 1961.

Stewart, James Brewer. *Holy Warriors: The Abolitionists and American Slavery.* New York, 1976.

———. *Joshua R. Giddings and the Tactics of Radical Politics.* Cleveland, 1970.

Stokes, Anson Phelps. *Memorials of Eminent Yale Men.* Vol. I of 2 vols. New Haven, Conn., 1914.

Sweet, William Warren. *Religion on the American Frontier, 1783–1850, Vol. III: The Congregationalists.* New York, 1936.

———. *Revivalism in America: Its Origin, Growth and Decline.* New York, 1944.

The Tercentenary History Committee, comp. and ed. *The Northampton Book: Chapters from 300 Years in the Life of a New England Town, 1654–1954.* Northampton, Mass., 1954.

Thistlethwaite, Frank. *America and the Atlantic Community: Anglo-American Aspects, 1790–1850.* New York, 1959.

Thomas, Benjamin P. *Theodore Weld, Crusader for Freedom.* New Brunswick, N.J., 1950.

Thomas, John L. *The Liberator: William Lloyd Garrison.* Boston, 1963.

Thompson, Dorothy. *The Chartists, Popular Politics in the Industrial Revolution.* New York, 1984.

Thompson, Ernest Trice. *Presbyterians in the South, Volume One: 1607–1861.* Richmond, Va., 1963.

Thompson, Francis M. *History of Greenfield, Shire Town of Franklin County, Massachusetts, 1682–1900.* 2 vols. Greenfield, Mass., 1904.

Tolis, Peter. *Elihu Burritt: Crusader for Brotherhood.* Hamden, Conn., 1968.

313

Walker, Peter. *Moral Choices: Memory, Desire, and Imagination in Nineteenth-Century American Abolition.* Baton Rouge, 1978.

Walters, Ronald G. *The Antislavery Appeal: American Abolitionism After 1830.* Baltimore, 1976.

Walvin, James, ed. *Slavery and British Society, 1776–1846.* Baton Rouge, 1982.

Ward, Susan Hayes. *The History of the Broadway Tabernacle Church: From Its Organization in 1840 to the Close of 1900, Including Factors Influencing Its Formation.* New York, 1901.

Warden, Robert B. *An Account of the Private Life and Public Services of Salmon Portland Chase.* Cincinnati, 1874.

Warner, Robert Austin. *New Haven Negroes: A Social History.* New Haven, Conn., 1940.

Warren, Israel P. *The Seamen's Cause; Embracing the History, Results, and Present Condition of the Efforts for the Moral Improvement of Seamen.* New York, 1858.

Webster, George S. *The Seamen's Friend: A Sketch of the American Seamen's Friend Society.* New York, 1932.

Weisberger, Bernard A. *They Gathered at the River: The Story of the Great Revivalists and Their Impact upon Religion in America.* Boston, 1958.

Whitman, Bennet. *Whittier: Bard of Freedom.* Chapel Hill, 1941.

Wiecek, William M. *The Sources of Antislavery Constitutionalism in America, 1760–1848.* Ithaca, N.Y., 1977.

Wilcoxson, William H. *History of Stratford, Connecticut, 1639–1939.* Stratford, Conn., 1939.

Wilentz, Sean. *Chants Democratic: New York City and the Rise of the American Working Class, 1788–1850.* New York, 1984.

Wolf, Hazel Catherine. *On Freedom's Altar: The Martyr Complex in the Abolition Movement.* Madison, Wis., 1952.

Wood, Ann Douglas. *The Feminization of American Culture.* New York, 1976.

Wyatt-Brown, Bertram. *Lewis Tappan and the Evangelical War Against Slavery.* Cleveland, 1969.

———. *Yankee Saints and Southern Sinners.* Baton Rouge, 1985.

York, Robert M. *George B. Cheever, Religious and Social Reformer, 1807–1890.* Orono, Me., 1955.

Young, Alfred, ed. *Dissent: Explorations in the History of American Radicalism.* DeKalb, Ill., 1968.

Zilversmit, Arthur. *The First Emancipation: The Abolition of Slavery in the North.* Chicago, 1967.

Zornow, William Frank. *Lincoln and the Party Divided.* Norman, Okla., 1954.

314

DISSERTATIONS

Henderson, Alice Hatcher. "The History of the New York State Anti-Slavery Society." Ph.D. dissertation, University of Michigan, 1963.

Hendricks, John R. "The Liberty Party in New York State, 1838–1848." Ph.D. dissertation, Fordham University, 1959.

Housley, Donald David. "The *Independent*: A Study in Religious and Social Opinion, 1848–1870." Ph.D. dissertation, Pennsylvania State University, 1971.

Pope, Earl A. "New England Calvinism and the Disruption of the Presbyterian Church." Ph.D. dissertation, Brown University, 1962.

Rice, Arthur Harry. "Henry B. Stanton as a Political Abolitionist." Ph.D. dissertation, Columbia University, Teachers College, 1968.

Seifman, Eli. "A History of the New-York State Colonization Society." Ph.D. dissertation, New York University, 1965.

Senior, Robert C. "New England Congregationalists and the Anti-Slavery Movement, 1830–1860." Ph.D. dissertation, Yale University, 1954.

Wayland, John Terrill. "The Theological Department in Yale College, 1822–1858." Ph.D. dissertation, Yale University, 1933.

INDEX

Abeel, David, 64
Abolitionists: ideology of, 9, 99–100, 119; motives of, 97–101; and colonization movement, 97, 105–106; and evangelicalism, 99–100; racial attitudes of, 107–109; and antiaboltionist riots, 110–12, 117–18; and postal campaign, 117, 119; and women's roles, 144–45; and political action, 146, 147, 148, 151; and questioning method, 146, 149, 150; and U.S. Constitution, 147, 228; and Texas annexation, 200, 202–204, 224–225; and fugitive slaves, 215–16; and disunionism, 230–31; and Mexican War, 231–32; and American Bible Society, 239–40. *See also* American Anti-Slavery Society; Liberty party
Adams, Charles Francis, 243, 244, 245, 249
Adams, John Quincy: and *Amistad* case, 177, 178; and Leavitt, 178, 192, 208; and antislavery insurgents, 188, 190, 191, 192, 211; censure trial of, 190–92; and Texas annexation, 200; mentioned, 151, 188–94 *passim,* 200, 208, 209
African Repository and Colonial Journal, 45
Alden, John, 212

Allmendinger, David, 11
American and Foreign Anti-Slavery Society, 162, 164, 182, 184, 185, 236, 238, 239
American and Foreign Anti-Slavery Society *Reporter,* 182, 183
American Anti-Slavery Society: founding of, 103; Leavitt's role in, 104, 106, 112, 117, 132, 136, 137, 141–45 *passim,* 152–60 *passim;* and benevolent societies, 106; and blacks, 107; and postal campaign, 117, 119; and nonresistance, 142; financial problems of, 143, 157; and Leavitt-Tappan feud, 152–54; schism of, 160–63; mentioned, 104, 106, 108, 131–35 *passim,* 144, 150, 152, 159, 163, 164. *See also* Abolitionists; Garrisonians
American Bible Society, 239–40, 259
American Board of Commissioners for Foreign Missions, 8, 64, 121
American Colonization Society: appeal of, 42–43; and abolitionists, 42, 95, 97, 100, 105, 106; and Leavitt, 45, 94, 96, 106
American Education Society, 126
American Free Trade League, 282–84
American Home Missionary Society, 121, 126
American Missionary Association, 238

317